Encounters I

Encounters I

A Cognitive Approach to Advanced Chinese

Jennifer Li-chia Liu

劉 力 嘉

with **Yan Li**

李 焱

Indiana University Press
Bloomington and Indianapolis

This book is a publication of

Indiana University Press
601 North Morton Street
Bloomington, Indiana 47404-3797 USA

www.iupress.indiana.edu

Telephone orders   800-842-6796
Fax orders   812-855-7931
Orders by e-mail   iuporder@indiana.edu

♾ The paper used in this publication meets the minimum requirements of
the American National Standard for Information Sciences—Permanence
of Paper for Printed Library Materials, ANSI Z39.48-1992.

Manufactured in the United States of America

Cataloging information is available from the Library of Congress

By Jennifer Li-chia Liu
ISBN 978-0-253-22111-7 paperback (Encounters I)
ISBN 978-0-253-22112-4 paperback (Encounters I: Workbook)

By Jennifer Li-chia Liu
ISBN 978-0-253-22113-1 paperback (Encounters II)
ISBN 978-0-253-22114-8 paperback (Encounters II: Workbook)

1 2 3 4 5   15 14 13 12 11 10

Contents

Tables

目錄

L	Theme	Communication/Skill	Grammar /Usage
6.	Literature and Performing Arts	Discussing the status of classical literature today	連A帶B…
			S不僅僅是…也/都V
		Talking about popular literature and its impact	S把A和B聯繫/結合/加起來
			S不VO…，一VO…
		Narrating the experience of going to a Beijing opera	先不談X，就Y來看/而言
		Reading a commentary on "best-sellers"	…有所V
7.	Advertisements and Commercials	Talking about being tricked	難道S…不成/嗎
		Returning a product to a store	（在）…以內/以外/以上/以下
		Narrating an experience of selling something	…毫無N/毫不V
			S應該…才對/才是/才好/才行
			一是…，二是…
		Comprehending a report on commercials	以X（為Y）來V　　把X當作/作為Y
8.	Love and Marriage	Urging someone to get married	都什麼N了
		Talking with a soon-to-be groom	S不妨V，（說不定）…
			S儘可能地快/早/多V
		Narrating an experience of being on a dating game show	S不再是N了/不再VO了
			S再也不/別VO了
		Comprehending a report on a population poll	S假如…也/就V
			A向B表示好感/關心/同情/歡迎/友好
9.	Education and Career	Talking about student behavior	S一V就是NP
		Talking about the high school experience	S VO V₁個 不/沒 停/完
			瞧/看你V/Adj 的
		Narrating the experience of trying to get ahead of others in school	S在V₁O₁的同時，也V₂O₂
			S不僅不/沒V₁O₁，（甚至/反而）還V₂O₂
		Reading a commentary on the job search by recent college graduates	…，況且S（也/還/又）VO
10.	Social Commentary	Arguing with someone	O S V得/不著　S V得/不了O
		Making criticism	V了一N₁的N₂
			往輕點說是…，重說是…
		Comparing social phenomena	不單單是A，B還/都/也…
		Reading an authentic text with little glossary aid	…，…以V
			A為B（所）V
		Synthesizing reading and study skills acquired from previous chapters	

Preface

Encounters I and *II* is a complete course designed for students who have finished the equivalent of two years of Chinese in a typical college setting in the United States or abroad. This high-intermediate to advanced series is closely coordinated, in terms of vocabulary, grammatical structures, and approach, with its predecessor, *Connections I* and *II*. However, due to its overall flexibility, users of other intermediate texts will also find this advanced series accommodating. It is intended for learners with diverse interests and backgrounds and varying degrees of exposure to Chinese language and culture. Users will find these two learner-centered textbooks motivating and thought-provoking, no matter whether their skills are uneven, excellent in some respects but lacking in others (as is often found in the case of students with Chinese heritage), or whether they have had no other training in the language beyond a second-year course.

I. Learning Needs and Instructional Design

Students who want to progress from an intermediate to an advanced level in their Chinese studies are often confronted with a number of challenges. First of all, in mastering vocabulary, both the quantity and quality of their vocabulary must be increased, so that they are able to express themselves with more sophistication. This task, in and of itself, can be very daunting and time-consuming. Furthermore, they need to understand the differences between the written and spoken forms of Chinese expression, acquire a sense of various styles of writing, convey their ideas in clear, connected discourse, and use their acquired linguistic knowledge and skills to deal with real-life tasks. Students also need a deeper understanding of Chinese culture and contemporary society, rapidly changing in this age of globalization.

Encounters was designed to help students tackle these challenges as follows: First, to ensure that the majority of the vocabulary items presented in the textbooks are of high frequency usage, appropriate for high-intermediate to advanced learners of Chinese, the vocabulary conforms to the second and third categories in *The Frequency List of Chinese Vocabulary and Characters* 漢語水平詞匯與漢字等級大綱 (1992). This careful selection of vocabulary will help students maximize their study time and give them confidence to interact in Chinese beyond the classroom. Vocabulary items are recycled as much as possible, not only from chapter to chapter, but also within the three-text component of each chapter. This built-in repetition will lessen students' burden of rote memorization. Colloquialisms are included to acquaint students with expressions that will make them sound more like native speakers. To encourage students to start thinking in Chinese, the vocabulary items are annotated in Chinese whenever possible.

Vocabulary items are divided into two categories: productive and receptive. Productive words, numbered in the vocabulary list, are the lexical items with more generative power in terms of forming new compounds or those with more complex usages (e.g., verbs, adverbs, etc.). Therefore, they should be committed to memory and studied carefully. Receptive words, unnumbered items in the vocabulary list, are easier to understand (e.g., concrete nouns) and require less study. This distinction will not only help students prioritize their learning tasks, but also will help them understand that not all words are equally important. This key concept will come in handy when students start accessing authentic materials on their own. In addition, usage of all productive words is clearly laid out, so that students will know the context or collocation of these important lexical items. Two sample sentences are given for each lexical item, usually in the interrogative mode, so that interaction among students or between teacher and students is facilitated.

Most chapters are divided into three components: dialogue, narrative, and exposition, progressing gradually from colloquial to formal styles. This modular design affords many advantages: (1) it helps students see how expressions are phrased differently according to a distinctive rhetorical structure; (2) it allows the in-depth exploration of a particular issue from different points of view; (3) recycling vocabulary is easier; (4) it provides students with different models for various learning activities, role-playing, narration of events, etc.; (5) as each text component can be covered within an hour or two, it permits teachers to design their curricula with great flexibility; (6) it makes up for the traditional emphasis on reading at the advanced stage to the neglect of other skills. Chapters 5, 10, 15, and 20 include slightly adapted essays by well-known Chinese writers, so that students will have the experience of dealing with an authentic text as well as a sense of accomplishment, which rightly comes at the end of prolonged study.

Each chapter is designed to start with a problem scenario which serves to highlight the theme in focus and pique learners' interest about the chapters' contents. Such scenarios convey the idea that the ultimate goal for language study is not just studying isolated words and sentence patterns for their own sake, but to piece everything together, to keep reading and studying the whole chapter until the problem is solved.

To help students gain a better understanding of contemporary Chinese life and society, a variety of topics are covered, ranging from common personal interests to significant societal phenomena. Themes covered in **Encounters I** are: (1) Homecoming and Reunion; (2) Travel and Sightseeing; (3) Leisure and Sports; (4) Computing and the Internet; (5) Movies and Music; (6) Literature and the Performing Arts; (7) Advertisements and Commercials; (8) Love and Marriage; (9) Education and Careers; and (10) Social Commentary. In **Encounters II**, themes are: (11) Housing and Real Estate; (12) Traffic and Transportation; (13) Health and Medicine; (14) Social Roles and Social Welfare; (15) Crime and Justice; (16) Nature and the Environment; (17) Economics and Consumption; (18) Politics and Choices; (19) World and Future; and (20) Coming of Age. These themes allow students to access the elements of life in Chinese society and become familiar with current practices and preferences. Lesson topics raise issues of long-lasting interest and global concern, providing food for thought. They are sure to provoke many class discussions.

II. Organization of the Text
In this advanced series, all chapters except the last one contain eight sections: (1) Objectives and Problem Scenario, (2) Dialogue One, (3) Dialogue Two, (4) Narrative, (5) Exposition, (6)

Word Summary, (7) Grammar, and (8) Background Notes. Dialogue One, Dialogue Two, Narrative, and the Exposition sections all have the following components: comprehension check, vocabulary list (by order of appearance), words in context (usage), and free discussion and class activities. To provide an easy review of the words covered in the chapter, the Word Summary section presents productive and receptive vocabulary by grammatical categories and by alphabetical order in pinyin. In the Grammar section, there are six patterns in each chapter. These are not "sentence patterns" per se, but distinctive rhetorical structures, for example, to express emotion, make logical transitions, use an expression in context, and so forth. Each pattern is labeled by its function; then follows a contextual example, further examples, and exercises to be done either orally or in writing. To observe the principle of maximum contextualization, the grammar examples are always presented with both questions and answers. The exercises in the Workbooks have eight sections, each responding to the specific learning needs outlined previously. They are: (1) Productive Words, (2) Word Power, (3) Coherent Passages, (4) Colloquial and Written Expressions, (5) Listening, (6) Supplemental Reading, (7) Writing, and (8) Problem-Solving Tasks. Both **Encounters I** and **II** conclude with two indexes: (1) lesson vocabulary and (2) sentence patterns.

In most cases, both traditional and simplified characters are provided in each section. Whenever possible, each is listed side by side in columns rather than one beneath the other. Although it may look a bit crowded at first glance, this layout allows students to easily scan each of the columns and figure out the corresponding character form or meaning. If there are differences in lexical items used in mainland China and Taiwan, both are noted. Although most of the "new words" are annotated, there are times students may need to resort to a dictionary. This is especially the case in the Supplementary Reading exercise section, in which new words are purposely left unglossed. While the **Encounters** textbooks were designed to keep students from becoming overburdened looking up characters, mastery of dictionaries is an important aspect of Chinese language learning, and the textbooks' design encourages use of dictionaries to some extent.

Although students are exposed to a "finer" selection of words and sentence patterns, appropriate to the advanced level, the fundamental principle of **Encounters** is the same as in **Interactions** and **Connections**. All the texts are composed from a learner's perspective and the examples are relevant to students' lives. The method of instruction is a cognitive approach, which focuses on students' thought processes so as to promote active and meaningful learning. A special emphasis is on synthesizing all the linguistic resources to solve problems and handle real-life tasks. While in **Connections** we learn many aspects of Chinese life through the eyes of a foreign student, this time we experience Chinese life from the insiders' perspective, as Li Ming, one of the dramatis personae created in **Interactions** and developed in **Connections**, returns to China to reunite with his family and friends.

I wish to express special thanks to Yan Li, whose participation in this project was invaluable to me in the way of providing insight into mainland Chinese usage and access to mainland Chinese resources as well as for her collaboration in drafting this edition. I am also grateful to Brian Baumann and Denise Gigliotti for their editorial help. Thanks must also be extended to the students and teachers at Indiana University as well as at the University of

Virginia, University of Oregon, and Hamilton College for their feedback and suggestions, particularly to Professor Hsin-hsin Liang and Professor Hong Gang Jin for their willingness to work with the drafts of this series. Any remaining errors and infelicities are of course my own responsibility.

Jennifer Liu
Bloomington, Indiana

Encounters I

第一課　從美國回來，我變得小氣了？

Theme: Homecoming and Reunion

Communicative Objectives
- Reminiscing about an old friend
- Inviting friends out
- Narrating a reunion

Skill Focus
Comprehending an essay on social etiquette

Grammar Focus
- 在…的N中
- …，其中…
- O S V得/不起
- S要麼VO，要麼VO
- A Adj於B
- 即使/就算…，S也…

Problem Scenario
　　Since you went abroad, you haven't seen your high school classmates for a couple of years. Now that you are back, you are anxious to meet all of them and share your experience. While planning for a reunion, you realize that many of your friends have gone their separate ways and now have different views on life, money, and friendship, not to mention the change in their appearance. What activities should be planned for such an event? How do you persuade everyone to come to this function?

對話 Dialogue

(1)Reminiscing about an old friend

李明的高中同學討論李明這個人怎麼樣。

男同學：李明後天就要從美國回來了，這個週末我們老同學一起吃飯
　　　　怎麼樣？

女同學：時間過得真快，他已經去了三年了吧！不知道從前那個活潑
　　　　的小李現在變成什麼樣子了？

男同學：我記得，那時候他個子高高的，總是打扮得很時髦。

女同學：是啊！咱們班數他最受歡迎。不過[1]在我的印象中，小李的性
　　　　格有點矛盾。

男同學：為什麼這麼說？

女同學：他很貪玩，但成績卻不錯；他有點驕傲，可是對朋友又很有
　　　　耐心。

男同學：就是因為這些原因，他才會受到大家的歡迎。

女同學：尤其受女生的歡迎！我知道有很多女生喜歡他！

男同學：我猜你也是[2]其中之一吧！

女同學：別胡說！

閱讀理解 Comprehension Check

1. 李明是誰？他原來住在哪裡？現在呢？
2. 小李從前長得怎麼樣？打扮得怎麼樣？
3. 小李的性格矛盾嗎？為什麼？
4. 小李的女同學覺得小李怎麼樣？

(1)Reminiscing about an old friend

李明的高中同学讨论李明这个人怎么样。

男同学：李明后天就要从美国回来了，这个周末我们老同学一起吃饭怎么样？

女同学：时间过得真快，他已经去了三年了吧！不知道从前那个活泼的小李现在变成什么样子了？

男同学：我记得，那时候他个子高高的，总是打扮得很时髦。

女同学：是啊！咱们班数他最受欢迎，不过[1]**在**我的印象**中**，小李的性格有点矛盾。

男同学：为什么这么说？

女同学：他很贪玩，但成绩却不错；他有点骄傲，可是对朋友又很有耐心。

男同学：就是因为这些原因，他才会受到大家的欢迎。

女同学：尤其受女生的欢迎！我知道有很多女生喜欢他！

男同学：我猜你也是[2]**其中**之一吧！

女同学：别胡说！

阅读理解 Comprehension Check

1. 李明是谁？他原来住在哪里？现在呢？
2. 小李从前长得怎么样？打扮得怎么样？
3. 小李的性格矛盾吗？为什么？
4. 小李的女同学觉得小李怎么样？

對話一生詞 Vocabulary

Study the numbered vocabulary (productive vocabulary) for its usage. The unnumbered items (receptive vocabulary) are to facilitate reading comprehension.

◎By Order of Appearance

1.	小氣	小气	xiǎoqi	Adj	stingy, mean	[petty-spirit]
2.	活潑	活泼	huópō	Adj	lively, vivacious	[lively-impetuous]
	變成	变成	biànchéng	RV	to change into	[to change-to become]
	個子	个子	gèzi	N	height, stature, build	[individual-suffix]
3.	打扮		dǎbàn	V/N	to dress/make up, to pose as	[to do-to dess up as]
	時髦	时髦	shímáo	Adj	fashionable, in vogue	[current-long hair]
4.	數	数	shǔ	V	<口> to count, to be reckoned as	
5.	性格		xìnggé	N	nature, disposition, temperament	[nature-style]
	矛盾		máodùn	Adj/N	contradictory, contradiction	[spear-shield]
6.	貪	贪	tān	V	to have an insatiable desire for, to covet	
	驕傲	骄傲	jiāo'ào	Adj/N	arrogant, conceited, to be proud, pride	[proud-haughty]
	耐心		nàixīn	N	patience	[to bear-heart]
7.	歡迎	欢迎	huānyíng	V	to welcome	[happy-to receive]
8.	尤其		yóuqí	Adv	especially	[especially-such]
	猜		cāi	V	to guess	
9.	其中		qízhōng	N	in/among (it/them/which/etc.)	[such-interior]
10.	胡說	胡说	húshuō	IE	<口> to talk nonsense	[recklessly-say]

Characters with Many Strokes

潑 變 髦 數 盾 貪 驕 傲 耐 歡

詞匯用法 Words in Context

1. 小氣：花錢小氣；太小氣；小氣　小气：花钱小气；太小气；小气

鬼

鬼

在什麼地方請客會被認為特別
小氣？

在什么地方请客会被认为特别
小气？

在錢包裏放很多錢的人是不是一
定很大方？

在钱包里放很多钱的人是不是一
定很大方？

2. 活潑：活潑的孩子、樣子；上課
很活潑

活泼：活泼的孩子、样子；上课
很活泼

你小的時候活潑嗎？長大了以後
呢？

你小的时候活泼吗？长大了以后
呢？

你覺得什麼時候應該表現得活潑
一點？

你觉得什么时候应该表现得活泼
一点？

3. 打扮：打扮得很漂亮、時髦；愛
打扮

打扮：打扮得很漂亮、时髦；爱
打扮

什麼時候需要打扮得漂亮一點？

什么时候需要打扮得漂亮一点？

什麼樣的人算愛打扮的人？

什么样的人算爱打扮的人？

4. 數：數他最小氣、笨、貪玩
你覺得同學中誰最貪玩？

数：数他最小气、笨、贪玩
你觉得同学中谁最贪玩？

誰給你的零花錢最多？

谁给你的零花钱最多？

5. 性格：性格活潑；有什麼性格；
性格不合

性格：性格活泼；有什么性格；
性格不合

你的性格像自己的父親還是母
親？

你的性格象自己的父亲还是母
亲？

夫妻離婚的原因可能是什麼？

夫妻离婚的原因可能是什么？

6. 貪：貪玩、吃、睡；貪錢、嘴

贪：贪玩、吃、睡；贪钱、嘴

他為什麼和一個比自己大二十歲
的女人結婚了呢？

他为什么和一个比自己大二十岁
的女人结婚了呢？

你的功課到現在還沒完成？

你的功课到现在还没完成？

7. 歡迎：受到歡迎；歡迎你到北京
來

欢迎：受到欢迎；欢迎你到北京
来

現在什麼專業最受學生的歡迎？　　現在什么专业最受学生的欢迎？

聽說你們週末有一個晚會，我可　　听说你们周末有一个晚会，我可
以參加嗎？　　　　　　　　　　以参加吗？

8.　尤其：

當學生真辛苦，尤其那些一邊工　　当学生真辛苦，尤其那些一边工
作一邊上課的學生。　　　　　　作一边上课的学生。

陳方很會說笑話，尤其喝了酒以　　陈方很会说笑话，尤其喝了酒以
後，笑話可多了。　　　　　　　后，笑话可多了。

9.　其中：（句型）

10.　胡說：別胡說　　　　　　　　胡说：别胡说

你打扮得這麼漂亮是不是要去　　你打扮得这么漂亮是不是要去
約會？　　　　　　　　　　　　约会？

今天沒來上課的學生都嫌中文太　　今天没来上课的学生都嫌中文太
難。　　　　　　　　　　　　　难。

自由發揮與課堂活動　Free Discussion and Class Activities

1.　你覺得最讓你難忘的是什麼時候　　你觉得最让你难忘的是什么时候
的朋友？為什麼？　　　　　　　的朋友？为什么？

2.　請介紹一位讓你最難忘的朋友。　　请介绍一位让你最难忘的朋友。

👤👤 (2) Inviting friends out

李明和高中同學討論請大家吃飯的事。

小李：　　這次回來，我發現北京到處都是「洋快餐」，沒想到麥當勞和肯德基在中國這麼受年輕人的歡迎。

同學：　　因為「洋快餐」的環境非常舒服，點餐也不用花很多時間。

小李：　　而且自己點自己的，省得幾個朋友一起吃飯還要考慮誰請客的問題。

同學：　　可是那兒的東西不是漢堡就是薯條，既沒營養，也不好吃。

小李：　　好了，我不是來和你討論快餐的。三年沒見了，我想請老朋友在我家附近的一家自助餐廳吃飯，那兒的環境不錯，而且有免費的卡拉OK，你覺得怎麼樣？

同學：　　別開玩笑了！在那種地方請客難道你不怕丟面子嗎？

小李：　　面子和在什麼地方請客有關係嗎？

同學：　　當然了，你從美國回來，至少要去酒店訂一桌才可以，不然大家會笑話你，以為你[3]**請不起**。

小李：　　那好吧！週六晚上七點，麗都酒店門口，不見不散。

閱讀理解 Comprehension Check

5.　小李回國後，發現北京有什麼變化？
6.　小李的同學認為洋快餐有什麼特色？
7.　小李想在什麼地方和他的老同學見面？為什麼？
8.　最後小李決定在哪裏請客？為什麼？

(2) Inviting friends out

李明和高中同学讨论请大家吃饭的事。

小李：　这次回来，我发现北京到处都是"洋快餐"，没想到麦当劳和肯德基在中国这么受年轻人的欢迎。

同学：　因为"洋快餐"的环境非常舒服，点餐也不用花很多时间。

小李：　而且自己点自己的，省得几个朋友一起吃饭还要考虑谁请客的问题。

同学：　可是那儿的东西不是汉堡就是薯条，既没营养，也不好吃。

小李：　好了，我不是来和你讨论快餐的。三年没见了，我想请老朋友在我家附近的一家自助餐厅吃饭，那儿的环境不错，而且有免费的卡拉OK，你觉得怎么样？

同学：　别开玩笑了！在那种地方请客难道你不怕丢面子吗？

小李：　面子和在什么地方请客有关系吗？

同学：　当然了，你从美国回来，至少要去酒店订一桌才可以，不然大家会笑话你，以为你[3]**请不起**。

小李：　那好吧！周六晚上七点，丽都酒店门口，不见不散。

阅读理解 Comprehension Check

5.　小李回国后，发现北京有什么变化？

6.　小李的同学认为洋快餐有什么特色？

7.　小李想在什么地方和他的老同学见面？为什么？

8.　最后小李决定在哪里请客？为什么？

對話二生詞 Vocabulary

	洋		yáng	Adj	foreign	
	快餐		kuàicān	N	quick meal, fast food	[fast-meal]
	麥當勞	麦当劳	Màidāngláo	N	McDonald's	
	肯德基		Kěndéjī	N	KFC (Kentucky Fried Chicken)	
	環境	环境	huánjìng	N	environment, surroundings	[circle-area]
11.	點	点	diǎn	V	to order (dishes), to check one by one, to hint	
12.	省得		shěngde	Conj	lest	[to save-(complement)]
13.	考慮	考虑	kǎolǜ	V	想一想	[check-consider]
	請客	请客	qǐngkè	VO	to treat sb. (to meal/show/etc.)	[invite-guest]
	營養	营养	yíngyǎng	N	nutrition, nourishment	[nourish-raise]
	附近		fùjìn	N/	vicinity, nearby	[enclose-near]
	自助餐廳	自助餐厅	zìzhù cāntīng	N	restaurant that serves buffet	[self-helf-eat-hall]
	免費	免费	miǎnfèi	Adj/VO	不要錢的	[exempt-fee]
	卡拉OK		kǎlā OK	N	karaoke	
	別開玩笑了！	别开玩笑了！	bié kāi wánxiào le!	IE	<口> Stop joking around!	[not-start-fun-laugh]
14.	難道	难道	nándào	MA	Do you really mean to say that…	[difficult-to say]
15.	丟		diū	V/N	to lose, to misplace	
16.	至少		zhìshǎo	Adv	最少	[till-little]
	酒店		jiǔdiàn	N	hotel	[wine-inn]
17.	訂	订	dìng	V	to book (seats), to order (books, etc.)	
18.	笑話	笑话	xiàohuà	V/N	to laugh at, joke	[laugh-words]
	不見不散	不见不散	bú jiàn bú sàn	IE	Be there or be square.	[not-see-not-break up]

Characters with Many Strokes

頓　點　通　餐　環　境　費　難　笑　散

詞匯用法 Words in Context

11. 點：點菜；不會點；點不出來；　　点：点菜；不会点；点不出来；
    點了一大桌子菜；由誰點；點　　点了一大桌子菜；由谁点；点名；
    名；為你點一首歌　　　　　　　为你点一首歌

    如果你和家人出去吃飯，一般由　　如果你和家人出去吃饭，一般由
    誰點菜？　　　　　　　　　　　谁点菜？

    什麼時候你會為朋友點歌？　　　什么时候你会为朋友点歌？

12. 省得:省得麻煩/浪費時間/他擔　　省得:省得麻烦/浪费时间/他担
    心　　　　　　　　　　　　　　心

    你為什麼買這麼多紙盤？　　　　你为什么买这么多纸盘？

    你為什麼每個星期打電話回家？　你为什么每个星期打电话回家？

13. 考慮：考慮問題；考慮一下；考　　考虑：考虑问题；考虑一下；考
    慮考慮　　　　　　　　　　　　虑考虑

    這個晚會你打算穿中式服裝還是　　这个晚会你打算穿中式服装还是
    西式服裝？　　　　　　　　　　西式服装？

    老師，下個學期我們可不可以每　　老师,下个学期我们可不可以每个
    個星期五考試？　　　　　　　　星期五考试？

14. 難道：　　　　　　　　　　　　难道：

    你難道不嫌學中文辛苦嗎？　　　你难道不嫌学中文辛苦吗？

    你怎麼這麼亂花錢，難道掙錢很　　你怎么这么乱花钱，难道挣钱很
    容易嗎？　　　　　　　　　　　容易吗？

15. 丟：丟錢、人、臉；丟東西、垃圾　丟：丢钱、人、脸；丢东西、垃圾

    難道你自己沒有自行車嗎？為什　　难道你自己没有自行车吗？为什
    麼要借我的？　　　　　　　　　么要借我的？

    你覺得做了什麼事情會讓自己丟　　你觉得做了什么事情会让自己丢
    臉？　　　　　　　　　　　　　脸？

16. 至少：至少三十塊錢、五十歲；　　至少：至少三十块钱、五十岁；
    至少工作兩個小時　　　　　　　至少工作两个小时

買一輛奔馳汽車要多少錢？　　　　　买一辆奔驰汽车要多少钱？

你每天得花多長時間準備中文
課？

你每天得花多长时间准备中文
课？

17. 訂：訂位子、飛機票、火車票、　　17. 订：订位子、飞机票、火车票、
　　旅館、房間　　　　　　　　　　　旅馆、房间

如果感恩節要去旅行，得什麼時
候訂機票？

如果感恩节要去旅行，得什么时
候订机票？

去什麼樣的餐廳吃飯需要訂位
子？

去什么样的餐厅吃饭需要订位
子？

18. 笑話：被別人笑話；笑話別人；　　18. 笑话：被别人笑话；笑话别人；
　　講笑話；鬧笑話　　　　　　　　　讲笑话；闹笑话

你為什麼一工作就把那輛舊的汽
車賣了？

你为什么一工作就把那辆旧的汽
车卖了？

什麼樣的人喜歡笑話自己的同
學？

什么样的人喜欢笑话自己的同
学？

自由發揮與課堂活動　Free Discussion and Class Activities

3. 和朋友聚會的時候，你會選擇在　　3. 和朋友聚会的时候，你会选择在
　　快餐店、自助餐廳還是高級酒　　　快餐店、自助餐厅还是高级酒
　　店？為什麼？　　　　　　　　　　店？为什么？

4. 你喜歡「洋快餐」嗎？為什麼？　　4. 你喜欢"洋快餐"吗？为什么？
　　「洋快餐」和「中快餐」有什麼　　　"洋快餐"和"中快餐"有什么
　　不同？　　　　　　　　　　　　　不同？

敘述 Narrative

我變了？

　　高中一畢業我就去美國留學，這是我三年來第一次回國，當然我得請客。請客第一就要選擇地方。按照美國的習慣，中學生聚會，[4]**要麼**到自助餐廳，**要麼**到快餐廳。我記得在我出國以前，大家都挺喜歡麥當勞的，於是我建議去麥當勞聚會。可是沒想到我的同學卻說，「你在麥當勞請客，難道不覺得太小氣了嗎？」聽了他們的話，我的臉都紅了。為了不丟面子，我只好在一家五星級酒店訂了位子。

　　在點菜的時候我請大家各點各的，這又引起了大家的不滿。他們覺得我這樣做是為了省錢。他們建議西

餐中吃，點一桌子菜，然後大家一起吃。如果我嫌太貴的話，可以AA制。這時我只好讓大家想點什麼就點什麼，但是點多少就要吃多少，不可以剩。我覺得那頓飯大家吃得一點也不愉快。第二天我的一個同學對我說，她覺得我比三年以前小氣多了。從美國回來，不但沒給大家帶禮物，吃飯的時候還不讓大家多點菜。是啊，我以前不是這樣的。在上初中的時候，我們彼此喜歡，可是誰也不敢說出來，因為中學生不可以早

戀。可是在我出國的前一天，我帶她去這裏最高級的商店，對她說，「你去挑一套最喜歡的衣服，不管多少錢，我都給你買！」和那時比，現在的我真的小氣多了。可是我告訴她，我之所以變小氣了，是因為我了解到掙錢不容易。在美國，我的零花錢都是自己掙來的。每天除了上課以外，我要打兩個小時的工，非常辛苦。雖然每天可以賺十幾塊美金，但是我捨不得亂花錢！

可能她把我的話告訴了朋友們，後來大家要回請我。這一次他們選擇了麥當勞，而且說好用AA制的方法付帳！那天大家都非常開心。我想他們原諒了我這個「小氣鬼」！這次回國，收穫真不少，不但見到了老朋友，而且讓我發現了自己的變化。我喜歡這種變化！

閱讀理解 Comprehension Check

9. 小李是什麼時候到美國的？回中國的時候，他得做什麼？
10. 小李打算在哪裏請客？為什麼？他的同學覺得怎麼樣？
11. 點菜的時候，小李和他的同學又有什麼不同的看法？
12. 最後小李用什麼方法讓大家點菜？還有什麼要求？
13. 在中國，高中的學生可以交男女朋友嗎？
14. 小李覺不覺得自己比從前小氣？為什麼？
15. 在美國，小李的零花錢是怎麼來的？
16. 小李怎麼知道他的同學「原諒了我這個小氣鬼」？
17. 小李對自己這次回國的經驗滿意嗎？為什麼？

我变了？

高中一毕业我就去美国留学，这是我三年来第一次回国，当然我得请客。请客第一就要选择地方。按照美国的习惯，中学生聚会，[4]**要么**到自助餐厅，**要么**到快餐厅。我记得在我出国以前，大家都挺喜欢麦当劳的，于是我建议去麦当劳聚会。可是没想到我的同学却说，"你在麦当劳请客，难道不觉得太小气了吗？"听了他们的话，我的脸都红了。为了不丢面子，我只好在一家五星级酒店订了位子。

在点菜的时候我请大家各点各的，这又引起了大家的不满。他们觉得我这样做是为了省钱。他们建议西餐中吃，点一桌子菜，然后大家一起吃。如果我嫌太贵的话，可以AA制。这时我只好让大家想点什么就点什么，但是点多少就要吃多少，不可以剩。我觉得那顿饭大家吃得一点也不愉快。第二天我的一个同学对我说，她觉得我比三年以前小气多了。从美国回来，不但没给大家带礼物，吃饭的时候还不让大家多点菜。是啊，我以前不是这样的。在上初中的时候，我们彼此喜欢，可是谁也不敢说出来，因为中学生不可以早恋。可是在我出国的前一天，我带她去这里最高级的商店，对她说，"你去挑一套最喜欢的衣服，不管多少钱，我都给你买！"和那时比，现在的我真的小气多了。可是我告诉她，我之所以变小气了，是因为我了解到挣钱不容易。在美国，我的零花钱都是自己挣来的。每天除了上课以外，我要打两个小时的工，非常辛苦。

虽然每天可以赚十几块美金，但是
我舍不得乱花钱！

　　可能她把我的话告诉了朋友
们，后来大家要回请我。这一次
他们选择了麦当劳，而且说好用
AA制的方法付帐！那天大家都非

常开心。我想他们原谅了我这个
"小气鬼"！这次回国，收获真
不少，不但见到了老朋友，而且
让我发现了自己的变化。我喜欢
这种变化！

阅读理解 Comprehension Check

9. 小李是什么时候到美国的？回中国的时候，他得做什么？
10. 小李打算在哪里请客？为什么？他的同学觉得怎么样？
11. 点菜的时候，小李和他的同学又有什么不同的看法？
12. 最后小李用什么方法让大家点菜？还有什么要求？
13. 在中国，高中的学生可以交男女朋友吗？
14. 小李觉不觉得自己比从前小气？为什么？
15. 在美国，小李的零花钱是怎么来的？
16. 小李怎么知道他的同学"原谅了我这个小气鬼"？
17. 小李对自己这次回国的经验满意吗？为什么？

敘述生詞 Vocabulary

19.	敘述	叙述	xùshù	N/V	narration, to narrate	[to recount-to relate]
	聚會	聚会	jùhuì	N	gathering, to get together	[to gather-to meet]
20.	要麼	要么	yàome	Conj	either, or	[be about to-suffix]
21.	挺		tǐng	Adv	<口> quite, very	
	五星級	五星级	wǔxīngjí	N	five-star	[five-star-grade]
	位子		wèizi	N	seat, place	[place-(noun suffix)]
22.	引起		yǐnqǐ	V	to give rise to, to lead to	[to draw-to rise]
23.	不滿	不满	bùmǎn	N/Adj	discontent, unsatisfied	[not-full]
	西餐中吃		xīcān zhōng chī	N	用吃中國菜的方法吃西餐	[west-meal-Chinese-eat]

24.	嫌		xián	V	覺得…不好	
	AA制		…zhì	IE	各付各的 to go Dutch treat, to each pay his own	[AA-system]
25.	剩(下)		shèng(xià)	V	to be left (over), to remain	[remain-down]
26.	彼此		bǐcǐ	Adv	互相	[that-this]
	早戀	早恋	zǎoliàn	N	很早開始談戀愛	[early-love]
	高級	高级	gāojí	Adj	high in rank/grade/ quality	[high-grade]
27.	挑		tiāo	V	to choose	
28.	掙	挣	zhèng	V	to earn	
	零花錢	零花钱	línghuāqián	N	pocket money <TW>零用錢	[odd-spend-money]
29.	辛苦		xīnkǔ	Adj	hard, laborious	[suffering-bitter]
30.	捨不得	舍不得	shěbùdé	RV	to begrudge doing sth., to loathe to part with or use	[give up-not-able]
31.	亂	乱	luàn	Adv	(to do something) carelessly, randomly	
32.	也許	也许	yěxǔ	Adv	可能	[also-allow]
	回請	回请	huíqǐng	V	to return hospitality, to give return banquet	[to return-to invite]
	付帳	付帐	fùzhàng	VO	to pay a bill	[to pay-debt]
33.	原諒	原谅	yuánliàng	V	to excuse, to pardon	[pardon-to forgive]
	鬼		guǐ	Suf	term of abuse (e.g., 小氣鬼、酒鬼), ghost	
34.	收穫	收获	shōuhuò	N	gains, results	[to receive-to reap]

Characters with Many Strokes

敘 聚 挺 嫌 剩 戀 掙 零 亂 穫

詞匯用法 Words in Context

19. 敘述：敘述一件事情；敘述得不太清楚　　　叙述：叙述一件事情；叙述得不太清楚
這本書每一課的第二個部分是什麼？　　　这本书每一课的第二个部分是什么？

怎麼樣才能把一件事情敘述得很　　怎么样才能把一件事情叙述得很
清楚？　　　　　　　　　　　　　清楚？

20. 要麼：（句型）　　　　　　　　　要么：（句型）

21. 挺：挺好的；挺貪玩的；挺驕傲　　挺：挺好的；挺贪玩的；挺骄傲
　　的；挺捨不得的　　　　　　　　的；挺舍不得的

你覺得今天的天氣怎麼樣？　　　　你觉得今天的天气怎么样？

離開家回學校的時候，你捨得　　　离开家回学校的时候，你舍得
嗎？　　　　　　　　　　　　　　吗？

22. 引起：引起不滿、興趣、討論；　　引起：引起不满、兴趣、讨论；
　　沒引起什麼不滿　　　　　　　　没引起什么不满

如果一個學生上課的時候總是遲　　如果一个学生上课的时候总是迟
到，會怎麼樣？　　　　　　　　　到，会怎么样？

什麼話題會引起大家的討論？　　　什么话题会引起大家的讨论？

23. 不滿：對……不滿；引起學生的　　不满：对……不满；引起学生的
　　不滿　　　　　　　　　　　　　不满

你對這兒的什麼方面不滿？　　　　你对这儿的什么方面不满？

父母的哪些做法會引起你的不　　　父母的哪些做法会引起你的不
滿？　　　　　　　　　　　　　　满？

24. 嫌：嫌冷、遠、麻煩；嫌孩子貪　　嫌：嫌冷、远、麻烦；嫌孩子贪
　　玩；嫌這個工作掙的錢少　　　　玩；嫌这个工作挣的钱少

為什麼有些學生要從宿舍搬到學　　为什么有些学生要从宿舍搬到学
校外面的公寓？　　　　　　　　　校外面的公寓？

你為什麼很少去麥當勞吃東西？　　你为什么很少去麦当劳吃东西？

25. 剩(下)：剩飯、菜；剩下兩個小　　剩(下)：剩饭、菜；剩下两个小
　　時；剩下我一個人　　　　　　　时；剩下我一个人

在飯館吃飯的時候，剩下的菜，　　在饭馆吃饭的时候，剩下的菜，
你怎麼辦？　　　　　　　　　　　你怎么办？

還有多長時間就要考試了？　　　　还有多长时间就要考试了？

26. 彼此：彼此了解、幫助、關心、　　彼此：彼此了解、帮助、关心、

不滿　　　　　　　　　　　　　　　　不满

什麼樣的人才算你的朋友？　　　　　什么样的人才算你的朋友？

這兩個人為什麼從來都不說話？　　　这两个人为什么从来都不说话？

27.　挑：挑東西、男（女）朋友；挑　　挑：挑东西、男（女）朋友；挑
　　不出合適的來；把喜歡的挑出來　　不出合适的来；把喜欢的挑出来

　　你每次去買衣服的時候怎麼都要　　你每次去买衣服的时候怎么都要
　　花那麼長的時間？　　　　　　　　花那么长的时间？

　　每個學期你怎麼選擇自己要上什　　每个学期你怎么选择自己要上什
　　麼課？　　　　　　　　　　　　　么课？

28.　掙：掙錢　　　　　　　　　　　　挣：挣钱

　　做什麼工作掙的錢比較多？　　　　做什么工作挣的钱比较多？

　　在學校工作，每個小時可以掙多　　在学校工作，每个小时可以挣多
　　少錢？　　　　　　　　　　　　　少钱？

29.　辛苦：工作、生活辛苦；辛苦地　　辛苦：工作、生活辛苦；辛苦地
　　掙錢　　　　　　　　　　　　　　挣钱

　　你覺得什麼樣的工作很辛苦？　　　你觉得什么样的工作很辛苦？

　　你最近為什麼看起來很累？　　　　你最近为什么看起来很累？

30.　捨不得：（句型）　　　　　　　　舍不得：（句型）

31.　亂：亂花、買、說、走、寫、畫　　乱：乱花、买、说、走、写、画

　　你父母剛剛給了你零花錢，你怎　　你父母刚刚给了你零花钱，你怎
　　麼就花完了？　　　　　　　　　　么就花完了？

　　你的書上怎麼有這麼多奇怪的　　　你的书上怎么有这么多奇怪的
　　畫？　　　　　　　　　　　　　　画？

32.　也許：也許會來；也許錯了　　　　也许：也许会来；也许错了

　　張麗今天怎麼沒來上課？　　　　　张丽今天怎么没来上课？

　　他不喜歡開玩笑，可是今天為什　　他不喜欢开玩笑，可是今天为什
　　麼講了那麼多笑話？　　　　　　　么讲了那么多笑话？

33.　原諒：原諒別人；不可原諒的錯　　原谅：原谅别人；不可原谅的错

誤　　　　　　　　　　　　　　　误

如果你的朋友約會的時候遲到　　　如果你的朋友约会的时候迟到
了，你怎麼樣才會原諒他？　　　　了，你怎么样才会原谅他？

忘記女朋友的生日是不可原諒的　　忘记女朋友的生日是不可原谅的
嗎？　　　　　　　　　　　　　　吗？

34. 收穫：收穫很大；有很多收穫　　　收获：收获很大；有很多收获

你覺得學中文最大的收穫是什　　　你觉得学中文最大的收获是什
麼？　　　　　　　　　　　　　　么？

農民辛苦地工作為的是什麼？　　　农民辛苦地工作为的是什么？

自由發揮與課堂活動　Free Discussion and Class Activities

5. 如果你可以出國留學，你打算去　　如果你可以出国留学，你打算去
哪個國家？為什麼？　　　　　　　哪个国家？为什么？

6. 你覺得出國留學對一個學生來說　　你觉得出国留学对一个学生来说
有什麼好處？有哪那些壞處？　　　有什么好处？有哪那些坏处？

7. 你出過國、留過學嗎？在國外的　　你出过国、留过学吗？在国外的
經驗對你有什麼影響？回國後你　　经验对你有什么影响？回国后你
發現自己有了什麼變化？　　　　　发现自己有了什么变化？

8. 一個中國朋友在你們學中文的時　　一个中国朋友在你们学中文的时
候給了你們很多幫助，所以你們　　候给了你们很多帮助，所以你们
想在這個週末和他一起吃中國　　　想在这个週末和他一起吃中国
飯。在吃飯之前，你們要討論下　　饭。在吃饭之前，你们要讨论下
面幾個問題：　　　　　　　　　　面几个问题：

● 你們對這位中國朋友的印象；　● 你们对这位中国朋友的印象；

● 去哪家中國飯館：同學甲要去　● 去哪家中国饭馆：同学甲要去
　A飯館，同學乙要去B飯館；　　　A饭馆，同学乙要去B饭馆；

● 怎麼付帳：同學甲希望大家　　● 怎么付帐：同学甲希望大家
　AA制，同學乙希望學生請中　　　AA制，同学乙希望学生请中
　國朋友；　　　　　　　　　　　国朋友；

● 最後決定去什麼地方，怎麼通　● 最后决定去什么地方，怎么通
　知那位老同學，怎麼見面。　　　知那位老同学，怎么见面。

說明 Exposition

為何「聚會」不能少

　　自古以來，中國人一直有衣錦還鄉的觀念，那些留學生當然也不例外。由於中國的經濟水平仍然[5]**低於**美國，所以不管是沒畢業的學生，還是事業有成的人，回國的時候都要考慮為親人和朋友準備什麼禮物。要送禮，就得所有的人都送，要不然，沒收到禮物的人一定會很不滿意。除此以外，給什麼人送什麼禮物也是一件讓人頭疼的問題。禮物的輕重跟關係的遠近有很密切的關係，所以收到禮物的人也會根據禮物的輕重來判斷自己在送禮人心中的地位。

　　老朋友見面當然應該一起聚會，但是選擇聚會的地點也得小心。一般來說，請大家聚會的人要結帳。所以選擇太貴的地方恐怕付不起，選擇太便宜的地方，又要被別人笑話。雖然同學的聚會有很多讓人頭疼的問題，但是聚會仍然是一個和朋友聯絡感情、建立聯繫的好辦法。

　　剛回國的學生由於對國內的情況已經不太熟悉了，他們需要很快的建立一個關係網，為自己以後的發展做準備。[6]**即使**沒有打算回國工作的人，**也**希望和國內的朋友保持好的關係，因為在國際化的今天，多個朋友多條路。

閱讀理解 Comprehension Check

18. 留學生一般有什麼觀念？這對他們回國的時候有什麼影響？
19. 為什麼送禮是一件讓人頭疼的問題？
20. 為什麼和同學聚會也是一件讓人頭疼的問題？
21. 作者認為對誰來說聚會不能少？為什麼？

为何"聚会"不能少

自古以来，中国人一直有衣锦还乡的观念，那些留学生当然也不例外。由于中国的经济水平仍然[5]**低于**美国，所以不管是没毕业的学生，还是事业有成的人，回国的时候都要考虑为亲人和朋友准备什么礼物。要送礼，就得所有的人都送，要不然，没收到礼物的人一定会很不满意。除此以外，给什么人送什么礼物也是一件让人头疼的问题。礼物的轻重跟关系的远近有很密切的关系，所以收到礼物的人也会根据礼物的轻重来判断自己在送礼人心中的地位。

老朋友见面当然应该一起聚会，但是选择聚会的地点也得小心。一般来说，请大家聚会的人要结帐。所以选择太贵的地方恐怕付不起，选择太便宜的地方，又要被别人笑话。虽然同学的聚会有很多让人头疼的问题，但是聚会仍然是一个和朋友联络感情、建立联系的好办法。

刚回国的学生由于对国内的情况已经不太熟悉了，他们需要很快的建立一个关系网，为自己以后的发展做准备。[6]**即使**没有打算回国工作的人，**也**希望和国内的朋友保持好的关系，因为在国际化的今天，多个朋友多条路。

阅读理解 Comprehension Check

18. 留学生一般有什么观念？這对他們回国的時候有什么影响？
19. 为什么送礼是一件让人头疼的问题？
20. 为什么和同學聚会也是一件让人头疼的问题？
21. 作者认为对谁来說聚会不能少？为什么？

說明生詞 Vocabulary

35.	說明	说明	shuōmíng	N/V	explanation, to explain	[to say-clear]
	為何	为何	wèihé	QW	<書>為什麼	[for-what]
	自古以來	自古以来	zìgǔyǐlái	IE	since ancient times	[from-ancient-till-come]
	衣錦還鄉	衣锦还乡	yījǐnhuánxiāng	IE	to return home after making good	[clothes-brocade-return-home town]
	例外		lìwài	N	exception	[example-outside]
36.	仍然		réngrán	Adv	still, yet	[still-(adv marker)]
37.	事業	事业	shìyè	N	career, undertaking	[matter-enterprise]
	有成		yǒuchéng	VO	to have achieved success	[to have-result]
	親人	亲人	qīnrén	N	close relatives, dear ones	[kin-people]
	除此以外		chúcǐyǐwài	IE	except for this, in addition	[except-this-beyond]
	密切		mìqiè	Adj	close, intimate	[intimate-be close to]
38.	判斷	判断	pànduàn	V	to judge, to determine	[to decide-to break]
	地位		dìwèi	N	position, status	[place-location]
39.	結帳	结帐	jiézhàng	VO	to settle accounts	[to conclude-accounts]
40.	聯絡	联络	liánluò	V	to contact	[to unite-to twine]
41.	建立		jiànlì	V	to establish, to set up	[to build-to stand]
42.	發展	发展	fāzhǎn	N/V	to develop, to expand	[to send out-to expand]
43.	即使		jíshǐ	Conj	even, even if/though	[even if-if]
44.	保持		bǎochí	V	to keep (up a good thing going)	[to guarantee-to hold]
	國際化	国际化	guójìhuà	V/N	to internationalize, internationalization	[country-among-ize]

Characters with Many Strokes

還　鄉　業　慮　親　斷　帳　聯　建　際

詞匯用法 Words in Context

35. 說明：說明看法；說明電腦怎麼
　　用；說明書

　　電器裏面的說明書有什麼作用？

35. 说明：说明看法；说明电脑怎么
　　用；说明书

　　电器里面的说明书有什么作用？

如果你和朋友的意見不同，你會
做什麼？

如果你和朋友的意见不同，你会
做什么？

36. 仍然：仍然流行；仍然沒精神

大家都覺得中文難學，為什麼仍
然有那麼多人喜歡學中文呢？

如果你的朋友都去酒吧，可是你
的功課還沒寫完，你會和他們去
酒吧嗎？

仍然：仍然流行；仍然没精神

大家都觉得中文难学，为什么仍
然有那么多人喜欢学中文呢？

如果你的朋友都去酒吧，可是你
的功课还没写完，你会和他们去
酒吧吗？

37. 事業：事業有成

什麼樣的人算是事業有成的人？

事業和家庭有矛盾的時候，你會
選擇哪個？

事业：事业有成

什么样的人算是事业有成的人？

事业和家庭有矛盾的时候，你会
选择哪个？

38. 判斷：判斷對錯、好壞；判斷出
來

你怎麼判斷學校的好壞？

你覺得新聞裏說的事情一定都是
真的嗎？

判断：判断对错、好坏；判断出
来

你怎么判断学校的好坏？

你觉得新闻里说的事情一定都是
真的吗？

39. 結帳：誰結帳；怎麼結帳；用現
金（信用卡）結帳

和父母出去吃飯的時候，一般來
說誰結帳？

我帶的錢不多，我們不要去那家
很貴的飯館吧！

结帐：谁结帐；怎么结帐；用现
金（信用卡）结帐

和父母出去吃饭的时候，一般来
说谁结帐？

我带的钱不多，我们不要去那家
很贵的饭馆吧！

40. 聯絡：聯絡感情；和朋友聯絡

上大學以後你還經常和高中的同
學聯絡嗎？

你覺得什麼事情可以幫你和朋友
聯絡感情？

联络：联络感情；和朋友联络

上大学以后你还经常和高中的同
学联络吗？

你觉得什么事情可以帮你和朋友
联络感情？

41. 建立：建立好關係；建立民主制

建立：建立好关系；建立民主制

度；建立國家、部門

為什麼人們都說哈佛是美國最古老的大學？

中國的領導訪問美國的目的是什麼？

42. 發展：發展經濟、社會、教育；發展得很快、慢

你覺得最近十幾年，哪個國家的經濟發展得最快？

你覺得政府發展教育的政策怎麼樣？

43. 即使：（句型）

李明現在變得小氣了，大家是不是不把他當朋友了？

事業有成的人一定有幸福的家庭嗎？

44. 保持：保持好的習慣、關係、聯繫、衛生、健康；保持下去

你還在和中學的同學聯繫嗎？

怎麼做才能保持健康？

自由發揮與課堂活動　Free Discussion and Class Activities

9. 在你的國家，一般人怎麼和別人建立聯繫？

10. 在你的國家，朋友聚會一般會做些什麼？有什麼需要注意的地方？

11. 對你來說，送禮是個頭疼的問題嗎？為什麼？

度；建立国家、部门

为什么人们都说哈佛是美国最古老的大学？

中国的领导访问美国的目的是什么？

发展：发展经济、社会、教育；发展得很快、慢

你觉得最近十几年，哪个国家的经济发展得最快？

你觉得政府发展教育的政策怎么样？

即使：（句型）

李明现在变得小气了，大家是不是不把他当朋友了？

事业有成的人一定有幸福的家庭吗？

保持：保持好的习惯、关系、联系、卫生、健康；保持下去

你还在和中学的同学联系吗？

怎么做才能保持健康？

在你的国家，一般人怎么和别人建立联系？

在你的国家，朋友聚会一般会做些什么？有什么需要注意的地方？

对你来说，送礼是个头疼的问题吗？为什么？

應用詞 Productive Vocabulary

◎By Grammatical Categories

Nouns/Pronouns/Measure Words

性格	xìnggé	nature, disposition, temperament	不滿	bùmǎn	discontent, unsatisfied
事業	shìyè	career, undertaking	敘述	xùshù	narration, to narrate
收穫	shōuhuò	gains, results	說明	shuōmíng	explanation, to explain
其中	qízhōng	in/among (it/them/which/etc.)	發展	fāzhǎn	to develop, to expand

Verbs/Stative Verbs/Adjectives

數	shǔ	to count, to be reckoned as	剩(下)	shèng(xià)	to be left (over), to remain
點	diǎn	to order (dishes), to check one by one, to hint	原諒	yuánliàng	to excuse, to pardon
訂	dìng	to book (seats), to order (books, etc.)	笑話	xiàohuà	to laugh at, joke
挑	tiāo	to choose	建立	jiànlì	to establish, to set up
掙	zhèng	to earn	保持	bǎochí	to keep (up a good thing going)
貪	tān	to have an insatiable desire for, to covet	聯絡	liánluò	to contact
嫌	xián	to dislike that...	結帳	jiézhàng	to settle accounts
丟	diū	to lose, to misplace	捨不得	shěbùdé	to begrudge doing sth., to loathe to part with or use
打扮	dǎbàn	to dress/make up, to pose as	小氣	xiǎoqi	stingy, mean
歡迎	huānyíng	to welcome	活潑	huópō	lively, vivacious
考慮	kǎolǜ	to think over, to consider	辛苦	xīnkǔ	hard, laborious
判斷	pànduàn	to judge, to determine			
引起	yǐnqǐ	to give rise to, to lead to			

Adverbs and Others

挺	tǐng	quite, very	省得	shěngde	lest
亂	luàn	(to do something) carelessly, randomly	要麼	yàome	either, or
尤其	yóuqí	especially	即使	jíshǐ	even, even if/though
至少	zhìshǎo	at (the) least	難道	nándào	Do you really mean to say that...?
也許	yěxǔ	perhaps, maybe	胡說	húshuō	to talk nonsense
仍然	réngrán	still, yet			
彼此	bǐcǐ	mutually			

理解詞 Receptive Vocabulary

◎ By Grammatical Categories

Nouns/Pronouns/Measure Words

親人	qīnrén	close relatives, dear ones	位子	wèizi	seat, place
個子	gèzi	height, stature, build	例外	lìwài	exception
耐心	nàixīn	patience	零花錢	línghuāqián	pocket money
早戀	zǎoliàn	puppy love	五星級	wǔxīngjí	five-star
地位	dìwèi	position, status	酒店	jiǔdiàn	hotel
聚會	jùhuì	gathering, to get together	自助餐廳	zìzhù cāntīng	restaurant that serves buffet
快餐	kuàicān	quick meal, fast food	卡拉OK	kǎlā OK	karaoke
營養	yíngyǎng	nutrition, nourishment	西餐中吃	xīcān zhōng chī	to eat Western-style food in the Chinese way
附近	fùjìn	vicinity, nearby			
環境	huánjìng	environment, surroundings			

Verbs/Stative Verbs/Adjectives

猜	cāi	to guess	時髦	shímáo	fashionable, in vogue
變成	biànchéng	to change into	高級	gāojí	high in rank/grade/quality
請客	qǐngkè	to treat sb. (to meal/show/etc.)	免費	miǎnfèi	to be free of charge
回請	huíqǐng	to return hospitality, to give return banquet	密切	mìqiè	close, intimate
付帳	fùzhàng	to pay a bill	矛盾	máodùn	contradictory, contradiction
有成	yǒuchéng	to have achieved success	驕傲	jiāo'ào	arrogant, conceited, to be proud, pride
國際化	guójìhuà	to internationalize, internationalization			
洋	yáng	foreign			

Adverbsand Others

鬼	guǐ	term of abuse (e.g., 小氣鬼、酒鬼), ghost	衣錦還鄉	yījǐnhuán xiāng	to return home after making good
為何	wèihé	why	除此以外	chúcǐ yǐwài	except for this, in addition
AA制	…zhì	to go Dutch treat, to each pay his own	別開玩笑了！	bié kāi wánxiào le!	Stop joking around!
不見不散	bú jiàn bú sàn	Be there or be square.			
自古以來	zìgǔyǐlái	since ancient times			

本课词表 Chapter Vocabulary

◎By Pinyin

Words with asterisk* are productive vocabulary which needs to be memorized and studied for its usage.

Pinyin	汉字	Definition
bǎochí*	保持	to keep (up a good thing going)
biànchéng	变成	to change into
bǐcǐ*	彼此	mutually
bié kāi wánxiào le!	别开玩笑了！	<口> Stop joking around!
bú jiàn bú sàn	不见不散	Be there or be square.
bùmǎn*	不满	discontent, unsatisfied
cāi	猜	to guess
chúcǐ yǐwài	除此以外	except for this, in addition
dǎbàn*	打扮	to dress/make up, to pose as
diǎn*	点	to order (dishes), to check one by one, to hint
dìng*	订	to book (seats), to order (books, etc.)
diū*	丢	to lose, to misplace
dìwèi	地位	position, status
fāzhǎn*	发展	to develop, to expand
fùjìn	附近	vicinity, nearby
fùzhàng	付帐	to pay a bill
gāojí	高级	high in rank/grade/quality
gèzi	个子	height, stature, build
guǐ	鬼	term of abuse (e.g., 小氣鬼、酒鬼), ghost
guójìhuà	国际化	to internationalize, internationalization
húshuō*	胡说	<口> to talk nonsense
huánjìng	环境	environment, surroundings
huānyíng*	欢迎	to welcome
huíqǐng	回请	to return; hospitality, to give return banquet
huópō*	活泼	lively, vivacious
jiànlì*	建立	to establish, to set up
jiāo'ào	骄傲	arrogant, conceited, to be proud, pride
jiézhàng*	结帐	to settle accounts
jíshǐ*	即使	even, even if/though
jiǔdiàn	酒店	hotel
jùhuì	聚会	gathering, to get together
kǎlā OK	卡拉OK	karaoke
kǎolǜ*	考虑	to think over, to consider
kuàicān	快餐	quick meal, fast food
liánluò*	联络	to contact
línghuāqián	零花钱	pocket money
lìwài	例外	exception
luàn*	乱	(to do something) carelessly, randomly
máodùn	矛盾	contradictory, contradiction
miǎnfèi	免费	to be free of charge
mìqiè	密切	close, intimate
nàixīn	耐心	patience
nándào*	难道	Do you really mean to say that...
pànduàn*	判断	to judge, to determine
qǐngkè	请客	to treat sb. (to meal/show/etc.)
qīnrén	亲人	close relatives, dear ones
qízhōng*	其中	in/among (it/them/which/etc.)
réngrán*	仍然	still, yet

shěbùdé*	舍不得	to begrudge doing sth., to loathe to part with or use
shèng(xià)*	剩(下)	to be left (over), to remain
shěngde*	省得	lest
shímáo	时髦	fashionable, in vogue
shìyè*	事业	career, undertaking
shōuhuò*	收获	gains, results
shǔ*	数	<口> to count, to be reckoned as
shuōmíng*	说明	explanation, to explain
tān*	贪	to have an insatiable desire for, to covet
tiāo*	挑	to choose
tǐng*	挺	<口> quite, very
wèihé	为何	why
wèizi	位子	seat, place
wǔxīngjí	五星级	five-star
xián*	嫌	to dislike that...
xiàohuà*	笑话	to laugh at, joke
xiǎoqi*	小气	stingy, mean
xīcān zhōng chī	西餐中吃	to eat Western-style food in the Chinese way
xìnggé*	性格	nature, disposition,

xīnkǔ*	辛苦	temperament hard, laborious
xùshù*	叙述	narration, to narrate
yáng	洋	foreign
yàome*	要么	either, or
yěxǔ*	也许	perhaps, maybe
yījǐnhuán xiāng	衣锦还乡	to return home after making good
yíngyǎng	营养	nutrition, nourishment
yǐnqǐ*	引起	to give rise to, to lead to
yǒuchéng	有成	to have achieved success
yóuqí*	尤其	especially
yuánliàng*	原谅	to excuse, to pardon
zǎoliàn	早恋	puppy love
zhèng*	挣	to earn
zhì	AA制	to go Dutch treat, to each pay his own
zhìshǎo*	至少	at (the) least
zìgǔyǐlái	自古以来	since ancient times
zìzhù cāntīng	自助餐厅	restaurant that serves buffet

語法和用法 Grammar and Usage

Pay attention to the function of the structure and then study the example sentences. When blanks are provided, either answer the questions or complete the sentences.

1. Expressing perspective

在sb. 的N 中，S	zài...de N zhōng	from the perspective of sb.

- 不過在我的印象中，小李的性格有點矛盾。

1. 在我的印象中，中學生喜歡在麥當勞聚會。

    在我的印象中，中学生喜欢在麦当劳聚会。

    My impression is that middle school students like to hang around at MacDonalds.

    那已經是過去的事情了，現在去麥當勞聚會要被人笑話的。

    那已经是过去的事情了，现在去麦当劳聚会要被人笑话的。

    That's already a thing of the past. Now if you go to MacDonalds to hang out, you will be ridiculed.

2. 我不太喜歡李明，我覺得他有點驕傲。

    我不太喜欢李明，我觉得他有点骄傲。

    I don't like Li Ming very much. I think he is a bit arrogant.

    可是在女孩子的心中，他卻是一個沒有缺點的人。

    可是在女孩子的心中，他却是一个没有缺点的人。

    But from the girls' perspective, he is flawless.

3   那個孩子又調皮又不聽話。

    那个孩子又调皮又不听话。

    That child is naughty and doesn't listen to his parents.

    但是在父母的眼中，自己的孩子都是完美的。

    但是在父母的眼中，自己的孩子都是完美的。

    Yet, from the parents' perspective, their own children are perfect.

4. 朋友對你來說很重要嗎？   朋友对你来说很重要吗？

5. 你對中國的年輕人有什麼印　　　你对中国的年轻人有什么印
　　象？　　　　　　　　　　　　象？

---

6. 你為什麼來這兒念大學？　　　你为什么来这儿念大学？

The pattern 在sb. 的 N 中 takes on a limited number of N (印象/心/眼)to indicate someone's perspective. Thus it's similar to the use of 對 sb. 來說. So it's repetitive to say 在我的心中，對我來說朋友很重要。

2. Expressing a subset

| …，其中… | …, qízhōng… | …, of which/of whom/among whom/among which… |
| 其中之一 | qízhōng zhī yī | one of them |

● 我猜你也是其中之一吧！

1. 中國每年有多少人　　中国每年有多少人　　How many students graduate
　　從大學畢業？多少　　从大学毕业？多少　　from colleges each year in
　　人會出國留學？　　人会出国留学？　　China? How many of them
　　　　　　　　　　　　　　　　　　study abroad?

　　中國每年有幾十萬　　中国每年有几十万　　In China every year there are
　　大學畢業生，其中　　大学毕业生，其中　　over one hundred thousand
　　百分之五會出國留　　百分之五会出国留　　college graduates, five percent
　　學。　　　　　　　学。　　　　　　　of whom will study abroad.

2. 中文課要學的生詞　　中文课要学的生词　　Are there a lot of vocabulary
　　多嗎？一共多少　　多吗？一共多少　　terms to study in Chinese
　　個？　　　　　　　个？　　　　　　class? How many all together?

　　中文課每課都有很　　中文课每课都有很　　In Chinese class there are many
　　多生詞，其中要會　　多生词，其中要会　　new words to study every
　　用，而且會寫的差　　用，而且会写的差　　chapter, about forty of which
　　不多有四十個。　　不多有四十个。　　one has to know how to use
　　　　　　　　　　　　　　　　　　and how to write.

3. 美國哪些大學很漂亮？這所大學怎麼樣？   美国哪些大学很漂亮？这所大学怎么样？   Which U.S. universities are beautiful? How about this one?

美國有五所大學最漂亮，這所大學是其中之一。   美国有五所大学最漂亮，这所大学是其中之一。   There are five colleges in the U.S. that are most beautiful. This university is one of them.

4. 你每天花多長時間準備功課？中文課呢？   你每天花多长时间准备功课？中文课呢？

---

5. 你去過哪些城市旅行？你最喜歡的是哪兒？   你去过哪些城市旅行？你最喜欢的是哪儿？

---

6. 這個學期你選了哪些課？你最喜歡哪門課？   这个学期你选了哪些课？你最喜欢哪门课？

Note that when 其中 is used, 其中 immediately follows a preceding statement. Thus, it's wrong to say 我去過四個城市，芝加哥其中我最喜歡 or 我去過四個城市，我其中最喜歡芝加哥. Instead, one should say我去過四個城市，其中芝加哥是我最喜歡的 or 我去過四個城市，其中我最喜歡的是芝加哥. When 其中之一 is used, it's often located at the end of a sentence, e.g., 我去過四個城市，芝加哥是其中之一.

3. Expressing the affordability of a proposition

O S V 得起	…de qǐ	S can afford to VO
O S V 不起	…bù qǐ	S cannot afford to VO

- 你從美國回來，至少要去酒店訂一桌才可以，不然大家會笑話你，以為你請不起。

1. 這個週末我們一起去「長城」吃晚飯   这个周末我们一起去"长城"吃晚饭   This weekend let's go to the "Great Wall" to have dinner.

吧。	吧。	
每個週末都到外面吃飯，我可吃不起。	每个周末都到外面吃饭，我可吃不起。	(If) we go out to have dinner every weekend, I can't afford it.
2. 為什麼你們每次開學的時候都買舊書，不買新書？	为什么你们每次开学的时候都买旧书，不买新书？	At the beginning of each semester why do you buy used books instead of new ones?
新書比舊書貴幾倍，開學的時候如果都買新書，誰買得起？	新书比旧书贵几倍，开学的时候如果都买新书，谁买得起？	New ones are several times more expensive than the used ones. If one buys all new books at the beginning of the semester, who could afford it?
3. 我要去印地買東西，你知道坐出租汽車要多少錢嗎？	我要去印地买东西，你知道坐出租汽车要多少钱吗？	I want to go buy something at Indianapolis; do you know how much it costs to go by taxi?
要一百多塊錢，太貴了，你坐得起也不要坐。	要一百多块钱，太贵了，你坐得起也不要坐。	It'll be more than one hundred dollars. That's too expensive. Even if you can afford it, you shouldn't do it.
4. 校園裏有很多又大又好的房子，你為什麼要住在校外呢？	校园里有很多又大又好的房子，你为什么要住在校外呢？	
5. 李明過生日的時候，我想送他一瓶香水，你呢？	李明过生日的时候，我想送他一瓶香水，你呢？	
6. 你這輛車已經開了好幾年了，為什麼不換一輛新的？	你这辆车已经开了好几年了，为什么不换一辆新的？	

The pattern V 得起 or V 不起 indicates mostly one can or cannot afford to V because it's (not) costly. Verbs used, such as 買、住、吃、送, often involve monetary resources. So, it's wrong to say 這輛車常給我帶來好運，所以我換不起 'this car often brings me good luck, so I can't afford to change it.' Note that the thing one can(not) afford will go after 得起/不起, or at the beginning of the sentence as a topic, e.g., 我住不起校內的房子 or 校內的房子我住不起. Also, in English, one often says 'I can't afford to buy a new car.' However, in Chinese when the thing one can(not) afford is a generic noun, there is no need to indicate "a" as it often is in English. So, the incorrect sentence 我買不起一輛新車 should be rephrased to 我買不起新車. Never say 這東西太貴，我沒有錢買得起. One should simply say 這東西太貴，我買不起 'This thing is too expensive. I can't afford to buy it.'

The meaning of V得起 or V 不起 can be extended to indicate senses involving no monetary resources, and expresses whether or not one can take/stand something, e.g., 他這個人開不起玩笑/經不起批評/經得起考驗 'He can't take any jokes/can't take criticism/can take a challenge'; 他們一輸了球就說裁判不公平，一點兒都輸不起 'Whenever they lose the game, they say the referee is not fair. They can't take the loss at all.'

4. Expressing binding alternative

S要麼VO，要麼VO	yàome…yàome	either…or…

- 按照美國的習慣，中學生聚會，要麼到自助餐廳，要麼到快餐廳。

1. 你週末的時候打算作什麼？	你周末的时候打算作什么？	What do you plan to do this weekend?
沒什麼特別的事情，要麼去運動，要麼去圖書館做功課。	没什么特别的事情，要么去运动，要么去图书馆做功课。	I don't have anything special. I either exercise or go to the library to do homework.
2. 小王特貪玩，我從來沒看他學習過。	小王特贪玩，我从来没看他学习过。	Xiao Wang really loves to have fun. I've never seen him studying.
是啊，他要麼去看電影，要麼去酒吧，就是不去學習。	是啊，他要么去看电影，要么去酒吧，就是不去学习。	That's right. He either goes to see a movie or goes to a bar, but he never goes to study.

3. | 聽說你不太喜歡現在的同屋，嫌他有什麼不好嗎？ | 听说你不太喜欢现在的同屋，嫌他有什么不好吗？ | I heard that you don't like your current roommate. What don't you like about him? |

| 他要麼亂用我的東西，要麼大聲地放音樂，我想我最好找別的房子。 | 他要么乱用我的东西，要么大声地放音乐，我想我最好找别的房子。 | He either uses my stuff without my consent or plays loud music. I think I had better find another place to stay. |

4. | 你大學畢業以後打算做什麼？ | 你大学毕业以后打算做什么？ | |

_____

5. | 我打算學習商業，你覺得我上哪所大學比較好？為什麼？ | 我打算学习商业，你觉得我上哪所大学比较好？为什么？ | |

_____

6. | 下個星期天是爸爸的生日，我們怎麼慶祝呢？ | 下个星期天是爸爸的生日，我们怎么庆祝呢？ | |

_____

Note that what goes after 要麼 is often a verb phrase, not a noun and that the verb phrases after two 要麼 are often parallel. So, one should not say 我覺得你上要麼印大，要麼哈佛. Instead, one should say 我覺得你要麼上印大，要麼上哈佛. The pattern 要麼⋯，要麼⋯ is used to indicate just two binding alternatives, not one's comments on the alternatives. So, phrases like 都好 or 比較好 should not follow the pattern. It's wrong to say 畢業以後，要麼去找工作，要麼繼續學習都好。

5. Expressing comparison

A Adj於B	yú	A is more/less Adj than B
A 高於/低於B	gāoyú/dīyú	A is higher/lower than B
A 多於/少於B	duōyú/shǎoyú	A is more/lesser than B
A 大於/小於B	dàyú/xiǎoyú	A is bigger/smaller than B

● 由於中國的經濟水平仍然低於美國⋯⋯

1. 農村和城市有什麼
不同？

农村和城市有什么
不同？

What are the differences between the countryside and cities?

在農村，人們的生
活水平和教育水平
低於城市。

在农村，人们的生
活水平和教育水平
低于城市。

In the countryside, people's living and educational standards are lower than that in the city.

2. 中國有多少大學？
他們有什麼不同？

中国有多少大学？
他们有什么不同？

How many colleges are there in China? What are the differences among them?

在中國有幾百所大
學，不同的大學對
學生的要求也不一
樣，一般來說，重
點大學的要求高於
普通大學。

在中国有几百所大
学，不同的大学对学
生的要求也不一样，
一般来说，重点大学
的要求高于普通大
学。

There are several hundred colleges in China. Different colleges have different requirements of their students. Generally speaking, the standards of famous colleges are higher than those of ordinary colleges.

3. 現在年輕人花的錢
多嗎？花多少？都
花在什麼方面？

现在年轻人花的钱
多吗？花多少？都
花在什么方面？

Do young people spend much money nowadays? How much do they spend and in what areas?

現在年輕人都愛打
扮，每個月花在買
衣服上的錢不會少
於五百塊。

现在年轻人都爱打
扮，每个月花在买
衣服上的钱不会少
于五百块。

Nowadays young people love to dress up. The money they spend on clothing each month is no less than five hundred dollars.

4. 在美國公立大學和私立大學的
學費有什麼不同？

在美国公立大学和私立大学的学
费有什么不同？

---

5. 他畢業以後好不容易才找到工
作，為什麼現在又不做了？

他毕业以后好不容易才找到工
作，为什么现在又不做了？

---

6. | 我聽說，現在回國的留學生比　　我听说，现在回国的留学生比从
從前的多，你知道為什麼嗎？　　前的多，你知道为什么吗？

於 is often used in literary, formal Chinese such as that found in news articles or headlines. In this pattern 於 goes after an adjective to indicate comparision. Its usage is equivalent to the colloquial expression of 和A比，B···. So, to state "he prefers study to work" colloquially, one can say 和工作比，他更喜歡學習. To express the same idea more literally, one can say 他對學習的興趣大於工作. It's odd to say 他高於我 'he is taller than I,' but all right to say 美國人均收入高於我國 'the average income of Americans is higher than that in our country' because the style of the latter is in literary formal Chinese.

6. Expressing a concessive condition

| 即使/就算··· ，S 也 ··· | jíshǐ/jiùsuàn..., S yě | even if...S still; even |

- **即使**沒有打算回國工作的人，**也**希望和國內的朋友保持好的關係……

1. | 你們要去看自己的老同學，為什麼總要我一起去？我和你們這個年紀的人談不來。 | 你们要去看自己的老同学，为什么总要我一起去？我和你们这个年纪的人谈不来。 | When you guys want to go see your own classmates, why do you always want me to go with you? I can't talk to people your age. |

| 就算你和大家談不來，為了禮貌，你也要和我們一起去！ | 就算你和大家谈不来，为了礼貌，你也要和我们一起去！ | Even if you can't talk to anyone, to show courtesy, you have to go with us. |

2. | 我每天上班又忙又累，下班以後真的懶得做飯。 | 我每天上班又忙又累，下班以后真的懒得做饭。 | Every day at work I am tired and busy. After work, I really don't feel like cooking at all. |

| 就算你再忙再累，你也得做飯，這是我們結婚的時候就說好的！ | 就算你再忙再累，你也得做饭，这是我们结婚的时候就说好的！ | Even if you are busy and tired, you have to cook. This was what we agreed upon when we got married. |

3. | 我是一個很健康的人，你不要每天都對我說多吃蔬菜、注意營養行不行？ | 我是一个很健康的人，你不要每天都对我说多吃蔬菜、注意营养行不行？ | I'm a very healthy person. Don't tell me every day that I need to eat more vegetables and pay more attention to my diet, okay? |
|---|---|---|
| 即使再健康的人，也會有營養的問題，你不注意的話一定會發福的！ | 即使再健康的人，也会有营养的问题，你不注意的话一定会发福的！ | Even those who are healthy can have a problem with their diet. If you don't pay attention to this, you will certainly gain weight. |

4. | 我不覺得張新有什麼優點，為什麼張麗會那麼喜歡他？ | 我不觉得张新有什么优点，为什么张丽会那么喜欢他？ | |

5. | 那些洋快餐沒有營養，又不好吃，我不明白為什麼那麼多人喜歡吃？ | 那些洋快餐没有营养，又不好吃，我不明白为什么那么多人喜欢吃？ | |

6. | 吃飯的時候，我從来不給別人夾菜或者盛湯，因為我覺得那太不衛生了！ | 吃饭的时候，我从来不给别人夹菜或者盛汤，因为我觉得那太不卫生了！ | |

The pattern "即使/就算…，S 也" expresses a concessive condition. It often indicates the volition of the speaker to do or not to do an action, regardless of the circumstance stated in the 即使/就算 clause. It is not used simply to designate two different aspects of a thing, as often expressed by 雖然…但是…. So, it's wrong to say 就算快餐不好吃，快餐也很便宜 'Even though fast-food does not taste good, it is cheap.' Instead, it is more appropriate to rephrase it into something like 雖然快餐不好吃，可是很便宜 'Although fast food does not taste good, it is cheap' or 就算快餐不好吃，也有很多人喜歡 'Even though fast-food does not taste good, there are many people who like it.' Remember that 也 should always go after the subject, if there is one.

背景常識 Background Notes

1. 「AA」制：八十年代末，九十年代初流行起來的一種吃飯的時候各付各的帳的方法。吃飯的時候，大家一起點菜，然後大家平分所有的費用。這是年輕人比較喜歡的一種方法。

2. 旅館、酒店：在中國旅館有很多不同的說法，包括旅館、賓館、飯店、酒店。雖然他們的意思差不多，但是每個詞代表了不同檔次的旅館。一般來說，旅館是指那些規模比較小的，比較便宜的地方；飯店和酒店的檔次最高，賓館在兩者之間。

3. 早戀：在初中和高中，學校認為學生的主要工作應該是學習，所以禁止學生談戀愛。如果有學生談戀愛的話，就被稱為「早戀」，會受到老師的批評。一般的家長也非常反對中學生談戀愛。不過現在，學校和家長慢慢地認識到應該正確的認識這個問題，所以對早戀學生的態度比以前好得多，但他們還是會限制學生早戀。

背景常识 Background Notes

1. "AA"制：八十年代末，九十年代初流行起来的一种吃饭的时候各付各的帐的方法。吃饭的时候，大家一起点菜，然后大家平分所有的费用。这是年轻人比较喜欢的一种方法。

2. 旅馆、酒店：在中国旅馆有很多不同的说法，包括旅馆、宾馆、饭店、酒店。虽然他们的意思差不多，但是每个词代表了不同档次的旅馆。一般来说，旅馆是指那些规模比较小的，比较便宜的地方；饭店和酒店的档次最高，宾馆在两者之间。

3. 早恋：在初中和高中，学校认为学生的主要工作应该是学习，所以禁止学生谈恋爱。如果有学生谈恋爱的话，就被称为"早恋"，会受到老师的批评。一般的家长也非常反对中学生谈恋爱。不过现在，学校和家长慢慢地认识到应该正确的认识这个问题，所以对早恋学生的态度比以前好得多，但他们还是会限制学生早恋。

第二課　沒有錢，能走多遠？

Theme: Travel and Sightseeing

Communicative Objectives
- Talking about places and weather
- Talking about ways of traveling
- Narrating a travel experience

Skill Focus
Comprehending a travel guide

Grammar Focus
- X 被稱為 Y
- S 不僅⋯而且⋯
- S V 於 X
- A⋯，而 B (卻)⋯
  S Adj 而 Adj
- S 固然 X 但是／可是／
  不過 Y
- 首先⋯其次⋯最後

Problem Scenario
Your friend has told you that if you go to China, you should visit Kunming by all means because the weather there is very nice. In addition, you should definitely join a tour group. With a very limited budget (￥$4,000), how would you plan your trip to China this summer? Which cities are you going to visit (your itinerary)? By what means of transportation? What preparations should you make beforehand?

對話 Dialogue

(1)Talking about places and weather

李明鄰居的女兒張麗，和剛考上北大的同學王方聊天。

王方：　請問，去中文系怎麼走？

張麗：　我正要去中文系，跟我走吧！

王方：　太謝謝你了！我是大一的新生，從昆明來的。

張麗：　我是大三的老生，歡迎到北京來。聽說昆明[1]**被稱為**「春城」，那裏的氣候一定很好吧？

王方：　是啊！昆明[2]**不僅**四季都像春天一樣溫暖，**而且**比較潮濕，不像北京這麼乾！

張麗：　我知道昆明在中國的西南部，那裏是不是有很多少數民族？

王方：　對，少數民族佔人口的三分之一。

張麗：　你們可以互相溝通嗎？

王方：　大部分的少數民族都有自己的方言。當然他們也會說普通話，但是口音很重！

張麗：　聽起來真有意思，希望我以後有機會去昆明旅行。

王方：　那我可以做你的導遊！

閱讀理解 Comprehension Check

1. 王方是誰？她是從哪兒來的？
2. 張麗去過昆明嗎？昆明的氣候怎麼樣？
3. 昆明在中國的什麼地方？那兒有什麼特色 tèsè 'characteristics'？
4. 張麗想去昆明嗎？為什麼？

(1)Talking about places and weather

李明邻居的女儿张丽，和刚考上北大的同学王方聊天。

王方： 请问，去中文系怎么走？

张丽： 我正要去中文系，跟我走吧！

王方： 太谢谢你了！我是大一的新生，从昆明来的。

张丽： 我是大三的老生，欢迎到北京来。听说昆明[1]**被称为**"春城"，那里的气候一定很好吧？

王方： 是啊！昆明[2]**不仅**四季都象春天一样温暖，**而且**比较潮湿，不象北京这么干！

张丽： 我知道昆明在中国的西南部，那里是不是有很多少数民族？

王方： 对，少数民族占人口的三分之一。

张丽： 你们可以互相沟通吗？

王方： 大部分的少数民族都有自己的方言。当然他们也会说普通话，但是口音很重！

张丽： 听起来真有意思，希望我以后有机会去昆明旅行。

王方： 那我可以做你的导游！

阅读理解 Comprehension Check

1. 王方是谁？她是从哪儿来的？
2. 张丽去过昆明吗？昆明的气候怎么样？
3. 昆明在中国的什么地方？那儿有什么特色tèsè 'characteristics'？
4. 张丽想去昆明吗？为什么？

對話一生詞 Vocabulary

Study the numbered vocabulary (productive vocabulary) for its usage. The unnumbered items (receptive vocabulary) are to facilitate reading comprehension.

◎By Order of Appearance

	鄰居	邻居	línjū	N	neighbor	[near-to dwell]
1.	請問	请问	qǐngwèn	N	May I ask...?	[please-ask]
	大一		dàyī	N	大學一年級的學生 → 大二、大三、大四	[univerity-one]
	昆明		Kūnmíng	N	capital of Yunnan province	[descendant-bright]
	上海		Shànghǎi	N	Shanghai	[over-sea]
2.	稱	称	chēng	V	to call, to say, to weigh	
3.	氣候	气候	qìhòu	N	climate, situation	[air-situation]
4.	不僅	不仅	bùjǐn	Conj	不只	[not-only]
5.	季節	季节	jìjié	N	season	[season-joint]
6.	溫暖		wēnnuǎn	Adj	warm	[warm-genial]
7.	潮濕	潮湿	cháoshī	Adj	wet, moist, damp	[damp-wet]
8.	乾	干	gān	Adj	dry	
9.	少數	少数	shǎoshù	N	small number, few, minority	[few-number]
	民族		mínzú	N	ethnic group, nationality	[people-clan]
10.	佔	占	zhàn	V	to occupy	
11.	溝通	沟通	gōutōng	V	to communicate	[trench-to connect]
	導遊	导游	dǎoyóu	N	tour guide	[to lead-travel]

Characters with Many Strokes

鄰 稱 僅 節 暖 潮 濕 乾 溝 導

詞匯用法 Words in Context

1. 請問：請問，現在幾點？請問，　　　请问：请问，现在几点？请问，
   去圖書館怎麼走？　　　　　　　　去图书馆怎么走？

   你想去圖書館，會怎麼問路？　　　你想去图书馆，会怎么问路？

你想知道現在幾點了，你會怎麼問你的同學？

你想知道现在几点了，你会怎么问你的同学？

2. 稱：（句型）

    称：（句型）

3. 氣候：氣候很好；氣候潮濕、很乾、溫暖、寒冷

    你覺得這兒的氣候怎麼樣？

    人們為什麼都那麼喜歡去佛羅里達旅遊？

    你觉得这儿的气候怎么样？

    人们为什么都那么喜欢去佛罗里达旅游？

4. 不僅：（句型）

    不仅：（句型）

5. 季節：四季如春

    春、夏、秋、冬，你最喜歡哪個季節？為什麼？

    你覺得春天是旅行的季節嗎？

    季节：四季如春

    春、夏、秋、冬，你最喜欢哪个季节？为什么？

    你觉得春天是旅行的季节吗？

6. 溫暖：氣候溫暖；溫暖的房間、教室；溫暖的手、家

    為什麼一到週末你就回家？

    外面的雪那麼好看，你為什麼還待在屋子裏？

    温暖：气候温暖；温暖的房间、教室；温暖的手、家

    为什么一到周末你就回家？

    外面的雪那么好看，你为什么还待在屋子里？

7. 潮濕：氣候、房間潮濕；潮濕的空氣

    你喜歡下雨天嗎？為什麼？

    你為什麼不喜歡住在那兒？

    潮湿：气候、房间潮湿；潮湿的空气

    你喜欢下雨天吗？为什么？

    你为什么不喜欢住在那儿？

8. 乾：氣候比較乾；嘴很乾；嗓子乾死了

    上中文課的時候大家都要帶一瓶水，你知道為什麼嗎？

    如果你從圖書館跑到教室會有什麼感覺？

    干：气候比较干；嘴很干；嗓子干死了

    上中文课的时候大家都要带一瓶水，你知道为什么吗？

    如果你从图书馆跑到教室会有什么感觉？

9. 少數：佔少數；少數人同意

    少数：佔少数；少数人同意

↔多數 | ↔多数

在這個大學，和美國學生比，外國學生多嗎？

你覺得在美國，人們喜不喜歡看足球比賽？

10. 佔：佔少數、多數；佔1/3；佔重要的地位；佔很多時間

準備中文課會佔你多少時間？

三年級的中文課男生多還是女生多？

11. 溝通：用中文溝通；無法溝通；溝通不了

你有中國朋友嗎？你們怎麼溝通？

多學幾種外語有什麼好處？

在这个大学，和美国学生比，外国学生多吗？

你觉得在美国，人们喜不喜欢看足球比赛？

佔：佔少数、多数；佔1/3；佔重要的地位；佔很多时间

准备中文课会占你多少时间？

三年级的中文课男生多还是女生多？

沟通：用中文沟通；无法沟通；沟通不了

你有中国朋友吗？你们怎么沟通？

多学几种外语有什么好处？

自由發揮與課堂活動 Free Discussion and Class Activities

1. 旅行的時候你喜歡去一個有朋友的地方還是沒有朋友的地方？為什麼？

旅行的时候你喜欢去一个有朋友的地方还是没有朋友的地方？为什么？

2. 你喜歡旅行嗎？你喜歡一個人去旅行，還是和朋友一起去？為什麼？

你喜欢旅行吗？你喜欢一个人去旅行，还是和朋友一起去？为什么？

3. 有機會的話，你想去哪兒旅行？為什麼？

有机会的话，你想去哪儿旅行？为什么？

(2) Talking about ways of traveling

李明鄰居的女兒張麗，和一個愛旅行的同學陳文聊天。

陳文：　國慶節快到了，這個季節去昆明旅行最舒服，有沒有什麼打算？

張麗：　當然有，可是我一個月的生活費恐怕還不夠買一張飛機票呢！

陳文：　那你為什麼不參加旅行團呢？

張麗：　跟旅行團會便宜嗎？

陳文：　便宜多了！三千塊錢包括機票、酒店、一日三餐和旅行景點的門票。

張麗：　真的嗎？可是我知道從北京到昆明的來回飛機票就要三千二。

陳文：　所以現在人們都[3]**熱衷於**跟團旅行，既省錢又省心。

張麗：　可是昆明在高原上，我會不會不習慣那裏的氣候和飲食？

陳文：　一定會碰到不習慣的地方，可是旅行就是要去經歷不同的東西！

閱讀理解 Comprehension Check

5.　什麼時候去昆明最好？

6.　跟團旅行有什麼好處？

7.　張麗擔心在昆明會遇到什麼問題？

8.　在陳文看來，旅行的目的是什麼？

(2) Talking about ways of traveling

李明邻居的女儿张丽，和一个爱旅行的同学陈文聊天。

陈文： 国庆节快到了，这个季节去昆明旅行最舒服，有没有什么打算？

张丽： 当然有，可是我一个月的生活费恐怕还不够买一张飞机票呢！

陈文： 那你为什么不参加旅行团呢？

张丽： 跟旅行团会便宜吗？

陈文： 便宜多了！三千块钱包括机票、酒店、一日三餐和旅行景点的门票。

张丽： 真的吗？可是我知道从北京到昆明的来回飞机票就要三千二。

陈文： 所以现在人们都[3]**热衷于**跟团旅行，既省钱又省心。

张丽： 可是昆明在高原上，我会不会不习惯那里的气候和饮食？

陈文： 免不了会碰到不习惯的地方，可是旅行就是要去经历不同的东西！

阅读理解 Comprehension Check

5. 什么时候去昆明最好？
6. 跟团旅行有什么好处？
7. 张丽担心在昆明会遇到什么问题？
8. 在陈文看来，旅行的目的是什么？

對話二生詞 Vocabulary

	國慶節	国庆节	Guóqìngjié	N	National Day	[country-to celebrate-holiday]
12.	打算		dǎsuàn	N/V	plan, to plan	[to do-to calculate]
13.	恐怕		kǒngpà	Adv	perhaps, I think, I'm afraid	[fear-perhaps]
14.	包括		bāokuò	V	to include	[to contain-to draw together]
15.	景點	景点	jǐngdiǎn	N	scenic spot	[scene-spot]
	門票	门票	ménpiào	N	admission fee	[door-ticket]
16.	熱衷於	热衷于	rèzhōngyú	V	to be keen on, to be very fond of	[hot-inner feelings-at]
17.	省		shěng	V	to save	
	高原		gāoyuán	N	plateau, highland	[high-plain]
18.	碰到		pèngdào	RV	to run into	[to run into-(complement)]
19.	經歷	经历	jīnglì	V/N	to experience, experience	[to undergo-through]
	飲食	饮食	yǐnshí	N	food and drink, diet	[drink-meal]

Characters with Many Strokes

慶 算 景 熱 衷 於 省 碰 經 歷

詞匯用法 Words in Context

12. 打算：有什麼打算；打算做什麼
你畢業以後打算做什麼工作？
你這個寒假有什麼打算嗎？

打算：有什么打算；打算做什么
你毕业以后打算做什么工作？
你这个寒假有什么打算吗？

13. 恐怕：恐怕我幫不了你；恐怕不
能用中文溝通；恐怕會下雨
我打算感恩節的時候去南部旅
遊，你願意和我一起去嗎？
你覺得我在麥當勞慶祝我的生日
怎麼樣？

恐怕：恐怕我帮不了你；恐怕不
能用中文沟通；恐怕会下雨
我打算感恩节的时候去南部旅
游，你愿意和我一起去吗？
你觉得我在麦当劳庆祝我的生日
怎么样？

14. 包括：英語包括美國英語和英國
英語；包括我

你每個月的房租包括水費和電費
嗎？

這個週末有多少人參加你們的晚
會？

包括：英语包括美国英语和英国
英语；包括我

你每个月的房租包括水费和电费
吗？

这个周末有多少人参加你们的晚
会？

15. 景點：旅遊景點；有不少景點

美國哪個州的旅遊景點最多？

你最想去哪個旅遊景點？

景点：旅遊景点；有不少景点

美国哪个州的旅游景点最多？

你最想去哪个旅游景点？

16. 熱衷於：（句型）

热衷于：（句型）

17. 省：省錢、時、油、電、水、
紙；省心、事

為什麼大家都熱衷於買日本車？

你覺得什麼樣的旅遊方法比較省
心？

省：省钱、时、油、电、水、
纸；省心、事

为什么大家都热衷于买日本车？

你觉得什么样的旅游方法比较省
心？

18. 碰到：碰到朋友；碰到困難、麻
煩

學中文的時候，你碰到最大的困
難是什麼？

在路上碰到你的同學，中國人和
美國人說的話有什麼不同？

碰到：碰到朋友；碰到困难、麻
烦

学中文的时候，你碰到最大的困
难是什么？

在路上碰到你的同学，中国人和
美国人说的话有什么不同？

19. 經歷：經歷過一個人的生活；有
意思的經歷

旅遊的時候，你有什麼有意思的
經歷？

你經歷過談戀愛的痛苦了嗎？

经历：经历过一个人的生活；有
意思的经历

旅游的时候，你有什么有意思的
经历？

你经历过谈恋爱的痛苦了吗？

自由發揮與課堂活動 Free Discussion and Class Activities

4. 你覺得什麼時候旅行最好？為什麼？

   你觉得什么时候旅行最好？为什么？

5. 去旅行的時候，你會怎麼解決錢的問題？用信用卡，旅行支票，還是現金？為什麼？

   去旅行的时候，你会怎么解决钱的问题？用信用卡，旅行支票，还是现金？为什么？

6. 旅行的時候你喜歡住在什麼地方？為什麼？

   旅行的时候你喜欢住在什么地方？为什么？

7. 介紹一個旅行的時候省錢的辦法。

   介绍一个旅行的时候省钱的办法。

8. 我打算去佛羅里達旅行，但是我不了解那裏的情況。請給我一些建議：

   1）怎麼訂機票和酒店；
   2）什麼時候去；
   3）哪些地方值得去；
   4）需要注意的事情。

   我打算去佛罗里达旅行，但是我不了解那裏的情况。请给我一些建议：

   1）怎么订机票和酒店；
   2）什么时候去；
   3）哪些地方值得去；
   4）需要注意的事情。

敘述 Narrative

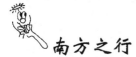

南方之行

熱衷於旅行的陳文已經跟她的旅行團到了昆明。[4]**而**我這個窮學生還在想，在這個什麼都要錢的社會裏，沒有錢我能走多遠？

我很幸運，王方請我國慶節和她一起回昆明，這樣我可以在她家裏白吃白住，既省錢又省心！從北京到昆明要坐兩天兩夜的火車，王方擔心路上不安全，就在她的內衣上縫了一個小口袋，把錢都放到裏面。這樣做[5]**固然**很安全，**但是**每次用錢都要去洗手間取。我覺得不方便，就建議先花我

的錢，到昆明時我已經沒有多少錢了。

不知為了什麼事，下火車的時候我倆吵了起來，我一生氣就對她說，「我們各走各的吧！」可是出了車站，我才想起來自己連吃飯的錢都沒有了。當我既生氣又失望地在街上亂走時，一輛公共汽車停在我面前，司機用有口音的

普通話大聲說：「快上，快上。」我隨便問了一句，「沒錢能上嗎？」「能！能！」他一定以為我在開玩笑，所以笑著回答。上了車以後，我正高興碰到了「雷鋒」，司機

卻叫我買票。我只好說：「我真的沒錢，是你非讓我上來的！」看了我的學生證以後，他就說「算了！」

　下車以後我就想，不花錢可不可以在昆明旅行？除了王方以外，在昆明我沒有朋友，住成了一個大問題。不過我想起來，在北京，學校的週末舞會結束後，常有外校的女孩來不及回去，就到我們的宿舍借住，我每次都熱情歡迎。我想好人有好報，所以就跟一個女學生聊起天來，結果沒到三分鐘，她就同意讓我借住了，而且成了我在昆明的導遊。

　雖然沒錢，可是我卻在昆明玩得很愉快。我現在還經常想起我的南方之行，那些坐飛機、住酒店的人恐怕不能明白我那種苦中找樂的愉快感覺。

閱讀理解 Comprehension Check

9. 張麗認為現在的社會有什麼問題？
10. 張麗國慶節的時候，上哪兒玩了？為什麼？
11. 為什麼王方把錢放在內衣的小口袋裏？
12. 為什麼張麗到昆明時，錢都花完了？
13. 張麗和王方一起在昆明玩嗎？為什麼？
14. 張麗沒有錢，為什麼還上公共汽車？
15. 張麗最後買沒買票？你怎麼知道？
16. 張麗在昆明最大的問題是什麼？為什麼會有這個問題？
17. 在北京，週末舞會完了以後，常有什麼事情？
18. 為什麼張麗跟一個女學生聊天？張麗相信什麼？結果怎麼樣？
19. 張麗對她的南方之行有什麼感覺？

南方之行

热衷于旅行的陈文已经跟她的旅行团到了昆明。[4]而我这个穷学生还在想，在这个什么都要钱的社会里，没有钱我能走多远？

我很幸运，王方请我国庆节和她一起回昆明，这样我可以在她家里白吃白住，既省钱又省心！从北京到昆明要坐两天两夜的火车，王方担心路上不安全，就在她的内衣上缝了一个小口袋，把钱都放到里面。这样做[5]固然很安全，但是每次用钱都要去洗手间取。我觉得不方便，就建议先花我的钱，到昆明时我已经没有多少钱了。

不知为了什么事，下火车的时候我俩吵了起来，我一生气就对她说，"我们各走各的吧！"可是出了车站，我才想起来自己连吃饭的钱都没有了。当

我既生气又失望地在街上乱走时，一辆公共汽车停在我面前，司机用有口音的普通话大声说："快上，快上"。我随便问了一句，"没钱能上吗？""能！能！"他一定以为我在开玩笑，所以笑着回答。上了车以后，我正高兴碰到了"雷锋"，司机却叫我买票。我只好说："我真的没钱，是你非让我上来的！"看了我的学生证以后，他就说"算了！"

下车以后我就想，不花钱可不可以在昆明旅行？除了王方以外，在昆明我没有朋友，住成了一个大问题。不过我想起来，在北京，学校的周末舞会结束后，常有外校的女孩来不及回去，就到我们的宿舍借

住，我每次都热情欢迎。我想好
人有好报，所以就跟一个女学生
聊起天来，结果没到三分钟，她
就同意让我借住了，而且成了我
在昆明的导游。

虽然没钱，可是我却在昆
明玩得很愉快。我现在还经常想
起我的南方之行，那些坐飞机、
住酒店的人恐怕不能明白我那种
苦中找乐的愉快感觉。

阅读理解 Comprehension Check

9. 张丽认为现在的社会有什么问题？

10. 张丽国庆节的时候，上哪儿玩了？为什么？

11. 为什么王方把钱放在内衣的小口袋里？

12. 为什么张丽到昆明时，钱都花完了？

13. 张丽和王方一起在昆明玩吗？为什么？

14. 张丽没有钱，为什么还上公共汽车？

15. 张丽最後买没买票？你怎么知道？

16. 张丽在昆明最大的问题是什么？为什么会有这个问题？

17. 在北京，周末舞会完了以後，常有什么事情？

18. 为什么张丽跟一个女学生聊天？张丽相信什么？结果怎么样？

19. 张丽对她的南方之行有什么感觉？

敘述生詞 Vocabulary

	之		zhī	Part	<書>的	
20.	幸運	幸运	xìngyùn	Adj	lucky	[luck-fortune]
21.	白		bái	Adv	free of charge, to do sth. in vain	
	内衣		nèiyī	N	underwear	[inside-clothes]
	縫	缝	féng	V	to sew	
	口袋		kǒudài	N	pocket	[hole-pouch]
22.	固然		gùrán	Conj	雖然	[firm-(adv marker)]
	洗手間	洗手间	xǐshǒujiān	N	廁所	[wash-hand-room]

23.	取		qǔ	V	拿
24.	建議	建议	jiànyì	V	to suggest	[to propose-discuss]
25.	吵		chǎo	V	to quarrel
26.	失望		shīwàng	V/Adj	to become disappointed, to lose (hope)	[to lose-hope]
27.	隨便	随便	suíbiàn	Adv	casually, to do as one pleases	[to follow-convenient]
	雷鋒	雷锋	Léi Fēng	N	a model citizen who is always ready to help others	[thunder-sharp]
28.	證	证	zhèng	N	certificate, card, credentials (e.g., 學生證)
29.	算了		suànle	IE	<口>Let it be. Forget it.	[let it pass-(particle)]
	舞會	舞会	wǔhuì	N	dancing party	[dance-gathering]
30.	結束	结束	jiéshù	V	to end	[to settle-to bind]
	借住		jièzhù	V	to stay over at sb. else's place	[to borrow-to stay]
31.	熱情	热情	rèqíng	Adv	enthusiastically	[hot-feeling]
	好人有好報	好人有好报	hǎorén yǒu hǎo bào	IE	One good turn deserves another.	[good-people-have-good-to recompense]

Characters with Many Strokes

運 縫 袋 建 議 望 隨 證 算 舞

詞匯用法 Words in Context

20. 幸運：很幸運；幸運兒；幸運的是　　幸运：很幸运；幸运儿；幸运的是

你覺得自己算是一個幸運兒嗎？為什麼？　　你觉得自己算是一个幸运儿吗？为什么？

我昨天沒準備，幸運的是今天老師沒叫我回答問題。　　我昨天没准备，幸运的是今天老师没叫我回答问题。

21. 白：白吃、喝、玩、送、寫、準備　　白：白吃、喝、玩、送、写、准备

參加學校的一些晚會是免費的　　参加学校的一些晚会是免费的

嗎？

為什麼如果老師說今天不考聽寫，準備了的同學會不高興？

22. 固然：（句型）

23. 取：取東西、錢

下樓以後發現沒帶車鑰匙，你怎麼辦？

去銀行取錢的時候要做些什麼？

24. 建議：提建議；有一些建議；請給我一些建議

在選擇專業的時候，你的父母給你提了什麼建議？

如果學中文的學生要有一次聚會，對地點你有什麼建議嗎？

20. 吵：吵架；吵起來了；吵個不停

和男/女朋友吵架以後，怎麼讓他/她原諒自己？

你會為什麼事情和父母吵起來？

21. 失望：對成績很失望；這裏的氣候讓我失望；覺得失望

來到這兒以後，有什麼事情讓你失望？

旅遊的時候發生什麼事情你會覺得失望？

22. 隨便：隨便走走；隨便吃點東西；隨便吧；覺得很隨便

下午還有課，中午咱們吃點什麼

呢？

人們為什麼不太喜歡去不熟悉的
人家裏做客？

23. 證：學生、工作、借書、駕駛、
畢業證

你的學生證有什麼作用？

你有駕駛證嗎？什麼時候考到
的？

24. 算了：太麻煩，算了吧！算了，
不說了。

你的朋友不接受你的建議，你會
怎麼辦？

我對這次的考試成績很失望，怎
麼辦？

25. 結束：三點結束；還沒結束；會
議結束；我和女朋友結束了

這個學期的課什麼時候結束？

怎麼很長時間沒看到小王和他的
女朋友一起參加晚會了？

26. 熱情：熱情的朋友；熱情地幫助
別人

你覺得哪些方面可以說明這兒的
人很熱情？

張麗的導遊對她怎麼樣？

呢？

人们为什么不太喜欢去不熟悉的
人家里做客？

证：学生、工作、借书、驾驶、
毕业证

你的学生证有什么作用？

你有驾驶证吗？什么时候考到
的？

算了：太麻烦，算了吧！算了，
不说了。

你的朋友不接受你的建议，你会
怎么办？

我对这次的考试成绩很失望，怎
么办？

结束：三点结束；还没结束；会
议结束；我和女朋友结束了

这个学期的课什么时候结束？

怎么很长时间没看到小王和他的
女朋友一起参加晚会了？

热情：热情的朋友；热情地帮助
别人

你觉得哪些方面可以说明这儿的
人很热情？

张丽的导游对她怎么样？

自由發揮與課堂活動 Free Discussion and Class Activities

9. 你去過什麼地方旅遊？說說你難
忘的旅遊經歷。

你去过什么地方旅游？说说你难
忘的旅游经历。

10. 為你的客戶 kèhù 'customer' 安排旅行計劃

根據下面這些人的背景和特點，為他們選擇地點、時間、旅行的方法。說明你這麼安排的原因是什麼。

- 小張：女，中文系大三的學生
- 老李：男，商人。已退休，身體不太好
- 美華：家庭主婦

11. 為了慶祝媽媽50歲的生日，孩子打算安排爸爸媽媽去旅行，可是他們的觀點有差別。

A: 想讓父母去佛羅里達。

B: 想讓父母去北京。

A和B討論這個問題，說明自己的理由，然後決定父母應該去什麼地方。

为你的客户 kèhù 'customer' 安排旅行计划

根据下面这些人的背景和特点，为他们选择地点、时间、旅行的方法。说明你这么安排的原因是什么。

- 小张：女，中文系大三的学生
- 老李：男，商人。已退休，身体不太好
- 美华：家庭主妇

为了庆祝妈妈50岁的生日，孩子打算安排爸爸妈妈去旅行，可是他们的观点有差别。

A: 想让父母去佛罗里达。

B: 想让父母去北京。

A和B讨论这个问题，说明自己的理由，然后决定父母应该去什么地方。

說明 Exposition

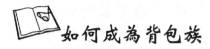 如何成為背包族

　　現在越來越多的年輕人熱衷於背起背包到各地旅行。那麼，怎麼樣才能成為一個「背包族」呢？

　　[6]**首先**，在旅行以前應該了解那裏的環境、氣候、民族、宗教、飲食習慣、居住條件等情況。不同的地區在各方面的差別很大。如果了解了這些情況，不僅可以避免麻煩，而且可以增加樂趣，讓旅行更有意思。

　　其次，要了解可用交通工具的時刻表。熟悉了這些情況，才能安排好時間。

　　最後，要旅行千萬別怕麻煩。應該多閱讀旅遊方面的雜誌，當然也可以向有經驗的朋友請教。不過，不要以為別人有趣而難忘的經歷你一定會碰到。每個人的旅行都是不同的。

閱讀理解 Comprehension Check

20. 「背包族」是什麼意思？
21. 「背包族」第一應該了解什麼？
22. 「背包族」第二應該了解什麼？
23. 最後「背包族」應該做什麼？
24. 所有人旅遊的經歷都是很有趣的，對嗎？

如何成为背包族

现在越来越多的年轻人热衷于背起背包到各地旅行。那么，怎么样才能成为一个"背包族"呢？

⁶**首先**，在旅行以前应该了解那里的环境、气候、民族、宗教、饮食习惯、居住条件等情况。不同的地区在各方面的差别很大。如果了解了这些情况，不仅可以避免麻烦，而且可以增加乐趣，让旅行更有意思。

其次，要了解可用交通工具的时刻表。熟悉了这些情况，才能安排好时间。

最后，要旅行千万别怕麻烦。应该多阅读旅游方面的杂志，当然也可以向有经验的朋友请教。不过，不要以为别人有趣而难忘的经历你一定会碰到。每个人的旅行都是不同的。

阅读理解 Comprehension Check

20. "背包族"是什么意思？
21. "背包族"第一应该了解什么？
22. "背包族"第二应该了解什么？
23. 最后"背包族"应该做什么？
24. 所有人旅游的经历都是很有趣的，对吗？

說明生詞 Vocabulary

32.	如何		rúhé	Adv	<書>怎麼樣	[if-what/why/how]
33.	成為	成为	chéngwéi	V	to become, to turn into (+ N) cp. 變成+ Adj	[to become-to be]
	背包		bēibāo	N	knapsack, backpack	[to carry on the back-bag]
34.	族		zú	N	a group of, clan	
35.	背		bēi	V	to carry on the back	

36.	首先		shǒuxiān	Adv	第一	[first-earlier]
37.	居住		jūzhù	N	住	[to reside-to live]
38.	地區	地区	dìqū	N	area, region	[place-district]
39.	差別		chābié	N	不同	[differ-to separate]
40.	避免		bìmiǎn	V	to avoid	[to avoid-to exempt]
41.	增加		zēngjiā	V	to increase	[to increase- to add]
	樂趣	乐趣	lèqù	N	delight, pleasure, joy	[happy-fun]
42.	其次		qícì	Adv	第二	[its-second]
	工具		gōngjù	N	tool	[work-utensil]
	時刻表	时刻表	shíkèbiǎo	N	timetable, schedule	[time-quarter hour-list]
43.	安排		ānpái	V/N	to arrange, to plan, to fix up	[to fix-to arrange]
	旅遊	旅游	lǚyóu	N	tour, tourism	[to travel-to travel]
	雜誌	杂志	zázhì	N	magazine	[composite-magazine]
44.	難忘	难忘	nánwàng	Adj	很難忘記	[hard-to forget]

Characters with Many Strokes

為 族 首 差 避 增 趣 旅 雜 難

詞彙用法 Words in Context

32. 如何：如何和別人溝通，如何給別人提建議

如何：如何和别人沟通，如何给别人提建议

大四的學生最關心的問題是什麼？

大四的学生最关心的问题是什么？

在請朋友吃飯以前你要考慮什麼？

在请朋友吃饭以前你要考虑什么？

33. 成為：會成為問題；成為朋友、鄰居、背包族、音樂家

成为：会成为问题；成为朋友、邻居、背包族、音乐家

你覺得中國會成為發達國家嗎？

你觉得中国会成为发达国家吗？

怎麼才能成為背包族？

怎么才能成为背包族？

34. 族：背包、上班、開車、打工、愛貓族

族：背包、上班、开车、打工、爱猫族

夫妻都是上班族會有什麼不方便的地方？

現在北京的開車族越來越多，你覺得這對城市的環境有什麼影響？

35. 背：背書包；背不動；背起來；背在背上

爬山的時候為什麼不要帶太多的東西？

騎自行車來上課，你的書包放在哪兒？

36. 首先：（句型）

37. 居住：居住在這兒；在這兒居住了三年；居住條件不好

你喜歡這兒的居住環境嗎？為什麼？

美國哪個城市最適合人居住？

38. 地區：不同的地區；安全、危險地區

美國南部人和西部人為什麼會有很大的差別？

在大城市裏什麼地區比較安全？

39. 差別：有差別；差別很大；沒什麼差別

你覺得英文和中文最大的差別是什麼？

這兒的氣候和你老家的氣候有什麼差別？

40. 避免：避免引起大家的不滿；避免問題、矛盾；無法避免

夫妻都是上班族会有什么不方便的地方？

现在北京的开车族越来越多，你觉得这对城市的环境有什么影响？

背：背书包；背不动；背起来；背在背上

爬山的时候为什么不要带太多的东西？

骑自行车来上课，你的书包放在哪儿？

首先：（句型）

居住：居住在这儿；在这儿居住了三年；居住条件不好

你喜欢这儿的居住环境吗？为什么？

美国哪个城市最适合人居住？

地区：不同的地区；安全、危险地区

美国南部人和西部人为什么会有很大的差别？

在大城市里什么地区比较安全？

差别：有差别；差别很大；没什么差别

你觉得英文和中文最大的差别是什么？

这儿的气候和你老家的气候有什么差别？

避免：避免引起大家的不满；避免问题、矛盾；无法避免

你嫌同屋太活潑，為什麼不告訴　　　你嫌同屋太活泼，为什么不告诉

他呢？　　　　　　　　　　　　　　　他呢？

怎麼樣才能避免考試以後失望？　　　怎么样才能避免考试以后失望？

41.　增加：增加樂趣；功課增加了不　　增加：增加乐趣；功课增加了不

少；人口一直在增加；↔減少　　　　少；人口一直在增加；↔减少

全世界的人口有什麼變化？　　　　　全世界的人口有什么变化？

什麼事情可以增加你旅遊的樂　　　　什么事情可以增加你旅游的乐

趣？　　　　　　　　　　　　　　　　趣？

42.　其次：（句型）　　　　　　　　　其次：（句型）

43.　安排：安排時間、課程、假期；　　安排：安排时间、课程、假期；

安排得很好；不知道如何安排；　　　安排得很好；不知道如何安排；

週末怎麼安排　　　　　　　　　　　　周末怎么安排

快考試了，你打算如何安排自己　　　快考试了，你打算如何安排自己

的時間？　　　　　　　　　　　　　　的时间？

你是不是一個很會安排自己生活　　　你是不是一个很会安排自己生活

的人？為什麼？　　　　　　　　　　　的人？为什么？

44.　難忘：難忘的經歷、過去、生　　　难忘：难忘的经历、过去、生

活、朋友；大學生活很難忘　　　　　活、朋友；大学生活很难忘

你最難忘的人是誰？　　　　　　　　你最难忘的人是谁？

什麼樣的經歷讓你很難忘？　　　　　什么样的经历让你很难忘？

自由發揮與課堂活動　Free Discussion and Class Activities

12.　通過旅行你可以學到什麼？舉例　　通过旅行你可以学到什么？举例

說明。　　　　　　　　　　　　　　　说明。

13.　你覺得在旅行中最應該注意的問　　你觉得在旅行中最应该注意的问

題是什麼？　　　　　　　　　　　　题是什么？

14.　上網找一個你想去的旅行景點，　　上网找一个你想去的旅行景点，

了解那個地方的環境、飲食、宗　　　了解那个地方的环境、饮食、宗

教情況和可用的交通工具，並向　　　教情况和可用的交通工具，并向

同學介紹。　　　　　　　　　　　　同学介绍。

應用詞 Productive Vocabulary

◎By Grammatical Categories

Nouns/Pronouns/Measure Words

證	zhèng	certificate, card, credentials	景點	jǐngdiǎn	scenic spot
族	zú	a group of, clan	居住	jūzhù	living
請問	qǐngwèn	May I ask…?	地區	dìqū	area, region
打算	dǎsuàn	plan, to plan	少數	shǎoshù	small number, few, minority
氣候	qìhòu	climate, situation	差別	chābié	difference
季節	jìjié	season			

Verbs/Stative Verbs/Adjectives

稱	chēng	to call, to say, to weigh	增加	zēngjiā	to increase
佔	zhàn	to occupy	避免	bìmiǎn	to avoid
省	shěng	to save	失望	shīwàng	to become disappointed, to lose (hope)
取	qǔ	to take, to get, to fetch	成為	chéngwéi	to become, to turn into
吵	chǎo	to quarrel	熱衷於	rèzhōngyú	to be keen on, to be very fond of
背	bēi	to carry on the back	乾	gān	dry
碰到	pèngdào	to run into	溫暖	wēnnuǎn	warm
溝通	gōutōng	to communicate	潮濕	cháoshī	wet, moist, damp
經歷	jīnglì	to experience, experience	幸運	xìngyùn	lucky
包括	bāokuò	to include	難忘	nánwàng	unforgettable, memorable
安排	ānpái	to arrange, to plan, to fix up			
建議	jiànyì	to suggest			
結束	jiéshù	to end			

Adverbs and Others

白	bái	free of charge, to do sth. in vain	首先	shǒuxiān	first
熱情	rèqíng	enthusiastically	其次	qícì	second
隨便	suíbiàn	casually, to do as one pleases	不僅	bùjǐn	not only
恐怕	kǒngpà	perhaps, I think, I'm afraid	固然	gùrán	although
如何	rúhé	how, how about it	算了	suànle	Let it be. Forget it.

理解詞 Receptive Vocabulary

◎ **By Grammatical Categories**

Nouns/Pronouns/Measure Words

鄰居	línjū	neighbor	內衣	nèiyī	underwear
大一	àyī	freshman	背包	bēibāo	knapsack, backpack
導遊	dǎoyóu	tour guide	口袋	kǒudài	pocket
民族	mínzú	ethnic group, nationality	雜誌	zázhì	magazine
門票	ménpiào	admission fee	工具	gōngjù	tool
高原	gāoyuán	plateau, highland	時刻表	shíkèbiǎo	timetable, schedule
飲食	yǐnshí	food and drink, diet	洗手間	xǐshǒujiān	bathroom
旅遊	lǚyóu	tour, tourism	國慶節	Guóqìngjié	National Day
樂趣	lèqù	delight, pleasure, joy			
舞會	wǔhuì	dancing party			

Verbs/Stative Verbs/Adjectives

縫	féng	to sew
借住	jièzhù	to stay over at sb. else's place

Adverbs and Others

之	zhī	of
好人有好報	hǎorén yǒu hǎobào	One good turn deserves another.

本課詞表 Chapter Vocabulary

◎**By Pinyin**

Words with asterisk* are productive vocabulary which needs to be memorized and studied for its usage.

ānpái*	安排	to arrange, to plan, to fix up	bāokuò*	包括	to include
àyī	大一	freshman	bēi*	背	to carry on the back
bái*	白	free of charge, to do sth. in vain	bēibāo	背包	knapsack, backpack
			bìmiǎn*	避免	to avoid

bùjǐn*	不仅	not only
chābié*	差别	difference
chǎo*	吵	to quarrel
cháoshī*	潮湿	wet, moist, damp
chēng*	称	to call, to say, to weigh
chéngwéi*	成为	to become, to turn into
dǎoyóu	导游	tour guide
dǎsuàn*	打算	plan, to plan
dìqū*	地区	area, region
féng	缝	to sew
gān*	干	dry
gāoyuán	高原	plateau, highland
gōngjù	工具	tool
gōutōng*	沟通	to communicate
Guóqìngjié	国庆节	National Day
gùrán*	固然	although
hǎorén yǒu hǎo bào	好人有好报	One good turn deserves another.
jiànyì*	建议	to suggest
jiéshù*	结束	to end
jièzhù	借住	to stay over at sb. else's place
jìjié*	季节	season
jǐngdiǎn*	景点	scenic spot
jīnglì*	经历	to experience, experience
jūzhù*	居住	living
kǒngpà*	恐怕	perhaps, I think, I'm afraid
kǒudài	口袋	pocket
lèqù	乐趣	delight, pleasure, joy
línjū	邻居	neighbor
lǚyóu	旅游	tour, tourism
ménpiào	门票	admission fee
mínzú	民族	ethnic group,

		nationality
nánwàng*	难忘	unforgettable, memorable
nèiyī	内衣	underwear
pèngdào*	碰到	to run into
qícì*	其次	second
qìhòu*	气候	climate, situation
qǐngwèn*	请问	May I ask...?
qǔ*	取	to take, to get, to fetch
rèqíng*	热情	enthusiastically
rèzhōngyú*	热衷于	to be keen on, to be very fond of
rúhé*	如何	how, how about it
shǎoshù*	少数	small number, few, minority
shěng*	省	to save
shíkèbiǎo	时刻表	timetable, schedule
shīwàng*	失望	to become disappointed, to lose (hope)
shǒuxiān*	首先	first
suànle*	算了	Let it be. Forget it.
suíbiàn*	随便	casually, to do as one pleases
wēnnuǎn*	温暖	warm
wǔhuì	舞会	dancing party
xìngyùn*	幸运	lucky
xǐshǒujiān	洗手间	bathroom
yǐnshí	饮食	food and drink, diet
zázhì	杂志	magazine
zēngjiā*	增加	to increase
zhàn*	占	to occupy
zhèng*	证	certificate, card, credentials
zhī	之	of
zú*	族	a group of, clan

語法和用法 Grammar and Usage

Pay attention to the function of the structure and then study the example sentences.   When blanks are provided, either answer the questions or complete the sentences.

1. Naming

S把X稱為Y	bǎ...chēngwéi...	S call X as Y
X被(S)稱為Y	bèichēngwéi...	X be called Y (by S)

● 聽說昆明被稱為「春城」，那裏的氣候一定很好吧？

1. 聽說芝加哥的風很   听说芝加哥的风很   I heard that it's very windy in
    大。   大。   Chicago.

    對，所以人們把芝   对，所以人们把芝   That's right, so people call
    加哥稱為「風   加哥称为 "风   Chicago the "wind city."
    城」。   城"。

2. 什麼是「少數民   什么是 "少数民   What is a "minority"?
    族」？   族"？

    我們把人口很少的   我们把人口很少的   We call those ethnic groups
    民族稱為少數民   民族称为少数民   with low population
    族。   族。   "minorities."

3. 什麼人是導遊呢？   什么人是导游呢？   Who is a tour guide?

    那些帶別人去旅行   那些带别人去旅行   Those who take others on tours
    的人被稱為導遊。   的人被称为导游。   are called tour guides.

4. 我們把什麼樣的人稱為「背包   我们把什么样的人称为 "背包
    族」？   族"？

5. 我常聽中國人說「老外」，那   我常听中国人说 "老外" ，那
    是什麼意思？   是什么意思？

6. 請問，BIG TEN 說的是什麼？   请问，BIG TEN 说的是什么？

The pattern S把X稱為Y is used for naming something. Note that X is often a noun preceded by a relatively long modifier. So, one should not say 我們把年輕人熱衷於背起背包到各地旅行稱為「背包族」。 Instead, the sentence should be我們把熱衷於背起背包到各地旅行的年輕人稱為「背包族」。 When X is used as subject, remember to use the passive marker 被 instead of 把. Thus, it's wrong to say 背著背包到處旅行的人稱為「背包族」。 Don't confuse 稱為 chēngwéi 'to call' with 成為 chéngwéi 'to become.'

2. Expressing an additional condition

不僅…而且/也…	bùjǐn…érqiě/yě	<書> not only…but also… <口> 不但…而且…

- 昆明不僅四季都像春天一樣溫暖，而且比較潮濕，不像北京這麼乾！

1. 放假的時候，你喜歡去哪兒玩？

   放假的时候，你喜欢去哪儿玩？

   Where do you like to go when you have a break?

   放假的時候，我喜歡去同學家玩，因為這樣做不僅可以省下吃和住的錢，而且會有一個好導遊。

   放假的时候，我喜欢去同学家玩，因为这样做不仅可以省下吃和住的钱，而且会有一个好导游。

   When I have a break, I like to go to my classmate's place for fun, because this will not only save eating and living expenses, but also get me a good tour guide.

2. 在旅行以前我應該準備什麼？

   在旅行以前我应该准备什么？

   Before I go on vacation, what should I prepare?

   在旅行以前你應該多了解那個地方的情況，不僅要閱讀旅行方面的雜誌，

   在旅行以前你应该多了解那个地方的情况，不仅要阅读旅行方面的杂志，

   Before you go on vacation, you should better understand the conditions of the place. You not only have to read travel magazines but also consult friends who have experience.

而且要向有經驗的
朋友請教。

而且要向有经验的
朋友请教。

3. 王紅旅行的時候幸運嗎？為什麼？

王紅旅行的时候幸运吗？为什么？

Was Wang Hong lucky when she traveled? Why?

王紅旅行的時候很幸運，她碰到的那個女孩不僅讓她借住，而且成了她的好朋友，所以王紅的假期才這麼愉快。

王红旅行的时候很幸运，她碰到的那个女孩不仅让她借住，而且成了她的好朋友，所以王红的假期才这么愉快。

Wang Hong was very lucky when she travelled. The girl she ran into not only let her stay overnight but also became her good friend. Thus, Wang Hong's vacation was so enjoyable.

4. 我一到這裏就很喜歡，因為這裏不僅＿＿＿＿＿＿＿＿＿＿
而且＿＿＿＿＿＿＿＿＿＿

我一到这里就很喜欢，因为这里不仅＿＿＿＿＿＿＿＿＿＿
而且＿＿＿＿＿＿＿＿＿＿

5. 跟團旅行比自己去旅行便宜多了，不僅＿＿＿＿＿＿＿＿＿＿
而且＿＿＿＿＿＿＿＿＿＿

跟团旅行比自己去旅行便宜多了，不仅＿＿＿＿＿＿＿＿＿＿
而且＿＿＿＿＿＿＿＿＿＿

6. 你喜歡住在大城市還是小城市？為什麼？

你喜欢住在大城市还是小城市？为什么？

The pattern 不僅⋯而且/也⋯ should connect two parallel clauses which provide additional information about the subject of the sentence, e.g., 我喜歡住大城市，因為大城市不僅交通方便，而且環境很好 'I like to live in a big city, because big cities not only have convenient transportation, but also good environment.' Note that 交通 cannot go before 不僅, because the subject of the sentence is 大城市, not 交通. It's wrong to say 我喜歡住大城市，因為大城市交通不僅方便，而且環境很好。 Similarly, the following sentence is odd because the clause following 而且 does not bring out any additional information about the implied subject of the sentence: 我喜歡住大城市，因為不僅更好玩，而且我認為小城市沒有意思。

3. Expressing the target/location/time of an action

S 熱衷於VO	rèzhōngyú	S is very fond of …
S 習慣於VO	xíguànyú	S is used to…
S 生於Place/Time	shēngyú	S was born in…
S 死於Place/Time	sǐyú	S died in…

●   所以現在人們都熱衷於跟團旅行，既省錢又省心。

1.   現在北京的年輕人
     喜歡做什麼？

     現在北京的年轻人
     喜欢做什么？

     What do young people in
     Beijing like to do nowadays?

     北京的年輕人都熱
     衷於上網和旅行。

     北京的年轻人都热
     衷于上网和旅行。

     Young people in Beijing are
     eager to log on to the internet
     and to travel.

2.   你第一次自己生
     活，適應了嗎？

     你第一次自己生
     活，适应了吗？

     This is the first time you've
     lived by yourself. Have you
     gotten used to it?

     我已經習慣於一個
     人生活了。

     我已经习惯于一个
     人生活了。

     I've already gotten used to
     living alone.

3.   聽說李白是一個很
     有名的詩人。他是
     什麼時候的人？活
     了多久？

     听说李白是一个很
     有名的诗人。他是
     什么时候的人？活
     了多久？

     I heard that Li Bo was a very
     famous poet. What period of
     history did he live in? How
     long did he live?

     他生於西元701年，
     死於762年，活到61
     歲。

     他生于西元701年，
     死于762年，活到61
     岁。

     He was born in 701 C.E., and
     died in 762 C.E. He lived to
     61 years old.

4.   你知道這一陣子大家都在討論什
     麼問題？

     你知道这一阵子大家都在讨论什
     么问题？

---

5.   住宿舍比住公寓省錢，你為什麼
     不住宿舍呢？

     住宿舍比住公寓省钱，你为什麼
     不住宿舍呢？

6.　你對甘奈迪總統有什麼了解？　　你对肯尼迪总统有什么了解？

In this pattern 於 is used after verbs like 熱衷、習慣、生、死 to indicate the target/location/time of an action. Note that there is often verb or verb phrase after 熱衷、習慣 instead of a noun. So, one cannot say 最近美國人熱衷於功夫電影. Instead, one should say 最近美國人熱衷於看功夫電影. Also, it's odd to say 美國人最近熱衷於看電視 because the VO has to be something special. Although 我習慣於早起 and 我習慣早起 are basically the same, the sentence with 於 in it is often more formal and literary. To say "he was born in 1998" colloquially, one can say 他是一九九八年生的. In a literary manner, one can say 他生於一九九八年. Compare this to Adj 於 (L1, G5).

4. Expressing a change of condition or supplementary information

A⋯，而B（卻）⋯	...., ér....(què)	A..., but B...
S Adj 而 Adj	...ér...	S is Adj and Adj

- 熱衷於旅行的陳文已經跟她的旅行團到了昆明。而我這個窮學生還在想……沒有錢我能走多遠？
- 不要以為別人有趣而難忘的經歷你一定會碰到

1.　我和她一見如故，很快就成了好朋友，但是我們有很多不同：我習慣於早睡早起，而她卻喜歡熬夜；我喜歡在家看書，而她卻常去旅行。

我和她一见如故，很快就成了好朋友，但是我们有很多不同：我习惯于早睡早起，而她却喜欢熬夜；我喜欢在家看书，而她却常去旅行。

We hit it off very quickly and became good friends, but we have several differences: I'm used to going to bed early and getting up early. Yet, she likes to stay up late. I like to read at home, but she often goes to travel.

2.　她是從台灣來的，而我是從大陸來的！

她是从台湾来的，而我是从大陆来的！

She is from Taiwan, but I'm from Mainland China.

3. 很多人覺得寫簡體
   字既容易又省時
   間，而我卻覺得繁
   體字比簡體字漂亮
   得多！

   很多人觉得写简体
   字既容易又省时
   间，而我却觉得繁
   体字比简体字漂亮
   得多！

   Many people think that writing
   simplified characters is both
   easy and timesaving, but I think
   traditonal characters are nicer
   looking than simplified ones.

4. 你知道北京和昆明的氣候有什
   麼不同嗎？

   你知道北京和昆明的气候有什
   么不同吗？

---

5. 學生和生意人會選擇什麼方式
   旅行？

   学生和生意人会选择什么方式
   旅行？

---

6. 我習慣於用寫的方法記生詞，
   而

   我习惯于用写的方法记生词，
   而

而, similar to 於, is another element often found in formal, literary Chinese.
Depending on the context, 而 can have two very different meanings. When it means
"but," 而 is often preceded by another clause and the clause with 而 often has 卻 to
reinforce the meaning of transition. When it means "and," 而 often connects two
adjectives, e.g., 他的說法幽默而準確 'the way he spoke was both humorous and
incisive.' Note that with a sense of "but," 而 should connect two clauses with opposite
meanings. So, it's odd to say 北京的氣候很乾，而昆明的氣候很溫暖 'Beijing's
climate is dry and Kunming's is warm.' It's more appropriate to say 北京的氣候很
乾，而昆明很潮濕. For the same reason, it's odd to say 北京人很熱情，而昆明很
安全.

5. Expressing contradiction of a factual statement

S固然X,但是 / 可是 /　　不過Y	guràn…dànshì /kěshì/ búguò…	S no doubt X, but Y
固然X, Y 也	gùrán…, …yě	Admittedly X, Y

• 這樣做固然很安全，但是每次用錢都要去洗手間取。

1. 您的孩子太貪玩了，其他同學在圖書館看書的時候，他要麼在踢足球，要麼在打網球，這樣會影響他的成績。

您的孩子太貪玩了，其他同学在图书馆看书的时候，他要么在踢足球，要么在打网球，这样会影响他的成绩。

Your kid likes to have fun too much. When other students are studying at the library, he is either playing football or tennis. This will affect his grades.

我的孩子固然貪玩，但是這並沒有影響他的成績，他的功課都是A，我覺得除了學習以外，他也應該有自己的生活。

我的孩子固然贪玩，但是这并没有影响他的成绩，他的功课都是A，我觉得除了学习以外，他也应该有自己的生活。

Admittedly, my kid likes to have too much fun. Yet, this hasn't had any impact on his grade at all. He gets all As. I think in addition to studying, he should have his own life.

2. 現在中學生聚會喜歡「AA制」，我覺得朋友之間算得那麼清楚不好。

现在中学生聚会喜欢"AA制"，我觉得朋友之间算得那么清楚不好。

Nowadays when middle-school students get together, they like to go Dutch. I don't think it is good when friends keep such close tabs on things.

朋友之間算得太清楚固然不好，不過如果大家每次吃飯的時候都要爭著付帳，也很不好。

朋友之间算得太清楚固然不好，不过如果大家每次吃饭的时候都要争着付帐，也很不好。

No doubt it is not good to keep close tabs among friends. Yet, if everyone has to fight to pay for the bill when they get together, that is not good, either.

3. 我覺得跟團去一個陌生的地方旅行比較方便，因為所有的事情都由他們安排，非常省心。

我觉得跟团去一个陌生的地方旅行比较方便，因为所有的事情都由他们安排，非常省心。

I think when going to a strange place, it is more convenient to join a tour group. This is because they will take care of everything and this saves a lot of worries.

跟團旅行固然很省心，但是你不能自己安排時間，也少

跟团旅行固然很省心，但是你不能自己安排时间，也少

No doubt it saves worries to travel with a tour group, but you can't arrange your own schedule this way and you

了很多自由。   了很多自由。   have less freedom.

4. 他上課的時候態度
很不好，既不注意
聽我說，又不和別
的同學合作。

他上课的时候态度
很不好，既不注意
听我说，又不和别
的同学合作。

When he goes to classes, his attitude is very bad. He not only does not pay attention to what I said, but also does not cooperate with other classmates.

他的態度固然不太
好，你也不應該罵
他。

他的态度固然不太
好，你也不应该骂
他。

Indeed, his attitude is not good. Yet, you shouldn't scold him, either.

5. 西班牙文和法文比中文簡單得
多，你為什麼不選那兩種語
言？

西班牙文和法文比中文简单得
多，你为什么不选那两种语
言？

---

6. 我覺得李明現在太小氣了，根
本不像一個從美國回來的人。

我觉得李明现在太小气了，根
本不象一个从美国回来的人。

---

7. 我找到了一個工作，可是我覺
得那個工作太辛苦，我還沒決
定要不要接受。

我找到了一个工作，可是我觉
得那个工作太辛苦，我还没决
定要不要接受。

When used with 但是/可是/不過, 固然 is very much like 雖然. Yet, it sounds more formal than 雖然. Note that 固然 should go after the subject, e.g., 中文固然比法文難，但是……. One shouldn't say 中文比法文固然難，但是……. When used with 也, 固然 often goes before the subject, e.g., 青少年出了問題，固然家庭有責任，學校也不能說沒有關係 'When teenagers run into problems, admittedly their family bears responsibility, yet schools aren't without responsibility also.'

6. Expressing sequence

首先…其次…最後…	shǒuxiān…qícì… zuìhòu…	first…second…at last

● 首先，在旅行以前應該了解那裏的…其次，要了解可用交通工具的時刻表…最後，要旅行千萬別怕麻煩。

1. 寫報告容易不容易？為什麼？

   写报告容易不容易？为什么？

   Is it easy to write a paper? Why?

   寫一篇報告真不容易！首先，你要看看自己對什麼有興趣，決定題目；其次，你得閱讀這方面的研究資料；最後找到自己的看法，才能開始寫報告。

   写一篇报告真不容易！首先，你要看看自己对什么有兴趣，决定题目；其次，你得阅读这方面的研究资料；最后找到自己的看法，才能开始写报告。

   Writing a paper is not easy at all. First, you have to see what you are interested in and decide on a topic. Then, you have to read the related research materials. Finally, you have to find your own perspective. Only then can you start to write a paper.

2. 你找工作的時候，會考慮哪些問題？

   你找工作的时候，会考虑哪些问题？

   What things do you consider when you look for a job?

   在找工作的時候，我首先要考慮這個工作賺的錢多不多；其次要考慮這個工作有沒有意思；最後還要考慮工作環境好不好。

   在找工作的时候，我首先要考虑这个工作赚的钱多不多；其次要考虑这个工作有没有意思；最后还要考虑工作环境好不好。

   When looking for a job, I'll first consider if the salary is good or not; then I'll consider if the job is interesting or not; finally, I will see if the working environment is good or not.

3. 你喜歡這裏嗎？為什麼？

   你喜欢这里吗？为什么？

   Do you like it here? Why?

   我很喜歡這裏，首先是因為這裏的商學院非常有名；其

   我很喜欢这里，首先是因为这里的商学院非常有名；其

   I like it here a lot. First of all, the Business School here is very famous. Second, the tuition and living expense are

次是這裏的學費和生活費都不貴；最後這裏的氣候不乾也不濕，所以在這裏生活很舒服。

次是这里的学费和生活费都不贵；最后这里的气候不干也不湿，所以在这里生活很舒服。

not too expensive. Lastly, the weather here is neither too dry nor too humid. Thus, it's very comfortable to live here.

4. 你覺得中文和英文有什麼不同？

你觉得中文和英文有什么不同？

---

5. 你買車的時候會考慮什麼？

你买车的时候会考虑什么？

---

6. 你會怎麼選擇住的地方？

你会怎么选择住的地方？

The pattern 首先…其次…最後… is used to indicate a sequence of events, actions, or priorities. It's a simple but very useful structure to organize and present one's ideas. It's slightly more formal than 第一…第二…最後…. Note that when one uses 考慮 (example 2), the clause that follows should use "A not A" structure.

背景常識 Background Notes

1. 國慶節：1949年10月1日是中華人民共和國成立的日子，大陸的中國人把每年的10月1日叫做「國慶節」，或者「十一」。從九十年代末，每年的國慶節全國各地都放一個星期的假，所以從那個時候起，旅遊成了國慶節期間人們的一個重要活動。

2. 雷鋒：雷鋒是六十年代中國大陸一個軍人的名字。雷鋒因為做了很多的好事兒出名，所以後來他的名字就變成了榜樣的意思。每年三月是全國的「雷鋒月」，那個時候會有很多關於雷鋒的故事，大家都要學習雷鋒去做好事，幫助別人。所以「雷鋒」已經變成了榜樣的意思，看到有人做了好事或者幫助了別人，我們就會叫他「活雷鋒」。

3. 週末舞會：在中國的大學，一般來說星期五和星期六的晚上都會在學校的活動中心舉行一個舞會。不管是本校的學生、外校的學生，還是已經工作的人，只要買票，就可以參加這樣的舞會。在大學裏，參加舞會是一個很好的認識朋友的機會。

4. 交通工具：在中國，雖然坐飛機的人越來越多，但是火車仍然是一種重要的交通工具。一般來說，一列火車包括十幾個車廂，這些車廂的安排並不完全一樣，有硬座、軟座、硬臥、軟臥。硬座的價格最便宜，軟臥的價格最貴。火車上還有一節車廂是餐車，不過餐車上飯菜的價格會比一般飯館裏的價格高好幾倍。

背景常识 Background Notes

1. 国庆节：1949年10月1日是中华人民共和国成立的日子，大陆的中国人把每年的10月1日叫做"国庆节"，或者"十一"。从九十年代末，每年的国庆节全国各地都放一个星期的假，所以从那个时候起，旅游成了国庆节期间人们的一个重要活动。

2. 雷锋：雷锋是六十年代中国大陆一个军人的名字。雷锋因为做了很多的好事儿出名，所以后来他的名字就变成了榜样的意思。每年三月是全国的"雷锋月"，那个时候会有很多关于雷锋的故事，大家都要学习雷锋去做好事，帮助别人。所以"雷锋"已经变成了榜样的意思，看到有人做了好事或者帮助了别人，我们就会叫他"活雷锋"。

3. 周末舞会：在中国的大学，一般来说星期五和星期六的晚上都会在学校的活动中心举行一个舞会。不管是本校的学生、外校的学生，还是已经工作的人，只要买票，就可以参加这样的舞会。在大学里，参加舞会是一个很好的认识朋友的机会。

4. 交通工具：在中国，虽然坐飞机的人越来越多，但是火车仍然是一种重要的交通工具。一般来说，一列火车包括十几个车厢，这些车厢的安排并不完全一样，有硬座、软座、硬卧、软卧。硬座的价格最便宜，软卧的价格最贵。火车上还有一节车厢是餐车，不过餐车上饭菜的价格会比一般饭馆里的价格高好几倍。

第三課　週末人們在做什麼？

Theme: Leisure and Sports

Communicative Objectives
- Talking about exercise
- Talking about sports
- Narrating an experience of getting back in shape

Skill Focus
- Comprehending a report on the changing common expressions among people in Beijing

Grammar Focus
- S 趁(著)…(的時候) VO
- (O)有什麼好V的？　V什麼O？
- S 把…掛/放在N上
- X有害於/有利於/有助於Y
- O S V(得/不)下去
- …，(而) S 則VO
  (S)…則X; …則Y

Problem Scenario
With the approach of an important meeting (e.g., reunion, job interview, visiting your future parents-in-law), you realize that you can't get into the dresses in your closet any more. You need to lose some extra pounds in one month. You log on your computer and find out all sorts of information about losing weight. You consult your parents, friends and neighbors and they all have different kinds of advice and beliefs. Who would you listen to? When choosing a diet program, what factors would you consider? What plan will work for you?

對話 Dialogue

♟♟ (1)Talking about exercise

李明的爸爸李鐵和鄰居趙平聊天。

老趙：　這麼早，去哪兒啊？

老李：　去跳交際舞，[1]趁現在還不太熱，出去鍛鍊鍛鍊。

老趙：　現在跳交際舞好像很時髦，不過那是年輕人的活動，你這麼大年紀還跳，有點不像話！

老李：　您這種想法太落伍了。跳交際舞是一種健身運動，誰都可以參加。我建議您也試一試。

老趙：　我自己在家裡安安靜靜地練太極拳不是也挺好的嗎？

老李：　一個人練習免不了會覺得無聊，如果很多人一邊跳交際舞，一邊聊天，不僅能達到健身的目的，而且讓人心情愉快。

老趙：　聽起來不錯，我發現這種運動吸引了越來越多的老百姓。

老李：　跳交際舞既不需要花錢，又可以豐富自己的生活，當然受老百姓歡迎了！

閱讀理解 Comprehension Check

1. 老李每天一早都去做什麼？為什麼？
2. 老趙覺得年紀大的人不應該做什麼？老李同意他的想法嗎？
3. 老趙每天都做什麼運動？老李為什麼覺得跳交際舞更好？
4. 現在在中國流行跳交際舞嗎？為什麼？

对话 Dialogue

(1)Talking about exercise

李明的爸爸李铁和邻居赵平聊天。

老赵： 这么早，去哪儿啊？

老李： 去跳交际舞，[1]趁现在还不太热，出去锻炼锻炼。

老赵： 现在跳交际舞好象很时髦，不过那是年轻人的活动，你这么大年纪还跳，有点不象话！

老李： 您这种想法太落伍了。跳交际舞是一种健身运动，谁都可以参加。我建议您也试一试。

老赵： 我自己在家里安安静静地练太极拳不是也挺好的吗？

老李： 一个人练习免不了会觉得无聊，如果很多人一边跳交际舞，一边聊天，不仅能达到健身的目的，而且让人心情愉快。

老赵： 听起来不错，我发现这种运动吸引了越来越多的老百姓。

老李： 跳交际舞既不需要花钱，又可以丰富自己的生活，当然受老百姓欢迎了！

阅读理解 Comprehension Check

1. 老李每天一早都去做什么？为什么？
2. 老赵觉得年纪大的人不应该做什么？老李同意他的想法吗？
3. 老赵每天都做什么运动？老李为什么觉得跳交际舞更好？
4. 现在在中国流行跳交际舞吗？为什么？

對話一生詞 Vocabulary

Study the numbered vocabulary (productive vocabulary) for its usage. The unnumbered items (receptive vocabulary) are to facilitate reading comprehension.

◎**By Order of Appearance**

	交際舞	交际舞	jiāojìwǔ	N	ballroom/social dancing [to meet-occasion-dance]
1.	趁		chèn	V/ Conj	to take advantage of (sth.), while (doing sth. else)
2.	不像話	不象话	bú xiànghuà	IE	ridiculous, outrageous, unreasonable [not-to be like-words]
3.	落伍		luòwǔ	Adj	to be outdated [to fall-ranks]
4.	健身		jiànshēn	VO	to keep fit [to strengthen-body]
	參加	参加	cānjiā	V	to join, to attend, to take part in [to enter-to add]
5.	安靜	安静	ānjìng	Adj	quiet, peaceful [peaceful-still]
	太極拳	太极拳	Tàijíquán	N	a kind of shadowboxing [great-extreme-fist]
6.	不是…嗎	不是…吗	búshì...ma	IE	<口>Isn't it right? [not-to be-(question marker)]
7.	免不了		miǎnbuliǎo	RV	to be unavoidable, to be bound to [to avoid-not-can]
8.	無聊	无聊	wúliáo	Adj	沒有意思 [without-to endure]
9.	達到	达到	dádào	V	to achieve, to reach, to attain [to reach-to arrive]
10.	老百姓		lǎobǎixìng	N	common people, civilians [old-hundred-surname]
11.	豐富	丰富	fēngfù	V/ Adj	to enrich, rich, abundant [plentiful-wealthy]

Characters with Many Strokes

際 趁 靜 極 拳 無 聊 達 豐 富

詞匯用法 Words in Context

1. 趁：（句型）　　　　　　　　　　趁：（句型）

2. 不像話：亂扔垃圾太不像話了　　不像话：乱扔垃圾太不像话了

你覺得在桌子上亂寫字的做法怎麼樣？

你喜不喜歡別人問你多大了？

3. 落伍：思想、衣服、家具落伍；太落伍了

你怎麼每個星期都要去買新衣服？

你覺得你父母有哪些落伍的思想？

4. 健身：去健身房健身；健身的運動

你經常去健身房健身嗎？為什麼？

你覺得什麼樣的健身的運動對老人合適？

5. 安靜：安靜的生活；圖書館很安靜；安安靜靜地看書　↔吵

你喜歡自己去圖書館看書，還是和朋友一起去？為什麼？

你覺得大城市和小鎮的生活有什麼不同？

6. 不是…嗎：導遊不是很熱情嗎？健身不是很流行嗎？

張麗是不是覺得她的南方之行很無聊？

我以為中國不同民族的人不能溝通。

7. 免不了：免不了碰到困難、覺得失望；辛苦是免不了的

你一個人生活會不會覺得無聊？

你一个人生活会不会觉得无聊？

不經常看書的人，思想會不會慢慢地落伍？

不经常看书的人，思想会不会慢慢地落伍？

8. 無聊：無聊的電影；讓人覺得無聊

　　无聊：无聊的电影；让人觉得无聊

你覺得哪部電影很無聊？為什麼？

你觉得哪部电影很无聊？为什么？

有人說這兒的生活有點無聊，你覺得呢？

有人说这儿的生活有点无聊，你觉得呢？

9. 達到：達到目的、要求；達到八十分；達到一百人；沒有達到；達不到

　　达到：达到目的、要求；达到八十分；达到一百人；没有达到；达不到

現在這個學校的留學生已經達到多少了？

现在这个学校的留学生已经达到多少了？

你學習中文是為了要達到什麼樣的目的？

你学习中文是为了要达到什么样的目的？

10. 老百姓：老百姓的生活；受到老百姓的歡迎；我只是老百姓

　　老百姓：老百姓的生活；受到老百姓的欢迎；我只是老百姓

最近什麼樣的健身活動受到了老百姓的歡迎？

最近什么样的健身活动受到了老百姓的欢迎？

你覺得買得起汽車的人一定都是有錢人嗎？

你觉得买得起汽车的人一定都是有钱人吗？

11. 豐富：豐富的生活、資源、思想

　　丰富：丰富的生活、资源、思想

你覺得豐富的生活應該是什麼樣的？

你觉得丰富的生活应该是什么样的？

美國的哪些資源很豐富？

美国的哪些资源很丰富？

自由發揮與課堂活動 Free Discussion and Classroom Activities

1. 介紹一個你喜歡的運動，並說明喜歡的原因以及這種運動對身體的好處。

   介绍一个你喜欢的运动，并说明喜欢的原因以及这种运动对身体的好处。

2. 你覺得老人應該做哪些運動，不應該做哪些運動？為什麼？

   你觉得老人应该做哪些运动，不应该做哪些运动？为什么？

3. 最近什麼運動吸引了越來越多的老百姓？

   最近什么运动吸引了越来越多的老百姓？

(2) Talking about sports

李明約鄰居趙平的兒子趙強出去看球。

小李：　後天北京和上海有一場足球比賽，我買了兩張票，一起去看吧！

小趙：　恐怕不行。我已經答應小麗明天教她玩滑板。

小李：　滑板[2]**有什麼好教的**？北京隊和上海隊是全國水平最高的球隊，他們的比賽一定很精彩。

小趙：　上一次你也說一定精彩，結果踢得那麼臭！

小李：　我好不容易才買到票！不去太可惜了！

小趙：　你可以找小王這個球迷一起去，他很積極，即使是臭球，我估計他也願意看。

小李：　既然你對足球這麼不感興趣，那就算了吧！如果晚上沒事的話，我們一起去酒吧坐坐？

小趙：　不好意思，晚上我要陪小麗去學校門口新開的那家網吧。

小李：　你現在總是[3]**把小麗掛在嘴上**，我看你已經成了她的跟屁蟲了！

小趙：　別拿我開心了！

閱讀理解 Comprehension Check

5. 小李想找小趙去做什麼？小趙能去嗎？為什麼？
6. 小李認為這次的比賽很值得看？為什麼？小趙同意嗎？
7. 小趙建議小李找誰一起去看球賽？為什麼？
8. 小李又約小趙和他去做什麼？結果呢？
9. 最後小李怎麼跟小趙開玩笑？

(2) Talking about sports

李明约邻居赵平的儿子赵强出去看球。

小李：　后天北京和上海有一场足球比赛，我买了两张票，一起去看吧！

小赵：　恐怕不行。我已经答应小丽明天教她玩滑板。

小李：　滑板[2]有什么好教的？北京队和上海队是全国水平最高的球队，他们的比赛一定很精彩。

小赵：　上一次你也说一定精彩，结果踢得那么臭！

小李：　我好不容易才买到票！不去太可惜了！

小赵：　你可以找小王这个球迷一起去，他很积极，即使是臭球，我估计他也愿意看。

小李：　既然你对足球这么不感兴趣，那就算了吧！如果晚上没事的话，我们一起去酒吧坐坐？

小赵：　不好意思，晚上我要陪小丽去学校门口新开的那家网吧。

小李：　你现在总是[3]把小丽挂在嘴上，我看你已经成了她的跟屁虫了！

小赵：　别拿我开心了！

阅读理解 Comprehension Check

10. 小李想找小赵去做什么？小赵能去吗？为什么？
11. 小李认为这次的比赛很值得看？为什么？小赵同意吗？
12. 小赵建议小李找谁一起去看球赛？为什么？
13. 小李又约小赵和他去做什么？结果呢？
14. 最后小李怎么跟小赵开玩笑？

對話二生詞 Vocabulary

12.	答應	答应	dāying	V	to agree to do sth., to promise, to answer	[to answer-to respond]
	滑板		huábǎn	N	skateboard	[slippery-board]
	球隊	球队	qiúduì	N	sports team	[ball-team]
13.	精彩		jīngcǎi	Adj	brilliant, splendid	[perfect-splendor]
14.	臭		chòu	Adj	<PRC> foul, stinking, <TW>爛 làn	
15.	可惜		kěxī	Adj/Ph	unfortunately, it's a pity!	[can-to feel sorry for sb.]
	球迷		qiúmí	N	非常喜歡看球賽的人	[ball-fan]
16.	積極	积极	jījí	Adj	active, energetic, positive	[to amass-extreme]
17.	估計	估计	gūjì	V	to estimate, to appraise, to reckon	[to estimate-to count]
	酒吧		jiǔbā	N	喝酒的地方	[wine-(place marker)]
	網吧	网吧	wǎngbā	N	上網的地方 <TW>網咖	[net-(place marker)]
18.	掛	挂	guà	V	to hang, to put up	
	跟屁蟲	跟屁虫	gēnpìchóng	N	a tagalong	[to follow-buttocks-worm]
	拿…開心	拿…开心	ná...kāixīn	IE	to make fun of…	[to take-open-heart]

Characters with Many Strokes

應 滑 隊 精 彩 臭 積 極 網 蟲

詞匯用法 Words in Context

12. 答應：答應別人的事情一定要做　　答应：答应别人的事情一定要做
　　到；別隨便答應別人　　　　　　到；别随便答应别人

　　如果你想提前考試，你覺得老師　　如果你想提前考试，你觉得老师
　　會答應嗎？　　　　　　　　　　会答应吗？

　　這個週末你為什麼不和大家去健　　这个周末你为什么不和大家去健
　　身房鍛鍊？　　　　　　　　　　身房锻炼？

13. 精彩：精彩的比賽、電視節目　　　精彩：精彩的比赛、电视节目

你覺得哪兩個籃球隊的比賽會很
精彩？為什麼？

你觉得哪两个篮球队的比赛会很
精彩？为什么？

你覺得哪個電視節目很精彩？

你觉得哪个电视节目很精彩？

14. 臭：臭味；球打得很臭；臭球；
↔香

臭：臭味；球打得很臭；臭球；
↔香

你覺得這個大學的籃球隊裏，誰
打得最臭？

你觉得这个大学的篮球队里，谁
打得最臭？

看比賽的時候，你怎麼總是說
「臭球」？

看比赛的时候，你怎么总是说
"臭球"？

15. 可惜：真可惜！覺得可惜　　　可惜：真可惜！觉得可惜

你覺得上大學的時候，沒做什麼
很可惜？

你觉得上大学的时候，没做什么
很可惜？

聽說昆明是個旅遊的好地方，你
去過了嗎？

听说昆明是个旅游的好地方，你
去过了吗？

16. 積極：很積極；不積極；積極參
加

积极：很积极；不积极；积极参
加

你喜歡參加大學裏的學生活動
嗎？

你喜欢参加大学里的学生活动
吗？

上課的時候，你是不是很願意回
答老師的問題？

上课的时候，你是不是很愿意回
答老师的问题？

17. 估計：我估計；無法估計；據估
計

估计：我估计；无法估计；据估
计

你估計到2050年，世界會有多少
人？

你估计到2050年，世界会有多少
人？

你估計這次的考試會不會很難？

你估计这次的考试会不会很难？

18. 掛：把衣服掛起來；把籃球掛在
嘴上

挂：把衣服挂起来；把篮球挂在
嘴上

你回家以後都把衣服掛在哪兒？

你回家以后都把衣服挂在哪儿？

球迷應該是什麼樣的人？ 球迷应该是什么样的人？

自由發揮與課堂活動 Free Discussion and Classroom Activities

4. 邀請一個同學去看球賽，至少 說出兩個要去看的理由。

    邀请一个同学去看球赛，至少 说出两个要去看的理由。

5. 你週末的時候常常做什麼？這 跟你的生活有什麼關係？

    你週末的时候常常做什么？这 跟你的生活有什么关系？

6. 選出最好的籃球運動員： 幾個同學一組，討論選出最好 的籃球運動員（比如：喬丹 Michael Jordan、姚明Ming Yao）， 並向大家介紹選擇這個運動員 的原因。

    选出最好的籃球运动员： 几个同学一组，讨论选出最好 的籃球运动员（比如：乔丹 Michael Jordan、姚明Ming Yao）， 并向大家介绍选择这个运动员 的原因。

敘述Narrative

怎麼才能減肥

從前一直為自己苗條的身材驕傲，沒想到結婚以後卻一天比一天胖。開始我沒有太注意，可是後來發現衣服越來越緊，才知道我真的該減肥了。

第一個想到的方法就是吃減肥藥，可是商店裏有各種各樣的減肥藥，我不知道選哪一種好。不過後來看到報紙上說，最有效的減肥方法不是吃藥，而是有好的飲食和運動習慣，於是我開始「檢查」自己。

我想我之所以胖有兩個原因：首先是貪吃，其次是懶惰！我既不喜歡像公公那樣每天跳交際舞，也不會跟兒子玩滑板，生活中最大的享受就是一邊看電視，一邊吃零食，尤其是一個人無聊的時

候。人們常說：「一口吃不出個胖子。」所以我也不可能一下子變成個瘦子，得有一個長期計劃才行。第一我要改變不好的飲食習慣。由於工作的關係，我的早飯和午飯都吃得很少，有時候甚至不吃，而晚飯卻吃得很多。這不僅[4]**有害於**健康，而且也是長胖的主要原因。好的飲食習慣應該是「早吃飽，午吃好，晚吃少」。而且要多吃蔬菜和水果，少吃零食。

第二，我參加了一個健身班。我的班有30多個學生，在我看來，50%的人應該增肥，30%的人身材合適，大約只有20%的人需要減肥。當然身材最好的要數老師。

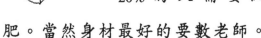

從上課到下課，她可以一直不停地跳，而且眼睛不會忽視房間的任何人。如果看到有人想偷懶，她就會站在前面大聲叫：「夏天想不想穿裙子？」當然想！所以就算再累也得堅持。

運動減肥是長期的，不可能讓人一下子變瘦。開始的時候由於沒有什麼效果，我失望得想放棄。但是一想起班裏那些苗條的年輕人，就告訴自己一定要堅持 5下去。兩個月以後，我減了大約12斤。看到這個結果，我覺得自己經歷的辛苦是值得的。

閱讀理解 Comprehension Check

10. 「我」從前覺得自己什麼很好？結婚後有什麼變化？她是怎麼發現這種變化的？
11. 「我」要減肥，想到的第一個方法是什麼？她用了這個方法沒有？為什麼？
12. 「我」認為自己胖的原因是什麼？她覺得什麼是一種享受？
13. 「一口吃不出個胖子」是什麼意思？
14. 「我」要減肥，首先要做什麼？她從前的飲食習慣怎麼樣？
15. 「我」要減肥，其次要做什麼？
16. 在「我」看來，真正需要減肥的人有多少？
17. 「我」對她健身班的老師有什麼看法？老師教得好嗎？為什麼？
18. 運動減肥很花時間，「我」為什麼沒有放棄？最後結果怎麼樣？

怎么才能减肥

从前一直为自己苗条的身材骄傲，没想到结婚以后却一天比一天胖。开始我没有太注意，可是后来发现衣服越来越紧，才知道我真的该减肥了。

第一个想到的方法就是吃减肥药，可是商店里有各种各样的减肥药，我不知道选哪一种好。不过后来看到报纸上说，最有效的减肥方法不是吃药，而是有好的饮食和运动习惯，于是我开始"检查"自己。

我想我之所以胖有两个原因：首先是贪吃，其次是懒惰！我既不喜欢象公公那样每天跳交际舞，也不会跟儿子玩滑板，生活中最大的享受就是一边看电视，一边吃零食，尤其是一个人无聊的时候。人们常说："一口吃不出个胖子。"所以我也不可

能一下子变成个瘦子，得有一个长期计划才行。第一我要改变不好的饮食习惯。由于工作的关系，我的早饭和午饭都吃得很少，有时候甚至不吃，而晚饭却吃得很多。这不仅[4]**有害于**健康，而且也是长胖的主要原因。好的饮食习惯应该是"早吃饱，午吃好，晚吃少"。而且要多吃蔬菜和水果，少吃零食。

第二，我参加了一个健身班。我的班里有30多个学生，在我看来，50%的人应该增肥，30%的人身材合适，大约只有20%的人需要减肥。当然身材最好的要数老师。从上课到下课，她可以一直不停地跳，而且眼睛不会忽

视房间里的任何人。如果看到有人想偷懒，她就会站在前面大声叫："夏天想不想穿裙子？"当然想！所以就算再累也得坚持。

运动减肥是长期的，不可能让人一下子变瘦。开始的时候由于没有什么效果，我失望得想放弃。但是一想起班里那些苗条的年轻人，就告诉自己一定要坚持[5]下去。两个月以后，我减了大约12斤。看到这个结果，我觉得自己经历的辛苦是值得的。

阅读理解 Comprehension Check

10. "我"从前觉得自己什么很好？结婚后有什么变化？她是怎么发现这种变化的？
11. "我"要减肥，想到的第一个方法是什么？她用了这个方法没有？为什么？
12. "我"认为自己胖的原因是什么？她觉得什么是一种享受？
13. "一口吃不出个胖子"是什么意思？
14. "我"要减肥，首先要做什么？她从前的饮食习惯怎么样？
15. "我"要减肥，其次要做什么？
16. 在"我"看来，真正需要减肥的人有多少？
17. "我"对她健身班的老师有什么看法？老师教得好吗？为什么？
18. 运动减肥很花时间，"我"为什么没有放弃？最后结果怎么样？

敘述生詞 Vocabulary

19.	减肥	减肥	jiǎnféi	VO	to lose weight	[to reduce-fat]
	苗條	苗条	miáotiáo	Adj	slim, slender	[seedling-strip]
20.	身材		shēncái	N	figure, stature	[body-material]
21.	緊	紧	jǐn	Adj	tight	
22.	有效		yǒuxiào	Adj	effective, valid	[to have-effect]
23.	檢查	检查	jiǎnchá	N/V	examination, to check	[to check-to investigate]
	一口吃不出個胖子	一口吃不出个胖子	yì kǒu chību chū ge pàngzi	IE	<口>one can't get fat after only one bite	[one-mouth-eat-not-out-a-fat-person]

	懶惰	懒惰	lǎnduò	Adj	lazy, indolent	[lazy-indolent]
	公公		gōnggong	N	先生的爸爸	[husband's father-husband's father]
24.	享受		xiǎngshòu	N/V	to enjoy	[to enjoy-to receive]
	零食		língshí	N	between-meal nibbles, snacks	[odd-meal]
25.	改變	改变	gǎibiàn	V	to change, to transform	[to change-to change]
26.	甚至		shènzhì	Conj	even (to the point of), so much so that	[very-to]
27.	有害於	有害于	yǒuhàiyú	VP	對…不好	[to have-harm-at]
28.	主要		zhǔyào	Adj	main, chief, principal, major	[main-vital]
29.	蔬菜		shūcài	N	vegetables, greens	[vegetables-greens]
30.	合適	合适	héshì	Adj	suitable, appropriate, right	[to accord with-suit]
31.	大約	大约	dàyuē	Adv	probably, about, around	[big-approximately]
32.	忽視	忽视	hūshì	V	to overlook, to neglect, to ignore	[to disregard-look]
33.	任何		rènhé	Adj	any, whatever	[any-what]
34.	偷懶	偷懒	tōulǎn	V	to slack off, to shirk one's duty	[secretly-lazy]
	裙子		qúnzi	N	skirt	[skirt-(noun suffix)]
35.	堅持	坚持	jiānchí	V	to persist in, to insist on	[firm-to hold]
36.	長期	长期	chángqī	Adj/N	很長時間的	[long-term]
37.	效果		xiàoguǒ	N	effect, result	[effect-fruit]
38.	放棄	放弃	fàngqì	V	to give up, to abandon	[to release-to discard]
	斤		jīn	N	half of a kilogram	
39.	值得		zhíde	Adj/V	to merit, to deserve	[to be worth-(complement)]

Characters with Many Strokes

減　緊　檢　懶　惰　零　蔬　適　偷　棄

詞匯用法 Words in Context

19. 減肥：減肥的方法；減肥藥；減肥糖　　　減肥：减肥的方法；减肥药；减肥糖

你覺得怎麼做才是減肥的好方　　　你觉得怎么做才是减肥的好方

法？

你相信減肥藥可以幫人減肥嗎？為什麼？

20. 身材：身材苗條、高大、矮小、好

什麼樣的人打籃球不太合適？

什麼樣的人才能當模特兒？

21. 緊：衣服越來越緊；時間很緊；考試安排得很緊 ↔鬆sōng

你喜歡穿緊一點還是鬆一點的衣服？

什麼情況會讓你在星期五的晚上去圖書館看書？

22. 有效：有效的方法、做法

你覺得用什麼方法學漢字更有效？

據說喝咖啡能提神'refresh oneself'，這個做法對你有效嗎？

23. 檢查：檢查身體、作業、學生準備功課了沒有；健康檢查

中文課聽寫生詞的目的是什麼？

你每年都做健康檢查嗎？

24. 享受：享受生活、好聽的音樂；最大的享受；是一種享受

對你來說，做什麼是最大的享受？

你覺得聽什麼樣的音樂是一種享受？

25. 改變：改變看法、安排；有一些

法？

你相信减肥药可以帮人减肥吗？为什么？

身材：身材苗条、高大、矮小、好

什么样的人打篮球不太合适？

什么样的人才能当模特儿？

紧：衣服越来越紧；时间很紧；考试安排得很紧 ↔松sōng

你喜欢穿紧一点还是松一点的衣服？

什么情况会让你在星期五的晚上去图书馆看书？

有效：有效的方法、做法

你觉得用什么方法学汉字更有效？

据说喝咖啡能提神，这个做法对你有效吗？

检查：检查身体、作业、学生准备功课了没有；健康检查

中文课听写生词的目的是什么？

你每年都做健康检查吗？

享受：享受生活、好听的音乐；最大的享受；是一种享受

对你来说，做什么是最大的享受？

你觉得听什么样的音乐是一种享受？

改变：改变看法、安排；有一些

改變

想減肥的人應該改變哪些不好的飲食習慣？

學中文以後，你對中文的了解有什麼改變？

26. 甚至：麥當勞很受歡迎，甚至老人都喜歡麥當勞；他很忙，甚至週末都工作

現在學中文的人越來越多嗎？

你是一個貪玩的人嗎？為什麼？

27. 有害於：（句型）

28. 主要：主要原因；主要是因為；主要討論健康的問題

中文的小班課和大班課有什麼不一樣？

你為什麼會選擇學習中文？

29. 蔬菜：蔬菜水果；綠葉蔬菜

你最愛吃哪一種蔬菜？

吃蔬菜對身體健康有什麼好處？

30. 合適：很合適；不太合適

你覺得自己穿紅色的衣服怎麼樣？

中文課每天的功課多不多？

31. 大約：大約三個小時；一百塊錢；大約還有十天就放假了

你估計一個最好的筆記本電腦要多少錢？

還有多長時間感恩節就到了？

改变

想减肥的人应该改变哪些不好的饮食习惯？

学中文以后，你对中文的了解有什么改变？

甚至：麦当劳很受欢迎，甚至老人都喜欢麦当劳；他很忙，甚至周末都工作

现在学中文的人越来越多吗？

你是一个贪玩的人吗？为什么？

有害于：（句型）

主要：主要原因；主要是因为；主要讨论健康的问题

中文的小班课和大班课有什么不一样？

你为什么会选择学习中文？

蔬菜：蔬菜水果；绿叶蔬菜

你最爱吃哪一种蔬菜？

吃蔬菜对身体健康有什么好处？

合适：很合适；不太合适

你觉得自己穿红色的衣服怎么样？

中文课每天的功课多不多？

大约：大约三个小时；一百块钱；大约还有十天就放假了

你估计一个最好的笔记本电脑要多少钱？

还有多长时间感恩节就到了？

32. 忽視：忽視問題、朋友；孩子被　　　　忽视：忽视问题、朋友；孩子被
    父母忽視了　　　　　　　　　　　　　父母忽视了

    如果夫妻兩個人都工作的話，對　　　　如果夫妻两个人都工作的话，对
    孩子會有什麼影響？　　　　　　　　　孩子会有什么影响？

    說中文的時候，你很注意自己的　　　　说中文的时候，你很注意自己的
    發音嗎？　　　　　　　　　　　　　　发音吗？

33. 任何：任何人、事情、時間　　　　　　任何：任何人、事情、时间

    哪些學生可以選中文課？　　　　　　　哪些学生可以选中文课？

    如果我有問題，什麼時候可以給　　　　如果我有问题，什么时候可以给
    你打電話？　　　　　　　　　　　　　你打电话？

34. 偷懶：經常偷懶；別偷懶；少偷　　　　偷懒：经常偷懒；别偷懒；少偷
    點懶　　　　　　　　　　　　　　　　点懒

    你在哪些方面會偷懶？　　　　　　　　你在哪些方面会偷懒？

    你覺得怎麼樣可以讓你的成績變　　　　你觉得怎么样可以让你的成绩变
    得更好？　　　　　　　　　　　　　　得更好？

35. 堅持：堅持一年；堅持（不）下　　　　坚持：坚持一年；坚持（不）下
    去；堅持觀點；對自己的看法很　　　　去；坚持观点；对自己的看法很
    堅持　　　　　　　　　　　　　　　　坚持

    去健身多長時間就可以減肥了？　　　　去健身多长时间就可以减肥了？

    如果別人不同意你的看法，你會　　　　如果别人不同意你的看法，你会
    怎麼做？　　　　　　　　　　　　　　怎么做？

36. 長期：長期打算、工作；長期堅　　　　长期：长期打算、工作；长期坚
    持　↔短期　　　　　　　　　　　　　持　↔短期

    學一個學期的中文就可以看中文　　　　学一个学期的中文就可以看中文
    報紙嗎？　　　　　　　　　　　　　　报纸吗？

    你會不會一直在那個飯館工作？　　　　你会不会一直在那个饭馆工作？

37. 效果：有很好的效果；效果不　　　　　效果：有很好的效果；效果不
    好；沒有效果　　　　　　　　　　　　好；没有效果

    吃減肥藥對減肥有幫助嗎？　　　　　　吃减肥药对减肥有帮助吗？

你覺得什麼樣的方法對記漢字有好的效果？

你觉得什么样的方法对记汉字有好的效果？

38. 放棄：放棄工作、家庭、傳統；捨不得放棄；放棄不了

你會不會為了愛情放棄工作？

你覺得為了健康，自己得放棄哪些不好的飲食習慣？

放弃：放弃工作、家庭、传统；舍不得放弃；放弃不了

你会不会为了爱情放弃工作？

你觉得为了健康，自己得放弃哪些不好的饮食习惯？

39. 值得：值得買、看、聽、去；不值得

這兒最值得去的地方是哪兒？

你覺得花五十塊美金買一輛二手自行車怎麼樣？

值得：值得买、看、听、去；不值得

这儿最值得去的地方是哪儿？

你觉得花五十块美金买一辆二手自行车怎么样？

自由發揮與課堂活動 Free Discussion and Classroom Activities

7. 介紹一下你自己的飲食習慣，想一想哪些地方有助於健康，而哪些地方有害於健康？

介绍一下你自己的饮食习惯，想一想哪些地方有助于健康，而哪些地方有害于健康？

8. 請你給下面不同的人安排一個減肥計劃，請你先說明哪些習慣讓他們變得很胖，然後再提出你的減肥建議。
   1) 55歲的退休婦女
   2) 30歲的在辦公室工作的先生

请你给下面不同的人安排一个减肥计划，请你先说明哪些习惯让他们变得很胖，然后再提出你的减肥建议。
   1) 55岁的退休妇女
   2) 30岁的在办公室工作的先生

9. 辯論:什麼才是有效的減肥方法？
   甲方:吃減肥藥。請說明：
   1) 減肥藥有什麼效果；
   2) 其他的減肥方法為什麼不好

   乙方:運動。請說明：
   1) 運動為什麼是有效的減肥方法；
   2) 吃減肥藥有什麼不好

辩论:什么才是有效的减肥方法？
   甲方:吃减肥药。请说明：
   1) 减肥药有什么效果；
   2) 其他的减肥方法为什么不好

   乙方:运动。请说明：
   1) 运动为什么是有效的减肥方法；
   2) 吃减肥药有什么不好

説明 Exposition

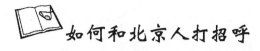如何和北京人打招呼

　「吃了嗎？」曾經是北京人見面打招呼必說的一句話，可是現在人們已經放棄了這個老傳統。也許是因為生活豐富了的緣故，人們也就不再把吃飯這個問題天天掛在嘴上了。

　如果你現在看到兩個七八十歲的老頭兒和老太太在路上見面時說「晚上老地方見！」你可千萬不要以為他們是黃昏戀，他們不是約好去跳交際舞，就是去打太極拳。

　以前年輕人見了面以後，免不了找個地方坐下來聊一聊，而現在[6]則急急忙忙地說：「把你的OICQ號碼給我，咱們網上聊！」中年人不像老年人那麼清閒，也不像年輕人那麼時髦，他們見面的時候，很可能會互相介紹介紹減肥或者健身的經驗。

　了解了這些以後，和北京人打招呼的時候也要學會「因人而異」。

閱讀理解 Comprehension Check

19. 從前的北京人怎麼跟人打招呼？現在呢？為什麼？
20. 老人彼此怎麼打招呼？有空的話，他們常做什麼活動？
21. 年輕人從前怎麼打招呼？現在呢？
22. 中年人見面的時候常說些什麼？

如何和北京人打招呼

"吃了吗？"曾经是北京人见面打招呼必说的一句话，可是现在人们已经放弃了这个老传统。也许是因为生活丰富了的缘故，人们也就不再把吃饭这个问题天天挂在嘴上了。

如果你现在看到两个七八十岁的老头儿和老太太在路上见面时说"晚上老地方见！"你可千万不要以为他们是黄昏恋，他们不是约好去跳交际舞，就是去打太极拳。

以前年轻人见了面以后，免不了找个地方坐下来聊一聊，而现在[6]则急急忙忙地说："把你的OICQ号码给我，咱们网上聊！"中年人不象老年人那么清闲，也不象年轻人那么时髦，他们见面的时候，很可能会互相介绍介绍减肥或者健身的经验。

了解了这些以后，和北京人打招呼的时候也要学会"因人而异"。

阅读理解 Comprehension Check

19. 从前的北京人怎么跟人打招呼？现在呢？为什么？
20. 老人彼此怎么打招呼？有空的话，他们常做什么活动？
21. 年轻人从前怎么打招呼？现在呢？
22. 中年人见面的时候常说些什么？

說明生詞 Vocabulary

40.	打招呼		dǎ zhāohu	VO	to say hello, to greet sb.	[to do-beckon-call]
41.	曾經	曾经	céngjīng	Adv	once, ever	[once-to undergo]
	緣故	缘故	yuángù	N	reason	[cause-therefore]
	老頭兒	老头儿	lǎotóur	N	<口> old man/chap	[old-head]
	黃昏戀	黄昏恋	huánghūnliàn	N	love between the elderly (lit. sunset love)	[yellow-dusk-love]
42.	則	则	zé	Adv	then, in that case	
43.	急忙		jímáng	Adv	in haste, hurriedly	[urgent-busy]
	OICQ			IE	O I seek you.	
44.	號碼	号码	hàomǎ	N	(serial) number	[number-code]
	清閑	清闲	qīngxián	Adj	at leisure, idle	[quiet-spare time]
	因人而異		yīn rén ér yì	IE	to change one's manner of speaking depending on whom he is addressing.	[on the basis of-people-and-different]

Characters with Many Strokes

曾 緣 戀 則 急 號 清 閑 異

詞匯用法 Words in Context

40. 打招呼：打個招呼；沒打招呼

在路上碰到一個很久沒見的朋友，你怎麼跟他打招呼？

如果你的朋友沒跟你打招呼，你會怎麼想？

打招呼：打个招呼；没打招呼

在路上碰到一个很久没见的朋友，你怎么跟他打招呼？

如果你的朋友没跟你打招呼，你会怎么想？

41. 曾經：曾經去過中國；不曾有過這樣的經歷；↔不曾

你現在熱衷於健身嗎？

你是一個貪玩的人嗎？

曾经：曾经去过中国；不曾有过这样的经历；↔不曾

你现在热衷于健身吗？

你是一个贪玩的人吗？

42. 則：（句型）

则：（句型）

43. 急忙：急忙跑進教室；急急忙忙 　　急忙：急忙跑进教室；急急忙忙

你怎麼每天都急急忙忙的？ 　　你怎么每天都急急忙忙的？

這幾天上課你都遲到了嗎？ 　　这几天上课你都迟到了吗？

44. 號碼（號）：電話號碼；房間號 　　号码（号）：电话号码；房间号

你的電話號碼是多少？ 　　你的电话号码是多少？

你住在這棟公寓的哪個房間？ 　　你住在这栋公寓的哪个房间？

自由發揮與課堂活動 Free Discussion and Classroom Activities

10. 介紹不同地方打招呼的方式，這 　　介绍不同地方打招呼的方式，这

些不同說明了什麼現象？ 　　些不同说明了什么现象？

11. 你對黃昏戀有什麼看法？ 　　你对黄昏恋有什么看法？

應用詞 Productive Vocabulary

◎By Grammatical Categories

Nouns/Pronouns/Measure Words

享受	xiǎngshòu	to enjoy
蔬菜	shūcài	vegetables, greens
身材	shēncái	figure, stature
檢查	jiǎnchá	examination, to check

效果	xiàoguǒ	effect, result
號碼	hàomǎ	(serial) number
老百姓	lǎobǎixìng	common people, civilians

Verbs/Stative Verbs/Adjectives

掛	guà	to hang, to put up
趁	chèn	to take advantage of (sth.), while (doing sth. else)
估計	gūjì	to estimate, to appraise, to reckon
達到	dádào	to achieve, to reach, to attain
改變	gǎibiàn	to change, to transform
答應	dāying	to agree to do sth., to promise, to answer
豐富	fēngfù	to enrich, rich, abundant
堅持	jiānchí	to persist in, to insist on
放棄	fàngqì	to give up, to abandon
忽視	hūshì	to overlook, to neglect, to ignore
偷懶	tōulǎn	to slack off, to shirk one's duty
健身	jiànshēn	to keep fit
減肥	jiǎnféi	to lose weight
打招呼	dǎ zhāohu	to say hello, to greet sb.
免不了	miǎnbuliǎo	to be unavoidable, to be bound to

有害於	yǒuhàiyú	to be harmful
臭	chòu	<PRC> foul, stinking
緊	jǐn	tight
安靜	ānjìng	quiet, peaceful
精彩	jīngcǎi	brilliant, splendid
積極	jījí	active, energetic, positive
有效	yǒuxiào	effective, valid
值得	zhíde	to merit, to deserve
合適	héshì	suitable, appropriate, right
主要	zhǔyào	main, chief, principal, major
任何	rènhé	any, whatever
長期	chángqī	long-term, long period of time
落伍	luòwǔ	to be outdated
無聊	wúliáo	bored, senseless, silly
可惜	kěxī	unfortunately, It's a pity!

Adverbs and Others

則	zé	then, in that case
大約	dàyuē	probably, about, around
曾經	céngjīng	once, ever
甚至	shènzhì	even (to the point of), so much so that

急忙	jímáng	in haste, hurriedly
不像話	bú xiànghuà	ridiculous, outrageous, unreasonable
不是…嗎	búshì...ma	Isn't it right?

理解词 Receptive Vocabulary

◎ **By Grammatical Categories**

Nouns/Pronouns/Measure Words

斤	jīn	half of a kilogram	公公	gōnggong	father-in-law
緣故	yuángù	reason	跟屁蟲	gēnpìchóng	a tagalong
零食	língshí	between-meal nibbles, snacks	老頭兒	lǎotóur	<口> old man/chap
滑板	huábǎn	skateboard	太極拳	Tàijíquán	a kind of shadowboxing
酒吧	jiǔbā	bar	交際舞	jiāojìwǔ	ballroom/social dancing
網吧	wǎngbā	Internet café	黃昏戀	huánghūnliàn	love between the elderly (lit. sunset love)
裙子	qúnzi	skirt			
球隊	qiúduì	sports team			
球迷	qiúmí	sports fan			

Verbs/Stative Verbs/Adjectives

參加	cānjiā	to join, attend, take part in	清閑	qīngxián	at leisure, idle
苗條	miáotiáo	slim, slender	懶惰	lǎnduò	lazy, indolent

Adverbs and Others

拿…開心	ná...kāixīn	to make fun of…	一口吃不出個胖子	yì kǒu chību chū ge pàngzi	one can't get fat after only one bite
因人而異	yīn rén ér yì	different people do things in different ways			

本课词表 Chapter Vocabulary

◎ **By Pinyin**

Words with asterisk* are productive vocabulary which needs to be memorized and studied for its usage.

ānjìng*	安静	quiet, peaceful	chángqī*	长期	long-term, long period of time
bú xiànghuà*	不象话	ridiculous, outrageous, unreasonable	chèn*	趁	to take advantage of (sth.), while (doing sth. else)
búshì...ma*	不是…吗	<口>Isn't it right?	chòu*	臭	foul, stinking
cānjiā	参加	to join, to attend, to take part in	dǎ zhāohu*	打招呼	to say hello, to greet sb.
céngjīng*	曾经	once, ever	dádào*	达到	to achieve, to reach, to attain

dāying*	答应	to agree to do sth., to promise, to answer
dàyuē*	大约	probably, about, around
fàngqì*	放弃	to give up, to abandon
fēngfù*	丰富	to enrich, rich, abundant
gǎibiàn*	改变	to change, to transform
gēnpìchóng	跟屁虫	a tagalong
gūjì*	估计	to estimate, to appraise, to reckon
gōnggong	公公	father-in-law
guà*	挂	to hang, to put up
hàomǎ*	号码	(serial) number
héshì*	合适	suitable, right appropriate
hūshì*	忽视	to overlook, to neglect, to ignore
huábǎn	滑板	skateboard
huánghūn liàn	黄昏恋	love between the elderly (lit. sunset love)
jiǎnchá*	检查	examination, to check
jiānchí*	坚持	to persist in, to insist on
jiǎnféi*	减肥	to lose weight
jiànshēn*	健身	to keep fit
jiāojìwǔ	交际舞	ballroom/social dancing
jījí*	积极	active, energetic, positive
jímáng*	急忙	in haste, hurriedly
jīn	斤	half of a kilogram
jǐn*	紧	tight
jīngcǎi*	精彩	brilliant, splendid
jiǔbā	酒吧	bar
kěxī*	可惜	unfortunately, It's a pity!
lǎnduò	懒惰	lazy, indolent
lǎobǎixìng*	老百姓	common people, civilians
lǎotóur	老头儿	<口> old man/chap

língshí	零食	between-meal nibbles, snacks
luòwǔ*	落伍	to be outdated
miǎnbuliǎo*	免不了	to be unavoidable, to be bound to
miáotiáo	苗条	slim, slender
ná...kāixīn	拿…开心	to make fun of...
qīngxián	清闲	at leisure, idle
qiúduì	球队	sports team
qiúmí	球迷	sports fan
qúnzi	裙子	skirt
rènhé*	任何	any, whatever
shēncái*	身材	figure, stature
shènzhì*	甚至	even (to the point of), so much so that
shūcài*	蔬菜	vegetables, greens
Tàijíquán	太极拳	a kind of shadowboxing
tōulǎn*	偷懒	to slack off, to shirk one's duty
wǎngbā	网吧	Internet café
wúliáo*	无聊	bored, senseless, silly
xiǎngshòu*	享受	to enjoy
xiàoguǒ*	效果	effect, result
yì kǒu chību chū ge pàngzi	一口吃不出个胖子	<口>one can't get fat after only one bite
yīn rén ér yì	因人而异	different people do things in different ways
yǒuhàiyú*	有害于	to be harmful
yǒuxiào*	有效	effective, valid
yuángù	缘故	reason
zé*	则	then, in that case
zhíde*	值得	to merit, to deserve
zhǔyào*	主要	main, chief, principal, major

語法和用法 Grammar and Usage

Pay attention to the function of the structure and then study the example sentences. When blanks are provided, either answer the questions or complete the sentences.

1. Expressing expediency

S 趁(著)…(的 時候) VO	chèn(zhe)...(de shíhou)	S VO by taking advantage of...
S 趁早/熱/年輕	chènzǎo/rè/niánqīng	S does sth. while there is still time/while it is warm/while one is young

● 趁現在還不太熱，出去鍛鍊鍛鍊。

1. 你這次回國只有兩個星期的時間，好好在家裏休息一下，不要到處亂跑。

你这次回国只有两个星期的时间，好好在家里休息一下，不要到处乱跑。

You have only a two-week break coming back this time. Have a good rest at home and don't run around.

那怎麼行，我就是要趁回國的機會和朋友多聚一下。

那怎么行，我就是要趁回国的机会和朋友多聚一下。

How would that work? I'm going to take advantage of my return to meet with my friends.

2. 你十點鐘上課，現在才七點，怎麼就要走？

你十点钟上课，现在才七点，怎么就要走？

You have class at ten o'clock and now it's only seven o'clock. Why are you leaving?

我想趁早走，不然過一會兒恐怕會堵車。

我想趁早走，不然过一会儿恐怕会堵车。

I want to leave while it is still early. Otherwise, I'm afraid there could be a traffic jam after a while.

3. 飯做好了，大家趁熱吃吧，涼了就不好吃了。

饭做好了，大家趁热吃吧，凉了就不好吃了。

The meal is ready. Everybody, eat it while it is still warm. It won't taste good if it cools down.

我的文章還沒寫完，你們先吃吧！

我的文章还没写完，你们先吃吧！

My article is not finished yet. Why don't you go ahead and eat?

4.　我聽說秋天是北京最漂亮的季　　我听说秋天是北京最漂亮的季
　　節，你不打算去旅行嗎？　　　　节，你不打算去旅行吗？

5.　今天是週末，大家要麼去酒　　　今天是周末，大家要么去酒
　　吧、要麼和朋友約會，你為什　　吧、要么和朋友约会，你为什
　　麼還在看書？　　　　　　　　　么还在看书？

6.　每天早上，公園裏都有一個老　　每天早上，公园里都有一个老
　　人免費教大家跳交際舞，你要　　人免费教大家跳交际舞，你要
　　不要和我一起去學？　　　　　　不要和我一起去学？

The pattern S 趁 (著) … (的 時候) VO indicates one's intent of making use of an opportunity or occasion to do something incidentally, so there is often 要 (example 1), 想 (example 2), 得、打算 before 趁著. What goes between 趁著 and 的時候/機會 is often a noun phrase or a verb phrase, e.g., 趁著秋天天氣好的時候、趁著週末沒事的時候、趁著學校放長假的時候、趁著這個難得的好機會. To say "while there is still time/while it is warm/ while one is young," the following set expressions are used, 趁早/趁熱/趁年輕.

2. Expressing disagreement

(O) 有什麼好 V 的 ？	yǒushénme hǎo… de?	What's the point of Ving O?
V 什麼 O ？	…shénme…?	

● 滑板有什麼好教的？北京隊和上海隊是全國水平最高的球隊，他們的
　比賽一定很精彩。

1.　我的教授給我發電　　我的教授给我发电　　My professor sent me an e-
　　子郵件說，她要和　　子邮件说，她要和　　mail saying that she wanted to
　　我談一談我的功　　　我谈一谈我的功　　　talk with me about my
　　課，我有點害怕！　　课，我有点害怕！　　homework. I'm a bit scared.

這有什麼好怕的，也許她覺得你的功課非常好呢！	这有什么好怕的，也许她觉得你的功课非常好呢！	What's the point of being scared? Perhaps she thinks your homework is excellent.

2.

昨天大家嫌我在麥當勞請客太小氣，我也覺得非常不好意思。	昨天大家嫌我在麦当劳请客太小气，我也觉得非常不好意思。	Yesterday everyone thought that I was too stingy by taking them out at MacDonald's. I also felt very embarrassed.
你有什麼不好意思的，他們不小氣，為什麼不請客？	你有什么不好意思的，他们不小气，为什么不请客？	What's the point of feeling embarrassed? If they're not stingy, why don't they treat you?

3.

我好不容易買到兩張足球比賽的票，要不要一起去看？	我好不容易买到两张足球比赛的票，要不要一起去看？	It took me a long time to get these two tickets to the football game. Would you like to go with me?
那麼臭的比賽，一點也不精彩，有什麼好看的，你還是找別人吧！	那么臭的比赛，一点也不精彩，有什么好看的，你还是找别人吧！	Such a rotten game certainly won't be any good. What's the point of watching it? You'd better find someone else to go with you.

4.

我今天晚上九點要出去看一部最新的中國電影。	我今天晚上九点要出去看一部最新的中国电影。	I'm going out tonight at nine o'clock to see the latest Chinese movie.
那麼晚，看什麼電影？還是在家休息好了。	那么晚，看什么电影？还是在家休息好了。	It's too late to go to a movie. You'd better stay home and rest.

5.

李明是你的好朋友，為什麼昨天聚會的時候，你連一句話都沒跟他說？	李明是你的好朋友，为什么昨天聚会的时候，你连一句话都没跟他说？	

6.　昨天你逛了一天商店，難道什 昨天你逛了一天商店，难道什
　　麼東西都沒買嗎？ 么东西都没买吗？

7.　這是最近美國最流行的音樂， 这是最近美国最流行的音乐，
　　你聽聽看。 你听听看。

While the pattern (O)有什麼好V的 and V什麼O both indicate the speaker's disagreement of the proposition in the previous context, the former places more emphasis on the object and the latter on the action. Compare the preceding contexts and the use of the respective patterns in the following: 沒錢，買什麼東西？ 'If one has no money, what's the point of shopping.' 這家店很小，東西又少，有什麼好買 的？ 'This store is small and has few things. What's the point of shopping for things (here)?' Note that in "O有什麼好V的" the object is often omitted if it's understood within the context and does not need to be specified. Also, "O有什麼好V的" is a set expression; no element should be inserted in between 好 and V or V and 的. So, it's wrong to say 有什麼好跟他說的 or 有什麼好說話的. Instead, one should say 跟他有 什麼好說的 'What's the point of talking to him?'

3. Expressing preoccupation

S 把…掛在 N 上	bǎ…guàzài…shàng	to hang…on…
S 把…放在 N 上/裏	bǎ…fàngzài..shàng/lǐ	to put…on…

● 你現在總是把小麗掛在嘴上，我看你已經成了她的跟屁蟲了！

1.　你知道嗎，小麗在 你知道吗，小丽在 Did you know that Xiao Li is in
　　和小趙談戀愛。 和小赵谈恋爱。 love with Xiao Zhao?

　　怪不得，小趙最近 怪不得，小赵最近 No wonder, lately Xiao Zhao
　　天天把小麗掛在嘴 天天把小丽挂在嘴 talks about her all the time.
　　上。 上。

2.　聽說上海的一種減 听说上海的一种减 I heard that there is a very
　　肥藥非常有效，這 肥药非常有效，这 effective diet medicine in
　　次你去上海千萬別 次你去上海千万别 Shanghai. By all means
　　 　 remember to buy me some when
　　 　 you go to Shanghai this time.

忘了給我帶一點回　　　忘了给我带一点回
來。　　　　　　　　　來。

你說了好幾遍了，　　　你说了好几遍了，　　　You have mentioned it several
我一定把這件事放　　　我一定把这件事放　　　times. I surely will remember
在心上。　　　　　　　在心上。　　　　　　　it.

3.　明天德國和巴西有　　　明天德国和巴西有　　　Tomorrow Germany and
　　一場橄欖球比賽，　　　一场橄榄球比赛，　　　Brazil have a soccer match.
　　你覺得誰能贏？　　　　你觉得谁能赢？　　　　Who do you think will win?

　　德國的橄欖球隊不　　　德国的橄榄球队不　　　Germany's soccer team isn't
　　太好，巴西根本不　　　太好，巴西根本不　　　too good. Brazil's team won't
　　會把他們放在眼　　　　会把他们放在眼　　　　consider them a match at all.
　　裏。　　　　　　　　　里。

4.　我總是聽你媽媽說她要減肥，　　我总是听你妈妈说她要减肥，
　　可是她看起來好像沒瘦。　　　　可是她看起来好象没瘦。

5.　我打算寒假的時候去昆明旅　　　我打算寒假的时候去昆明旅
　　行，你答應過做我的導遊，是　　行，你答应过做我的导游，是
　　吧？　　　　　　　　　　　　吧？

6.　我覺得李明從美國留學回來以　　我觉得李明从美国留学回来以
　　後，好像比從前驕傲了，不太　　后，好象比从前骄傲了，不太
　　願意和同學們在一起。　　　　愿意和同学们在一起。

The pattern 把⋯V在N上/裏is very colloquial and has set expressions. When the
noun is "mouth" 嘴上, the verb is always 掛 and it means "one keeps on saying
something or someone" as a concern (example 1). When the noun is "mind" 心上, the
verb should be 放 and it means "one keeps something on one's mind." To say
someone doesn't heed of one's advice, one can say 他沒把我的話放在心上. Note that

when the noun is "eyes" 眼裏, the verb is still 放 and what follows 把 is always a person/team. In addition, it is always used with a negative marker before 把 to indicate "one doesn't have someone in one's eyes," that is, one considers the other no match for oneself or takes the other lightly, e.g., 他從來不把我放在眼裏.

4. Expressing the impact of one on another

X 有害於 Y	yǒuhàiyú...	X is harmful to Y
X 有利於 Y	yǒulìyú...	X is beneficial to Y
X 有助於 Y	yǒuzhùyú...	X is helpful to Y

● 這不僅有害於健康，而且也是長胖的主要原因。

1. 經常曬太陽好嗎？　　經常晒太阳好吗？　　Is it good to sunbathe often?

經常曬太陽有利於健康，但是長時間曝曬有害於皮膚。

经常晒太阳有利于健康，但是长时间曝晒有害于皮肤。

To sunbathe often is good for your health, but if you sunbathe for a long time, it will be harmful to your skin.

2. 留學生回不回國有什麼關係？

留学生回不回国有什么关系？

What does it matter if overseas students do not return to their home countries?

如果能有很多的留學生畢業以後回國工作的話，會有利於中國的經濟發展。

如果能有很多的留学生毕业以后回国工作的话，会有利于中国的经济发展。

If many overseas students after they graduate return to China to work, it will benefit China's economic development.

3. 你怎麼那麼了解李明？

你怎么那么了解李明？

How do you know Li Ming so well?

我和李明從小就是很好的朋友，所以我非常了解他有什麼樣的性格。我想了解一個人的經歷有助於了解他的想法。

我和李明从小就是很好的朋友，所以我非常了解他有什么样的性格。我想了解一个人的经历有助于了解他的想法。

Li Ming and I have been good friends since we were small, so I know his personality very well. I think understanding a person's experiences helps you understand his way of thinking.

4. 現在有很多美國人反對開汽車，他們建議所有的人都騎自行車，這是為什麼？

現在有很多美国人反对开汽车，他们建议所有的人都骑自行车，这是为什么？

---

5. 我知道你的專業是中國歷史，可是在美國有很多關於中國歷史的英文書，你不學中文也可以研究中國歷史。

我知道你的专业是中国历史，可是在美国有很多关于中国历史的英文书，你不学中文也可以研究中国历史。

---

6. 我不明白，為什麼在中國中學生不可以談戀愛？

我不明白，为什么在中国中学生不可以谈恋爱？

The pattern X有害於Y is a formal equivalent of X對Y有害. So never mix the two and say something like 汽車的污染對身體有害於. Since patterns involving 於, in general, are more literary. It's odd to say 學中文有利於我. Instead, it's more appropriate to use the phrase to express more abstract and elaborate ideas, e.g., 學中文有利於我了解中國歷史.

5. Expressing continuation or progression

O S V (得/不) 下去	V (de/bu) xiàqù	S (is able to) continue to V O

● 但是一想起班裏那些苗條的年輕人，就告訴自己一定要堅持下去。

1. 開學的時候，你告訴我，為了減肥，你打算每天去跑步，怎麼這兩天都沒看見你跑步呢？

开学的时候，你告诉我，为了减肥，你打算每天去跑步，怎么这两天都没看见你跑步呢？

When the semester started, you told me you would jog every day to lose weight, how come I haven't seen you jogging these last two days?

我堅持了兩個星

我坚持了两个星

I have been doing it for two

期，可是最近功課
太多，我堅持不下
去了。

期，可是最近功课
太多，我坚持不下
去了。

weeks, but recently I've had so much homework I can't keep it up.

2. 這部電影特別無
聊，我看了開頭就
看不下去了。

这部电影特别无
聊，我看了开头就
看不下去了。

This movie is so boring. After I saw the opening I can't stand to keep watching it.

我也覺得挺沒意思
的，不過也許看下
去就會有興趣了。

我也觉得挺没意思
的，不过也许看下
去就会有兴趣了。

I also think it is quite boring, but if we keep watching it, it might become more interesting.

3. 今天上課的時候，
總是有學生說話，
老師的課都上不下
去了。

今天上课的时候，
总是有学生说话，
老师的课都上不下
去了。

Today in class there were always students talking, so the teacher could not continue her lesson.

我覺得如果他們繼
續下去的話，老師
應該批評他們，不
然會影響其他的同
學。

我觉得如果他们继
续下去的话，老师
应该批评他们，不
然会影响其他的同
学。

I think if they continue talking this way, the teacher should criticize them; otherwise, it will affect other students.

4. 我沒想到中文這麼難學，尤其
是漢字，我每天花很多時間準
備功課，還是有問題，我打算
放棄中文課了。

我没想到中文这么难学，尤其
是汉字，我每天花很多时间准
备功课，还是有问题，我打算
放弃中文课了。

5. 我和我的同屋對彼此都非常不
滿意，他嫌我吵，我嫌他髒，
你說我們該怎麼辦？

我和我的同屋对彼此都非常不
满意，他嫌我吵，我嫌他脏，
你说我们该怎么办？

6. Michael Jordan離開籃球隊的時候

Michael Jordan离开篮球队的时候

很年輕，我覺得他可以再多打　　很年轻，我觉得他可以再多打
幾年。　　　　　　　　　　　　几年。

V(得/不)下去 expresses the continuation or progression of an action. If the verb takes on an object, the object should be topicalized and placed at the beginning of the sentence or after the subject, e.g., 中文我一定要學下去 or 我中文一定要學下去. If one cannot continue the action, one should use V不下去. So, never say 這種地方我不可以住下去. Instead, one should say 這種地方我住不下去. The verb is often a one-syllable verb such as 學、看、聽、住、上、打.

6. Expressing chronological sequence, causal relationship, contrast

...,（而）S 則 VO	zé	..., however SVO (= 卻)
(S) ... 則 X; ... 則 Y		S...thus X; ... thus Y (= 就)

- 以前年輕人見了面以後，免不了找個地方坐下來聊一聊，而現在則急急忙忙地說…

1. 中美年輕人聚會有　　中美年轻人聚会有　　What's the difference between
   什麼不同？　　　　　什么不同？　　　　　Chinese and American young
   　　　　　　　　　　　　　　　　　　　　people when they go out?

   在美國年輕人聚會　　在美国年轻人聚会　　In the U.S., when young
   喜歡「AA制」，而　　喜欢"AA制"，而　　people get together, they like
   中國的年輕人則喜　　中国的年轻人则喜　　to go dutchtreat; however,
   歡由一個人請客。　　欢由一个人请客。　　Chinese young people prefer
   　　　　　　　　　　　　　　　　　　　　one person to treat the others.

2. 李明留學以後，有　　李明留学以后，有　　How has Li Ming changed
   什麼變化？　　　　　什么变化？　　　　　since he studied abroad?

   李明去美國以前是　　李明去美国以前是　　Before going to the U.S., Li
   一個很大方的人，　　一个很大方的人，　　Ming was very generous.
   而從美國回來以後　　而从美国回来以后　　However, after coming back,
   則變得小氣多了，　　则变得小气多了，　　he has become stingier, but this
   不過這是因為他知　　不过这是因为他知　　is only because he now knows
   道了掙錢的辛苦。　　道了挣钱的辛苦。　　how hard it is to make money.

3. 吃藥或節食減肥怎 　吃药或节食减肥怎 　How about taking pills or
   麼樣？ 　　　　么样？ 　　　　skipping meals to lose weight?

   吃減肥藥、節食都 　吃减肥药、节食都 　Taking weight-losing pills and
   有害於健康，不是 　有害于健康，不是 　skipping meals are both harmful
   好的減肥方法；好 　好的减肥方法；好 　to your health. Neither is a good
   的飲食習慣和運動 　的饮食习惯和运动 　way to lose weight. Rather,
   則既有利於健康， 　则既有利于健康， 　good diet habits and exercise are
   又可以減肥。 　　　又可以减肥。 　　　good for your health and help
   　　　　　　　　　　　　　　　　　　　you lose weight.

4. 想學好中文得花多 　想学好中文得花多 　How long does it take to study
   長時間？ 　　　　长时间？ 　　　　Chinese well?

   想學好中文，少則 　想学好中文，少则 　To study Chinese well, it can
   三、四年，多則 　　三、四年，多则 　　take at least three to four years or
   七、八年。 　　　　七、八年。 　　　　at most seven to eight years.

5. 在中國，年輕人、中年人和老 　在中国，年轻人、中年人和老
   年人有什麼不同的活動？ 　　年人有什么不同的活动？

6. 學習電腦等專業的留學生留在 　学习电脑等专业的留学生留在
   美國可以找到一份薪水很高的 　美国可以找到一份薪水很高的
   工作，不久以後就可以買汽車 　工作，不久以后就可以买汽车
   和房子，回國則＿＿＿＿＿＿ 　和房子，回国则＿＿＿＿＿＿
   ＿＿＿＿＿＿＿＿＿＿＿＿ 　　＿＿＿＿＿＿＿＿＿＿＿＿

7. 你覺得我如果旅行的話，是自己 　你觉得我如果旅行的话，是自己
   去旅行還是跟團比較好？ 　　去旅行还是跟团比较好？

則, similar to 於 and 而, is an element which often marks more formal and literary
Chinese. It can mean "however" or "thus" depending on the context. Note that when
則 means "however," it always goes after the subject and is often preceded by 而.
When 則 means "thus," it is often preceded by a verb or adjective, and what follows

often comes in parallel form (example 4). This structure is often found in set, formal expressions, e.g., 他不說則已，一說則滔滔不絕 'If he dosen't speak, that's all right. Once he starts, he never stops.'

背景常識 Background Notes

1. 健身：最近幾年，除了年輕人熱衷於各種運動以外，老人也不像以前那樣每天呆在家裏看電視、聊天了。當然，由於經濟的原因，老人不太可能去健身房鍛鍊，於是他們自己組織起來，利用早上和晚上的時間鍛鍊身體。他們最喜愛的運動不僅包括傳統的太極拳，還有交際舞、扭秧歌。但是也有不少人認為老人扭秧歌的時候把音樂的聲音放得過大，會影響附近居民的生活。

2. 黃昏戀：和早戀相反，黃昏戀指的是老年人的戀愛。根據傳統的觀點，結過婚的人不應該離婚，更不應該再結婚。所以黃昏戀在很長一段時間裏受到人們的反對，尤其是子女，他們首先很難接受一個陌生人做自己的繼父或者繼母，其次他們認為父母有黃昏戀是因為孩子給他們的關心不夠，怕被別人批評不孝順。不過，現在所謂的黃昏戀慢慢的被大家接受了，也許以後就沒有黃昏戀這個詞了。

3. 網吧：網吧是電腦流行以後的一個新產物，由於電腦和上網的價格不低，所以網吧就以它的快速和低價吸引了很多網蟲，尤其是年輕人。

4. 足球：足球是很多中國人喜愛的運動。和美國的籃球一樣，中國也有足球的全國聯賽。每到這個時候，全國的球迷都會非常激動，關注自己喜歡的球隊。

5. 運動：隨著經濟水平的提高，年輕人不再滿足於週末呆在家裏看電視，而是走到外面進行各種運動。現在非常流行的球類運動有乒乓球、羽毛球、保齡球。由於價格比較貴，網球不如其他球類流行，但是也越來越受歡迎。年輕人還經常到郊外活動，常常是幾個要好的朋友一起開車到附近的郊區騎馬、射箭、吃一吃各地有特色的飯菜。

背景常识 Background Notes

1. 健身：最近几年，除了年轻人热衷于各种运动以外，老人也不象以前那样每天呆在家里看电视、聊天了。当然，由于经济的原因，老人不太可能去健身房锻炼，于是他们自己组织起来，利用早上和晚上的时间锻炼身体。他们最喜爱的运动不仅包括传统的太极拳，还有交际舞、扭秧歌。但是也有不少人认为老人扭秧歌的时候把音乐的声音放得过大，会影响附近居民的生活。

2. 黄昏恋：和早恋相反，黄昏恋指的是老年人的恋爱。根据传统的观点，结过婚的人不应该离婚，更不应该再结婚。所以黄昏恋在很长一段时间里受到人们的反对，尤其是子女，他们首先很难接受一个陌生人做自己的继父或者继母，其次他们认为父母有黄昏恋是因为孩子给他们的关心不够，怕被别人批评不孝顺。不过，现在所谓的黄昏恋慢慢的被大家接受了，也许以后就没有黄昏恋这个词了。

3. 网吧：网吧是电脑流行以后的一个新产物，由于电脑和上网的价格不低，所以网吧就以它的快速和低价吸引了很多网虫，尤其是年轻人。

4. 足球：足球是很多中国人喜爱的运动。和美国的篮球一样，中国也有足球的全国联赛。每到这个时候，全国的球迷都会非常激动，关注自己喜欢的球队。

5. 运动：随着经济水平的提高，年轻人不再满足于周末呆在家里看电视，而是走到外面进行各种运动。现在非常流行的球类运动有乒乓球、羽毛球、保龄球。由于价格比较贵，网球不如其他球类流行，但是也越来越受欢迎。年轻人还經常到郊外活动，常常是几个要好的朋友一起开车到附近的郊区骑马、射箭、吃一吃各地有特色的饭菜。

第四課　我是網絡俠客還是壞蛋？

Theme: Computing and the Internet

Communicative Objectives
- Talking about computer problems
- Talking about online shopping
- Narrating an experience about getting hooked on something

Skill Focus
- Comprehending a report on a new kind of computer

Grammar Focus
- 幸虧S⋯，不然⋯
- 所謂⋯指的是⋯
- X對Y起(⋯的)作用
- 通過⋯，SVO
- S一旦⋯，就/也⋯
- S因⋯而VO

Problem Scenario

Tired of all the computing problems that you have run into lately, you are planning to buy a new machine and have a great time surfing on the internet. Yet, you have heard a lot about hackers and computer viruses and are very concerned about the security issue. Will you ever become a net-lover? What machine will you get and which websites will you visit? What will you look out for when you surf on the net? Any dos and don'ts?

對話 Dialogue

(1)Talking about computer problems

張麗和趙強一起做功課，張麗的電腦出了一些毛病。

小張： 哎呀！我的電腦又死機了。

小趙： 沒什麼大不了的！你只要先把它關了，過一會兒再打開就可以了！不過你的功課可能會丟了。

小張： [1]幸虧我有隨時把文件存起來的習慣，不然就白做了。不知道怎麼搞的，我的電腦最近總是有些小毛病。

小趙： 也許你的電腦有病毒。

小張： 真的嗎？那怎麼辦？

小趙： 別緊張，電腦有病毒很容易處理，你買一個殺毒軟件就能對付了。

小張： 哪裏能買到這種軟件呢？

小趙： 哪兒都能買到，就是有點兒貴，我建議你上網去下載一個免費的。

小張： 網絡真是我們的好朋友，什麼都可以下載。

閱讀理解 Comprehension Check

1. 小張的電腦出了什麼問題？小趙給她什麼建議？
2. 小張的功課丟了嗎？為什麼？
3. 小趙認為小張的電腦可能有什麼問題？應該怎麼辦？
4. 小趙建議小張去買殺毒軟件嗎？為什麼？

(1) Talking about computer problems

张丽和赵强一起做功课，张丽的电脑出了一些毛病。

小张：   哎呀！我的电脑又死机了。

小赵：   没什么大不了的！你只要先把它关了，过一会儿再打开就可以了！不过你的功课可能会丢了。

小张：   [1]幸亏我有随时把文件存起来的习惯，不然就白做了。不知道怎么搞的，我的电脑最近总是有些小毛病。

小赵：   也许你的电脑有病毒。

小张：   真的吗？那怎么办？

小赵：   别紧张，电脑有病毒很容易处理，你买一个杀毒软件就能对付了。

小张：   哪里能买到这种软件呢？

小赵：   哪儿都能买到，就是有点儿贵，我建议你上网去下载一个免费的。

小张：   网络真是我们的好朋友，什么都可以下载。

阅读理解 Comprehension Check

1.   小张的电脑出了什么问题？小赵给她什么建议？
2.   小张的功课丢了吗？为什么？
3.   小赵认为小张的电脑可能有什么问题？应该怎么办？
4.   小赵建议小张去买杀毒软件吗？为什么？

對話一生詞 Vocabulary

Study the numbered vocabulary (productive vocabulary) for its usage. The unnumbered items (receptive vocabulary) are to facilitate reading comprehension.

◎By Order of Appearance

1.	網絡	网络	wǎngluò	N	\<PRC\> the internet \<TW\>網路	[net-twine]
	俠客	俠客	xiákè	N	a person adept in martial arts and given to chivalrous conduct (in old times), chivalrous warrior	[chivalrous-person engaged in a particular pursuit]
	壞蛋	坏蛋	huàidàn	N	scoundrel	[bad-egg]
	死機	死机	sǐjī	VO	\<PRC \> to crash (computer) \<TW\>當機	[dead-machine]
	沒什麼大不了的	没什么大不了的	méi shénme dàbùliǎode	IE	No big deal.	[not have-what-big-not-dispose of]
2.	幸虧	幸亏	xìngkuī	Adv	fortunately, luckily	[luck-thanks to]
3.	隨時	隨时	suíshí	Adv	at any time, whenever necessary	[to follow-time]
	文件		wénjiàn	N	documents, file	[writing-item]
4.	存		cún	V	to save, to deposit (money), to keep, to accumulate	
	不知道怎麼搞的	不知道怎么搞的	bù zhīdào zěnme gǎo de	IE	I don't know how this happened.	[not-know-how-to do]
	病毒		bìngdú	N	virus	[disease-poison]
5.	處理	处理	chǔlǐ	V	to handle, to deal with, to dispose of	[to manage-run]
	軟件	软件	ruǎnjiàn	N	\<PRC\> software \<TW\>軟體	[soft-item]
6.	對付	对付	duìfu	V	to deal/cope with, to tackle, to make do	[to treat-to comit to]
	上網	上网	shàngwǎng	VO	to log on　↔ 下網	[up-net]
	下載	下载	xiàzǎi	V	to download↔ 上傳	[down-to transport]

Characters with Many Strokes

網 壞 機 虧 隨 搞 毒 處 軟 載

詞彙用法 Words in Context

1. 網絡：網絡公司；網絡小說　　　网络：网络公司；网络小说

   現在在什麼地方工作最賺錢？　　現在在什么地方工作最賺钱？

   你覺得網絡小說和一般的小說有　你觉得网络小说和一般的小说有
   什麼不同？　　　　　　　　　　什么不同？

2. 幸虧：（句型）　　　　　　　　幸亏：（句型）

3. 隨時：隨時存起來；隨時問問　　随时：随时存起来；随时问问
   題；隨時來找我　→隨地　　　　题；随时来找我　→随地

   如果你有問題可不可以隨時找老　如果你有问题可不可以随时找老
   師？　　　　　　　　　　　　　师？

   你為什麼不管走到哪兒都帶著一　你为什么不管走到哪儿都带着一
   把雨傘？　　　　　　　　　　　把雨伞？

4. 存：存錢；把錢存在銀行；存一　存：存钱；把钱存在银行；存一
   年　　　　　　　　　　　　　　年

   你覺得存錢是不是一個好的投資　你觉得存钱是不是一个好的投资
   方法？　　　　　　　　　　　　方法？

   銀行的利息和存錢的時間有什麼　银行的利息和存钱的时间有什么
   關係？　　　　　　　　　　　　关系？

5. 處理：處理一下；處理好了；怎　处理：处理一下；处理好了；怎
   麼處理；處理不了　　　　　　　么处理；处理不了

   如果你的電腦有病毒，你會怎麼　如果你的电脑有病毒，你会怎么
   處理？　　　　　　　　　　　　处理？

   放假了你還沒回家，有什麼事情　放假了你还没回家，有什么事情
   需要處理嗎？　　　　　　　　　需要处理吗？

6. 對付：對付壞人；對付一下；很　对付：对付坏人；对付一下；很
   難對付　　　　　　　　　　　　难对付

   你覺得我們應該怎麼對付黑客？　你觉得我们应该怎么对付黑客？

   什麼樣的顧客特別難對付？　　　什么样的顾客特别难对付？

自由發揮與課堂活動 Free Discussion and Class Activities

1. 你用電腦的時候，遇到過什麼問題？你怎麼解決？

   你用电脑的时候，遇到过什么问题？你怎么解决？

2. 你常上網嗎？你覺得上網的時候，應該注意那些事情？

   你常上网吗？你觉得上网的时候，应该注意那些事情？

3. 你最喜歡哪些網站、網頁？為什麼它們能吸引你？

   你最喜欢哪些网站、网页？为什么它们能吸引你？

👥👥 (2) Talking about online shopping

張麗和她的同學陳文討論上網買東西。

小張：　聽說在網上買東西很便宜，是不是真的？

小陳：　網絡上的東西不見得都很便宜，但是在網上購買東西的確非常方便！你不用出去，就能買到想要的東西。

小張：　找到了喜歡的東西以後怎麼辦呢？

小陳：　你先點「購買」，然後他們會讓你填一些個人資料，你也可以選擇讓他們用什麼方式把東西寄給你。

小張：　那我怎麼付帳呢？

小陳：　最後你還要填信用卡的號碼和有效日期。

小張：　把我的信用卡號碼告訴別人會不會有危險？

小陳：　很多人在討論這個問題，不過到目前為止我還沒有碰到什麼問題。

小張：　你真有兩下子，什麼都懂。我也來試試網上購物吧！

小陳：　不過你要小心，自從我上網買東西以後，省了很多時間，但是浪費了很多錢。

閱讀理解 Comprehension Check

5. 小陳覺得網上買東西比較便宜嗎？最大的好處是什麼？
6. 網上買東西，第一步該做什麼？第二步該做什麼？
7. 網上買東西，怎麼付帳？可能會有什麼問題？
8. 小陳覺得在網上買東西，安全嗎？為什麼？
9. 最後小陳說，在網上買東西給她自己帶來什麼問題？

(2) Talking about online shopping

张丽和她的同学陈文讨论上网买东西。

小张： 听说在网上买东西很便宜，是不是真的？

小陈： 网络上的东西不见得都很便宜，但是在网上购买东西的确非常方便！你不用出去，就能买到想要的东西。

小张： 找到了喜欢的东西以后怎么办呢？

小陈： 你先点"购买"，然后他们会让你填一些个人资料，你也可以选择让他们用什么方式把东西寄给你。

小张： 那我怎么付帐呢？

小陈： 最后你还要填信用卡的号码和有效日期。

小张： 把我的信用卡号码告诉别人会不会有危险？

小陈： 很多人在讨论这个问题，不过到目前为止我还没有碰到什么问题。

小张： 你真有两下子，什么都懂。我也来试试网上购物吧！

小陈： 不过你要小心，自从我上网买东西以后，省了很多时间，但是浪费了很多钱。

阅读理解 Comprehension Check

5. 小陈觉得网上买东西比较便宜吗？最大的好处是什么？

6. 网上买东西，第一步该做什么？第二步该做什么？

7. 网上买东西，怎么付帐？可能会有什么问题？

8. 小陈觉得在网上买东西，安全吗？为什么？

9. 最后小陈说，在网上买东西给她自己带来什么问题？

對話二生詞 Vocabulary

7.	不見得	不见得	bújiànde	Adv	not necessarily/likely	[not-see-(complement)]
8.	購買	购买	gòumǎi	V	買	[to buy-to buy]
9.	的確	的确	díquè	Adv	certainly, indeed	[in reality-true]
10.	填		tián	V	to fill in (form)	
11.	資料	资料	zīliào	N	data, material	[record-material]
12.	方式		fāngshì	N	way, fashion, pattern	[way-form]
	信用卡		xìnyòngkǎ	N	credit card →耶誕卡、生日卡	[trust-use-card]
	日期		rìqī	N	date	[day-period]
13.	危險	危险	wēixiǎn	N/Adj	danger, dangerous	[danger-danger]
	有兩下子	有两下子	yǒu liǎngxiàzi	IE	<口> to know one's stuff	[to have-two-(frequency of occurrences)]
14.	浪費	浪费	làngfèi	V/Adj	to waste, to squander, extravagant	[frivolous-cost]

Characters with Many Strokes

購　確　填　資　危　險　浪　費

詞匯用法 Words in Context

7. 不見得：好東西不見得貴；不吃飯不見得能減肥

一個人看籃球比賽很無聊嗎？

北京人和別人打招呼的時候是不是總是說「吃了嗎」？

不见得：好东西不见得贵；不吃饭不见得能减肥

一个人看篮球比赛很无聊吗？

北京人和别人打招呼的时候是不是总是说"吃了吗"？

8. 購買：購買東西；購物

你常去哪兒購物？

在網上購買電腦安全嗎？

购买：购买东西；购物

你常去哪儿购物？

在网上购买电脑安全吗？

9. 的確：的確有效、可惜；的確值得買

的确：的确有效、可惜；的确值得买

多吃蔬菜真的有助於一個人的健康嗎？

聽說佛羅里達州的氣候溫暖潮濕，是這樣嗎？

10. 填：填表、填空、填名字；填出生日期

申請學校的時候要填哪些表？

申請信用卡的時候要在表上填什麼？

11. 資料：找資料

寫論文的時候你怎麼找需要的資料？

在網上購物的時候，你需要填哪些關於自己的資料？

12. 方式：購物、思考、生活方式

你喜歡什麼樣的購物方式？

生活方式不同的人結婚會幸福嗎？

13. 危險：很危險；不怕危險
↔安全

你覺得哪些運動比較危險？

開快車有什麼危險？

14. 浪費：浪費時間、錢、水、電、資源；不要浪費；太浪費

為什麼一些父母不讓孩子上網？

去飯館吃飯，剩下的飯菜怎麼辦？為什麼？

多吃蔬菜真的有助于一个人的健康吗？

听说佛罗里达州的气候温暖潮湿，是这样吗？

填：填表、填空、填名字；填出生日期

申请学校的时候要填哪些表？

申请信用卡的时候要在表上填什么？

资料：找资料

写论文的时候你怎么找需要的资料？

在网上购物的时候，你需要填哪些关于自己的资料？

方式：购物、思考、生活方式

你喜欢什么样的购物方式？

生活方式不同的人结婚会幸福吗？

危险：很危险；不怕危险
↔安全

你觉得哪些运动比较危险？

开快车有什么危险？

浪费：浪费时间、钱、水、电、资源；不要浪费；太浪费

为什么一些父母不让孩子上网？

去饭馆吃饭，剩下的饭菜怎么办？为什么？

自由發揮與課堂活動 Free Discussion and Class Activities

4. 你的朋友從來沒有網上購物的經歷，請你告訴她應該怎麼做。

你的朋友从来没有网上购物的经历，请你告诉她应该怎么做。

5. 電腦給你的生活帶來了什麼好的影響和壞的影響？

电脑给你的生活带来了什么好的影响和坏的影响？

6. 辯論：要不要鼓勵人們網上購物
正方：支持
反方：反對

辩论：要不要鼓励人们网上购物
正方：支持
反方：反对

敘述 Narrative

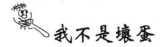 **我不是壞蛋**

　　我是一個電腦迷，也是人們經常說的「黑客」。也許看到「黑客」這兩個字，人們就會想到那些破壞網絡的壞蛋，但是這個印象並不對。因為[2]**所謂**的「HACKER」本來**指的是**那些喜歡思考、熱衷於解決問題的人，不見得所有的「黑客」都是破壞者。

　　我剛開始用電腦的時候，也只是用它發發電子郵件，交一些網友或者找找資料什麼的。不過有一件事情讓我對電腦產生了另一種興趣。有一天，我在朋友家借用他的電腦做功課，忽然發現有個文件需要密碼才可以打開。

PASSWORD?

　　我當時懷疑那是朋友寫給女孩子的情書，所以就特別想看看裏面寫的是什麼，可是試了幾種辦法都沒成功。不過我並沒有放棄，用了一天的時間，終於打開了那個文件，結果並不是情書，而是一些色情的圖片。

　　我這個不願意放棄的性格在我玩遊戲的時候[3]**起**了很大**的作用**。對一個電腦遊戲迷來說，那些便宜但簡單的遊戲沒什麼意思，可是好的遊戲貴得要命，如果我捨不得花錢買遊戲的話，就得想辦法打開密碼。有時候我要花幾天幾夜才能把密碼打開，可是只要能玩遊戲，花多長時間都值得。後來，只要看到有密碼的軟件我就會覺得手癢癢，想去試著打開。這種感覺就像吸了毒品一樣，很難戒掉。

其實做個黑客並不一定要有很高的學歷，很多有名的黑客都和我一樣是十幾歲的青少年。我們之所以可以成為黑客，是因為我們對新鮮的東西有好奇

壞蛋！

心，喜歡問為什麼，而且喜歡自己思考去找出答案來。有時候我發現一些網站有問題，我也會幫助他們解決。希望人們有一天能把黑客看成網絡上的俠客，而不是網絡上的

閱讀理解 Comprehension Check

10. 人們對「黑客」有什麼看法？這種看法對不對？為什麼？
11. 「我」一開始用電腦就是個黑客嗎？怎麼知道？
12. 什麼事情讓「我」變成一個黑客？
13. 打開密碼對「我」還有什麼特別的好處？
14. 後來「我」為什麼非開密碼不可？他開密碼時有什麼感覺？
15. 「黑客」的學歷一定很高嗎？他們都有些什麼特點？
16. 「我」希望別人對黑客的印象有什麼改變？為什麼？

我不是坏蛋

我是一个电脑迷，也是人们经常说的"黑客"。也许看到"黑客"这两个字，人们就会想到那些破坏网络的坏蛋，但是这个印象并不对。因为[2]**所谓**的"HACKER"本来**指的是**那些喜欢思考、热衷于解决问题的人，不见得所有的"黑客"都是破坏者。

我刚开始用电脑的时候，也只是用它发发电子邮件，交一些网友或者找找资料什么的。不过有一件事情让我对电脑产生了另一种兴趣。有一天，我在朋友家借用他的电脑做功课，忽然发现有个文件需要密码才可以打开。我当时怀疑那是朋友写给女孩子的情书，所以就特别想看看里面写的是什么，可是试了几种办法都没成功。不过我并没有放弃，用了一天的时间，终于打开了那个文件，结果并不是情书，而是一些色情的图片。

我这个不愿意放弃的性格在我玩游戏的时候[3]**起了很大的作用**。对一个电脑游戏迷来说，那些便宜但简单的游戏没什么意思，可是好的游戏贵得要命，如果我舍不得花钱买游戏的话，就得想办法打开密码。有时候我要花几天几夜才能把密码打开，可是只要能玩游戏，花多长时间都值得。后来，只要看到有密码的软件我就会觉得手痒痒，想去试着打开。这种感觉就象吸了毒品一样，很难戒掉。

其实做个黑客并不一定要有很高的学历，很多有名的黑客都和我一样是十几岁的青少年。我们之所以可以成为黑客，是因为我们对新鲜的东西有好奇心，喜欢问为什么，而且喜欢自己思考去找出答案来。有时候我发现一些网站有问题，我也会帮助他们解决。希望人们有一天能把黑客看成网络上的侠客，而不是网络上的坏蛋！

阅读理解 Comprehension Check

10. 人们对"黑客"有什么看法？这种看法对不对？为什么？
11. "我"一开始用电脑就是个黑客吗？怎么知道？
12. 什么事情让"我"变成一个黑客？
13. 打开密码对"我"还有什么特别的好处？
14. 后来"我"为什么非开密码不可？他开密码时有什么感觉？
15. "黑客"的学历一定很高吗？他们都有些什么特点？
16. "我"希望别人对黑客的印象有什么改变？为什么？

敘述生詞 Vocabulary

	黑客		hēikè	N	<PRC>hacker <TW>駭客hàikè	[black-person engaged in a particular pursuit]
15.	破壞	破坏	pòhuài	V	to destroy, to wreck	[to smash-bad]
16.	所謂	所谓	suǒwèi	Adj	so-called	[that which-to say]
17.	指		zhǐ	V	to point at, to refer to	
18.	思考		sīkǎo	V	to ponder over, to reflect on	[to think-to check]
	網友	网友	wǎngyǒu	N	netpal →筆友	[net-friend]
19.	產生	产生	chǎnshēng	V	to create (problems, influence), to emerge	[to produce-to grow]
20.	忽然		hūrán	Adv	suddenly	[suddenly-(adv marker)]
	密碼	密码	mìmǎ	N	password	[secret-code]
	打開	打开	dǎkāi	V	to open, to unfold, to turn on	[to hit-to open]
21.	懷疑	怀疑	huáiyí	V/N	to suspect, doubt	[to think of-to doubt]
	情書	情书	qíngshū	N	寫給情人的信	[feeling-letter]
22.	終於	终于	zhōngyú	Adv	最後	[to end-at]
	色情		sèqíng	N/Adj	pornography, pornographic	[sexual-feeling]

圖片	图片	túpiàn	N	picture, photograph	[drawing-piece]
遊戲	游戏	yóuxì	N/V	game, to play	[to rove-to play]
23. 作用		zuòyòng	N	effect	[to make-to use]
24. 手癢癢	手痒痒	shǒuyǎngyang	IE	<口> to have an itch to do sth.	[hand-itch-itch]
25. 毒品		dúpǐn	N	drugs, narcotics	[poison-goods]
26. 戒掉		jièdiào	RV	to stop/kick (bad habit)	[to give up-to drop]
27. 學歷	学历	xuélì	N	record of formal schooling	[study-experience]
28. 新鮮	新鲜	xīnxiān	Adj	novel, new, fresh	[new-fresh]
29. 好奇心		hàoqíxīn	N	curiosity	[to like-rare-mind]
30. 答案		dá'àn	N	solution, answer, key	[to answer-solution]
31. 網站	网站	wǎngzhàn	N	website	[net-station]

Characters with Many Strokes

壞　謂　網　產　碼　懷　疑　癢　毒　案

詞匯用法 Words in Context

15. 破壞：破壞東西、環境、關係；
被破壞了；破壞者

破坏：破坏东西、环境、关系；
被破坏了；破坏者

為什麼有人建議少開汽車，多騎
自行車？

为什么有人建议少开汽车，多骑
自行车？

什麼事情曾經破壞中美關係？

什么事情曾经破坏中美关系？

16. 所謂：（句型）

所谓：（句型）

17. 指：指的是我；用手指著一個人
說話

指：指的是我；用手指着一个人
说话

所謂的背包族指的是哪些人？

所谓的背包族指的是哪些人？

上中文課老師讓大家讀生詞的時
候，會怎麼做？

上中文课老师让大家读生词的时
候，会怎么做？

18. 思考：

思考：

你是一個喜歡思考的人嗎？

你是一个喜欢思考的人吗？

你思考問題的時候喜歡聽音樂還是走路？

你思考问题的时候喜欢听音乐还是走路？

19. 產生：產生興趣、影響、好感、懷疑

产生：产生兴趣、影响、好感、怀疑

你是什麼時候對中文產生興趣的？

你是什么时候对中文产生兴趣的？

什麼事情會讓你對自己的朋友產生懷疑？

什么事情会让你对自己的朋友产生怀疑？

20. 忽然：忽然死機；忽然想起沒帶車鑰匙；忽然發現問題

忽然：忽然死机；忽然想起没带车钥匙；忽然发现问题

用電腦的時候為什麼要有隨時存盤的習慣？

用电脑的时候为什么要有随时存盘的习惯？

據說英國人出門一定要帶雨傘，這是為什麼？

据说英国人出门一定要带雨伞，这是为什么？

21. 懷疑：懷疑有人故意破壞；懷疑…不是真的；懷疑他是小偷

怀疑：怀疑有人故意破坏；怀疑…不是真的；怀疑他是小偷

警察什麼時候會要求看一個人的身份證？

警察什么时候会要求看一个人的身份证？

你為什麼懷疑他的文章不是自己寫的？

你为什么怀疑他的文章不是自己写的？

22. 終於：終於寫完了；終於放假了

终于：终于写完了；终于放假了

你今天為什麼這麼高興？

你今天为什么这么高兴？

警察找到那個破壞學校電腦網絡的黑客了嗎？

警察找到那个破坏学校电脑网络的黑客了吗？

23. 作用：起作用（句型）；有（沒）什麼作用；作用很大

作用：起作用（句型）；有（没）什么作用；作用很大

感冒的時候，打針和吃藥哪個作用比較大？

感冒的时候，打针和吃药哪个作用比较大？

你覺得哪種減肥方法的作用比較大？

你觉得哪种减肥方法的作用比较大？

24. 手癢癢：覺得手癢癢
    →心癢癢、腳癢癢
    看別人做什麼的時候你會覺得手癢癢？
    看別人做什麼的時候你會覺得腳癢癢？

    手痒痒：觉得手痒痒
    →心痒痒、脚痒痒
    看别人做什么的时候你会觉得手痒痒？
    看别人做什么的时候你会觉得脚痒痒？

25. 毒品：買賣毒品　→吸毒
    你覺得什麼東西可以算是毒品？
    人為什麼要吸毒呢？

    毒品：买卖毒品　→吸毒
    你觉得什么东西可以算是毒品？
    人为什么要吸毒呢？

26. 戒掉：戒掉毒癮、壞習慣
    →吃掉、賣掉、忘掉、改掉
    為什麼吸毒的人很難戒掉毒癮？
    你覺得自己有什麼壞習慣需要改掉？

    戒掉：戒掉毒瘾、坏习惯
    →吃掉、卖掉、忘掉、改掉
    为什么吸毒的人很难戒掉毒瘾？
    你觉得自己有什么坏习惯需要改掉？

27. 學歷：學歷高、低；重視學歷
    學歷高低對找工作有什麼影響？
    你覺得對一個公司來說，學歷和工作經驗哪個更重要？為什麼？

    学历：学历高、低；重视学历
    学历高低对找工作有什么影响？
    你觉得对一个公司来说，学历和工作经验哪个更重要？为什么？

28. 新鮮：空氣新鮮；新鮮的水果、蔬菜、事情
    你剛來的時候，覺得什麼事情很新鮮？
    你覺得什麼地方的空氣很新鮮？

    新鲜：空气新鲜；新鲜的水果、蔬菜、事情
    你刚来的时候，觉得什么事情很新鲜？
    你觉得什么地方的空气很新鲜？

29. 好奇心：對…有好奇心；好奇心很強；對…很好奇
    你對哪些事情的好奇心很強？
    年輕人為什麼容易對電腦上癮？

    好奇心：对…有好奇心；好奇心很强；对…很好奇
    你对哪些事情的好奇心很强？
    年轻人为什么容易对电脑上瘾？

30. 答案：找到答案；選擇合適的答案；沒有答案

    答案：找到答案；选择合适的答案；没有答案

中文考試中的選擇題是怎麼樣
的？

你覺得科學可以給所有奇怪的事
情找到答案嗎？

31. 網站：最受歡迎的網站；十大網
站　　　→網頁、網址

我到哪兒能找到關於這個大學的
資料？

你最喜歡哪個網站？為什麼？

中文考试中的选择题是怎么样
的？

你觉得科学可以给所有奇怪的事
情找到答案吗？

网站：最受欢迎的网站；十大网
站　　　→网页、网址

我到哪儿能找到关于这个大学的
资料？

你最喜欢哪个网站？为什么？

自由發揮與課堂活動　Free Discussion and Class Activities

7. 以前你覺得什麼樣的人算是「黑
客」，你怎麼看這些人？現在
呢？

8. 你能不能想像一下，如果沒有電
腦我們的生活會是什麼樣？

9. 孩子要想辦法讓媽媽同意給她買
一個筆記本電腦，如果你是她，
你打算從哪些方面來說服媽媽？
試試看！

10. 把全班分為兩組：
甲組：準備介紹PC機的好處以
及Mac機的壞處，建議大家選擇
PC機。
乙組：準備介紹Mac機的好處以
及PC機的壞處，建議大家選擇
Mac機。

以前你觉得什么样的人算是"黑
客"，你怎么看这些人？现在
呢？我

你能不能想像一下，如果没有电
脑我们的生活会是什么样？

孩子要想办法让妈妈同意给她买
一个笔记本电脑，如果你是她，
你打算从哪些方面来说服妈妈？
试试看！

把全班分为两组：
甲组：准备介绍PC机的好处以及
Mac机的坏处，建议大家选择PC
机。
乙组：准备介绍Mac机的好处以
及PC机的坏处，建议大家选择
Mac机。

說明 Exposition

 電腦會說體貼話

電腦的計算速度雖然不斷提高，但是始終給人一種冷冷的感覺。人們一直都希望這個給自己的生活帶來很多方便的工具，有一天能變得體貼一些。最近科學家就發明了一種能 4**通過**聲音了解使用者情緒，並根據不同的情況「說話」的體貼電腦。

這種電腦是由日本科學家發明的。它們經過「訓練」以後，能判斷人的情緒。如果 5**一旦**發現使用者生氣、失望時，電腦就會自動發一封電子信安慰他。如果使用者 6**因**電腦出了毛病**而**生氣的話，電腦也會向他道歉。

閱讀理解 Comprehension Check

17. 電腦一直給人什麼樣的感覺？人們一直希望什麼？
18. 最近科學家發明了什麼樣的電腦？是哪兒的科學家發明的？
19. 這種電腦能做什麼？

电脑会说体贴话

电脑的计算速度虽然不断提高，但是始终给人一种冷冷的感觉。人们一直都希望这个给自己的生活带来很多方便的工具，有一天能变得体贴一些。最近科学家就发明了一种能⁴通过声音了解使用者情绪，并根据不同的情况"说话"的体贴电脑。

这种电脑是由日本科学家发明的。它们经过"训练"以后，能判断人的情绪。如果⁵一旦发现使用者生气、失望时，电脑就会自动发一封电子信安慰他。如果使用者⁶因电脑出了毛病而生气的话，电脑也会向他道歉。

阅读理解 Comprehension Check

17. 电脑一直给人什么样的感觉？人们一直希望什么？
18. 最近科学家发明了什么样的电脑？是哪儿的科学家发明的？
19. 这种电脑能做什么？

說明生詞 Vocabulary

	體貼	体贴	tǐtiē	Adj	showing consideration for	[body-to stay close to]
32.	計算	计算	jìsuàn	V/N	to compute, planning	[to count-to figure]
33.	速度		sùdù	N	speed	[fast-degree]
34.	提高		tígāo	V	to raise, to heighten, to enhance	[to lift-tall]
35.	始終	始终	shǐzhōng	Adv	一直	[beginning-end]
	科學家	科学家	kēxuéjiā	N	scientist	[rules-study-ist]
36.	發明	发明	fāmíng	V/N	to invent, invention	[to discover-bright]
37.	通過	通过	tōngguò	Prep/V	by (means/way of), to pass, to carry (motion)	[to go through-to pass]
38.	使用		shǐyòng	V	to use, to employ, to apply	[to use-to use]
	情緒	情绪	qíngxù	N	emotions, feelings, mood	[feeling-mood]
39.	經過	经过	jīngguò	Prep/V	after, through, as a result of, to go through	[to undergo-to pass]
40.	訓練	训练	xùnliàn	N/V	training, to drill	[to teach-to practice]
41.	一旦		yídàn	Conj	once, some time or other	[one-day]
42.	自動	自动	zìdòng	Adj	automatic	[self-to move]
43.	安慰		ānwèi	V/N	to comfort, consolation	[to set at ease-to console]
44.	道歉		dàoqiàn	VO	to apologize	[to say-apology]

Characters with Many Strokes

體 算 度 終 通 緒 練 斷 慰 歉

詞匯用法 Words in Context

32. 計算：計算機；計算速度　　　計算：计算机；计算速度

這幾十年來，電腦的計算速度有　　这几十年来，电脑的计算速度有
什麼變化？　　　　　　　　　　　什么变化？

你怎麼計算每個月掙了多少、花　　你怎么计算每个月挣了多少、花
了多少？　　　　　　　　　　　　了多少？

33. 速度：計算、提高速度；說話的
速度；速度太快、慢

你覺得你的中文老師中誰說話的
速度最快？

哪個電腦公司發展的速度最快？

速度：计算、提高速度；说话的
速度；速度太快、慢

你觉得你的中文老师中谁说话的
速度最快？

哪个电脑公司发展的速度最快？

34. 提高：提高水平、速度；被提高

你覺得中國人的生活水平在最近
二十年有什麼變化？

你的中文水平有什麼變化？

提高：提高水平、速度；被提高

你觉得中国人的生活水平在最近
二十年有什么变化？

你的中文水平有什么变化？

35. 始終：始終堅持鍛鍊/不同意

上一次旅遊的經歷真的那麼難忘
嗎？

為什麼你始終不願意在網上購
物？

始终：始终坚持锻炼/不同意

上一次旅游的经历真的那么难忘
吗？

为什么你始终不愿意在网上购
物？

36. 發明：發明燈泡；發明家；了不
起的發明

世界上最了不起的發明是什麼？

為什麼人們說愛迪生是偉大的發
明家？

发明：发明灯泡；发明家；了不
起的发明

世界上最了不起的发明是什么？

为什么人们说爱迪生是伟大的发
明家？

37. 通過：（句型）；通（不）過考
試；通過檢查

老師每天都要檢查學生是不是準
備了考試，怎麼樣才可以通過這
個檢查？

要拿到律師執照，要通過什麼考
試嗎？

通过：（句型）；通（不）过考
试；通过检查

老师每天都要检查学生是不是准
备了考试，怎么样才可以通过这
个检查？

要拿到律师执照，要通过什么考
试吗？

38. 使用：不知道怎麼使用電腦；使
用者；使用說明書

使用電腦時應該注意什麼？

使用：不知道怎么使用电脑；使
用者；使用说明书

使用电脑时应该注意什么？

所謂說明書指的是什麼？　　　所谓说明书指的是什么？

39. 經過：經過一年的生活、努力；　　经过：经过一年的生活、努力；
事情的經過　　　　　　　　　事情的经过

你們是怎麼成為好朋友的？　　你们是怎么成为好朋友的？

二十年的改革的結果是什麼？　二十年的改革的结果是什么？

40. 訓練：接受訓練；嚴格的訓練　　训练：接受训练；严格的训练

這個大學的籃球運動員在哪兒接　这个大学的篮球运动员在哪儿接
受訓練？　　　　　　　　　　受训练？

狗為什麼可以按照主人的要求做　狗为什么可以按照主人的要求做
事？　　　　　　　　　　　　事？

41. 一旦：（句型）　　　　　　　　一旦：（句型）

42. 自動：自動門、洗衣機；全自動　　自动：自动门、洗衣机；全自动
（照相機）→主動、被動　　　（照相机）→主动、被动

你每次都自己洗衣服嗎？　　　你每次都自己洗衣服吗？

什麼是自動門？　　　　　　　什么是自动门？

43. 安慰：安慰朋友；安慰的話；無　　安慰：安慰朋友；安慰的话；无
法安慰　　　　　　　　　　　法安慰

什麼時候你最需要朋友的安慰？　什么时候你最需要朋友的安慰？

他剛剛和朋友分手，你為什麼不　他刚刚和朋友分手，你为什么不
去安慰他？　　　　　　　　　去安慰他？

44. 道歉：向朋友道歉　　　　　　　道歉：向朋友道歉

你為什麼要向朋友道歉？　　　你为什么要向朋友道歉？

如果你的朋友約會遲到，你怎麼　如果你的朋友约会迟到，你怎么
才會原諒他？　　　　　　　　才会原谅他？

自由發揮與課堂活動　Free Discussion and Class Activities

11. 你希望將來的電腦會有什麼功　　你希望将来的电脑会有什么功
能？為什麼？　　　　　　　　能？为什么？

應用詞 Productive Vocabulary

◎By Grammatical Categories

Nouns/Pronouns/Measure Words

學歷	xuélì	record of formal schooling	網站	wǎngzhàn	website
訓練	xùnliàn	training, to drill	資料	zīliào	data, material
速度	sùdù	speed	毒品	dúpǐn	drugs, narcotics
方式	fāngshì	way, fashion, pattern	危險	wēixiǎn	danger, dangerous
作用	zuòyòng	effect	好奇心	hàoqíxīn	curiosity
答案	dá'àn	solution, answer, key			
網絡	wǎngluò	the net, the internet			

Verbs/Stative Verbs/Adjectives

存	cún	to save, to deposit (money), to keep, to accumulate	計算	jìsuàn	to compute, planning
填	tián	to fill in (form)	發明	fāmíng	to invent, invention
指	zhǐ	to point at, to refer to	安慰	ānwèi	to comfort, consolation
購買	gòumǎi	to purchase	道歉	dàoqiàn	to apologize
使用	shǐyòng	to use, to employ	懷疑	huáiyí	to suspect, doubt
思考	sīkǎo	to ponder over, to reflect on	戒掉	jièdiào	to stop/kick (bad habit)
處理	chǔlǐ	to handle, to deal with, to dispose of	浪費	làngfèi	to waste, to squander, extravagant
對付	duìfu	to deal/cope with, to tackle, to make do	破壞	pòhuài	to destroy, to wreck
產生	chǎnshēng	to create (problems, influence), to emerge	所謂	suǒwèi	so-called
提高	tígāo	to raise, to heighten	自動	zìdòng	automatic
			新鮮	xīnxiān	novel, new, fresh

Adverbs and Others

幸虧	xìngkuī	fortunately, luckily	通過	tōngguò	by (means/way of), to pass, to carry (motion)
隨時	suíshí	at any time, whenever necessary	經過	jīngguò	after, through, as a result of, to go through
忽然	hūrán	suddenly	一旦	yídàn	once, some time or other
終於	zhōngyú	finally	不見得	bújiànde	not necessarily/likely
始終	shǐzhōng	from beginning to end	手癢癢	shǒuyǎngyang	to have an itch to do sth.
的確	díquè	certainly, indeed			

理解詞 Receptive Vocabulary

◎ **By Grammatical Categories**

Nouns/Pronouns/Measure Words

文件	wénjiàn	documents, file	俠客	xiákè	a person adept in martial arts and given to chivalrous conduct (in old times), chivalrous warrior
軟件	ruǎnjiàn	<PRC> software			
圖片	túpiàn	picture, photograph			
密碼	mìmǎ	password	黑客	hēikè	<PRC>hacker
日期	rìqī	date	網友	wǎngyǒu	netpal
遊戲	yóuxì	game, to play	壞蛋	huàidàn	scoundrel
情書	qíngshū	love letter	科學家	kēxuéjiā	scientist
色情	sèqíng	pornography, pornographic	信用卡	xìnyòngkǎ	credit card
病毒	bìngdú	virus			
情緒	qíngxù	emotions, feelings, mood			

Verbs/Stative Verbs/Adjectives

打開	dǎkāi	to open, to unfold, to turn on	死機	sǐjī	<PRC>to crash (computer)
上網	shàngwǎng	to log on	體貼	tǐtiē	showing consideration for
下載	xiàzǎi	to download			

Adverbs and Others

有兩下子	yǒu liǎng xiàzi	to know one's stuff	沒什麼大不了的	méi shénme dàbùliǎode	No big deal.
不知道怎麼搞的	bù zhīdào zěnme gǎo de	I don't know how this happened.			

本课词表 Chapter Vocabulary

◎ **By Pinyin**

Words with asterisk* are productive vocabulary which needs to be memorized and studied for its usage.

ānwèi*	安慰	to comfort, consolation	zěnme gǎo de	么搞的	this happened.
bìngdú	病毒	virus	chǎnshēng*	产生	to create (problems, influence), to emerge
bújiànde*	不见得	not necessarily/likely	chǔlǐ*	处理	to handle, to deal with, to dispose of
bù zhīdào	不知道怎	I don't know how			

cún*	存	to save, to deposit (money), to keep, to accumulate
dá'àn*	答案	solution, answer, key
dǎkāi	打开	to open, to unfold, to turn on
dàoqiàn*	道歉	to apologize
díquè*	的确	certainly, indeed
dúpǐn*	毒品	drugs, narcotics
duìfu*	对付	to deal/cope with, to tackle, to make do
faming*	发明	to invent, invention
fāngshì*	方式	way, fashion, pattern
gòumǎi*	购买	to purchase
hàoqíxīn*	好奇心	curiosity
hēikè	黑客	<PRC>hacker
hūrán*	忽然	suddenly
huàidàn	坏蛋	scoundrel
huáiyí*	怀疑	to suspect, doubt
jièdiào*	戒掉	to stop/kick (bad habit)
jīngguò*	经过	after, through, as a result of
jìsuàn*	计算	to compute, planning
kēxuéjiā	科学家	scientist
làngfèi*	浪费	to waste, to squander, extravagant
méi shénme dàbùliǎode	没什么大不了的	No big deal.
mìmǎ	密码	password
pòhuài*	破坏	to destroy, to wreck
qíngshū	情书	love letter
qíngxù	情绪	emotions, feelings
rìqī	日期	date
ruǎnjiàn*	软件	<PRC> software
sèqíng	色情	pornography, pornographic
shàngwǎng	上网	to log on
shǐyòng*	使用	to use, to employ
shǐzhōng*	始终	from beginning to end
shǒuyǎng yang*	手痒痒	<口> to have an itch to do sth.
sǐjī	死机	<PRC > to crash (computer)
sīkǎo*	思考	to ponder over, to reflect on
sùdù*	速度	speed
suíshí*	随时	at any time, whenever necessary
suǒwèi*	所谓	so-called
tián*	填	to fill in (form)
tígāo*	提高	to raise, to heighten, to enhance
tǐtiē	体贴	showing consideration for
tōngguò*	通过	by (means/way of), to pass, to carry (motion)
túpiàn	图片	picture, photograph
wǎngluò*	网络	the net, the internet
wǎngyǒu	网友	netpal
wǎngzhàn*	网站	website
wēixiǎn*	危险	danger, dangerous
wénjiàn*	文件	documents, file
xiákè	侠客	chivalrous warrior
xiàzǎi	下载	to download
xìngkuī*	幸亏	fortunately, luckily
xīnxiān*	新鲜	novel, new, fresh
xìnyòngkǎ	信用卡	credit card
xuélì*	学历	record of formal schooling
xùnliàn*	训练	training, to drill
yídàn*	一旦	once, some time or other
yǒu liǎng xiàzi	有两下子	to know one's stuff
yóuxì	游戏	game, to play
zhǐ*	指	to point at, to refer to
zhōngyú*	终于	finally
zìdòng*	自动	automatic
zīliào*	资料	data, material
zuòyòng*	作用	effect

用法 Grammar and Usage

ay attention to the function of the structure and then study the example sentences. When blanks are provided, either answer the questions or complete the sentences.

1. Expressing a fortunate condition

幸虧 S …，不然 … (一定)	xìngkuī…bùrán	Fortunately S…, otherwise….
好在 S …，不然 …	hǎozài…bùrán	

● 幸虧我有隨時把文件存起來的習慣，不然就白做了。

1. 聽說你國慶節的時候，在昆明有一個難忘的旅行。

   听说你国庆节的时候，在昆明有一个难忘的旅行。

   I heard that you had an unforgettable trip in Kunming during National Day.

   幸虧我遇到了一個熱情的女孩，不然我恐怕連住的地方都沒有。

   幸亏我遇到了一个热情的女孩，不然我恐怕连住的地方都没有。

   Fortunately, I ran into a warm-hearted girl. Otherwise, I'm afraid I wouldn't even have had a place to stay.

2. 聽說你的電腦有病毒，現在修好了嗎？

   听说你的电脑有病毒，现在修好了吗？

   I heard that your computer has a virus. Have you fixed it yet?

   好在李明送了我一張消毒軟件。不然我的電腦一定不能用了。

   好在李明送了我一张消毒软件。不然我的电脑一定不能用了。

   Fortunately, Li Ming gave me some anti-virus software. Otherwise, my computer would not work at all.

3. 你知道嗎？小張最近交了一個網友，每天都要和那個人在網上聊天。

   你知道吗？小张最近交了一个网友，每天都要和那个人在网上聊天。

   Do you know what? Xiao Zhang has recently found a net friend. Every day he chats with that person on-line.

   幸虧我沒有電腦，不然一定像小張一樣浪費很多的時間

   幸亏我没有电脑，不然一定象小张一样浪费很多的时间

   Fortunately I don't have a computer. Otherwise, I'd certainly be wasting a lot of time and money just like Xiao

和錢。	和钱。	Zhang.

4. 很多減肥藥都有害於健康，還是運動減肥的方法比較好。 | 很多减肥药都有害于健康，还是运动减肥的方法比较好。

---

5. 昨天我去看了那兩個大學的籃球比賽，可是不知怎麼搞的，運動員們好像都很累，比賽一點也不精彩。 | 昨天我去看了那两个大学的篮球比赛，可是不知怎么搞的，运动员们好象都很累，比赛一点也不精彩。

---

6. 李明經常在網上購物，可是前兩天他發現有人偷了他的信用卡號碼，用他的信用卡買東西。 | 李明经常在网上购物，可是前两天他发现有人偷了他的信用卡号码，用他的信用卡买东西。

The pattern 幸虧 S ⋯ ，不然 ⋯ expresses a fortunate condition. What follows 幸虧 is always something good and what follows 不然 is an otherwise anticipated bad result. Remember if the subject is established in the previous context, it may be subsequently dropped. If the subject of two adjoining clauses is the same, either may be dropped. If the subject does exist, it often follows 幸虧/好在.

2. Clarifying a term

所謂⋯ 指的是⋯	suǒwèi…zhǐde shì	so-called…refers to…

• 所謂的「HACKER」本來指的是那些喜歡思考、熱衷於解決問題的人，不見得所有的「黑客」都是破壞者。

1. 在中國的時候，我常常聽人說「AA制」，可是不明白是什麼意思。 | 在中国的时候，我常常听人说 "AA制"，可是不明白是什么意思。 | When I was in China, I always heard people say "the AA way," but I never knew what it meant.

所謂「AA制」指的是在吃飯的時候，各付各的帳。

所谓"AA制"指的是在吃饭的时候，各付各的帐。

The so-called "AA way" means that one pays for one's own meal when dining out.

2. 什麼是「家庭主夫」？

什么是"家庭主夫"？

What is a "house-husband"?

所謂「家庭主夫」指的是那些不出去工作，專門待在家裏做家務、照顧孩子的先生。

所谓"家庭主夫"指的是那些不出去工作，专门待在家里做家务、照顾孩子的先生。

The so-called "house-husband" refers to those men who do not work outside, but instead stay home doing household chores and taking care of children.

3. 現在各種各樣的「迷」非常多，到底什麼是電腦迷？

现在各种各样的"迷"非常多，到底什么是电脑迷？

Nowadays there are many kinds of "fan." What does a "computer fan" mean?

所謂電腦迷指的是那些特別喜歡電腦的人。

所谓电脑迷指的是那些特别喜欢电脑的人。

The so-called "computer fan" refers to those who are infatuated with computers.

4. 李明要請大家在一個自助餐廳吃飯，不好意思，我還不知道什麼是自助餐廳。

李明要请大家在一个自助餐厅吃饭，不好意思，我还不知道什么是自助餐厅。

5. 請你給大家解釋一下，交際舞是一種什麼樣的舞？

请你给大家解释一下，交际舞是一种什么样的舞？

6. 「土包子」到底是什麼意思？

"土包子"到底是什么意思？

To clarify a term, one can use the pattern 所謂…指的是…. Note that what goes after 指的是 is often a noun preceded by a long modifier which clarifies the term. So, both of the following sentences are wrong: (1) 所謂自助餐廳指的是沒有服務生，吃什麼就自己去拿; (2) 所謂「家庭主夫」指的是那些先生在家做事，太太有工作. The first is missing a noun and the second switches the order of modifier and modified.

3. Expressing an effect

X 對 Y 起(… 的)作用   duì...qǐ (...de) zuòyòng   X has an ...effect on Y

• 我這個不願意放棄的性格在我玩遊戲的時候起了很大的作用。

1. 電腦對我們有什麼作用？

   有了電腦以後，我們的生活方便多了，所以我覺得電腦對我們的生活起了很大的作用。

   电脑对我们有什么作用？

   有了电脑以后，我们的生活方便多了，所以我觉得电脑对我们的生活起了很大的作用。

   What effect does the computer have on our life?

   After getting a computer, our lives are more convenient. Thus, I think computers have a great effect on our lives.

2. 交中國朋友對你學中文有什麼影響？

   以前我不喜歡說中文，所以我的口語不太好；不過後來我交了一些中國朋友，我的口語有了進步。我想和中國朋友說中文對我的口語起了好的作用。

   交中国朋友对你学中文有什么影响？

   以前我不喜欢说中文，所以我的口语不太好；不过后来我交了一些中国朋友，我的口语有了进步。我想和中国朋友说中文对我的口语起了好的作用。

   What impact does making Chinese friends have on your study of Chinese?

   Before I didn't like to speak Chinese, so my oral proficiency was not very good. Yet afterwards, I made a few Chinese friends and my oral skill has improved. I think speaking Chinese with Chinese friends has made a great impact on my speaking ability.

3. 咖啡對人好嗎？

   我每天都要喝好幾杯咖啡，不然就會很不舒服，我覺得

   咖啡对人好吗？

   我每天都要喝好几杯咖啡，不然就会很不舒服，我觉得

   Is coffee good for people?

   I have to drink several cups of coffee every day. Otherwise, I'll feel very uncomfortable. I think coffee has an invigorating

咖啡對我起了提神   咖啡对我起了提神   effect on me.
的作用。   的作用。

4. 爺爺以前很少運動，但是他的   爷爷以前很少运动，但是他的
    一個醫生朋友告訴他運動有助   一个医生朋友告诉他运动有助
    於健康，特別是老人更應該多   于健康，特别是老人更应该多
    運動，從那以後，他每天早上   运动，从那以后，他每天早上
    都去跳交際舞。   都去跳交际舞。

---

5. 中國以前人口增長得很快，但   中国以前人口增长得很快，但
    是實行人口政策以後，人口增   是实行人口政策以后，人口增
    長得比從前慢了很多。   长得比从前慢了很多。

---

6. 我聽說喝太多的茶對身體不   我听说喝太多的茶对身体不
    好，你還是少喝一點吧！   好，你还是少喝一点吧！

The pattern X對Y起 (… 的) 作用 is used to express an effect. Note that Y can be a noun or a verb phrase, e.g., 交中國朋友對我學中文起了作用. To express negation, one can say 不/沒起作用 'do/did not have an effect' or 起不了作用 'cannot have an effect.' To indicate the degree of the effect, 很好、很大 can be added before 作用. Phrases such as 提醒 'to remind,' 提神 'to refresh oneself,' 帶頭 'to set an example,' 交流 'to exchange' can also precede 作用 to specify the effect.

4. Expressing the instrument of an action

S 通過 … VO	tōngguò...	S VO by means of...
通過 … S VO		By means of..., S V O

● 最近科學家就發明了一種能通過聲音了解使用者情緒…的體貼電腦。

1. 今天的語法你學得   今天的语法你学得   How was today's grammar
    怎麼樣？   怎么样？   lesson?

今天的語法非常難，我都不懂，不過上課的時候，通過老師的解釋，我已經學會怎麼用了。

今天的语法非常难，我都不懂，不过上课的时候，通过老师的解释，我已经学会怎么用了。

Today's grammar is very hard. I didn't understand it at all, but with the teacher's explanation in class, I'm already able to use it.

2. 怎麼樣可以了解一個國家的文化？

怎么样可以了解一个国家的文化？

How can one get to understand a country's culture?

我想了解一個國家有很多種方法，比如通過看他們的電影、去那個國家旅行，都可以了解他們的文化。

我想了解一个国家有很多种方法，比如通过看他们的电影、去那个国家旅行，都可以了解他们的文化。

I think there are many ways to understand a country. For example, we can get to understand their culture by seeing their movies or traveling in that country.

3. 電腦對我們的生活起了什麼作用？

电脑对我们的生活起了什么作用？

What effect do computers have on our life?

電腦給我們的生活帶來很多方便，比如我們可以通過電腦購物、聊天、找資料什麼的。

电脑给我们的生活带来很多方便，比如我们可以通过电脑购物、聊天、找资料什么的。

Computers have made our life much more convenient. For example, with computers we can now go shopping, chat with friends, look up information, etc.

4. 我經常可以看到很多老年人在街上練太極拳或者跳交際舞，不知道他們為什麼那麼迷這些運動？

我经常可以看到很多老年人在街上练太极拳或者跳交际舞，不知道他们为什么那么迷这些运动？

5. 一個人如果吸毒的話，有什麼方法可以幫他戒毒？

一个人如果吸毒的话，有什么方法可以帮他戒毒？

6. 你覺得通過一個人的打扮是不　　你觉得通过一个人的打扮是不
　　是可以判斷他的性格？　　　　　是可以判断他的性格？

The pattern 通過…VO is used to express the instrument of an action.　通過… can go after the subject or, if it's too long, at the beginning of a sentence, e.g., 通過跳交際舞和打太極拳，老年人可以鍛煉身體 'Through ballroom dance and taiji, old people can exercise their body.'　The usage of 通過 is similar to that of 透過.

5.　Expressing a contingency

S 一旦…，S 就/也	yídàn...jiù/yě	If (once) S..., then S will

● 如果一旦發現使用者生氣、失望時，電腦就會自動發一封電子信安慰他。

1. 玩電腦會上癮嗎？　　　玩电脑会上瘾吗？　　　Can one get addicted to playing with computers?

　　會，有人說電腦是一種新的毒品，一旦上癮的話，就很難戒掉。　　会，有人说电脑是一种新的毒品，一旦上瘾的话，就很难戒掉。　　Yes, some said computers are a new kind of drugs. Once you get addicted, it's very hard to quit.

2. 中國的中學生為什麼不可以早戀？　　中国的中学生为什么不可以早恋？　　Why aren't Chinese middle school students allowed to have a boy friend or girl friend?

　　因為父母認為孩子一旦交了朋友，就很難專心學習。　　因为父母认为孩子一旦交了朋友，就很难专心学习。　　Because parents think that once their kids have boy friends or girl friends, they won't be able to concentrate on their studies.

3. 我能在一個星期裏減掉二十磅嗎？　　我能在一个星期里减掉二十磅吗？　　Can I lose twenty pounds in a week?

　　人們常說：「一口　　人们常说："一口　　People often say, "you can't get fat after only one bite,"

吃不出個胖子」，　　吃不出个胖子"，　　which means one can't get fat
也就是說人不可能　　也就是说人不可能　　suddenly. Thus, once you get
一下子突然變胖，　　一下子突然变胖，　　fat, you can't lose weight all of
那麼人一旦變胖，　　那么人一旦变胖，　　a sudden.
也不可能一下子變　　也不可能一下子变
瘦。　　　　　　　　瘦。

4. 你開車這麼小心，到現在都沒　　你开车这么小心，到现在都没
有什麼問題，所以我覺得你大　　有什么问题，所以我觉得你大
概不用花那麼多錢買汽車保險　　概不用花那么多钱买汽车保险
了。　　　　　　　　　　　　　　了。

---

5. 你們同學聚會為什麼選那麼貴　　你们同学聚会为什么选那么贵
的酒店，在普通的餐廳不可以　　的酒店，在普通的餐厅不可以
嗎？　　　　　　　　　　　　　　吗？

---

6. 我已經參加了一個下個月去北　　我已经参加了一个下个月去北
京的旅行團，可是我發現我的　　京的旅行团，可是我发现我的
錢不夠，我可不可以不去？　　　钱不够，我可不可以不去？

The pattern 一旦…，就/也 is used to express a contingency. 一旦 often follows the
subject and there is often 就 or sometimes 也 in the other clause. If a subject is present
in the 就 clause, it should precede 就. So, it's wrong to say 你一旦這次不去，就你
以後都不能去 'If you don't go this time, you won't be able to go in the future.' Note
that 一旦 is different from 如果. The consequence expressed by 一旦 is often
unexpected or serious. So, it's odd to say 你一旦花很多錢買新車，就不能買老的
車. Yet, it's all right to say 你不買保險，汽車一旦有問題，就要花很多錢.

6. Expressing a rationale

| S 因 … 而 VO | yīn...ér... | <書> because of …, S VO |
| | | <口> S因為…所以 VO |

● 如果使用者因電腦出了毛病而生氣的話，電腦也會向他道歉。

1. 李明為什麼在學校這麼受到歡迎？

   李明为什么在学校这么受到欢迎？

   Why was Li Ming so popular in school?

   李明上中學的時候，因個子高而受到大家的歡迎，尤其是女生的歡迎。

   李明上中学的时候，因个子高而受到大家的欢迎，尤其是女生的欢迎。

   When Li Ming was in middle school, , he was popular because of his height, particularly with the girls.

2. 為什麼現在這麼多學生選擇電腦專業？

   为什么现在这么多学生选择电脑专业？

   Why are there so many students choosing computer science as their major nowadays?

   電腦專業的學生畢業以後，很容易找到收入好的工作，很多中學生因此而選擇在大學的時候念電腦專業。

   电脑专业的学生毕业以后，很容易找到收入好的工作，很多中学生因此而选择在大学的时候念电脑专业。

   Those who major in computer science can easily find a well-paying job after graduation. Thus, many high school graduates choose to major in computer science at college.

3. 為什麼你總是受到老師的批評？

   为什么你总是受到老师的批评？

   Why were you always criticized by the teacher?

   上健身班的時候，別人可以堅持跳40分鐘，而我只能堅持20分鐘，所以我總是因偷懶而受到老師的批評。

   上健身班的时候，别人可以坚持跳40分钟，而我只能坚持20分钟，所以我总是因偷懒而受到老师的批评。

   When I was in gym class, other people could exercise forty minutes, but I could only do twenty minutes. So, my teacher always criticized me for slacking off.

4. 現在有很多軟件可以從網絡上下載，可是那些軟件的質量並不是最好的，為什麼大家還用呢？

   现在有很多软件可以从网络上下载，可是那些软件的质量并不是最好的，为什么大家还用呢？

5. 很多學生都喜歡選張老師的　　　　很多学生都喜欢选张老师的
　　課，大家為什麼都那麼喜歡他　　　课，大家为什么都那么喜欢他
　　呢？　　　　　　　　　　　　　呢？

6. 你一直都沒覺得自己胖，為什　　　你一直都没觉得自己胖，为什
　　麼忽然要減肥？　　　　　　　　么忽然要减肥？

The pattern S 因 ...而 VO is a more formal and literary way to express a rationale. Note that what follows 因 is the cause/reason and what follows 而 is the action the subject takes due to the cause. Remember 因 always follows the subject and what goes after 而 is often a verb phrase rather than a clause. So, it's wrong to say 因我朋友說我胖而我要減肥. Instead, the sentence should be 我因朋友說我胖而要減肥 'I wanted to lose weight because my friend said I was fat.'

背景常識 Background Notes

1. 網上購物：隨著電腦的普遍使用，網上購物也因為方便和低價吸引了越來越多的年輕人。一般來說，人們主要從網上購買書籍和一些禮物。因為在中國用信用卡的人還不是很多，所以選擇用信用卡付款的人比較少。不過很多的公司都會送貨上門，所以大家一般會在收到東西的時候付錢，這樣既方便又安全。

背景常识 Background Notes

1. 网上购物：随着电脑的普遍使用，网上购物也因为方便和低价吸引了越来越多的年轻人。一般来说，人们主要从网上购买书籍和一些礼物。因为在中国用信用卡的人还不是很多，所以选择用信用卡付款的人比较少。不过很多的公司都会送货上门，所以大家一般会在收到东西的时候付钱，这样既方便又安全。

第五課　中國人愛看什麼電影？

Theme: Movies and Music

Communicative Objectives
- Commenting on a film
- Commenting on a singer
- Narrating the experience of finding a movie that's right for everyone

Skill Focus
Reading a movie review

Grammar Focus
- X歸功於/歸因於/歸罪於Y
- S V QW(O) 不好，卻要/偏要…
- S不外乎是X, Y, (Z)
- S乾脆…吧，省得…
- X不過/只是Y罷了
- S以…為N

Problem Scenario

    You are a journalist and will have a rare opportunity to interview a celebrity (e.g., a director, an actress, an opera singer, etc.) and write an essay about him/her. This will be your chance to submit a leading article to a magazine. You are thinking of reading and viewing everything this celebrity has done so far. What else would you do to prepare for this interview? What questions will you ask? How would you present his/her views on your questions, while adding your own critical comments?

對話 Dialogue

(2) Commenting on a film

張麗和趙強看完《臥虎藏龍》之後，一起討論。

張麗：　這部電影真感人，我忍不住哭了好幾次。

趙強：　我覺得它一點意思也沒有，看到一半我就看不下去了。真不明白這樣的電影怎麼能得奧斯卡獎？

張麗：　既然得獎了，就一定有比別的電影好的地方。你不覺得這部電影拍得很美，和一般的功夫片不一樣嗎？

趙強：　儘管拍得很美，可是它根本沒表現出中國功夫的精彩，這樣的片子大概只能吸引老外。

張麗：　這部電影的演員來自大陸、台灣和香港三個地方，而且都是有名的明星。

趙強：　可是導演李安自己也承認，他選演員的時候更注意演員的形象，而不是演技。而且聽到男、女主角有香港口音的普通話，我就覺得很難受。

張麗：　你不喜歡李安，就批評他的電影。可是以前都是我們看有中文字幕的外國電影，現在外國人也開始看有英文字幕的中國電影了，這都要[1]**歸功於**李安。

趙強：　好吧，既然你那麼喜歡李安，我也不批評他了。不過我真的認為他不適合拍功夫片。

閱讀理解 Comprehension Check

1. 張麗認為《臥虎藏龍》這部片子的什麼很好？
2. 趙強喜歡《臥虎藏龍》嗎？為什麼？這部片子有哪些問題？
3. 張麗認為李安成功的地方在哪兒？

(1) Commenting on a film

张丽和赵强看完《卧虎藏龙》之后，一起讨论。

张丽：　这部电影真感人，我忍不住哭了好几次。

赵强：　我觉得一点意思也没有，看到一半我就看不下去了。真不明白这样的电影怎么能得奥斯卡奖。

张丽：　既然得奖了，就一定有比别的电影好的地方。你不觉得这部电影拍得很美，和一般的功夫片不一样吗？

赵强：　尽管拍得很美，可是它根本没表现出中国功夫的精彩，这样的片子大概只能吸引老外。

张丽：　这部电影的演员来自大陆、台湾和香港三个地方，而且都是有名的明星。

赵强：　可是导演李安自己也承认，他选演员的时候更注意演员的形象，而不是演技。而且听到男、女主角有香港口音的普通话，我就觉得很难受。

张丽：　你不喜欢李安，就批评他的电影。可是以前都是我们看有中文字幕的外国电影，现在外国人也开始看有英文字幕的中国电影了，这都要[1]归功于李安。

赵强：　好吧，既然你那么喜欢李安，我也不批评他了。不过我真的认为他不适合拍功夫片。

阅读理解 Comprehension Check

1. 张丽认为《卧虎藏龙》这部片子的什么很好？
2. 赵强喜欢《卧虎藏龙》吗？为什么？这部片子有哪些问题？
3. 张丽认为李安成功的地方在哪儿？

對話一生詞 Vocabulary

Study the numbered vocabulary (productive vocabulary) for its usage.　The unnumbered items (receptive vocabulary) are to facilitate reading comprehension.

◎By Order of Appearance

	臥虎藏龍	臥虎藏龙	Wò Hǔ Cáng Lóng	N	Crouching Tiger, Hidden Dragon, name of a film	[to lie down-tiger-to hide-dragon]
	感人		gǎnrén	Adj	讓人覺得感動	[to move-people]
1.	忍不住		rěnbuzhù	RV	can't bear, can't help but do sth.	[to bear-not-tightly]
2.	得獎	得奖	déjiǎng	VO	to win a prize	[to get-prize]
	奥斯卡		Aòsīkǎ	N	Oscar (e.g., Academy Award)	
3.	拍		pāi	V	to shoot film	
4.	一般		yìbān	Adj	general, ordinary, common	[one-kind]
	功夫		gōngfu	N	martial art, skill	[skill-skill]
	片		piàn	N	films	
5.	儘管	尽管	jǐnguǎn	Conj	even though, despite	[utmost-to run]
6.	表現	表现	biǎoxiàn	V/N	to display, performance	[show-to appear]
7.	吸引		xīyǐn	V	to attract, to draw, to fascinate	[to attract-to draw]
	演員	演员	yǎnyuán	N	performer	[to perform-person]
	來自	来自	láizì	V	to come/stem from	[to come-from]
	香港		Xiānggǎng	N	Hong Kong	[fragrant-port]
8.	導演	导演	dǎoyǎn	N/V	director, to direct (film/play/etc.)	[to guide-to perform]
	李安		Lǐ Ān	N	導演名 Ang Lee	
9.	承認	承认	chéngrèn	V	to admit, to acknowledge, to recognize	[to bear-to recognize]
10.	形象		xíngxiàng	N	image	[shape-appearance]
	演技		yǎnjì	N	acting	[to perform-skill]
	主角		zhǔjué	N	leading role, lead, protagonist	[main-role]
	難受	难受	nánshòu	Adj	to feel unwell/unhappy/pained	[hard-to endure]
11.	批評	批评	pīpíng	V/N	to criticize, criticism	[to comment-to review]

	字幕		zìmù	N	subtitle, caption	[word-screen]
12.	歸功於	归功于	guīgōngyú	V	to attribute success to, to give credit to	[to return-achievement-to]
13.	適合	适合	shìhé	V	to suit, to fit	[appropriate-to accord with]

Characters with Many Strokes

藏 獎 奧 儘 演 導 承 難 幕 歸

詞彙用法 Words in Context

1. 忍不住：忍不住哭了

    你一回家就忍不住要做什麼？

    為什麼抽煙的人都覺得戒煙特別難？

    忍不住：忍不住哭了

    你一回家就忍不住要做什么？

    为什么抽烟的人都觉得戒烟特别难？

2. 得獎：得獎了；得獎的人；得了大獎

    哪個導演得的獎最多？

    你在學校得過什麼獎？

    得奖：得奖了；得奖的人；得了大奖

    哪个导演得的奖最多？

    你在学校得过什么奖？

3. 拍：拍電影；拍武俠片；拍完了；拍不了；拍了三年

    哪個演員拍的電影最多？

    《星際大戰》這部電影拍了多長時間？

    拍：拍电影；拍武侠片；拍完了；拍不了；拍了三年

    哪个演员拍的电影最多？

    《星球大战》这部电影拍了多长时间？

4. 一般：這個工作的收入一般；我一般八點起床；一般說來

    有房子又有車的人是很有錢的人嗎？

    你每天在什麼地方吃午飯？

    一般：这个工作的收入一般；我一般八点起床；一般说来

    有房子又有车的人是很有钱的人吗？

    你每天在什么地方吃午饭？

5. 儘管：儘管這部電影我已經看過三遍了，但我還是忍不住哭了。

    尽管：尽管这部电影我已经看过三遍了，但我还是忍不住哭了。

聽說為了減肥，你已經節食一個
星期了，效果怎麼樣？

最近美國的經濟不景氣，你的工
作一定很不好找吧？

6. 表現：表現得很好；表現自己；
表現情緒、性格、不滿

你怎麼知道他昨天沒準備？

和朋友約會的時候，如果你心情
不好你會表現出來嗎？

7. 吸引：

你那麼喜歡哈里波特這部電影，
到底是什麼吸引了你？

為什麼現在有這麼多的學生選中
文課？

8. 導演：由李安導演的電影

你最喜歡哪個導演？

今年由誰導演的電影得了奧斯卡
獎？

9. 承認：承認錯誤；承認那個導演
不簡單；不願意承認；不得不承
認

導演有沒有找到這部電影不吸引
人的原因？

你是否有過一些破壞環境的行
為？

10. 形象：演員、公司的形象很重
要；破壞了形象；形象不好

你覺得形象和演技對演員來說哪
個更重要？

如果一個公司的產品有質量問題，對這個公司有什麼影響？

如果一个公司的产品有质量问题，对这个公司有什么影响？

11. 批評：批評朋友、政府；不要總是批評別人

批评：批评朋友、政府；不要总是批评别人

環保主義者為什麼批評布什總統？

环保主义者为什么批评布什总统？

如果你沒有準備功課，老師會做什麼？

如果你没有准备功课，老师会做什么？

12. 歸功於：（句型）

归功于：（句型）

13. 適合：這個工作適合你，你不適合學電腦

适合：这个工作适合你，你不适合学电脑

你覺得自己適合學什麼專業？

你觉得自己适合学什么专业？

你覺得我適合穿紅的衣服嗎？

你觉得我适合穿红的衣服吗？

自由發揮與課堂活動　Free Discussion and Class Activities

1. 介紹一部你喜歡的電影，包括演員、導演、故事以及你喜歡的原因。

介绍一部你喜欢的电影，包括演员、导演、故事以及你喜欢的原因。

2. 你喜歡《臥虎藏龍》嗎？你覺得這部電影最成功的地方是什麼？最失敗的呢？你覺得它在美國為什麼這麼受歡迎？

你喜欢《卧虎藏龙》吗？你觉得这部电影最成功的地方是什么？最失败的呢？你觉得它在美国为什么这么受欢迎？

3. 要成為明星，形象與演技哪個更重要？為什麼？

要成为明星，形象与演技哪个更重要？为什么？

(2) Commenting on a singer

張麗和趙強在往書店走的路上。

趙強：　這麼早就叫我出來和你逛書店，要買什麼書？

張麗：　不是買書，我要買成龍新出版的專輯。

趙強：　買誰的專輯²不好，卻要買他的情呀、愛呀的過時的專輯。

張麗：　你喜歡的那種亂七八糟，說不像說，唱不像唱的東西才容易過時。我崇拜成龍，因為他不管是做演員還是歌手，都很有自己的風格。

趙強：　你要知道，明星表現出來的不一定是真實的自己，他們的形象、風格、接受採訪的時候說的話、每天的生活都是公司為他們設計的。

張麗：　成龍也承認，有的時候他需要考慮商業利益，但是他還是一直努力讓觀眾看到他真實的一面。

趙強：　我聽說成龍為了維持自己的偶像地位，不敢公開他的婚姻。為了維持形象，他甚至還要不停地運動、節食。

張麗：　明星做什麼都會受人注意，為了成功，他們當然要付出一些代價。可是我們也不應該這麼討論別人的隱私。

趙強：　好好好，我不批評你的偶像了，我們快點走吧，去買他的專輯，讓你大飽耳福。

閱讀理解 Comprehension Check

4.　張麗喜歡聽誰的音樂？趙強呢？他喜歡聽哪種流行音樂？

5.　張麗覺得自己崇拜的明星什麼地方好？

6.　趙強怎麼批評張麗崇拜的明星？

(2) Commenting on a singer

张丽和赵强在往书店走的路上。

赵强：　这么早就叫我出来和你逛书店，要买什么书？

张丽：　不是买书，我要买成龙新出版的专辑。

赵强：　买谁的专辑[2]**不好，却**要买他的情呀、爱呀的过时的专辑。

张丽：　你喜欢的那种乱七八糟，说
　　　　不象说，唱不象唱的东西才
　　　　容易过时。我崇拜成龙，因
　　　　为他不管是做演员还是歌
　　　　手，都很有自己的风格。

赵强：　你要知道，明星表现出来的
　　　　不一定是真实的自己，他们
　　　　的形象、风格、接受采访的
　　　　时候说的话、每天的生活都
　　　　是公司为他们设计的。

张丽：　成龙也承认，有的时候他需要考虑商业利益，但是他还是一
　　　　直努力让观众看到他真实的一面。

赵强：　我听说成龙为了维持自己的偶像地位，不敢公开他的婚姻。
　　　　为了维持形象，他甚至还要不停地运动、节食。

张丽：　明星做什么都会受人注意，为了成功，他们当然要付出一些
　　　　代价。可是我们也不应该这么讨论别人的隐私。

赵强：　好好好，我不批评你的偶像了，我们快点走吧，去买他的专
　　　　辑，让你大饱耳福。

阅读理解 Comprehension Check

5.　张丽喜欢听谁的音乐？赵强呢？他喜欢听哪种流行音乐？

6.　张丽觉得自己崇拜的明星什么地方好？

7.　赵强怎么批评张丽崇拜的明星？

對話二生詞 Vocabulary

	成龍	成龙	Chéng Lóng	N	name of a movie star, Jacky Chan	[success-dragon]
	出版		chūbǎn	V	to publish, to come out	[to issue-edition]
	專輯	专辑	zhuānjí	N	album, special issue/collection of periodicals/films, etc.	[special-volume]
	過時	过时	guòshí	Adj	out-of-date	[to pass-time]
14.	亂七八糟	乱七八糟	luànqībāzāo	IE	at sixes and sevens, in a mess	[messy-seven-eight-rotten]
	崇拜		chóngbài	V	to worship, to adore	[high-to salute]
	歌手		gēshǒu	N	singer, vocalist	[to sing-person skilled in sth.]
	風格	风格	fēnggé	N	style	[common practice-standard]
	真實	真实	zhēnshí	Adj	true, real	[true-real]
15.	採訪	采访	cǎifǎng	V	to cover, to interview (for news report), to gather news	[to gather-to visit]
16.	設計	设计	shèjì	V/N	to design, plan	[to set up-to plan]
17.	利益		lìyì	N	interest, benefit, profit	[profit-advantage]
1.	維持	维持	wéichí	V	to keep, to maintain (a modicum of sth.)	[to maintain-to hold]
	偶像		ǒuxiàng	N	image, idol, model	[idol-picture]
18.	公開	公开	gōngkāi	V	to make public	[public-open]
19.	不停		bùtíng	Adv	without stopping, incessantly	[not-to stop]
	節食	节食	jiéshí	VO	to go on diet	[to restrain-food]
20.	付出		fùchū	V	to expend (time, efforts, life (but not money))	[to pay-out]
21.	代價	代价	dàijià	N	price, cost	[to take the place of-price]
	隱私	隐私	yǐnsī	N	personal secrets, privacy	[hidden-personal]
	大飽耳福	大饱耳福	dàbǎo ěrfú	IE	to have a treat for the ears, to listen to good music	[great-to satisfy-ear-blessing]

Characters with Many Strokes

專 輯 亂 糟 實 慮 維 偶 價 隱

詞匯用法 Words in Context

14. 亂七八糟：房間亂七八糟；總是
    亂七八糟的

    如果你一個星期不收拾自己的臥
    室，會怎麼樣？

    你覺得哪個城市的交通亂七八
    糟？為什麼？

15. 採訪：採訪得獎的導演；被採
    訪；接受採訪

    記者為什麼要採訪李安？

    所有的演員都會接受記者的採訪
    嗎？

16. 設計：設計房間；不會設計；這
    個設計很不錯

    你自己的房間是誰設計的？

    你覺得這個大學的圖書館怎麼
    樣？

17. 利益：商人的利益；保護自己的
    利益

    買東西的時候，注意什麼才能保
    護自己的利益？

    所謂「現實的人」是什麼樣的
    人？

18. 維持：維持生活、關係、地位；
    難以維持；維持不了

    每個月要多少錢才能維持你基本
    的生活？

    那對夫妻為什麼最後還是離婚
    了？

乱七八糟：房间乱七八糟；总是
乱七八糟的

如果你一个星期不收拾自己的卧
室，会怎么样？

你觉得哪个城市的交通乱七八
糟？为什么？

采访：采访得奖的导演；被采
访；接受采访

记者为什么要采访李安？

所有的演员都会接受记者的采访
吗？

设计：设计房间；不会设计；这
个设计很不错

你自己的房间是谁设计的？

你觉得这个大学的图书馆怎么
样？

利益：商人的利益；保护自己的
利益

买东西的时候，注意什么才能保
护自己的利益？

所谓"现实的人"是什么样的
人？

维持：维持生活、关系、地位；
难以维持；维持不了

每个月要多少钱才能维持你基本
的生活？

那对夫妻为什么最后还是离婚
了？

19.　公開：公開自己的隱私、秘密；
　　　公開地承認自己的錯誤

　　你會不會把自己的秘密告訴你的
　　朋友？

　　什麼樣的書不可以公開出版？

20.　不停：不停地說話、改變風格

　　張學友為什麼會一直受到歌迷的
　　支持？

　　怎麼做才不會讓自己的中文水平
　　下降？

21.　付出：付出很大的代價；付出了
　　　很多努力

　　你覺得一個人怎麼樣才能成功？

　　你覺得中文難學嗎？

22.　代價：很高的代價；成功的代價
　　　是失去自己的生活

　　不少國家為發展經濟付出了什麼
　　樣的代價？

　　你覺得成功的代價是什麼？

自由發揮與課堂活動　Free Discussion and Class Activities

4.　你最喜歡的電影明星、歌星是
　　誰？她、他為什麼能吸引你？

5.　每個人在一張紙上寫下一部電
　　影、或者一個演員的名字，然後
　　老師把這些寫著名字的紙貼在學
　　生背上。每個學生需要請別的同
　　學介紹那部電影的內容，或者那
　　個演員的特點，然後猜一猜他背
　　後的紙上寫的是什麼。

敘述 Narrative

大家都滿意的電影

忙了一個星期，好不容易到了週末。吃過晚飯以後，我拿出一張在街上買的光盤《安娜與國王》，想和大家一起放鬆一下。聽說這個片子在美國的票房不錯，而且又是中國演員當主角，所以引起了我的興趣。可是我剛說了片名，媽媽就不滿地說：「《安娜與國王》？為什麼不是《國王與安娜》？」這個問題我從來沒想過，不過媽媽問的也不是沒有道理，因為國王應該是最有權力的人，叫《國王與安娜》好像更合理！「就因為國王是亞洲的國王，而安娜卻是美國的安娜，情況就不同了。還有這張海報，朱迪·福斯特的照片特大，可是周潤發就只能遠遠地站

在她後邊。難道周潤發不是主角嗎？」

記得從前外國電影在國內被稱為「進口大片」，儘管票價比國產電影高幾倍，但還是非常有市場，怎麼現在卻開始給他們挑毛病了呢？原來幾年以前，國內的電影水平不高，而且人們沒有機會接觸外國片，所以好萊塢電影一下子流行起來，可是看多了

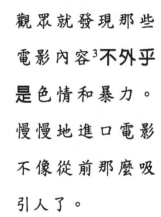

觀眾就發現那些電影內容[3]**不外乎是**色情和暴力。慢慢地進口電影不像從前那麼吸引人了。

近年來中國導演也拍了不少好電影，於是我就找了部張藝謀的新片。弟弟看了一眼卻說：「張藝謀的電影我

看膩了，他的每部電影都拍得很美，可是悶得要命，而且老講農村的生活。這也許會滿足外國人對中國的好奇，但是我更想看那些反映一般人現實生活的電影。」

還好，我還有幾部賀歲片，這幾年這些電影票房也非常好。

爸爸卻說：「這些片子明星多，過年時看看倒熱鬧，但是沒有什麼深度。」大家怎麼這麼挑剔呢？一個晚上竟然沒找到一部讓大家都滿意的電影。[4] **乾脆**別看電影，去唱卡拉 OK 吧，**省得**大家都不高興。

閱讀理解 Comprehension Check

10. 「我」週末的時候想做什麼？為什麼？
11. 為什麼媽媽對《安娜與國王》不滿？
12. 從前中國人喜歡看進口片嗎？為什麼？現在呢？為什麼？
13. 弟弟想看張藝謀拍的電影嗎？為什麼？
14. 爸爸想看賀歲片嗎？為什麼？
15. 「我」對大家有什麼看法？她覺得大家最好做什麼？為什麼？

大家都满意的电影

忙了一个星期，好不容易到了周末。吃过晚饭以后，我拿出一张在街上买的光盘《安娜与国王》，想和大家一起放松一下。听说这个片子在美国的票房不错，而且又是中国演员当主角，所以引起了我的兴趣。可是我刚说了片名，妈妈就不满地说："《安娜与国王》？为什么不是《国王与安娜》？"这个问题我从来没想过，不过妈妈问的也不是没有道理，因为国王应该是最有权力的人，叫《国王与安娜》好象更合理！"就因为国王是亚洲的国王，而安娜却是美国的安娜，情况就不同了。还有这张海报，朱迪·福斯特的照片特大，可是周润发就只能远远地站在她后边。难道周润发不是主角吗？"

记得从前外国电影在国内被叫做"进口大片"，尽管票价比国产电影高几倍，但还是非常有市场，怎么现在却开始给他们挑毛病了呢？原来几年以前，国内的电影水平不高，而且人们没有机会接触外国片，所以好莱坞电影一下子流行起来，可是看多了观众就发现那些电影 **³不外乎是色情**和暴力。慢慢地进口电影不象从前那么吸引人了。

近年来中国导演也拍了不少好电影，于是我就找了部张艺谋的新片。弟弟看了一眼却说："张艺谋的电影我都看腻了，他的每部电影都拍得很美，可是闷得要命，而且老讲农村的生活。这也许会满足外国人对中国的好奇，但是我更想看那些反映一般人现实生活的电影。"

还好，我还有几部贺岁片，这几年这些电影票房也非常好。爸爸却说："这些片子明星

多，过年时看看倒热闹，但是没有什么深度。"大家怎么这么挑剔呢？一个晚上竟然没找到一部让大家都满意的电影。⁴**干脆**别看电影，去唱卡拉OK吧，**省得**大家都不高兴。

阅读理解 Comprehension Check

10. "我"周末的时候想做什么？为什么？
11. 为什么妈妈对《安娜与国王》不满？
12. 从前中国人喜欢看进口片吗？为什么？现在呢？为什么？
13. 弟弟想看张艺谋拍的电影吗？为什么？
14. 爸爸想看贺岁片吗？为什么？
15. "我"对大家有什么看法？她觉得大家最好做什么？为什么？

敘述生詞 Vocabulary

23.	滿意	滿意	mǎnyì	Adj	satisfied, pleased	[full-desire]
	光盤	光盘	guāngpán	N	V.C.D. <TW>光碟 guāngdié	[light-disk]
	安娜與國王	安娜与国王	Ānnà yǔ Guówáng	N	Anna and the King, name of a movie	
24.	放鬆	放松	fàngsōng	RV	to relax, to loosen	[to release-loose]
	票房		piàofáng	N	box office	[ticket-room]
	道理		dàoli	N	reason, rationality, the right way	[way-principle]
	權力	权力	quánlì	N	power, authority	[right-strength]
25.	合理		hélǐ	Adj	rational, reasonable, equitable	[to conform to-reason]
	亞洲	亚洲	Yàzhōu	N	Asia	[second-continent]

海報	海报	hǎibào	N	poster, playbill	[extremely large-bulletin]
朱迪福斯特		Zhūdí Fúsītè	N	Jodi Foster, name of an actress <TW> 茱蒂·福斯特	
周潤發	周润发	Zhōu Rùnfā	N	name of an actor: Chow Yun-fat	
26. 進口	进口	jìnkǒu	V	to import, to enter port	[to enter-entrance]
票價	票价	piàojià	N	電影票的價格	[ticket-price]
國產	国产	guóchǎn	N	國內生產的	[country-to produce]
27. 接觸	接触	jiēchù	V	to come into contact with, to get in touch with	[to come in contact with-to touch]
好萊塢	好莱坞	Hǎoláiwù	N	Hollywood	
觀眾	观众	guānzhòng	N	spectator, audience	[to view-crowd]
28. 不外乎		búwàihū	V	to be nothing more than	[not-other-than]
暴力		bàolì	N	violence	[violent-force]
張藝謀	张艺谋	Zhāng Yìmóu	N	name of a director	
29. 膩	腻	nì	Adj	bored/tired of …	
30. 悶	闷	mèn/mēn	Adj/V	bored, depressed, stuffy, to cover tightly	
農村	农村	nóngcūn	N	rural area, countryside	[farming-village]
31. 滿足	满足	mǎnzú	V	to satisfy, to be contented	[full-sufficient]
32. 反映		fǎnyìng	V	to reflect, to report	[to turn over-to shine]
33. 現實	现实	xiànshí	N/Adj	reality, practical	[present-reality]
賀歲片	贺岁片	hèsuìpiàn	N	慶祝過年的影片	[to celebrate-year-film]
深度		shēndù	N	profundity, depth	[deep-extent]
34. 挑剔		tiāotì	Adj	nitpicking	[to pick-to pick out]
竟然		jìngrán	Adv	unexpectedly, to one's surprise	[unexpected-(adv marker)]
35. 乾脆	干脆	gāncuì	Adv	simply, to make a quick decision to V	[only-crisp]

Characters with Many Strokes

盤　鬆　權　價　觸　觀　暴　膩　農　歲

詞匯用法 Words in Context

23. 滿意：對專業很滿意；讓人滿
    意；非常滿意

    你對這個大學最滿意的地方是什
    麼？

    你為什麼從宿舍裏搬出來住？

    滿意：对专业很满意；让人满
    意；非常满意

    你对这个大学最满意的地方是什
    么？

    你为什么从宿舍里搬出来住？

24. 放鬆：放鬆一下

    考試的時候你會不會很緊張？

    週末的時候你怎麼放鬆自己？

    放松：放松一下

    考试的时候你会不会很紧张？

    周末的时候你怎么放松自己？

25. 合理：合理的要求、建議、價
    格；很不合理

    老師會拒絕學生什麼樣的要求？

    你那麼喜歡那件衣服，為什麼沒
    買？

    合理：合理的要求、建议、价
    格；很不合理

    老师会拒绝学生什么样的要求？

    你那么喜欢那件衣服，为什么没
    买？

26. 進口：進口產品、影片；從美國
    進口 ↔ 出口

    每年中國從美國進口什麼東西？

    美國不許什麼東西進口？

    进口：进口产品、影片；从美国
    进口 ↔ 出口

    每年中国从美国进口什么东西？

    美国不许什么东西进口？

27. 接觸：和同學接觸；接觸中國文
    化；接觸不到別的朋友

    學習一個國家的語言對你有什麼
    好處？

    怎麼做才能接觸到更多的朋友？

    接触：和同学接触；接触中国文
    化；接触不到别的朋友

    学习一个国家的语言对你有什么
    好处？

    怎么做才能接触到更多的朋友？

28. 不外乎：（句型）

    不外乎：（句型）

29. 膩：看、吃、聽、玩、說（不）
    膩；V膩了；V不膩

    你以前總是聽這盤錄音帶，現在
    為什麼不聽了？

    腻：看、吃、听、玩、说（不）
    腻；V腻了；V不腻

    你以前总是听这盘录音带，现在
    为什么不听了？

哪部電影讓你怎麼看也看不膩？　　哪部电影让你怎么看也看不腻？

30. 悶：很悶；悶死了　　　　　　　　闷：很闷；闷死了

你覺得什麼樣的課很悶？　　　　　你觉得什么样的课很闷？

週末很悶的時候，你會做什麼？　　周末很闷的时候，你会做什么？

31. 滿足：滿足要求、需要；很滿　　　满足：满足要求、需要；很满
　　足；不滿足　　　　　　　　　　　足；不满足

你需要什麼，父母就會給你買什　　你需要什么，父母就会给你买什
麼嗎？　　　　　　　　　　　　　么吗？

你的工作那麼好，為什麼還要辭　　你的工作那么好，为什么还要辞
職呢？　　　　　　　　　　　　　职呢？

32. 反映：反映生活、現實、個人經　　反映：反映生活、现实、个人经
　　驗　　　　　　　　　　　　　　　验

你選擇的專業能不能反映你的興　　你选择的专业能不能反映你的兴
趣？　　　　　　　　　　　　　　趣？

為什麼不同的導演拍的電影有不　　为什么不同的导演拍的电影有不
同的風格？　　　　　　　　　　　同的风格？

33. 現實：這個人很現實；面對現　　　现实：这个人很现实；面对现
　　實；現實生活　　　　　　　　　　实；现实生活

你對現實生活有什麼不滿意的地　　你对现实生活有什么不满意的地
方？　　　　　　　　　　　　　　方？

你自己是一個很現實的人嗎？為　　你自己是一个很现实的人吗？为
什麼？　　　　　　　　　　　　　什么？

34. 挑剔：很挑剔，別那麼挑剔　　　　挑剔：很挑剔，别那么挑剔

你在哪些方面比較挑剔？　　　　　你在哪些方面比较挑剔？

你覺得觀眾應不應該挑剔？　　　　你觉得观众应不应该挑剔？

35. 乾脆：（句型）　　　　　　　　　干脆：（句型）

自由發揮與課堂活動　Free Discussion and Class Activities

6. 你覺得外國的演員或者導演在美國發展會碰到哪些困難？

你觉得外国的演员或者导演在美国发展会碰到哪些困难？

7. 張藝謀是一位在國際上很有名的導演，但是在中國不少人批評他的電影是專門拍給外國人看的，你怎麼看這種說法？

张艺谋是一位在国际上很有名的导演，但是在中国不少人批评他的电影是专门拍给外国人看的，你怎么看这种说法？

8. 老師從中文網站上找到最新的歐美電影排行榜，然後讓學生根據中文的名字判斷是哪一部電影，並說明他們對那部電影的看法。

老师从中文网站上找到最新的欧美电影排行榜，然后让学生根据中文的名字判断是哪一部电影，并说明他们对那部电影的看法。

說明 Exposition

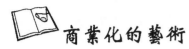 商業化的藝術

李安導演的《臥虎藏龍》得了奧斯卡的四項大獎。讓人難以相信的是，這部得獎電影在中國卻不太受人歡迎。

有些人認為，《臥虎藏龍》能得奧斯卡獎，要歸功於電影的藝術價值。導演李安非常了解西方觀眾，尤其是美國觀眾。所以他用美國人習慣的方式來講一個東方的故事，這樣給大家一種又熟悉、又新鮮的感覺。

當然，很多人不同意這個分析，他們認為影片之所以得獎，靠的是電影公司的安排，是一種純商業活動。在西方電影市場越來越不景氣的情況下，打開中國這個市場無疑會給電影公司帶來很好的經濟利益。《臥虎藏龍》一旦成功，就可以幫他們進入中國的市場。所以一直有人懷疑，所謂的「奧斯卡」獎⁵**不過**是商人手中賺錢的工具**罷了**！

其實，在現在的社會，無論是電影還是音樂，都變成了⁶**以賺錢為**目的的商業活動，而演員和歌手也不一定是藝術家，他們很可能也是被公司包裝出來賺錢的工具，真正得到好處的都是那些背後的公司。

閱讀理解 Comprehension Check

16. 有些人認為李安的《臥虎藏龍》為什麼會成功？
17. 另一些人有不同的看法，他們的看法是什麼？
18. 作者認為現在的電影和音樂是一種純藝術活動嗎？

商业化的艺术

　　李安导演的《卧虎藏龙》得了奥斯卡的四项大奖。让人难以相信的是，这部得奖电影在中国却不太受人欢迎。

　　有些人认为，《卧虎藏龙》能得奥斯卡奖，要归功于电影的艺术价值。导演李安非常了解西方观众，尤其是美国观众。所以他用美国人习惯的方式来讲一个东方的故事，这样给大家一种又熟悉、又新鲜的感觉。

　　当然，很多人不同意这个分析，他们认为影片之所以得奖，靠的是电影公司的安排，是一种纯商业活动。在西方电影市场越来越不景气的情况下，打开中国这个市场无疑会给电影公司带来很好的经济利益。《卧虎藏龙》一旦成功，就可以帮他们进入中国的市场。所以一直有人怀疑，所谓的「奥斯卡」奖[5]**不过**是商人手中赚钱的工具**罢了**！

　　其实，在现在的社会，无论是电影还是音乐，都变成了[6]**以**赚钱**为目的**的商业活动，而演员和歌手也不一定是艺术家，他们很可能也是被公司包装出来赚钱的工具，真正得到好处的都是那些背后的公司。

阅读理解 Comprehension Check

16. 有些人认为李安的《卧虎藏龙》为什么会成功？
17. 另一些人有不同的看法，他们的看法是什么？
18. 作者认为现在的电影和音乐是一种纯艺术活动吗？

説明生詞 Vocabulary

	商業	商业	shāngyè	N	business, commerce	[business-industry]
	藝術	艺术	yìshù	N	art	[skill-technology]
36.	難以	难以	nányǐ	V	to be difficult to…	[hard-so as to]
37.	價值	价值	jiàzhí	N	value, worth	[value-to be worth]
38.	分析		fēnxī	V/N	to analyze, analysis	[to divide-to separate]
	純	纯	chún	Adj	pure	
39.	景氣	景气	jǐngqì	N/Adj	prosperity, boom	[scene-spirit]
40.	無疑	无疑	wúyí	Adv	undoubtedly	[without-doubt]
41.	不過	不过	búguò	Adv	只是	[not-to surpass]
42.	罷了	罢了	bàle	Suf	(indicating limitation)	[to stop-(particle)]
43.	目的		mùdì	N	purpose, aim, goal	[goal-target]
44.	包裝	包装	bāozhuāng	V/N	to pack, to dress up, package	[to wrap-to pack]

Characters with Many Strokes

業 藝 術 難 價 純 無 疑 罷 裝

詞匯用法 Words in Context

36. 難以：難以相信、接受、理解、
忍受

我聽說很多藝術家為了藝術吸毒
品，你相信這是真的嗎？

我覺得你父母讓你學電腦專業的
建議不錯，你為什麼不接受呢？

37. 價值：有商業價值；價值很高；
毫無價值

你為什麼從來不看那些讓人發笑
的電影？

為什麼有些人喜歡看古書？

---

36. 难以：难以相信、接受、理解、
忍受

我听说很多艺术家为了艺术吸毒
品，你相信这是真的吗？

我觉得你父母让你学电脑专业的
建议不错，你为什么不接受呢？

37. 价值：有商业价值；价值很高；
毫无价值

你为什么从来不看那些让人发笑
的电影？

为什么有些人喜欢看古书？

38. 分析：分析一下這部電影；分析　　　分析：分析一下这部电影；分析
　　分析；你的分析很有深度　　　　　分析；你的分析很有深度

　　看過電影之後，你會不會分析導　　看过电影之后，你会不会分析导
　　演拍這部電影的目的？　　　　　　演拍这部电影的目的？

　　你喜不喜歡讀一些分析性的文　　　你喜不喜欢读一些分析性的文
　　章？為什麼？　　　　　　　　　　章？为什么？

39. 景氣：經濟不景氣　　　　　　　　景气：经济不景气

　　什麼時候會有很多人失業？　　　　什么时候会有很多人失业？

　　為什麼最近經濟不太景氣？　　　　为什么最近经济不太景气？

40. 無疑：經濟不景氣無疑會影響人　　无疑：经济不景气无疑会影响人
　　們的生活　　　　　　　　　　　　们的生活

　　兩個生活習慣不同的人住在一起　　两个生活习惯不同的人住在一起
　　會不會出問題？　　　　　　　　　会不会出问题？

　　週末去健身房能不能幫你放鬆一　　周末去健身房能不能帮你放松一
　　下？　　　　　　　　　　　　　　下？

41. 不過：（句型）　　　　　　　　　不过：（句型）

42. 罷了：（句型）　　　　　　　　　罢了：（句型）

43. 目的：生活的目的；學中文的目　　目的：生活的目的；学中文的目
　　的；達到目的　　　　　　　　　　的；达到目的

　　你為什麼選擇你現在學習的專　　　你为什么选择你现在学习的专
　　業？　　　　　　　　　　　　　　业？

　　商人為什麼要花那麼多錢做廣　　　商人为什么要花那么多钱做广
　　告？　　　　　　　　　　　　　　告？

44. 包裝：包裝明星；……的時候得　　包装：包装明星；……的时候得
　　包裝一下自己；禮物的包裝　　　　包装一下自己；礼物的包装

　　你覺得一個明星表現出來的是他　　你觉得一个明星表现出来的是他
　　自己嗎？　　　　　　　　　　　　自己吗？

　　送朋友禮物的時候，你在乎包裝　　送朋友礼物的时候，你在乎包装
　　嗎？為什麼？　　　　　　　　　　吗？为什么？

自由發揮與課堂活動 Free Discussion and Class Activities

9. 你認為誰最應該得奧斯卡最佳影片、導演、男主角、女主角獎？你的理由是什麼？

   你认为谁最应该得奥斯卡最佳影片、导演、男主角、女主角奖？你的理由是什么？

10. 辯論：是否應該取消奧斯卡獎？

    辩论：是否应该取消奥斯卡奖？

應用詞 Productive Vocabulary

◎**By Grammatical Categories**

Nouns/Pronouns/Measure Words

現實	xiànshí	reality, practical		目的	mùdì	purpose, aim, goal
景氣	jǐngqì	prosperity, boom		利益	lìyì	interest, benefit, profit
導演	dǎoyǎn	director, to direct (film/play/etc.)		價值	jiàzhí	value, worth
形象	xíngxiàng	image		代價	dàijià	price, cost

Verbs/Stative Verbs/Adjectives

拍	pāi	to shoot film		分析	fēnxī	to analyze, analysis
維持	wéichí	to keep, to maintain (a modicum of sth.)		包裝	bāozhuāng	to pack, package
接觸	jiēchù	to come into contact with, to get in touch with		付出	fùchū	to expend (time, efforts, life (but not money))
放鬆	fàngsōng	to relax, to loosen		進口	jìnkǒu	to import, to enter port
吸引	xīyǐn	to attract, to draw		得獎	déjiǎng	to win a prize
滿足	mǎnzú	to satisfy, to be contented		歸功於	guīgōngyú	to attribute success to, to give credit to
反映	fǎnyìng	to reflect, to dreport		不外乎	búwàihū	to be nothing more than
適合	shìhé	to suit, to fit		忍不住	rěnbuzhù	can't bear, can't help but do sth.
採訪	cǎifǎng	to cover, to interview (for news report)		悶	mèn/mēn	bored, depressed, stuffy, to cover tightly
批評	pīpíng	to criticize, criticism		膩	nì	bored/tired of …
公開	gōngkāi	to make public		挑剔	tiāotī	nitpicking
承認	chéngrèn	to admit, to acknowledge		滿意	mǎnyì	satisfied, pleased
難以	nányǐ	to be difficult to…		一般	yìbān	general, common
表現	biǎoxiàn	to display, performance		合理	hélǐ	rational, reasonable
設計	shèjì	to design, plan				

Adverbs and Others

罷了	bàle	(indicating limitation)		乾脆	gāncuì	simply, to make a quick decision to
不停	bùtíng	without stopping, incessantly		儘管	jǐnguǎn	even though, despite
不過	búguò	merely, no more than		亂七八糟	luànqībāzāo	at sixes and sevens, in a mess
無疑	wúyí	undoubtedly				

理解詞 Receptive Vocabulary

◎ By Grammatical Categories

Nouns/Pronouns/Measure Words

片	piàn	films	票價	piàojià	ticket price
字幕	zìmù	subtitle, caption	隱私	yǐnsī	personal secrets, privacy
光盤	guāngpán	V.C.D.	道理	dàoli	reason, rationality, the right way
功夫	gōngfu	martial art, skill	深度	shēndù	profundity, depth
演技	yǎnjì	acting	暴力	bàolì	violence
演員	yǎnyuán	performer	權力	quánlì	power, authority
觀眾	guānzhòng	spectator, audience	商業	shāngyè	business, commerce
主角	zhǔjué	leading role, lead, protagonist	藝術	yìshù	art
歌手	gēshǒu	singer, vocalist	國產	guóchǎn	domestically made
偶像	ǒuxiàng	image, idol, model	亞洲	Yàzhōu	Asia
風格	fēnggé	style	農村	nóngcūn	rural area, countryside
專輯	zhuānjí	album, special issue/collection of periodicals/films, etc.	賀歲片	hèsuìpiàn	films that celebrate Chinese New Year
海報	hǎibào	poster, playbill			
票房	piàofáng	box office			

Verbs/Stative Verbs/Adjectives

來自	láizì	to come/stem from	感人	gǎnrén	touching, moving
崇拜	chóngbài	to worship, to adore	過時	guòshí	out-of-date
出版	chūbǎn	to publish, to come out	難受	nánshòu	to feel unwell/unhappy/pained
節食	jiéshí	to go on diet			
純	chún	pure			
真實	zhēnshí	true, real			

Adverbs and Others

竟然	jìngrán	unexpectedly, to one's surprise
大飽耳福	dàbǎo ěrfú	to have a treat for the ears, to listen to good music

本课词表 Chapter Vocabulary

◎ By Pinyin

Words with asterisk* are productive vocabulary which needs to be memorized and studied for its usage.

bàle*	罢了	(indicating limitation)	gēshǒu	歌手	singer, vocalist
bàolì	暴力	violence	gōngfu	功夫	martial art, skill
bāozhuāng*	包装	to pack, to dress up, package	gōngkāi*	公开	to make public
biǎoxiàn*	表现	to display, performance	guāngpán	光盘	V.C.D.
búguò*	不过	merely, no more than	guānzhòng	观众	spectator, audience
búwàihū*	不外乎	to be nothing more than	guīgōngyú*	归功于	to attribute success to, to give credit to
bùtíng*	不停	without stopping, incessantly	guóchǎn	国产	domestically made
cǎifǎng*	采访	to cover, to interview (for news report), to gather news	guòshí	过时	out-of-date
			hǎibào	海报	poster, playbill
			hélǐ*	合理	rational, reasonable, equitable
chéngrèn*	承认	to admit, to acknowledge, to recognize	hèsuìpiàn	贺岁片	films that celebrate Chinese New Year
chūbǎn	出版	to publish, to come out	jiàzhí*	价值	value, worth
chún	纯	pure	jiēchù*	接触	to come into contact with, to get in touch with
chóngbài	崇拜	to worship, to adore	jiéshí	节食	to go on diet
dàbǎo ěrfú	大饱耳福	to have a treat for the ears, to listen to good music	jǐngqì*	景气	prosperity, boom
			jìngrán	竟然	unexpectedly, to one's surprise
dàijià*	代价	price, cost	jǐnguǎn*	尽管	even though, despite
dàoli	道理	reason, rationality, the right way	jìnkǒu*	进口	to import, to enter port
dǎoyǎn*	导演	director, to direct (film/play/etc.)	láizì	来自	to come/stem from
déjiǎng*	得奖	to win a prize	lìyì*	利益	interest, benefit, profit
fàngsōng*	放松	to relax, to loosen	luànqībāzāo*	乱七八糟	at sixes and sevens, in a mess
fǎnyìng*	反映	to reflect, to dreport	mǎnyì*	满意	satisfied, pleased
fēnggé	风格	style	mǎnzú*	满足	to satisfy, to be contented
fēnxī*	分析	to analyze, analysis	mèn/mēn*	闷	bored, depressed, stuffy, to cover tightly
fùchū*	付出	to expend (time, effort, life (but not money))	mùdì*	目的	purpose, aim, goal
gāncuì*	干脆	simply, to make a quick decision to V	nánshòu	难受	to feel unwell/ unhappy/pained
gǎnrén	感人	touching, moving			

nányǐ*	难以	to be difficult to...
nì*	腻	bored/tired of ...
nóngcūn	农村	rural area, countryside
ǒuxiàng	偶像	image, idol, model
pāi*	拍	to shoot film
piàn	片	films
piàofáng	票房	box office
piàojià	票价	ticket price
pīpíng*	批评	to criticize, criticism
quánlì	权力	power, authority
rěnbuzhù*	忍不住	can't bear, can't help but do sth.
shāngyè	商业	business, commerce
shèjì*	设计	to design, plan
shēndù	深度	profundity, depth
shìhé*	适合	to suit, to fit
tiāotì*	挑剔	nitpicking
wéichí*	维持	to keep, to maintain (a modicum of sth.)

wúyí*	无疑	undoubtedly
xiànshí*	现实	reality, practical
xíngxiàng*	形象	image
xīyǐn*	吸引	to attract, to draw, to fascinate
yǎnjì	演技	acting
yǎnyuán	演员	performer
Yàzhōu	亚洲	Asia
yībān*	一般	general, ordinary, common
yǐnsī	隐私	personal secrets, privacy
yìshù	艺术	art
zhēnshí	真实	true, real
zhuānjí	专辑	album, special issue/collection of periodicals/films, etc.
zhǔjué	主角	leading role, lead, protagonist
zìmù	字幕	subtitle, caption

語法和用法 Grammar and Usage

Pay attention to the function of the structure and then study the example sentences. When blanks are provided, either answer the questions or complete the sentences.

1. Expressing attribution

X 歸功於 Y	guīgōngyú	to give credit to Y for X
X 歸因於 Y	guīyīnyú	to attribute X to Y
X 歸罪於／歸咎於 Y	guīzuìyú/guījiùyú	to put the blame on Y for X

● 現在外國人也開始看有英文字幕的中國電影了，這都要歸功於李安。

1. 《臥》劇得了很多獎都是因為導演拍得好嗎？

    《卧》剧得了很多奖都是因为导演拍得好吗？

    Is the reason the movie "Crouching Tiger, Hidden Dragon" received so many awards all because the director did such a good job?

    《臥》劇的演員表演得非常精彩，所以有些人認為《臥》劇能得獎要歸功於演員，而不應該歸功於導演。

    《卧》剧的演员表演得非常精彩，所以有些人认为《卧》剧能得奖要归功于演员，而不应该归功于导演。

    In the movie, the actors and actresses performed brilliantly, so some people think the credit for the awards it received should be given to its actors and actresses, and shouldn't be given to the director.

2. 環境污染都是因為經濟發展的緣故嗎？

    环境污染都是因为经济发展的缘故吗？

    Is all environmental pollution because of economic development?

    不少國家在發展經濟的時候，沒有注意保護環境，但是環境被破壞有很多原因，不應該只歸咎於經濟的發展。

    不少国家在发展经济的时候，没有注意保护环境，但是环境被破坏有很多原因，不应该只归咎于经济的发展。

    When many countries developed their economy, they weren't concerned with protecting the environment. Yet, there are many reasons why our environment has deteriorated. We shouldn't just blame it on economic development.

3. 中國電影為什麼不如好萊塢的電影吸

    中国电影为什么不如好莱坞的电影吸

    Why can't Chinese movies attract audiences as well as

Logan freeman

引觀眾？是因為導演或演員不好嗎？	引观众？是因为导演或演员不好吗？	Hollywood films? Is it because directors and actors do not do a good job?
原因很多，不應該簡單地歸因於導演或者演員，更不應該歸咎於觀眾只喜歡看進口影片。	原因很多，不应该简单地归因于导演或者演员，更不应该归咎于观众只喜欢看进口影片。	There are many reasons. We shouldn't just simply attribute it to directors or actors, and furthermore we shouldn't blame it on the audience for only liking to see imported films.

4. 你參加健身班兩個月就減了12斤，值得恭喜，可不可以告訴我你有什麼好方法？

你参加健身班两个月就减了12斤，值得恭喜，可不可以告诉我你有什么好方法？

---

5. 我覺得電腦是一個偉大的發明，它給我們的生活帶來了很大的方便，你覺得呢？

我觉得电脑是一个伟大的发明，它给我们的生活带来了很大的方便，你觉得呢？

---

6. 這兩年我們的籃球隊表現得很不好，是什麼原因？

这两年我们的篮球队表现得很不好，是什么原因？

The pattern X歸功於/歸因於/歸罪於Y is a more formal way to express attribution. Their colloquial counterparts are X 是因為 Y 的幫助/緣故/錯誤. When one attributes X to Y, there is often an auxiliary verb 要 or 得 before 歸功於/歸因於/歸罪於. Y can be a noun, noun phrase, or a clause, e.g., 我們的球隊表現不好要歸因於教練/教練的訓練不足/訓練不夠 'Our team's poor performance can be attributed to the coach/the lack of training by the coach/the lack of training.'

2. Expressing a least favorable option

S V QW (O)不好， 卻要/偏要 VO	…bùhǎo,	<口> S could have Ved
S QW(O)不好 V， 卻要/偏要VO	quèyào/ piānyào	anything but O

● 買誰的專輯不好，卻要買他的情呀、愛呀的過時的專輯。

1. 今天我買了一張光盤《安娜與國王》，吃了飯以後我們一起看看吧！

今天我买了一张光盘《安娜与国王》，吃了饭以后我们一起看看吧！

Today I bought the V.C.D. "Anna and the King." After dinner, let's watch it together.

買什麼光盤不好，卻要買這張我最不喜歡的，還是你自己看吧！

买什么光盘不好，却要买这张我最不喜欢的，还是你自己看吧！

You could have bought any V.C.D but you had to buy this one that I hate. You'd better watch it yourself.

2. 爸爸現在迷上了交際舞，每天早上都到公園和別的老頭、老太太跳交際舞，少去一天都不舒服。

爸爸现在迷上了交际舞，每天早上都到公园和别的老头、老太太跳交际舞，少去一天都不舒服。

Now our dad is infatuated with ballroom dance. Every morning he has to go to the park to dance with other old folks. He doesn't miss a day.

交際舞有什麼好跳的，爸爸什麼不好學，卻要學那種摟摟抱抱的舞。

交际舞有什么好跳的，爸爸什么不好学，却要学那种搂搂抱抱的舞。

What is so good about ballroom dance? Dad could have learned anything but this kind of clinging and groping dance.

3. 我的朋友來看我，我想請他去「燕京」飯館吃飯，你覺得怎麼樣？

我的朋友来看我，我想请他去"燕京"饭馆吃饭，你觉得怎么样？

My friend is going to visit me and I want to take him to the "Yanjing" restaurant. What do you think?

你去哪兒請客不好，卻要去那個又貴又不好吃的地方。

你去哪儿请客不好，却要去那个又贵又不好吃的地方。

You should take him to any other places but that restaurant which not only is expensive but also has lousy food.

4. 下個星期我有三個大考，而且中文課也是下個星期考，想起

下个星期我有三个大考，而且中文课也是下个星期考，想起

來我就頭疼。   来我就头疼。

---

5. 小王21歲的生日就快到了，我問   小王21岁的生日就快到了，我问
    他打算怎麼慶祝，他說他想去   他打算怎么庆祝，他说他想去
    拉斯維加斯。   拉斯维加斯。

---

6. 你知道嗎，小張正在追和你一   你知道吗，小张正在追和你一
    起上中文課那個個子高高的女   起上中文课那个个子高高的女
    孩。   孩。

The pattern S …QW不好，卻要VO is a colloquial expression to indicate a least
favorable option. Remember the option indicated in the first clause is always
indefinite, so there is often a question word like 誰、哪兒、什麼. A sentence like 他
去紐約不好，卻要去芝加哥 should be rephrased as 他去哪兒不好，卻要去芝加哥
'He should have gone anywhere but to Chicago.' The verb in the first clause can go
before the question word or after 不好, and is often repeated in the second clause. So,
it's wrong to say 他追哪個女孩不好，卻要我先和她說過話的 'It would have been
better for him to go after any other girl than her. I talked to her first.'

3. Expressing constituent elements

S不外乎是 X, Y, (Z) búwàihū shì	S is nothing more than X, Y, (Z)

● 可是看多了觀眾就發現那些電影不外乎是色情和暴力。

1. 我這個星期五有一   我这个星期五有一   This Friday I have an exam.
    個大考，考完以   个大考，考完以   After that, I can take a good
    後，週末就可以好   后，周末就可以好   break on the weekend. What
    好休息一下了，你   好休息一下了，你   do you plan to do?
    打算做什麼？   打算做什么？

    哎，這麼悶的地   哎，这么闷的地   Well, what's there to do in this
    方，週末有什麼可   方，周末有什么可   boring place on the weekend?
                                                    There is nothing more than

做的，不外乎是運動和看電影，真無聊！

做的，不外乎是运动和看电影，真无聊！

exercise and watching movies. How dull!

2.　你剛剛的電話差不多說了一個小時，你和你媽媽怎麼有那麼多可聊的？

你剛剛的电话差不多说了一个小时，你和你妈妈怎么有那么多可聊的？

You were on the phone for over an hour. How can you and your mom have so much to talk about?

我們也沒聊什麼，而且每次她打電話來不外乎是問我這個星期做了什麼、吃飯怎麼樣、身體好不好，儘管每次的問題都一樣，但我還是得好好回答。

我们也没聊什么，而且每次她打电话来不外乎是问我这个星期做了什么、吃饭怎么样、身体好不好，尽管每次的问题都一样，但我还是得好好回答。

We didn't really chat about much. Besides, every time she calls me, she asks nothing more than what I did this week, how well I ate, how's my health. Though the questions are the same each time, I have to anwer properly.

3.　李明天天在電腦前要坐好幾個鐘頭，他到底在做什麼？

李明天天在电脑前要坐好几个钟头，他到底在做什么？

Li Ming always sits in front of his computer several hours a day. What on earth is he doing?

他眼裏只有電腦，可是他用電腦不外乎是上網和網友聊天，或者玩遊戲。

他眼里只有电脑，可是他用电脑不外乎是上网和网友聊天，或者玩游戏。

Every day he thinks only about computers, but when he uses them, he does nothing more than log on to chat with his net pals or to play games.

4.　我的很多朋友都不喜歡《臥虎藏龍》那部電影。我們根本不明白它為什麼能得獎。難道美國人和中國人的口味真的很不相同嗎？

我的很多朋友都不喜欢《臥虎藏龙》那部电影。我们根本不明白它为什么能得奖。难道美国人和中国人的口味真的很不相同吗？

5. 我這個暑假不打算選課，所以
    有時間去旅行，你覺得我可以
    選擇那些旅行的方法呢？

    我这个暑假不打算选课，所以
    有时间去旅行，你觉得我可以
    选择那些旅行的方法呢？

---

6. 你的同屋最近好像特別忙，很
    少見到他，他有什麼事情嗎？

    你的同屋最近好象特别忙，很
    少见到他，他有什么事情吗？

The pattern 不外乎是 is used to indicate the range of elements the subject includes.
So, what follows 不外乎是 is often a list of components (X, Y, Z), e.g., 得獎的電影不
外乎是有好的演員、導演、劇情. Thus, if a sentence starts with 在這兒旅行很簡
單, the following clause could be 不外乎是開車、騎自行車這兩種方法 'it's simple
to travel here; it's nothing more than these two methods: driving a car and riding a
bike.' Note that "nothing more than" is not used rhetorically, as it often is in English.
So, it's odd to say the following in Chinese 暑假去旅行不外乎是一個浪費錢的方法
'Going traveling during the summer is nothing more than a waste of money.'

4. Expressing an alternative

| S 乾脆…吧，省得… | gāncuì...ba, shěngde... | S might as well..., lest... |

- 乾脆別看電影，去唱卡拉OK吧，省得大家都不高興。

1. 今年夏天我想去中
    國旅行，可是我怕
    自己不適應那個地
    方，會拉肚子，還
    可能有別的問題。

    今年夏天我想去中
    国旅行，可是我怕
    自己不适应那个地
    方，会拉肚子，还
    可能有别的问题。

    This summer I want to go to
    China to travel, but I'm afraid I
    won't get used to the place,
    will get diarrhea, and have
    other problems.

    你乾脆在美國旅遊
    吧，省得擔心這
    個、擔心那個。

    你干脆在美国旅游
    吧，省得担心这
    个、担心那个。

    You might as well travel in the
    U.S., so as to avoid worrying
    about this and that.

2. 我每天要上網查資
    料都得跑到圖書館
    去，要給朋友發電

    我每天要上网查资
    料都得跑到图书馆
    去，要给朋友发电

    I have to go to the library every
    day to log on to the internet and
    look up information. When I
    want to send e-mails to friends,

子郵件也得去那兒，真不方便！

子邮件也得去那儿，真不方便！

I need to go there, too. It's real incovenient!

你乾脆買個電腦吧，省得這麼麻煩，每天跑來跑去。

你干脆买个电脑吧，省得这么麻烦，每天跑来跑去。

You might as well buy a computer, so as to avoid all these troubles running around each day.

3.　下星期六是她的生日，我想送她一條絲巾，怕她不喜歡；想送她一本書，又怕她已經看過了。

下星期六是她的生日，我想送她一条丝巾，怕她不喜欢；想送她一本书，又怕她已经看过了。

Next Saturday is her birthday. I want to give her a silk scarf, but she may not like it. I want to give her a book, but I fear that she's already read it.

你乾脆請她出去吃飯吧，省得猜來猜去，也不知道她到底喜歡什麼。

你干脆请她出去吃饭吧，省得猜来猜去，也不知道她到底喜欢什么。

You might as well take her out for a meal, so as to avoid guessing all the time what she really wants.

4.　我很想念我的家人，不知道爸爸的身體怎麼樣了，也不知道媽媽的病是不是好了一點兒。

我很想念我的家人，不知道爸爸的身体怎么样了，也不知道妈妈的病是不是好了一点儿。

5.　我很喜歡她，可是不敢告訴她。我送了她一點東西，也請她出去喝過咖啡。

我很喜欢她，可是不敢告诉她。我送了她一点东西，也请她出去喝过咖啡。

6.　我自己沒車，所以每次出去都要請朋友幫忙，有時候真覺得不好意思。

我自己没车，所以每次出去都要请朋友帮忙，有时候真觉得不好意思。

The pattern 乾脆⋯吧, 省得⋯ is used to express an alternative or a suggestion. What follows 乾脆 is the preferred option and what follows 省得 is the resulting problem experienced by the subject if the preferred option is not taken. So, it is wrong to say 你乾脆回家看你的父母吧，省得他們的病很嚴重 'You might as well go home and see your parents, lest their illness get worse.' Instead, the sentence should be 你乾脆回家看你的父母吧，省得你不放心 'You might as well go home and see your parents, otherwise you won't feel at ease.'

5. Expressing de-emphasis

| X 不過 Y 罷了 | búguò…bàle | X is only/merely/nothing |
| X 只是 Y 罷了 | zhǐshì…bàle | more than Y |

- 所謂的「奧斯卡獎」不過是商人手中賺錢的工具罷了！

1. 張藝謀是中國最有名的導演之一，你為什麼那麼不喜歡他拍的電影？

    张艺谋是中国最有名的导演之一，你为什么那么不喜欢他拍的电影？

    Zhang Yimou is one of the most famous directors in China. Why do you so dislike the movies he's made?

    我覺得他拍的電影沒有反映中國現實的情況，他不過是會吸引外國觀眾罷了。

    我觉得他拍的电影没有反映中国现实的情况，他不过是会吸引外国观众罢了。

    I think the movies he's made don't reflect the realities of China. He is merely trying to cater to a foreign audience.

2. 我每次請你參加我的晚會，你都不來，你是不是不喜歡我請的人？

    我每次请你参加我的晚会，你都不来，你是不是不喜欢我请的人？

    Each time I invited you to my party you haven't come. Is it because you don't like the people I invite?

    當然不是，我非常想參加你的晚會，我沒來只是因為我沒時間罷了，不是不喜歡。

    当然不是，我非常想参加你的晚会，我没来只是因为我没时间罢了，不是不喜欢。

    Of course not, I would like to go to your party very much. The reason I haven't come is because I haven't had time, not because I don't want to go.

3. 小張昨天告訴我，他打算從今天開始，每天看一個小時的中文報紙。他每天都有很多計劃，不過我想大部分的時候，他只是說說罷了，不會認真的。

小张昨天告诉我，他打算从今天开始，每天看一个小时的中文报纸。他每天都有很多计划，不过我想大部分的时候，他只是说说罢了，不会认真的。

Xiao Zhang told me yesterday that from now on he plans to read one hour from a Chinese newspaper every day.

He has a lot of plans every day, but I think most of the time it's just a lot of talk. He doesn't really mean it.

4. 上次張麗的電腦壞了，多虧你這個電腦專家，不然大概要花很多錢請別人來修了，你真了不起！

上次张丽的电脑坏了，多亏你这个电脑专家，不然大概要花很多钱请别人来修了，你真了不起！

5. 我經常聽別人說電腦黑客都特別厲害，我想他們一定都是受過很高教育的人吧？

我经常听别人说电脑黑客都特别厉害，我想他们一定都是受过很高教育的人吧？

6. 最近你總是把張麗掛在嘴上，你們是不是在談戀愛？

最近你总是把张丽挂在嘴上，你们是不是在谈恋爱？

In the pattern X 不過 Y 罷了, Y is used to de-emphasize X so Y is typically an understatement. For example, 別謝我，我不過幫你一個小忙罷了 'Don't thank me. I have only helped you a little bit.' Y can be a verb phrase or a noun, e.g., 我倆不過是朋友罷了 'We two are only friends.' 不過 can be exchanged by 只是 and 罷了 always occurs at the end of a sentence.

6. Expressing attribution

S 以 … 為 N	yǐ...wéi	to take … to be/act as N
S 以 … 為 例	yǐ...wéilì	to take...as an example
S 以 … 為 生	yǐ...wéishēng	to take...for a living
S 以 … 為 主	yǐ...wéizhǔ	to take...as main part or primary
S 以 … 為 重 (心)	yǐ...wéizhòng(xīn)	to take...as more important

● 在現在的社會，無論是電影還是音樂，都變成了以賺錢為目的的商業活動……。

1. 人口多對國家好嗎？

   人口多对国家好吗？

   Is it good for a country to have a large population?

   一個國家的人口太多不是一件好事，以中國為例，人口問題影響了經濟的發展。

   一个国家的人口太多不是一件好事，以中国为例，人口问题影响了经济的发展。

   A large population is not good for a country. Take China as an example, the population problem has an impact on its economic development.

2. 在中國殘疾人 cánjírén 以什麼為生？

   在中国残疾人以什么为生？

   In China, what do handicapped people do for a living?

   很多殘疾人，由於沒有受過很好的教育，不能找到一份好的工作，只能靠做一些非常辛苦的工作為生。

   很多残疾人，由于没有受过很好的教育，不能找到一份好的工作，只能靠做一些非常辛苦的工作为生。

   Many handicapped people, due to the lack of good education, can't find a good job. Thus, they can only make a living by doing various kinds of manual labor.

3. 傳統的中國女人生活以什麼為中心？

   传统的中国女人生活以什么为中心？

   What is the focus of life for traditional Chinese women?

   在傳統的社會，女人不可以出去工作，她們的生活都以家庭、丈夫和孩子為中心。

   在传统的社会，女人不可以出去工作，她们的生活都以家庭、丈夫和孩子为中心。

   In traditional society, women couldn't go and work, so their lives revolved around their family, husband, and children.

4.　我們的中文課，每天都會有不　　我们的中文课，每天都会有不
少生詞，可是哪些生詞是重點　　少生词，可是哪些生词是重点
呢？　　　　　　　　　　　　　　呢？

5.　美國人常吃什麼？中國人呢？　　美国人常吃什么？中国人呢？

6.　你每天好像都有很多事情要　　你每天好象都有很多事情要
做，我真不知道你到底要做什　　做，我真不知道你到底要做什
麼？　　　　　　　　　　　　　　么？

以⋯為 is a common pattern used in more formal and literary Chinese to express attribution. Many nouns can follow 為 and they are often one-syllable nouns such as 例、生、主、重. The use of 以⋯為例、以⋯為生 is straight-forward, e.g., 以我為 例 'use me as an example,' 他以說書為生 'he makes a living by story-telling.' Yet, beware of the use of 以⋯為主、以⋯為重. The former indicates a major component, while the latter indicates what is important. Study the following examples: (1) 美國人 的飲食多以肉為主，但中國人多以菜為主 'Americans eat mainly meat in their diet, but Chinese eat mainly vegetables in their diet'; (2) 你應該以學業、家庭為重, 不要 整天在外面打工 'You should put more importance on your studies and family, and not be out all day working part-time jobs.'

背景常識 Background Notes

1.　賀歲片：香港是最早拍賀歲片的地方。每個新年之前，有名的演員會 在一起拍一部輕鬆好笑的片子來慶祝新年。這樣的電影一般不是特別 有深度，只是為了讓大家在過年的時候放鬆一下。大陸是從九十年代 末期由導演馮小剛開始拍賀歲片的。最有名的賀歲片有《甲方乙 方》、《沒完沒了》等等。

2.　電影獎：在中國最有名的電影獎是金雞獎和百花獎。金雞獎是由電影 方面的專家評選出來的，而百花獎是由觀眾投票選出來的。

背景常识 Background Notes

1. 贺岁片：香港是最早拍贺岁片的地方。每个新年之前，有名的演员会在一起拍一部轻松好笑的片子来庆祝新年。这样的电影一般不是特别有深度，只是为了让大家在过年的时候放松一下。大陆是从九十年代末期由导演冯小刚开始拍贺岁片的。最有名的贺岁片有《甲方乙方》、《没完没了》等等。

2. 电影奖：在中国最有名的电影奖是金鸡奖和百花奖。金鸡奖是由电影方面的专家评选出来的，而百花奖是由观众投票选出来的。

第六課　現代人看什麼書？

Theme: Literature and Performing Arts

Communicative Objectives
- Discussing the status of classical literature today
- Talking about popular literature and its impact
- Narrating the experience of going to a Beijing opera

Skill Focus
- Reading a commentary on "best-sellers"

Grammar Focus
- 連A帶B…
- S不僅僅是…也/都V
- S把A和B聯繫/結合/加起來
- S不VO…，一VO…
- 先不談X，就Y來看/而言
- …有所V

Problem Scenario

Someone you know is going to have a birthday. You are thinking about taking the person out and treating him/her for an evening. Plus, you need to find a present for him/her. What plans will you make? If the activity were a show, what kind of show would it be? If the present were a book, which book would you get and why?

對話 Dialogue

(1) Discussing the status of classical literature today

李明的爸爸李鐵剛從書市回來，和妻子周紅對話。

妻子： 你每次去書市都抱一大堆書回來，可是卻沒時間看，不是浪費錢嗎？

丈夫： 這你就不懂了，我買的都是名著。每次書市打折最多的就是名著，你看這些，[1]連《水滸》帶《三國》才五十塊，我還不趁便宜多買點！

妻子： 現在誰還看名著啊？人們早就給這些書下了一個新的定義。

丈夫： 他們是怎麼定義名著的？

妻子： 所謂名著指的就是「人們都想說自己看過，可是又都不願意去看的書」。

丈夫： 哈哈！這個定義再恰當不過了！現在書市上最貴的要數那些怎麼學電腦，怎麼申請MBA或者考GRE的書，而最便宜的恐怕就是名著。連武俠和言情小說都比名著貴。

妻子： 哎，現在誰不是忙著工作賺錢，哪兒有時間和心情去看什麼文學作品啊？還是看報紙和雜誌更實際一點。

丈夫： 所以有人說現在流行的是快餐文學，看來這些名著要等我老了以後再慢慢看了！

閱讀理解 Comprehension Check

1. 丈夫在書市買了什麼？為什麼買這些書？
2. 妻子說現在名著的定義是什麼？丈夫同意嗎？為什麼？
3. 現在流行的是什麼文學？為什麼？

(1)Discussing the status of classical literature today

李明的爸爸李铁刚从书市回来，和妻子周红对话。

妻子：　你每次去书市都抱一大堆书回来，可是却没时间看，不是浪费钱吗？

丈夫：　这你就不懂了，我买的都是名著。每次书市打折最多的就是名著，你看这些，[1]连《水浒》带《三国》才五十块，我还不趁便宜多买点！

妻子：　现在谁还看名著啊？人们早就给这些书下了一个新的定义。

丈夫：　他们是怎么定义名著的？

妻子：　所谓名著指的就是"人们都想说自己看过，可是又都不愿意去看的书"。

丈夫：　哈哈！这个定义再恰当不过了！现在书市上最贵的要数那些怎么学电脑，怎么申请MBA或者考GRE的书，而最便宜的恐怕就是名著。连武侠和言情小说都比名著贵。

妻子：　哎，现在谁不是忙着工作赚钱，哪儿有时间和心情去看什么文学作品啊？还是看报纸和杂志更实际一点。

丈夫：　所以有人说现在流行的是快餐文学，看来这些名著要等我老了以后再慢慢看了！

阅读理解 Comprehension Check

1. 丈夫在书市买了什么？为什么买这些书？
2. 妻子说现在名著的定义是什么？丈夫同意吗？为什么？
3. 现在流行的是什么文学？为什么？

對話一生詞Vocabulary

Study the numbered vocabulary (productive vocabulary) for its usage. The unnumbered items (receptive vocabulary) are to facilitate reading comprehension.

◎By Order of Appearance

	市		shì	N	market (e.g., 書市、花市、菜市、魚市), city	
1.	堆		duī	N/M/V	pile, heap, to pile up	
	名著		míngzhù	N	有名的作品、書	[famous-book]
2.	打折		dǎzhé	VO	to have a discount	[to hit-to break]
	水滸	水浒	Shuǐhǔ	N	name of a classical novel: *Tale of Water Margin*	[water-waterside]
	三國	三国	Sānguó	N	name of a classical novel: *The Romance of the Three Kingdoms*	[three-kingdom]
3.	下定義	下定义	xià dìngyì	VO	to give a definition of, to define	[to form-fixed-meaning]
4.	恰當	恰当	qiàdàng	Adj	合適	[appropriate-proper]
	言情		yánqíng	N	love and romance	[words-feeling]
5.	實際	实际	shíjì	Adj/N	practical, reality (e.g., 實際上)	[real-circumstances]

Characters with Many Strokes

堆 著 義 當 實 際

詞匯用法 Words in Context

1. 堆：一大堆書、髒衣服、功課、人；東西亂堆；東一堆、西一堆
   週末到了，你為什麼不和大家一起出去？
   你手裏抱的是什麼東西？

   堆：一大堆书、脏衣服、功课、人；东西乱堆；东一堆、西一堆
   周末到了，你为什么不和大家一起出去？
   你手里抱的是什么东西？

2. 打折：商店在打折；給你打八

   打折：商店在打折；给你打八

折、打對折

為什麼大家都在聖誕節之後去買
東西？

這本書原來賣一百塊，你怎麼花
八十塊就買到了？

3. 下定義：給名著下個定義；怎麼
定義中文；好電影的定義是什麼

你覺得什麼樣的學生是好學生？

你喜歡人們給名著下的定義嗎？

4. 恰當：很恰當；不恰當

你不喜歡他做的飯為什麼不直接
告訴他呢？

用什麼話形容他不太恰當？

5. 實際：實際的情況；這個人很實
際；實際上

聽說中文的語法很難，是嗎？

為什麼我們不能相信報紙上所有
的報導？

折、打对折

为什么大家都在圣诞节之后去买
东西？

这本书原来卖一百块，你怎么花
八十块就买到了？

下定义：给名著下个定义；怎么
定义中文；好电影的定义是什么

你觉得什么样的学生是好学生？

你喜欢人们给名著下的定义吗？

恰当：很恰当；不恰当

你不喜欢他做的饭为什么不直接
告诉他呢？

用什么话形容他不太恰当？

实际：实际的情况；这个人很实
际；实际上

听说中文的语法很难，是吗？

为什么我们不能相信报纸上所有
的报道？

自由發揮與課堂活動 Free Discussion and Class Activities

1. 你喜歡看什麼樣的書？為什麼？

2. 你喜歡讀名著嗎？你怎麼看文章
中對名著的定義：「人們都想說
自己看過，可是又都不願意去看
的書」？

你喜欢看什么样的书？为什么？

你喜欢读名著吗？你怎么看文章
中对名著的定义："人们都想说
自己看过，可是又都不愿意去看
的书"？

♟♟(2) Talking about popular literature and its impact

李明的鄰居趙太太和兒子趙強討論電視劇和網上文學。

母親：　電視台從下個星期起開始播電視劇《三國》，每天一集，你們誰都不要和我搶電視。

兒子：　一部老掉牙的小說改編的電視劇有什麼吸引人的地方，值得您天天看？

母親：　當然值得，這可是名著，我是看這部小說長大的，我敢打賭，我們這一代人沒有幾個沒看過這本書的。

兒子：　您放心，最近網上恰好有部新小說，我才沒時間和您搶電視呢！

母親：　網上的小說能有什麼深度？今天看完，明天就忘了！

兒子：　那倒不一定！其實網絡小說更能反映我們實際的生活、更有讀者。

母親：　那麼人們怎麼在網上發表自己的文章呢？

兒子：　有一些網站專門發表網絡文章，網上有名的作家還有自己的聊天室，大家可以很快地發表對某一篇文章的看法，這樣 ²**不僅僅**是看別人的作品，**也**有參與感。

母親：　看來網絡文學會成為你們這一代人共同的回憶。

閱讀理解 Comprehension Check

4. 母親要孩子不要做什麼？為什麼她覺得這個電視劇值得看？
5. 孩子看不看這種電視劇？為什麼？他要看的是什麼？
6. 孩子說網上的作品受歡迎嗎？為什麼？
7. 孩子說現在的作者、讀者和從前的有什麼不同？

(2) Talking about popular literature and its impact

李明的邻居赵太太和儿子赵强讨论电视剧和网上文学。

母亲：　电视台从下个星期起开始播电视剧《三国》，每天一集，你们谁都不要和我抢电视。

儿子：　一部老掉牙的小说改编的电视剧有什么吸引人的地方，值得您天天看？

母亲：　当然值得，这可是名著，我是看这部小说长大的，我敢打赌，我们这一代人没有几个没看过这本书的。

儿子：　您放心，最近网上恰好有部新小说，我才没时间和您抢电视呢！

母亲：　网上的小说能有什么深度？今天看完，明天就忘了！

儿子：　那倒不一定！其实网络小说更能反映我们实际的生活、更有读者。

母亲：　那么人们怎么在网上发表自己的文章呢？

儿子：　有一些网站专门发表网络文章，网上有名的作家还有自己的聊天室，大家可以很快地发表对某一篇文章的看法，这样²**不仅仅**是看别人的作品，**也**有参与感。

母亲：　看来网络文学会成为你们这一代人共同的回忆。

阅读理解 Comprehension Check

4. 母亲要孩子不要做什么？为什么她觉得这个电视剧值得看？
5. 孩子看不看这种电视剧？为什么？他要看的是什么？
6. 孩子说网上的作品受欢迎吗？为什么？
7. 孩子说现在的作者、读者和从前的有什么不同？

對話二生詞 Vocabulary

	電視劇	电视剧	diànshìjù	N	TV series	[TV-drama]
	電視台	电视台	diànshìtái	N	TV station	[TV-station]
6.	播		bō	V	to broadcast	
	集		jí	M	volume, episode (as in a TV series)	
7.	搶	抢	qiǎng	V	to fight with, to snatch	
	老掉牙		lǎodiàoyá	Adj	old and shabby, obsolete	[old-to come off-tooth]
8.	改編	改编	gǎibiān	V	to adapt, to rearrange, to revise	[to change-to edit]
	代		dài	N	generation	
9.	敢		gǎn	V	to dare	
10.	打賭	打赌	dǎdǔ	VO	to make a bet, to bet	[to do-to bet]
11.	讀者	读者	dúzhě	N	看書的人	[to read-one who]
12.	發表	发表	fābiǎo	V	to publish, to issue	[to send out-show]
	文章		wénzhāng	N	essay, article, literary works	[writing-compositon]
13.	專門	专门	zhuānmén	Adj	special, specialized	[special-knack]
	作家		zuòjiā	N	寫文章的人	[to write-person]
14.	某		mǒu	Pre/Adj	certain, some	
15.	僅僅	仅仅	jǐnjǐn	Adv	only, merely	[only-only]
16.	參與	参与	cānyù	V	to participate in	[to join-to participate]
17.	回憶	回忆	huíyì	N/V	recollection, to recall	[to return-memory]

Characters with Many Strokes

劇 播 集 搶 編 敢 賭 讀 專 僅

詞匯用法 Words in Context

6.　播：播廣告；沒播過；播放時間　　播：播广告；没播过；播放时间
　　你最喜歡的節目什麼時候播？　　你最喜欢的节目什么时候播？
　　看電視的時候，你最討厭什麼？　看电视的时候，你最讨厌什么？

7.　搶：搶東西；搶位子；搶著付錢
　　你小時候會為什麼事情和兄弟姐妹吵架？
　　中國人和美國人吃完後付錢的習慣有什麼不同？

抢：抢东西；抢位子；抢着付钱
你小时候会为什么事情和兄弟姐妹吵架？
中国人和美国人吃完后付钱的习惯有什么不同？

8.　改編：把小說改編成電影；由小說改編的
　　羅密歐與茱利葉的電影是由什麼改編的？
　　現在流行把誰的書改編成電影？

改编：把小说改编成电影；由小说改编的
罗密欧与朱利叶的电影是由什么改编的？
现在流行把谁的书改编成电影？

9.　敢：敢看恐怖片；不敢說
　　你晚上不敢一個人做什麼？
　　你敢不敢一個人去外國生活？

敢：敢看恐怖片；不敢说
你晚上不敢一个人做什么？
你敢不敢一个人去外国生活？

10.　打賭：和朋友打賭；打賭打輸了；打什麼賭；賭什麼
　　你和朋友打賭時，會賭什麼？
　　你會為什麼事情和朋友打賭？

打赌：和朋友打赌；打赌打输了；打什么赌；赌什么
你和朋友打赌时，会赌什么？
你会为什么事情和朋友打赌？

11.　讀者：一般的讀者；讀者來信
　　什麼樣的書能吸引讀者？
　　美國哪家報紙的讀者最多？

读者：一般的读者；读者来信
什么样的书能吸引读者？
美国哪家报纸的读者最多？

12.　發表：發表文章、觀點
　　大學的老師除了上課以外，還應該做什麼？
　　在什麼情況下，你不會公開地發表自己的觀點？

发表：发表文章、观点
大学的老师除了上课以外，还应该做什么？
在什么情况下，你不会公开地发表自己的观点？

13.　專門：專門學習中文；受過專門訓練
　　為什麼他的功夫這麼好？

专门：专门学习中文；受过专门训练
为什么他的功夫这么好？

你以後打算專門學習中文嗎？　　　　你以后打算专门学习中文吗？

14. 某：某年、月、日；某位作家　　　　某：某年、月、日；某位作家

如果你忘了一位老師的名字，你　　　如果你忘了一位老师的名字，你
會怎麼說？　　　　　　　　　　　　会怎么说？

我們什麼時候能去月球生活？　　　　我们什么时候能去月球生活？

15. 僅僅：（句型）　　　　　　　　　　仅仅：（句型）

16. 參與：積極參與學校的活動；重　　　参与：积极参与学校的活动；重
在參與；熱心參與　　　　　　　　　在参与；热心参与

你覺得學生在學校除了學習以　　　　你觉得学生在学校除了学习以
外，還應該做什麼？　　　　　　　　外，还应该做什么？

你覺得參與和成功，哪個更重　　　　你觉得参与和成功，哪个更重
要？　　　　　　　　　　　　　　　要？

17. 回憶：回憶過去的生活；美好的　　　回忆：回忆过去的生活；美好的
回憶；童年回憶　　　　　　　　　　回忆；童年回忆

什麼事情會讓你回憶起過去的生　　　什么事情会让你回忆起过去的生
活？　　　　　　　　　　　　　　　活？

回憶過去的時候，什麼事情最讓　　　回忆过去的时候，什么事情最让
你難忘？　　　　　　　　　　　　　你难忘？

自由發揮與課堂活動 Free Discussion and Class Activities

3. 下面的小說你喜歡看哪一種？為　　　下面的小说你喜欢看哪一种？为
什麼？言情'romance,' 武俠, 偵探　　　什么？言情'romance,' 武侠, 侦探
'detective,' 科幻'science fiction'　　　　'detective,' 科幻'science fiction'

4. 你怎麼看網絡文學？你覺得這種　　　你怎么看网络文学？你觉得这种
作品有什麼優點和缺點？　　　　　　作品有什么优点和缺点？

5. 好萊塢把不少莎士比亞的作品改　　　好莱坞把不少莎士比亚的作品改
編成電影，你對這些電影有什麼　　　编成电影，你对这些电影有什么
印象？你覺得這種改編對宣傳古　　　印象？你觉得这种改编对宣传古
典文學有什麼影響？　　　　　　　　典文学有什么影响？

敘述 Narrative

父親節的感慨

我活了五十多歲，除了春節和國慶節以外，什麼節都不過。前幾天兒子突然跑回來說要慶祝什麼父親節，我猜又是一個洋節，我本來一點興趣也沒有，但是兒子的安排不好拒絕，只能聽他的了！兒子知道我是一個戲迷，所以就請我和老伴一起去看京劇。說句老實話，我這個戲迷有幾十年沒進過劇院了，不知道今天的劇院是不是還保持了傳統的風格，還是和其他的東西一樣都已經現代化、西化了！

兒子打了一輛車，直接把我們送到國安大劇院。下了車，我實在沒辦法[3]把眼前這座高樓**和**傳統的戲院**聯繫起來**。兒子向我解

釋，別看這座大樓外面很現代，其實裡面和從前的劇院是完全一樣的。果然像他說的，觀眾都坐在舞台前的桌子旁，一邊兒喝茶一邊兒看戲。服務員穿着清朝的衣服，手裡拿個水壺，為大家加茶倒水。感覺上彷彿回到了從前。

可是當我打開菜單的時候，卻大吃了一驚。一杯茶竟然要三十塊錢，簡直太黑了！我向兒子抱怨，這麼貴的地方老百姓怎麼來得起。兒子竟然說這種地方本來就不是為老百姓開的。我聽了就生氣，劇院不是給老百姓開的，那是給誰開的？回憶起過去北京的普通百姓沒幾個唸過書，可是個個都熟悉歷史，明白做人

的道理。這些事情是哪兒學來的？都是從劇院裡聽來的，通過看戲、聊戲，不知不覺地就有了這些道德觀念。可是看看坐在我週圍的人，這裡對他們來說更像是一個酒吧、一個朋友聚會的地方。哎！真不明白為什麼花那麼多錢到這兒來喝茶、聊天！

因為過兩天就是我的生日，從劇院回來以後，兒子還送了我一個生日禮物。打開一看，是《如何投資股票》。兒子勸我退休以後應該看看這些暢銷書，才不會落伍。他[4]不提暢銷書還好，一提暢銷書更讓我生氣。看看現在的書攤，所謂的暢銷書不是和電腦、股票、英語有關的，就是和什麼「隱私」有關的書，再不然就是那些無聊的言情小說。這些書不要說五十年，五年以後還會有人讀嗎？想想我們年輕時候的暢銷書，那才算是真正的好書，對人的一生都有很大的影響。我就是看了那些書以後，才決定去農村工作的。

我們的社會在不斷進步，生活也越來越豐富，但是我真擔心人們的精神會出現「營養不良」的現象。沒想到一個父親節引起了這麼多的感慨，恐怕這個父親節會讓我一生難忘了！

閱讀理解 Comprehension Check

8. 這個爸爸多大了？他平常過不過節？為什麼要過父親節？
9. 兒子請爸爸去做什麼？爸爸心裡覺得怎麼樣？
10. 現在的劇院和從前的什麼地方不同、相同？
11. 兒子認為現在的劇院是給誰開的？怎麼知道？爸爸怎麼想？為什麼？
12. 爸爸後來收到什麼生日禮物？他對暢銷書有什麼看法？
13. 爸爸擔心以後的人會有什麼問題？

父亲节的感慨

我活了五十多岁，除了春节和国庆节以外，什么节都不过。前几天儿子突然跑回来说要庆祝什么父亲节，我猜又是一个洋节，我本来一点兴趣也没有，但是儿子的安排不好拒绝，只能听他的了！

儿子知道我是一个戏迷，所以就请我和老伴一起去看京剧。说句老实话，我这个戏迷有几十年没进过剧院了，不知道今天的剧院是不是还保持了传统的风格，还是和其他的东西一样都已经现代化、西化了！

儿子打了一辆车，直接把我们送到国安大剧院。下了车，我实在没办法³把眼前这座高楼和传统的剧院联系起来。儿子向我解释，别看这座大楼外面很现代，里面和从前的

剧院是完全一样的。果然象他说的，观众坐在舞台前的桌子旁，一边儿喝茶一边儿看戏。服务员穿着清朝的衣服，手里拿个水壶，为大家加茶倒水。感觉上仿佛回到了从前。

可是当我打开菜单的时候，却大吃了一惊。一杯茶竟然要三十块钱，简直太黑了！我向儿子抱怨，这么贵的地方老百姓怎么来得起。儿子竟然说这种地方本来就不是为老百姓开的。我听了就生气，剧院不是给老百姓开的，那是给谁开的？回忆起过去北京的普通百姓没几个念过书，可是个个都熟悉历史，明白做人的道理，这些事情是哪儿学来的？都是从剧院里听来的，通

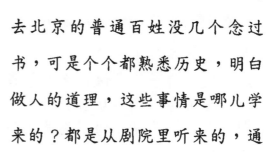

过看戏、聊戏，不知不觉地就有了这些道德观念。可是看看现在坐在我周围的人，这里对他们来说更象是一个酒吧、一个朋友聚会的地方。哎！真不明白为什么花那么多钱到这儿来喝茶、聊天！

因为过两天就是我的生日，从剧院回来以后，儿子还送了我一个生日礼物。打开一看，是《如何投资股票》。儿子劝我退休以后应该看看这些畅销书，才不会落伍。他[4]不提畅销书还好，一提畅销书更让我生气。看看现在的书摊，所谓的畅销书不是和电脑、股票、英语有关的，就

是和什么"隐私"有关的书，再不然就是那些无聊的言情小说。这些书不要说五十年，五年以后还会有人读吗？想想我们年轻时候的畅销书，那才算是真正的好书，对人的一生都有很大的影响。我就是看了那些书以后，才决定去农村工作的。

我们的社会在不断进步，生活也越来越丰富，但是我真担心人们的精神会出现"营养不良"的现象。没想到一个父亲节引起了这么多的感慨，恐怕这个父亲节会让我一生难忘了！

阅读理解 Comprehension Check

8. 这个爸爸多大了？他平常过不过节？为什么要过父亲节？
9. 儿子请爸爸去做什么？爸爸心里觉得怎么样？
10. 现在的剧院和从前的什么地方不同、相同？
11. 儿子认为现在的剧院是给谁开的？怎么知道？爸爸怎么想？为什么？

12. 爸爸后来收到什么生日礼物？他对畅销书有什么看法？
13. 爸爸担心以後的人会有什么问题？

敍述生詞 Vocabulary

	父親節	父亲节	Fùqīnjié	N	Father's Day [father-holiday]
	感慨		gǎnkǎi/ gǎnkài	N/V	feelings, to sign with emotion [to feel-to sigh with emotion]
18.	拒絕	拒绝	jùjué	V	to refuse, to reject, to decline [to resist-to cut off]
	老伴		lǎobàn	N	one's spouse, my wife/husband [old-companion]
	劇院	剧院	jùyuàn	N	theater [drama-facility]
19.	現代化	现代化	xiàndàihuà	V/N	to modernize, modernization [current-period-change]
	打車	打车	dǎ chē	VO	to take a taxi <TW>搭計程車 [to hit-car]
20.	直接		zhíjiē	Adj/ Adv	direct, immediate [straight-to connect]
21.	眼前		yǎnqián	N	before one's eyes, at present [eye-front]
	高樓	高楼	gāolóu	N	tall building [tall-building]
22.	結合	结合	jiéhé	V	to combine, to unite, to integrate [to tie-to combine]
23.	果然		guǒrán	Adv	really, as expected, sure enough [result-(adv marker)]
	舞台		wǔtái	N	stage, arena [dance-platform]
	清朝		qīngcháo	N	Qing dynasty (1644–1911) [Manchu-dynasty]
	水壺	水壶	shuǐhú	N	kettle, watering can [water-pot]
24.	彷佛	仿佛	fǎngfú	V	to seem, as if, to be more or less the same
	菜單	菜单	càidān	N	menu [dish-list]
25.	簡直		jiǎnzhí	Adv	simply [simple-directly]
26.	黑		hēi	Adj	greedy, wicked
27.	抱怨		bàoyuàn	V	to complain, to grumble [to hold-resentment]
	做人		zuòrén	VO	to conduct oneself, to behave, to be an upright person [to act-human]
	不知不覺	不知不觉	bùzhī-bùjué	Adv	unconsciously, unaware [not-to know-not-to feel]
28.	道德		dàodé	N	morality, ethics, morals [way-virtue]

29.	觀念	观念	guānniàn	N	concept	[view-idea]
30.	股票		gǔpiào	N	stock	[share in a company-ticket]
31.	投資	投资	tóuzī	VO	to invest	[to throw-capital]
32.	退休		tuìxiū	VO	to retire	[to retire from-to rest]
33.	暢銷	畅销	chàngxiāo	V	to sell well	[unimpeded-to sell]
34.	攤	摊	tān	N	bookstall, bookstand	
35.	不斷	不断	búduàn	Adv	unceasingly, continuously	[not-to stop]
36.	精神		jīngshén	N	spirit, mind	[essence-spirit]
37.	出現	出现	chūxiàn	V	to appear, to arise, to emerge	[to come out-to appear]
	不良		bùliáng	Adj	bad, harmful	[not-good]

Characters with Many Strokes

感 慨 絕 樓 壺 德 觀 暢 攤 營

詞匯用法 Words in Context

18. 拒絕：拒絕朋友的幫助、邀請；　　拒绝：拒绝朋友的帮助、邀请；
    無法拒絕　　↔答應　　　　　　无法拒绝　　↔答应

    如果朋友請你去酒吧，在什麼情　如果朋友请你去酒吧，在什么情
    況下你會拒絕？　　　　　　　况下你会拒绝？

    你怎麼拒絕別人的邀請？　　　你怎么拒绝别人的邀请？

19. 現代化：科學技術、農業現代　　现代化：科学技术、农业现代
    化；現代化的城市　　　　　化；现代化的城市

    你覺得生活中的一切都需要現代　你觉得生活中的一切都需要现代
    化嗎？為什麼？　　　　　　化吗？为什么？

    你覺得哪個城市是最現代化的城　你觉得哪个城市是最现代化的城
    市？　　　　　　　　　　市？

20. 直接：直接地拒絕；直接說出　　直接：直接地拒绝；直接说出
    來；太不直接　　↔間接　　　来；太不直接　　↔间接

    如果你不喜歡一個人的衣服，你　如果你不喜欢一个人的衣服，你

會不會直接告訴他？

你是不是總是直接發表自己的看法？

21. 眼前：眼前的風景、麻煩、困難

有人認為眼前的風景不如看不到的風景，你同意嗎？

你眼前最大的困難是什麼？

22. 結合：中西結合；把這些經驗結合起來

李安的電影為什麼能吸引那麼多的觀眾？

要把什麼結合起來才能學好中文呢？

23. 果然：果然很難

中文真的像人們說的那麼難學嗎？

電腦對人們的生活有越來越大的影響嗎？

24. 彷彿：彷彿回到了從前；彷彿真的看到了

電腦技術對拍星球大戰那部電影有什麼幫助？

你看小時候照片的時候,有什麼感覺？

25. 簡直：簡直冷死了；簡直不敢相信這是真的

你為什麼還沒寫完功課？

你為什麼從來不和他談話？

会不会直接告诉他？

你是不是总是直接发表自己的看法？

眼前：眼前的风景、麻烦、困难

有人认为眼前的风景不如看不到的风景，你同意吗？

你眼前最大的困难是什么？

结合：中西结合；把这些经验结合起来

李安的电影为什么能吸引那么多的观众？

要把什么结合起来才能学好中文呢？

果然：果然很难

中文真的象人们说的那么难学吗？

电脑对人们的生活有越来越大的影响吗？

彷佛：彷佛回到了从前；彷佛真的看到了

电脑技术对拍星球大战那部电影有什么帮助？

你看小时候照片的时候,有什么感觉？

简直：简直冷死了；简直不敢相信这是真的

你为什么还没写完功课？

你为什么从来不和他谈话？

26. 黑：這個商人很黑；黑店　　　　　　黑：这个商人很黑；黑店

你為什麼從來不去那家有名的餐　　你为什么从来不去那家有名的餐
館吃飯？　　　　　　　　　　　　馆吃饭？

為什麼人們不敢在旅遊景點買太　　为什么人们不敢在旅游景点买太
多東西？　　　　　　　　　　　　多东西？

27. 抱怨：抱怨天氣不好；愛抱怨；　　抱怨：抱怨天气不好；爱抱怨；
有很多抱怨　　　　　　　　　　　有很多抱怨

你覺得自己是不是一個愛抱怨　　　你觉得自己是不是一个爱抱怨
的人，為什麼？　　　　　　　　　的人，为什么？

你覺得你的同學一般會抱怨什　　　你觉得你的同学一般会抱怨什
麼？　　　　　　　　　　　　　　么？

28. 道德：有道德；不道德　　　　　　道德：有道德；不道德

你覺得隨地吐痰tùtán的行為怎麼　　你觉得随地吐痰的行为怎么样？
樣？

什麼樣的行為是不道德的？　　　　什么样的行为是不道德的？

29. 觀念：傳統的觀念；有不同的觀　　观念：传统的观念；有不同的观
念　　　　　　　　　　　　　　　念

你自己有哪些傳統的觀念？　　　　你自己有哪些传统的观念？

朋友之間有的時候為什麼會吵　　　朋友之间有的时候为什么会吵
架？　　　　　　　　　　　　　　架？

30. 股票：買賣股票；股票市場　　　　股票：买卖股票；股票市场

為什麼人們覺得買賣股票很危　　　为什么人们觉得买卖股票很危
險？　　　　　　　　　　　　　　险？

現在哪家公司的股票最貴？　　　　现在哪家公司的股票最贵？

31. 投資：投資股票；去中國投資；　　投资：投资股票；去中国投资；
投資很大　　　　　　　　　　　　投资很大

現在為什麼有很多商人都去中國　　现在为什么有很多商人都去中国
投資？　　　　　　　　　　　　　投资？

你認為開一家快餐店需要花很多　　你认为开一家快餐店需要花很多

錢嗎？   钱吗？

32. 退休：退休年齡；退休了；退休   退休：退休年龄；退休了；退休
老人   老人
一個人多大年紀就應該退休了？   一个人多大年纪就应该退休了？
退休以後，你打算做什麼？   退休以后，你打算做什么？

33. 暢銷：寫了幾本暢銷書；書、專   畅销：写了几本畅销书；书、专
輯很暢銷；不暢銷   辑很畅销；不畅销
現在美國誰的專輯最暢銷？   现在美国谁的专辑最畅销？
你最近看了哪本暢銷書？   你最近看了哪本畅销书？

34. 攤：書攤、小吃攤、服裝攤   摊：书摊、小吃摊、服装摊
你覺得北京哪裏的小吃攤最多、   你觉得北京哪里的小吃摊最多、
最好吃？   最好吃？
你平時喜歡去逛書攤嗎？   你平时喜欢去逛书摊吗？

35. 不斷：不斷發展、進步   不断：不断发展、进步
如果你一直學習中文，你的中文   如果你一直学习中文，你的中文
水平會怎麼樣？   水平会怎么样？
你覺得社會的進步會停下來嗎？   你觉得社会的进步会停下来吗？

36. 精神：豐富的精神生活；沒精   精神：丰富的精神生活；没精
神；物質   神；物质
你覺得對你來說物質生活和精神   你觉得对你来说物质生活和精神
生活，哪個更重要？   生活，哪个更重要？
你最近怎麼這麼沒精神？   你最近怎么这么没精神？

37. 出現：出現了新現象、問題；是   出现：出现了新现象、问题；是
八十年代出現的   八十年代出现的
嬉皮xīpí和雅皮yǎpí出現的時間有   嬉皮和雅皮出现的时间有什么不
什麼不同？   同？
最近出現了哪些暢銷書？   最近出现了哪些畅销书？

自由發揮與課堂活動 Free Discussion and Class Activities

6. 父母過生日的時候，你會怎麼給他們慶祝，會選什麼樣的禮物？為什麼？

父母过生日的时候，你会怎么给他们庆祝，会选什么样的礼物？为什么？

7. 你們家一般怎麼慶祝父親節和母親節？你覺得這兩個節日和父母的生日比，有什麼不同？

你们家一般怎么庆祝父亲节和母亲节？你觉得这两个节日和父母的生日比，有什么不同？

8. 你女/男朋友的媽媽過生日，你為了給他們留下一個好印象需要幫他們慶祝，你打算怎麼做？你這麼做的原因是什麼？

你女/男朋友的妈妈过生日，你为了给他们留下一个好印象需要帮他们庆祝，你打算怎么做？你这么做的原因是什么？

說明 Exposition

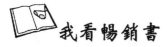 我看暢銷書

近幾年，各地開始流行暢銷書排行榜，但是仔細看看這些所謂的暢銷書，不難發現其中讓人不滿意的地方。

第一，所謂的暢銷書就是在某家書店中銷售量最大的書，可是在這家書店暢銷的書在別家書店也一定暢銷嗎？這是一個值得討論的問題。

第二，中國的四大名著在幾百年後仍然有許多讀者，而今天的暢銷書往往流行幾個月後，就被人們忘了。暢銷時間的長短似乎也可以用來判斷一本書的價值。

第三，不知從何時起，有了「名人出書熱」的現象。這些書多以自傳為主，⁵**先不談**這些名人的經歷是否有公開發表的價值，**就**從書本身**來看**，有些書明顯地因內容不夠而不得不加了很多照片。可悲的是，許多年輕的讀者根本不在乎書的質量如何，只在乎書的作者是不是自己崇拜的偶像。其實，暢銷書之所以暢銷，關鍵還是在讀者。如果讀者能夠挑剔一點，也許暢銷書的質量會⁶**有所**提高。

閱讀理解 Comprehension Check

14. 現在各地都流行什麼？但是這些流行的東西有什麼問題？
15. 什麼是暢銷書？所謂的暢銷書一定「暢銷」嗎？為什麼？
16. 暢銷書一定是好書嗎？為什麼？
17. 現在很多名人都流行做什麼？作者怎麼看這個現象？
18. 作者認為讀者和書的好壞有關係嗎？為什麼？

我看畅销书

近几年，各地开始流行畅销书排行榜，但是仔细看看这些所谓的畅销书，不难发现其中让人不满意的地方。

第一·所谓的畅销书就是在某家书店中销售量最大的书，可是在这家书店畅销的书在别家书店也一定畅销吗？这是一个值得讨论的问题。

第二·中国的四大名著在几百年后仍然有许多读者，而今天的畅销书往往流行几个月后，就被人们忘了。畅销时间的长短似乎也可以用来判断一本书的价值。

第三·不知从何时起，有了"名人出书热"的现象。这些书多以自传为主，[5]先不谈这些名人的经历是否有公开发表的价值，**就**从书本身**来看**，有些书明显地因内容不够而不得不加了很多照片。可悲的是，许多年轻的读者根本不在乎书的质量如何，只在乎书的作者是不是自己崇拜的偶像。

其实，畅销书之所以畅销，关键还是在读者。如果读者能够挑剔一点，也许畅销书的质量会[6]**有所**提高。

阅读理解 Comprehension Check

14. 现在各地都流行什么？但是这些流行的东西有什么问题？
15. 什么是畅销书？所谓的畅销书一定"畅销"吗？为什么？
16. 畅销书一定是好书吗？为什么？
17. 现在很多名人都流行做什么？作者怎么看这个现象？
18. 作者认为读者和书的好坏有关系吗？为什么？

說明生詞 Vocabulary

	排行榜		páihángbǎng	N	a rating board	[row-column-notice]
	銷售量	销售量	xiāoshòuliàng	N	sales volume	[to sell-to sell-amount]
	長短	长短	chángduǎn	N	length	[long-short]
38.	何		hé	Pron/Adv	who?, what?, why?, how? (e.g., 何時、何地、何必)	
39.	熱	热	rè	N	craze, fad	
	自傳	自传	zìzhuàn	N	autobiography	[self-biography]
40.	本身		běnshēn	N	itself, oneself, per se	[original-body]
41.	明顯	明显	míngxiǎn	Adj	clear, obvious	[bright-to show]
42.	質量	质量	zhìliàng	N	<PRC> quality, <TW>品質 pǐnzhí	[quality-amount]
43.	關鍵	关键	guānjiàn	N	key, crux	[critical juncture-key]
44.	有所		yǒusuǒ	Adv	to some extent, somewhat	[to have-that which]

Characters with Many Strokes

榜 銷 售 量 熱 傳 顯 質 關 鍵

詞匯用法 WordsinContext

38. 何：何時、何地、何人；為何　　何：何时、何地、何人；为何
你最近為何看起來總是很累？　　你最近为何看起来总是很累？
你計劃何時去中國旅遊？　　　　你计划何时去中国旅游？

39. 熱：出書、出國、學中文熱；電　　热：出书、出国、学中文热；电
腦專業很熱　　　　　　　　　　脑专业很热
美國出現過什麼熱？　　　　　　美国出现过什么热？
現在什麼專業最熱(門)？　　　　现在什么专业最热(门)？

40. 本身：條件、要求本身；這些書　　本身：条件、要求本身；这些书
本身就有問題　　　　　　　　　本身就有问题

你覺得學校哪些要求本身就有不合理的地方？

有人說很多暢銷書本身的質量不好，只不過宣傳得好罷了！你同意嗎？

你觉得学校哪些要求本身就有不合理的地方？

有人说很多畅销书本身的质量不好，只不过宣传得好罢了！你同意吗？

41. 明顯：很明顯；不太明顯；明顯的不同

你覺得中國人和美國人的飲食習慣很不一樣嗎？

退休的老人生活最明顯的特點是什麼？

明显：很明显；不太明显；明显的不同

你觉得中国人和美国人的饮食习惯很不一样吗？

退休的老人生活最明显的特点是什么？

42. 質量：質量良好、差

日本的電器質量好還是美國的電器質量好？

你買東西的時候重視質量還是重視價格？

质量：质量良好、差

日本的电器质量好还是美国的电器质量好？

你买东西的时候重视质量还是重视价格？

43. 關鍵：很關鍵；問題的關鍵；關鍵人物

要保護環境最關鍵的應該是什麼？

這個大學籃球隊的關鍵人物是誰？

关键：很关键；问题的关键；关键人物

要保护环境最关键的应该是什么？

这个大学篮球队的关键人物是谁？

44. 有所：（句型）

有所：（句型）

自由發揮與課堂活動 Free Discussion and Class Activities

9. 請介紹一本暢銷書，說明暢銷的原因，以及你對這本書的看法。

请介绍一本畅销书，说明畅销的原因，以及你对这本书的看法。

10. 在你的國家，什麼樣的書最暢銷？暢銷的原因是什麼？你覺得

在你的国家，什么样的书最畅销？畅销的原因是什么？你觉得

什麼樣的書才能成為暢銷書？

11. 美國有沒有暢銷書排行榜？哪個排行榜比較可信？為什麼？

12. 你買書或音樂專輯的時候會受到排行榜的影響嗎？什麼樣的影響？

13. 通過看一個社會的暢銷書，你能對這個社會有什麼樣的了解？為什麼？

14. "Living History"在美國是一本有名的暢銷書。請你1）上網找這本書的中文名字，並解釋為什麼這麼翻譯；2）介紹這本書的反對者是怎麼批評這本書的，而支持者是怎麼表揚這本書的；3）看看這本書是否有課文說明部分所介紹的暢銷書的缺點。

什么样的书才能成为畅销书？

美国有没有畅销书排行榜？哪个排行榜比较可信？为什么？

你买书或音乐专辑的时候会受到排行榜的影响吗？什么样的影响？

通过看一个社会的畅销书，你能对这个社会有什么样的了解？为什么？

"Living History"在美国是一本有名的畅销书。请你1）上网找这本书的中文名字，并解释为什么这么翻译；2）介绍这本书的反对者是怎么批评这本书的，而支持者是怎么表扬这本书的；3）看看这本书是否有课文说明部分所介绍的畅销书的缺点。

應用詞 Productive Vocabulary

◎By Grammatical Categories

Nouns/Pronouns/Measure Words

堆	duī	pile, heap, to pile up
攤	tān	bookstall, bookstand
熱	rè	craze, fad
何	hé	who?, what?, why?, how?
眼前	yǎnqián	before one's eyes, at present
本身	běnshēn	itself, oneself, per se
讀者	dúzhě	reader
道德	dàodé	morality, ethics, morals

觀念	guānniàn	concept
精神	jīngshén	spirit, mind
質量	zhǐliàng	<PRC> quality
關鍵	guānjiàn	key, crux
股票	gǔpiào	stock
回憶	huíyì	recollection, to recall

Verbs/Stative Verbs/Adjectives

播	bō	to broadcast
搶	qiǎng	to fight with, to snatch
敢	gǎn	to dare
彷佛	fǎngfú	to seem, as if, to be more or less the same
改編	gǎibiān	to adapt, to rearrange, to revise
發表	fābiǎo	to publish, to issue
暢銷	chàngxiāo	to sell well
參與	cānyù	to participate in
結合	jiéhé	to combine, to unite, to integrate
出現	chūxiàn	to appear, to arise, to emerge
投資	tóuzī	to invest
退休	tuìxiū	to retire
打折	dǎzhé	to have a discount

打賭	dǎdǔ	to make a bet, to bet
拒絕	jùjué	to refuse, to reject, to decline
抱怨	bàoyuàn	to complain, to grumble
現代化	xiàndàihuà	to modernize, modernization
下定義	xià dìngyì	to give a definition of, to define
黑	hēi	greedy, wicked
專門	zhuānmén	special, specialized
明顯	míngxiǎn	clear, obvious
直接	zhíjiē	direct, immediate
恰當	qiàdàng	appropriate, fitting, proper, suitable
實際	shíjì	practical, reality

Adverbs and Others

某	mǒu	certain, some
僅僅	jǐnjǐn	only, merely
果然	guǒrán	really, as expected, sure enough

簡直	jiǎnzhí	simply
不斷	búduàn	unceasingly, continuously
有所	yǒusuǒ	to some extent, somewhat

理解詞 Receptive Vocabulary

◎By Grammatical Categories

Nouns/Pronouns/Measure Words

市	shì	market, city		劇院	jùyuàn	theater
集	jí	volume, episode (as in a TV series)		高樓	gāolóu	tall building
代	dài	generation		舞台	wǔtái	stage, arena
長短	chángduǎn	length		菜單	càidān	menu
感慨	gǎnkǎi/gǎnkài	feelings, to sign with emotion		水壺	shuǐhú	kettle, watering can
自傳	zìzhuàn	autobiography		電視劇	diànshìjù	TV series
名著	míngzhù	famous book/work		電視台	diànshìtái	TV station
文章	wénzhāng	essay, article, literary works		排行榜	páihángbǎng	a rating board
言情	yánqíng	love and romance		銷售量	xiāoshòuliàng	sales volume
作家	zuòjiā	writer		父親節	Fùqīnjié	Father's Day
老伴	lǎobàn	one's spouse, my wife/husband				

Verbs/Stative Verbs/Adjectives

打車	dǎ chē	<PRC>to take a taxi		不良	bùliáng	bad, harmful
做人	zuòrén	to conduct oneself, to behave, to be an upright person		老掉牙	lǎodiàoyá	old and shabby, obsolete

Adverbs and Others

不知不覺	bùzhī-bùjué	unconsciously, unaware

本课词表 Chapter Vocabulary

◎By Pinyin

Words with asterisk* are productive vocabulary which needs to be memorized and studied for its usage.

duī*	堆	pile, to pile up		búduàn*	不斷	unceasingly
bàoyuàn*	抱怨	to complain, to grumble		bùliáng	不良	bad, harmful
běnshēn*	本身	itself, oneself, per se		bùzhī-bùjué	不知不覺	unconsciously
bō*	播	to broadcast		càidān	菜單	menu
				cānyù*	参与	to participate in

chángduǎn	长短	length
chàngxiāo*	畅销	to sell well
chūxiàn*	出现	to appear, to arise
dǎ chē	打车	<PRC>to take a taxi
dǎdǔ*	打赌	to bet
dài	代	generation
dǎzhé*	打折	to have a discount
diànshìjù	电视剧	TV series
diànshìtái	电视台	TV station
dàodé*	道德	morality, ethics, morals
dúzhě*	读者	reader
fābiǎo*	发表	to publish, to issue
fǎngfú*	仿佛	to seem, as if
Fùqīnjié	父亲节	Father's Day
gǎibiān*	改编	to adapt, to rearrange, to revise
gǎn*	敢	to dare
gǎnkǎi/gǎnkài	感慨	feelings, to sign with emotion
gāolóu	高楼	tall building
guānjiàn*	关键	key, crux
guānniàn*	观念	concept
guǒrán*	果然	really, sure enough
gǔpiào*	股票	stock
hé*	何	who?, what?, why?, how?
hēi*	黑	greedy, wicked
huíyì*	回忆	recollection, to recall
jí	集	volume, episode (as in a TV series)
jiǎnzhí*	简直	simply
jiéhé*	结合	to combine, to unite, to integrate
jīngshén*	精神	spirit, mind
jǐnjǐn*	仅仅	only, merely
jùjué*	拒绝	to refuse, to reject, to decline

jùyuàn	剧院	theater
lǎobàn	老伴	one's spouse, my wife/husband
lǎodiàoyá	老掉牙	old and shabby, obsolete
míngxiǎn*	明显	clear, obvious
míngzhù	名著	famous book
mǒu*	某	certain, some
páihángbǎng	排行榜	a rating board
qiàdàng*	恰当	appropriate, fitting, proper,
qiǎng*	抢	to fight with, to snatch
rè*	热	craze, fad
shì	市	market, city
shíjì*	实际	practical, reality
shuǐhú	水壶	kettle, watering can
tān*	摊	bookstall, bookstand
tóuzī*	投资	to invest
tuìxiū*	退休	to retire
wénzhāng	文章	essay, article, literary works
wǔtái	舞台	stage, arena
xià dìngyì*	下定义	to give a definition of, to define
xiàndàihuà*	现代化	to modernize, modernization
xiāoshòuliàng	销售量	sales volume
yǎnqián*	眼前	before one's eyes, at present
yánqíng	言情	love and romance
yǒusuǒ*	有所	to some extent
zhíjiē*	直接	direct, immediate
zhìliàng*	质量	<PRC> quality
zhuānmén*	专门	special, specialized
zìzhuàn	自传	autobiography
zuòjiā	作家	writer
zuòrén	做人	to conduct oneself, to behave,

語法和用法 Grammar and Usage

Pay attention to the function of the structure and then study the example sentences. When blanks are provided, either answer the questions or complete the sentences.

1. Expressing union

連A帶B⋯	lián…dài…	A as well as B; A and B

- 你看這些，連《水滸》帶《三國》才五十塊，我還不趁便宜多買點！

1. 上個週末你做了什麼？

   上個週末我和朋友逛商店的時候，碰到了大減價，所以連吃的，帶用的，買了一大堆。

   上个周末你做了什么？

   上个周末我和朋友逛商店的时候，碰到了大减价，所以连吃的，带用的，买了一大堆。

   What did you do this weekend?

   This weekend when my friend and I went window-shopping, we saw a big sale. So, we bought a lot of stuff to eat as well as stuff to use.

2. 昨天的晚會怎麼樣？

   昨天的晚會非常熱鬧，每個人都連說帶唱，一直鬧到半夜。

   昨天的晚会怎么样？

   昨天的晚会非常热闹，每个人都连说带唱，一直闹到半夜。

   How was the party last night?

   The party last night was a lot of fun. Everyone spoke and sang and carried on till midnight.

3. 她的東西都收拾得很好嗎？

   不，她每天做完功課以後，就連書帶本子一起扔進書包，結果第二天經常找不到要用的東西。

   她的东西都收拾得很好吗？

   不，她每天做完功课以后，就连书带本子一起扔进书包，结果第二天经常找不到要用的东西。

   Does she clean up her things well?

   No, after finishing her homework each day, she throws her books and notebooks into her bag. As a result, she always has trouble finding the things she needs the next day.

4. 我真的難以相信，你可以在商　　　我真的难以相信，你可以在商
　　店裏逛一整天。　　　　　　　　店里逛一整天。

---

5. 你知道在這裏租一輛汽車貴不　　　你知道在这里租一辆汽车贵不
　　貴？　　　　　　　　　　　　　贵？

---

6. 昨天你們去聽張學友的音樂　　　　昨天你们去听张学友的音乐
　　會，怎麼樣？　　　　　　　　　会，怎么样？

The pattern 連A帶B… is used to express unison. Though its meaning is similar to 和、跟, it's not a conjunction and its usage is more limited. A and B have to be parallel: either both nouns or verbs. So, one can use 連N帶N or 連V帶V, but never 連 VO帶VO. To use the pattern as a conjuction is incorrect, e.g., 我連買了鞋子帶買了 衣服, which should be rephrased as 我連鞋子帶衣服都買了. The wrongly worded sentence 這裏租車連很貴帶服務不好 should be rephrased as 這裏租車不貴，租一 天的車連租金帶保險才五十塊 'It's not expensive to rent a car here. It costs only fifty dollars to rent a car for a day, including rent and insurance.' Even if both A and B are parallel with respect to nouns or verbs, their forms must be similar as well. It's odd to say 這家店很大，連衣服帶吃的都買得到. Instead, one should say 這家店很大， 連穿的、用的、帶吃的都買得到 'This store is big, and one can buy anything including things to wear, to use, as well as to eat.'

2. Expressing an additional condition

S 不僅僅(是)…也/都…　bùjǐnjǐn(shì)…yě/dōu	S not only…but also…
不僅僅是A…B也/都…	Not only A….but also B….

* 大家可以很快地發表對某一篇文章的看法，這樣不僅僅是看別人的作
　品，也有參與感。

1. 你整天往書市跑，　　你整天往书市跑，　　You go to the bookfair all the
　　去那兒有什麼好　　　去那儿有什么好　　time. What's good about going
　　處？　　　　　　　　处？　　　　　　　there?

我每次去書市都可以買很多書，當然不僅僅是因為書市的書便宜，也是因為那些名著值得收藏shōucáng。

我每次去书市都可以买很多书，当然不仅仅是因为书市的书便宜，也是因为那些名著值得收藏。

Every time I go to the bookfair, I can buy a lot of books. Of course, this is not only because the books there are inexpensive, but also because the famous books are worth collecting.

2. 京劇為什麼能吸引人？

京剧为什么能吸引人？

Why is Beijing opera so appealing?

京劇是一種古老的藝術，演員的演唱和表演都非常精彩，所以京劇不僅僅讓觀眾大飽耳福，也讓大家大飽眼福。

京剧是一种古老的艺术，演员的演唱和表演都非常精彩，所以京剧不仅仅让观众大饱耳福，也让大家大饱眼福。

Beijing opera is a kind of ancient art. The singing and performance of the actors are excellent, so it not only gives the audience a listening treat, but also provides a feast for the eyes.

3. 很多名歌星都抱怨什麼？

很多名歌星都抱怨什么？

What are the complaints that many famous singers have?

很多歌星都抱怨出了名以後，反而受到了更多的限制，他們的公司不僅僅為他們設計形象，連他們什麼時候說什麼話，也要由公司安排。

很多歌星都抱怨出了名以后，反而受到了更多的限制，他们的公司不仅仅为他们设计形象，连他们什么时候说什么话，也要由公司安排。

Many singers complain that after becoming famous, they are put under a lot of constraints. Their company not only designs their image for them, but even arranges when they can talk and what they should say.

4. 周潤發在中國是個非常有名的演員，有很多的崇拜者，不知道美國人知不知道他？

周润发在中国是个非常有名的演员，有很多的崇拜者，不知道美国人知不知道他？

5. 你覺得一個非常懂電腦的人，
   是不是有可能成為黑客？

   你觉得一个非常懂电脑的人，
   是不是有可能成为黑客？

---

6. 我注意飲食習慣，而且不吃零
   食，這樣能不能減肥呢？

   我注意饮食习惯，而且不吃零
   食，这样能不能减肥呢？

As the pattern 不僅僅(是)⋯也/都⋯ expresses additional condition or proposition, what follows 不僅僅(是) and 也/都 should be similar in form and meaning (examples 1 and 2). It's odd to say 當黑客不僅僅是很簡單的工作，也可以在家做 'Being a hacker is not only a simple job, but also you can do it at home.' An optional 而且 can go before 也/都. This is a variant form of the pattern 不僅⋯而且也/都⋯ (L2, G2). The double 僅 in this pattern places more emphasis on the first condition. Note that if there is only one subject, it often goes before 不僅僅是. If there are two different subjects, the subject of the first clause goes after 不僅僅是.

3. Expressing union

S 把A和B 聯繫起來	bǎ... hé...liánxìqǐlái	to connect A and B
S 把A和B 結合起來	bǎ... hé...jiéhéqǐlái	to tie A and B together
S 把A和B 加起來	bǎ... hé...jiāqǐlái	to add A and B together

● 下了車，我實在沒辦法把眼前這座高樓和傳統的劇院聯繫起來。

1. 李明從美國回來以
   後，變了嗎？

   李明从美国回来以
   后，变了吗？

   Has Li Ming changed since
   he's come back from the U.S.?

   變化可大了！他變
   得安靜而且謙虛
   qiānxū，我真的沒辦
   法把現在的李明和
   從前的李明聯繫起
   來。

   变化可大了，他变
   得安静而且谦虚，
   我真的没办法把现
   在的李明和从前的
   李明联系起来。

   He has changed a lot. He's
   become quiet and modest. I
   really can't picture Li Ming
   now with the Li Ming of old.

2. 一般人對李安的電

   一般人对李安的电

   What do people think of Lee
   Ang's movies?

影有什麼看法？

影有什么看法？

雖然對李安的電影，觀眾的看法很不相同，但是大家都同意，李安在拍電影的時候把東方文化和西方文化結合起來，所以可以吸引很多西方的觀眾。

虽然对李安的电影，观众的看法很不相同，但是大家都同意，李安在拍电影的时候把东方文化和西方文化结合起来，所以可以吸引很多西方的观众。

Although the audience has different views of Lee Ang's movies, everyone agrees that Lee Ang combines eastern and western culture when he shoots movies. Thus, his movies are able to attract a large audience in the West.

3. 為什麼看京劇的人越來越少了？我們應該怎麼辦？

为什么看京剧的人越来越少了？我们应该怎么办？

Why is the number of people seeing Beijing opera becoming less and less? What should we do?

京劇雖然是中國古老的傳統藝術，但是由於它的節奏太慢，不適合現代觀眾的口味，所以要讓京劇繼續發展的話，應該把傳統藝術與現代藝術結合起來。

京剧虽然是中国古老的传统艺术，但是由于它的节奏太慢，不适合现代观众的口味，所以要让京剧继续发展的话，应该把传统艺术与现代艺术结合起来。

Although Beijing opera is China's traditional art, its rhythm is too slow for the taste of the modern audience. So, if we want to keep Beijing opera alive, we should combine traditional art with modern art.

4. 我對中國的文化感興趣，可是我應該怎麼去了解它呢？

我对中国的文化感兴趣，可是我应该怎么去了解它呢？

5. 為什麼中國和美國做生意的時候，總要考慮政治的問題呢？

为什么中国和美国做生意的时候，总要考虑政治的问题呢？

6. 為了減肥，我已經節食一個月

为了减肥，我已经节食一个月

了，可是一點效果都沒有，我　　了，可是一点效果都没有，我
該怎麼辦呢？　　　　　　　　　该怎么办呢？

The pattern S 把A和B 聯繫/結合/加起來 is used to express unison. 聯繫 indicates the association between A and B, e.g., 他受過很高的教育，我很難把他這種人和搞破壞的黑客聯繫起來 'He is highly educated. It's hard for me to associate someone like him with those destructive hackers.' Yet, 結合 emphasizes the combination of A and B, e.g., 把運動和飲食結合起來，減肥才有最好的效果 'Losing weight is best achieved with exercise and diet combined.' 加起來 is used mostly in a mathematical context.

4. Expressing a triggering precondition

S 不VO…（還好）， 一VO…（就/才）…	bù...(háihǎo), yī...(jiù/cái)	If S hadn't VO, it would be fine; once S VO …

* 他不提暢銷書還好，一提暢銷書更讓我生氣。

1.	你看書看了這麼久，為什麼不休息一下？	你看书看了这么久，为什么不休息一下？	You have been reading for such a long time. Why don't you take a break?
	這本書的故事情節非常精彩，不看還好，一看就放不下了，非把它看完不可。	这本书的故事情节非常精彩，不看还好，一看就放不下了，非把它看完不可。	The story of this book is brilliant. If I hadn't read it, it would have been fine, but once I started reading, I couldn't put it down. I've got to finish reading this book.
2.	你跟那個推銷員買了什麼東西？	你跟那个推销员买了什么东西？	What did you buy from that salesman?
	那個推銷員，一直向我推銷一種清潔用品，不用不知道，一用才發現真靈！	那个推销员，一直向我推销一种清洁用品，不用不知道，一用才发现真灵！	That salesman talked to me about a kind of cleaning product. I knew nothing about it before I used it, but once I tried, I found that it really does work.
3.	你現在的課上得怎	你现在的课上得怎	How are your classes going

麼樣？　　　　　　　　么样？　　　　　　　　now?

這個學期我選了五　　　这个学期我选了五　　　This semester I signed up for
門課，每天都有很　　　门课，每天都有很　　　five classes. I have so much
多作業，不想還　　　　多作业，不想还　　　　homework every day. I feel
好，一想我就覺得　　　好，一想我就觉得　　　fine when I don't think about
頭疼。　　　　　　　　头疼。　　　　　　　　it, but as soon as I do, my head
　　　　　　　　　　　　　　　　　　　　　　　hurts.

4. 這對夫妻的感情非常糟糕，　　　这对夫妻的感情非常糟糕，

___不超乎也好_____

5. 李明很少去商店買東西，可是　　　李明很少去商店买东西，可是

_____

6. 我的同屋平時很少說話，不過　　　我的同屋平时很少说话，不过

___不開口也好_____一開口及编即氣話。___

The pattern 不VO…，一VO…(就/才) expresses a triggering precondition and how
one will react if the action indicated by VO is taken. There are often 還好 at the end
of the first clause (see examples 1 and 3) and 就 in the second clause. Occasionally, 才
may be used if the perceived lateness of an action is emphasized (example 2).
Compare this to 一…就是 (L9, G1) and 要不是…也 (L12, G3).

5. Expressing an alternative aspect

先不談X，就Y來看	xiānbùtán, jiù…láikàn	to say nothing of X, just looking
先不談X，就Y而言	xiānbùtán, jiù…éryán	at Y

- 先不談這些名人的經歷是否有公開發表的價值，就從書本身來看，有
  些書明顯地因內容不夠而不得不加了很多照片。

1. 你看不看暢銷書？　　　你看不看畅销书？　　　Do you read best-sellers?

  我從來不看現在這　　　我从来不看现在这　　　I've never read today's so-
  些所謂的暢銷書，　　　些所谓的畅销书，　　　called best-sellers. To say
  先不談這些書到底　　　先不谈这些书到底　　　nothing of how long they stay
  能暢銷多久，就從　　　能畅销多久，就从　　　on the list, their subject matter
  　　　　　　　　　　　　　　　　　　　　　　doesn't interest me.

書的內容來看，就
不能引起我的興
趣。

书的内容来看，就
不能引起我的兴
趣。

2. 我想主修歷史。

我想主修历史。

I want to major in history.

你為什麼要選擇歷
史專業？先不談以
後能不能找到工
作，就從你的興趣
來看，你喜歡的並
不是歷史。

你为什么要选择历
史专业？先不谈以
后能不能找到工
作，就从你的兴趣
来看，你喜欢的并
不是历史。

Why do you want to choose
history as your major? To say
nothing of whether or not
you'll be able to find a job
later on, just looking at your
interests, what you like is
really not history.

3. 如果有錢的話，你
要買什麼車？

如果有钱的话，你
要买什么车？

If you had money, what car
would you buy?

如果有錢的話，我
要買日本車，它的
價格先不談，就從
質量來看，日本車
比美國車好多了。

如果有钱的话，我
要买日本车，它的
价格先不谈，就从
质量来看，日本车
比美国车好多了。

If I had money, I would buy a
Japanese car. To say nothing of
their price, just looking at their
quality, Japanese cars are much
better than American cars.

4. 下個星期是爸爸的生日，我們
出去慶祝呢，還是請朋友到家
裏來慶祝？

下个星期是爸爸的生日，我们
出去庆祝呢，还是请朋友到家
里来庆祝？

5. 你每天早上起得那麼早去跳交
際舞，真不明白那有什麼好跳
的？

你每天早上起得那么早去跳交
际舞，真不明白那有什么好跳
的？

6. 這些年輕人怎麼了？什麼音樂
不聽，非要聽搖滾樂，我一點
也不喜歡。

这些年轻人怎么了？什么音乐
不听，非要听摇滚乐，我一点
也不喜欢。

The pattern 先不談 X，就 Y 來看 expresses an alternative aspect. So, both X and Y should indicate different aspects of a topic, e.g., 先不談在哪兒慶祝生日，就時間來看，我覺得五點開始比較好 'To say nothing of the place for celebrating birthday, just looking at the time, I think it's better to start at five.' Remember 先不談 can go before or after X (example 3) and X often contains a question word (example 1) or an A-not-A form (example 2). 就 Y 而言 is a more literary counterpart of 就 Y 來看.

6. Expressing emphasis

⋯有所 V	yǒusuǒ V	there is V

● 如果讀者能夠挑剔一點，也許暢銷書的質量會有所提高。

1. 現在人們的生活水平提高了嗎？為什麼？

   現在人们的生活水平提高了吗？为什么？

   Have people's living standard risen nowadays? Why?

   從中國實行開放的政策以來，人們的生活水平已有所提高。

   从中国实行开放的政策以来，人们的生活水平已有所提高。

   Since China implemented an open policy, the people's living standard has improved.

2. 你對中國的了解多嗎？

   你对中国的了解多吗？

   Do you know a lot about China?

   從前我對中國的了解非常少，但是在學中文的時候，我交了不少中國朋友，現在我對中國文化已經有所了解。

   从前我对中国的了解非常少，但是在学中文的时候，我交了不少中国朋友，现在我对中国文化已经有所了解。

   Before I knew very little about China, but when I studied Chinese, I made quite a few Chinese friends. Now I have some understanding of Chinese culture.

3. 你和你的同屋各方面都一樣嗎？你們

   你和你的同屋各方面都一样吗？你们

   Do you and your roommate share many things in common? How is your relationship?

的關係好嗎？　　　　的关系好吗？

我和我同屋在生活習慣、學習方法方面有所不同，但是我們仍然是非常好的朋友。	我和我同屋在生活习惯、学习方法方面有所不同，但是我们仍然是非常好的朋友。	My roommate and I are quite different in terms of our life style and study methods. Yet, we are still very good friends.

4.　我覺得以前網絡上的文章質量都不怎麼好，現在怎麼樣？好一些了嗎？

　　我觉得以前网络上的文章质量都不怎么好，现在怎么样？好一些了吗？

5.　學了這麼長時間的中文，你覺得你的中文水平提高了嗎？

　　学了这么长时间的中文，你觉得你的中文水平提高了吗？

6.　改革開放以後，中國的經濟發展了嗎？

　　改革开放以后，中国的经济发展了吗？

The pattern ⋯有所V is a more formal expression to indicate emphasis. The verbs after 有所 are always two syllables, e.g., 進步、提高、發展、了解、改變、不同. There should not be anything between 有所 and the verb, or after the verb. So, each of the following sentences are wrong: 我的中文水平有所很提高; 我的中文水平有所好多了; 我的中文水平有所提高了很多 'My level in Chinese has improved a lot.'

Note this pattern cannot be negated by using 沒有 or 不. One cannot say 我的中文水平沒有所提高. To negate, just use a verb with negative meaning, e.g., 他一直忙著打工，沒時間好好念書，所以各門功課都有所退步 'He has been busy working part-time and has no time to study, so his study in every subject is slipping.' Compare this to the use of 所V (的N) '(the N) that was V-ed.'

背景常識 Background Notes

1. 書店：書店一般分為專業性書店和綜合書店。北京圖書大廈是目前北京最大的書店。風入松是在北京大學校園邊上的一家書店，這家書店因為有很濃的文化味道，所以受到了很多讀者的歡迎。中國書店是在北京城市中心的一家老牌書店，以賣古書為主。三聯書店也是著名的書店之一，有很多和藝術有關的書。這家書店裏也有咖啡屋和好聽的音樂，讀者可以邊喝咖啡邊讀書，環境非常舒服。

2. 電視連續劇：在中國幾乎每個電視台在每天的黃金時間（晚上八點到十點）都會放電視連續劇。以前香港和台灣的連續劇佔主要地位，但是近些年來，大陸自己的電視連續劇越來越多，質量也越來越高。在連續劇中，那些反映老百姓真實生活的片子很受歡迎。

3. 網絡文學：網絡文學現在很容易找到，網絡文章一般都比較短小，作者寫完以後可以很快地放到網上，讀者也可以隨時說明自己的感受。書庫是一個不錯的了解文學著作和網路文學的網站，你不妨去看看 www.shuku.net。

4. 生日晚會：老人過生日的時候，孩子一般要回家陪老人吃飯，而且要吃長壽麵。中國人習慣不給老人慶祝帶10的生日，比如80、90，但是要慶祝類似69、79、89這樣的生日。老人還不可以慶祝73和84歲的生日，因為孔子是73歲去世的，而老子是84歲去世的，所以中國人認為73和84是兩個不吉利的年紀，不要慶祝。年輕人過生日沒有什麼特別的講究，一般來說年輕人會為自己的生日舉辦晚會，酒吧和自己的家是比較常去的地方。

背景常识 Background Notes

1. 书店：书店一般分为专业性书店和综合书店。北京图书大厦是目前北京最大的书店。风入松是在北京大学校园边上的一家书店，这家书店因为有很浓的文化味道，所以受到了很多读者的欢迎。中国书店是在北京城市中心的一家老牌书店，以卖古书为主。三联书店也是著名的书店之一，有很多和艺术有关的书。这家书店里也有咖啡屋和好听的音乐，读者可以边喝咖啡边读书，环境非常舒服。

2. 电视连续剧：在中国几乎每个电视台在每天的黄金时间（晚上八点到十点）都会放电视连续剧。以前香港和台湾的连续剧占主要地位，但是近些年来，大陆自己的电视连续剧越来越多，质量也越来越高。在连续剧中，那些反映老百姓真实生活的片子很受欢迎。

3. 网络文学：网络文学现在很容易找到，网络文章一般都比较短小，作者写完以后可以很快地放到网上，读者也可以随时说明自己的感受。书库是一个不错的了解文学著作和网路文学的网站，你不妨去看看 www.shuku.net。

4. 生日晚会：老人过生日的時候，孩子一般要回家陪老人吃饭，而且要吃长寿面。中国人习惯不给老人庆祝带10的生日，比如80、90，但是要庆祝类似69、79、89这样的生日。老人还不可以庆祝73和84岁的生日，因为孔子是73岁去世的，而老子是84岁去世的，所以中国人认为73和84是两个不吉利的年纪，不要庆祝。年轻人过生日没有什么特别的讲究，一般来说年轻人会为自己的生日举办晚会，酒吧和自己的家是比较常去的地方。

第七課　真相哪兒找？

Theme: Advertisements and Commercials

Communicative Objectives
- Talking about being tricked
- Returning a product to a store
- Narrating an experience of selling something

Skill Focus
- Comprehending a report on commercials

Grammar Focus
- 難道S…不成/嗎
- (在)…以內/以外/以上/以下
- …毫無N/毫不V
- S 應該…才對/才是/才好/才行
- 一是…，二是…
- 以X(為Y)(來V)
  把X當作/作為Y

Problem Scenario

You wanted to buy a used laser printer and read ads on the newspaper carefully, in fear of getting gypped. You noticed a lot of hyperbole and gimmicks and thus, decided to go to a store instead to buy the printer. Unfortunately, the printer broke down after one month and you have lost your letter of guarantee. You want to return the printer to the store, and get a refund, if not for the full amount. What would you say to the salesman? How can you get your money back?

對話 Dialogue

(1)Talking about being tricked

記者張新的太太劉雲和李明的媽媽周紅在討論廣告。

張太太：聽說昨天有一家商場開業，所有的東西全打八折，你沒去看看嗎？

李太太：別提了，什麼八折，不過是騙人的廣告罷了。

張太太：[1]難道他們沒有打折**不成**？

李太太：不能說沒有，我看上了一件襯衣，原來賣兩百，打折以後是一百六。

張太太：那不是挺不錯的嗎？

李太太：可是我後來又去了旁邊的一家店，看見了一件完全一樣的襯衣，只賣一百二。

張太太：哎，現在的商家真是不像話，為了吸引顧客什麼辦法都用。上個月我也是看到一個廣告說他們那裏的皮衣「買一送一」。我覺得這真不錯，買一件給老公，送的那件就是我的。

李太太：結果你們買的時候他們卻不送。

張太太：他們送是送，不過送的不是皮衣，而是一件襯衣，他們說這也是「買一送一」！

李太太：看來，現在的廣告越來越不可信了，以後可要小心，別再上當了！

閱讀理解Comprehension Check

1. 張太太勸李太太去做什麼？為什麼李太太不去？
2. 張太太也有上當的經驗嗎？她是怎麼上當的？

(1)Talking about being tricked

记者张新的太太刘云和李明的妈妈周红在讨论广告。

张太太：听说昨天有一家商场开业，所有的东西全打八折，你没去看看吗？

李太太：别提了，什么八折，不过是骗人的广告罢了。

张太太：[1]难道他们没有打折**不成**？

李太太：不能说没有，我看上了一件衬衣，原来卖两百，打折以后是一百六。

张太太：那不是挺不错的吗？

李太太：可是我后来又去了旁边的一家店，看见了一件完全一样的衬衣，只卖一百二。

张太太：哎，现在的商家真是不像话，为了吸引顾客什么办法都用。上个月我也是看到一个广告说他们那的皮衣"买一送一"。我觉得这真不错，买一件给老公，送的那件就是我的。

李太太：结果你们买的时候他们却不送。

张太太：他们送是送，不过送的不是皮衣，而是一件衬衣，他们说这也是"买一送一"！

李太太：看来，现在的广告越来越不可信了，以后可要小心，别再上当了！

阅读理解 Comprehension Check

3. 张太太劝李太太去做什么？为什么李太太不去？
4. 张太太也有上当的经验吗？她是怎么上当的？

對話一生詞 Vocabulary

Study the numbered vocabulary (productive vocabulary) for its usage. The unnumbered items (receptive vocabulary) are to facilitate reading comprehension.

◎By Order of Appearance

	真相		zhēnxiàng	N	real situation, the real facts/truth	[true-appearance]
1.	廣告	广告	guǎnggào	N	advertisement	[wide-to announce]
	商場	商场	shāngchǎng	N	market, bazaar	[business-site]
2.	開業	开业	kāiyè	VO	<PRC> to start business <TW>開張	[to open-business]
3.	全		quán	Adj/Adv	全部、完全	
4.	別提了		bié tí le	IE	<口> 別說了	[not-to mention-(particle)]
5.	（欺）騙	（欺）骗	(qī)piàn	V	to deceive, to fool	[to cheat-to swindle]
6.	看上		kànshàng	RV	to take fancy to, to settle on	[to look-up]
	襯衣	衬衣	chènyī	N	<PRC> shirt <TW>襯衫	[shirt-clothes]
	商家		shāngjiā	N	merchant, business person	[business-person]
7.	顧客	顾客	gùkè	N	customer, shopper, client	[to look after-customer]
	皮衣		píyī	N	fur/leather clothing	[leather-clothes]
	買一送一	买一送一	mǎi yī sòngyī	IE	buy one, get one free	[to buy-one-to give as a present-one]
	老公		lǎogōng	N	先生、丈夫 ↔老婆	[prefix-husband]
8.	可信		kěxìn	Adj	可以相信	[to be worth-to believe]
9.	上當	上当	shàngdàng	VO	to be taken in, to be fooled/cheated	[to submit-trick]

Characters with Many Strokes

真　廣　場　業　提　欺　騙　襯　顧　當

詞彙用法 Words in Context

1. 廣告：登廣告；做廣告；播廣告　　　广告：登广告；做广告；播广告
    你覺得哪個廣告很成功？　　　　　你觉得哪个广告很成功？
    一個公司做廣告的方法有哪些？　　一个公司做广告的方法有哪些？

2. 開業：何時開業；剛剛開業；開　　开业：何时开业；刚刚开业；开
    不了業　　　　　　　　　　　　不了业
    那家中式快餐店是何時開業的？　　那家中式快餐店是何时开业的？
    一個商店剛剛開業的時候一般會　　一个商店刚刚开业的时候一般会
    做什麼？　　　　　　　　　　　做什么？

3. 全：全國、場、世界、校、班　　　全：全国、场、世界、校、班
    現在只有發展中國家有環境污染　　现在只有发展中国家有环境污染
    的問題嗎？　　　　　　　　　　的问题吗？
    這兒的學生都喜歡看籃球比賽　　　这儿的学生都喜欢看篮球比赛
    嗎？　　　　　　　　　　　　　吗？

4. 別提了：　　　　　　　　　　　别提了：
    上次的考試，你考得怎麼樣？　　　上次的考试，你考得怎么样？
    最近這個學校足球隊的表現如　　　最近这个学校足球队的表现如
    何？　　　　　　　　　　　　　何？

5. (欺)騙：騙人的方法；欺騙顧　　　(欺)骗：骗人的方法；欺骗顾
    客；被人騙；被欺騙；受騙；騙　　客；被人骗；被欺骗；受骗；骗
    子　　　　　　　　　　　　　　子
    你覺得商店什麼樣的廣告是欺騙　　你觉得商店什么样的广告是欺骗
    顧客的？　　　　　　　　　　　顾客的？
    你被別人騙過嗎？　　　　　　　你被别人骗过吗？

6. 看上：看上一件大衣；看上了那　　看上：看上一件大衣；看上了那
    個漂亮的女孩；看不上　　　　　个漂亮的女孩；看不上
    你怎麼一逛街，就要買那麼多東　　你怎么一逛街，就要买那么多东
    西呢？　　　　　　　　　　　　西呢？

小李的性格那麼好，你怎麼卻看
不上她？

小李的性格那么好，你怎么却看
不上她？

7. 顧客：對顧客很熱情；顧客很
多；多年的老顧客

顾客：对顾客很热情；顾客很
多；多年的老顾客

你覺得哪家商店的服務員對顧客
最熱情？

你觉得哪家商店的服务员对顾客
最热情？

你覺得顧客應不應該挑剔？

你觉得顾客应不应该挑剔？

8. 可信：廣告一般不可信；這件事
情不可信

可信：广告一般不可信；这件事
情不可信

你買東西的時候會受廣告的影響
嗎？為什麼？

你买东西的时候会受广告的影响
吗？为什么？

你覺得什麼人的話不可信？

你觉得什么人的话不可信？

9. 上當：上過當；上過朋友的當

上当：上过当；上过朋友的当

在什麼時候顧客容易上商家的
當？

在什么时候顾客容易上商家的
当？

在四月一號的時候，大家為什麼
都那麼小心？

在四月一号的时候，大家为什么
都那么小心？

自由發揮與課堂活動 Free Discussion and Class Activities

1. 買哪些東西的時候你會比較相信
廣告，而買哪些東西的時候比較
不相信廣告？為什麼？廣告在你
的生活中扮演什麼樣的角色？

买哪些东西的时候你会比较相信
广告，而买哪些东西的时候比较
不相信广告？为什么？广告在你
的生活中扮演什么样的角色？

2. 你覺得哪一類的廣告中不可信的
因素最多？舉例說明。

你觉得哪一类的广告中不可信的
因素最多？举例说明。

3. 人們對廣告的態度和他們的年
齡、性別、學歷有什麼關係？

人们对广告的态度和他们的年
龄、性别、学历有什么关系？

(2) Returning a product to a store

李明到商店裏退一個買了不久的手機

顧客： 您好，上個月我在這裏買了一個手機，可是我覺得它的式樣不夠時髦，功能也不全，所以我想退貨。

售貨員：我們這裏還有很多其他牌子的手機，您可以根據自己的需要換一個式樣新、功能全的。

顧客： 可是你們這裏的價格比別的地方貴很多。

售貨員：俗話說「便宜沒好貨」。我們的手機貴是貴，可是質量是最好的。

顧客： 我還是希望你能幫我退貨，這是收據。

售貨員：那好吧！（看收據）對不起，我們的商品[2]**在**一個月**以內**可以退換，您的手機已經超過退貨期了，我不能給您退。

顧客： 什麼，這個規定[3]**毫無**道理，而且我買的時候你也沒告訴我必須在一個月以內退換。我要見你的經理。

售貨員：對不起，他不在……

閱讀理解 Comprehension Check

3. 這個顧客想做什麼？為什麼？
4. 售貨員馬上答應他退貨嗎？他怎麼勸這位顧客？
5. 顧客覺得這家店沒有他要的手機嗎？為什麼不買別的呢？
6. 為什麼有收據，售貨員還是不給他退貨？
7. 最後這個顧客要做什麼？成功了沒有？

(2) Returning a product to a store

李明到商店里退一个买了不久的手机

顾客：   您好，上个月我在这里买了一个手机，可是我觉得它的式样不
          够时髦，功能也不全，所以我想退货。

售货员：   我们这里还有很多其他牌子的手机，您可以根据自己的需要换
          一个式样新、功能全的。

顾客：   可是你们这里的价格比别的地方贵很多。

售货员：   俗话说"便宜没好货"。我们的手机贵是贵，可是质量是最好
          的。

顾客：   我还是希望你能帮我退货，这是收据。

售货员：   那好吧！（看收据）对不起，我们的商品[2]在一个月**以内**可以退
          换，您的手机已经超过退货期了，我不能给您退。

顾客：   什么，这个规定[3]**毫无**道
          理，而且我买的时候你也没
          告诉我必须在一个月以内退
          换。我要见你的经理。

售货员：   对不起，他不在……

阅读理解 Comprehension Check

8.   这个顾客想做什么？为什么？
9.   售货员马上答应他退货吗？他怎么劝这位顾客？
10. 顾客觉得这家店没有他要的手机吗？为什么不买别的呢？
11. 为什么有收据，售货员还是不给他退货？
12. 最後这个顾客要做什么？成功了没有？

對話二生詞 Vocabulary

10.	退		tuì	V	to return, to refund	
	手機	手机	shǒujī	N	cellular phone	[hand-machine]
	式樣	式样	shìyàng	N	style, type, pattern	[form-shape]
11.	功能		gōngnéng	N	function	[effect-capability]
	售貨員	售货员	shòuhuòyuán	N	在店裏賣東西的人	[to sell-goods-person]
12.	牌子		páizi	N	brand, trademark, sign	[plate-noun suffix]
13.	換	换	huàn	V	to change, to exchange	
14.	價格	价格	jiàgé	N	price	[price-pattern]
	俗話	俗话	súhuà	N	common saying, proverb	[common-words]
	便宜沒好貨	便宜没好货	piányí méi hǎohuò	IE	<口>便宜的東西大概都不好	[cheap-not have-supeior-goods]
	收據	收据	shōujù	N	receipt	[to receive-proof]
	商品		shāngpǐn	N	commodity, goods, merchandise	[business-product]
15.	規定		guīdìng	N/V	rule, policy, to stipulate, to set	[regulation-fixed]
16.	毫無	毫无	háowú	V	完全沒有	[in the least-without]
	經理	经理	jīnglǐ	N	manager	[to manage-to run]

Characters with Many Strokes

機 樣 售 貨 牌 換 價 據 毫 無

詞匯用法 Words in Context

10. 退：要求、拒絕退貨/退錢；退不了貨；退學

如果你在商店買的東西有質量問題，你會怎麼辦？

在什麼情況下，商家會拒絕為顧客退貨？

11. 功能：功能很全、不全；多種功

退：要求、拒绝退货/退钱；退不了货；退学

如果你在商店买的东西有质量问题，你会怎么办？

在什么情况下，商家会拒绝为顾客退货？

功能：功能很全、不全；多种功

能

這個軟件有什麼功能？

你為什麼買這個手機？

12.　牌子：老牌子；講究牌子；有名
　　　的牌子（名牌）

你覺得哪個牌子的電腦好？

你一般穿什麼牌子的衣服？

13.　換：換衣服、房間、東西、錢；
　　　換不了；不給換

我應該在哪兒換錢？

你一天換幾次衣服？

14.　價格：價格高、低；商品價格；
　　　→原價、半價

麥當勞在全世界的價格都是一模
一樣的嗎？

你覺得這兒東西的價格怎麼樣？

15.　規定：有很多規定；這是規定；
　　　學校規定學生不許吸毒

在選課方面，學校有什麼規定？

你小的時候，父母是不是規定了
你看電視的時間？

16.　毫無：（句型）

能

这个软件有什么功能？

你为什么买这个手机？

牌子：老牌子；讲究牌子；有名
的牌子（名牌）

你觉得哪个牌子的电脑好？

你一般穿什么牌子的衣服？

换：换衣服、房间、东西、钱；
换不了；不给换

我应该在哪儿换钱？

你一天换几次衣服？

价格：价格高、低；商品价格；
→原价、半价

麦当劳在全世界的价格都是一模
一样的吗？

你觉得这儿东西的价格怎么样？

规定：有很多规定；这是规定；
学校规定学生不许吸毒

在选课方面，学校有什么规定？

你小的时候，父母是不是规定了
你看电视的时间？

毫无：（句型）

自由發揮與課堂活動　Free Discussion and Class Activities

4.　如果你想退掉剛買的手機，你打
　　算怎麼說服售貨員？

5.　你自己有沒有退貨的經歷？如果
　　有，請介紹一次讓你印象比較深
　　的退貨的經歷。如果沒有，談談

如果你想退掉刚买的手机，你打
算怎么说服售货员？

你自己有没有退货的经历？如果
有，请介绍一次让你印象比较深
的退货的经历。如果没有，谈谈

你為什麼買到不太滿意的東西而不去退貨。

6. 「無條件退貨」是不少中商場裏的廣告，你猜那是什麼意思？美國有哪些商店可以「無條件退貨」？「無條件退貨」對顧客和商店各有什麼好處和壞處？

你为什么买到不太满意的东西而不去退货。

"无条件退货"是不少中商场里的广告，你猜那是什么意思？美国有哪些商店可以"无条件退货"？"无条件退货"对顾客和商店各有什么好处和坏处？

敘述 Narrative

推銷員也能為顧客著想

　　每當說起「推銷員」的時候，人們免不了會想到那些想盡辦法向顧客推銷商品的人，認為他們總是想欺騙顧客。然而真正成功的推銷員應該是一個誠實、為顧客著想的人。

　　我開始做推銷員的時候是推銷一種清潔劑。我記得第一天我去一個公寓推銷我的商品。我準備了許多要對顧客說的話，可是得到的卻是拒絕。然而為了生活我不能放棄，只能硬著頭皮繼續。不知道敲了多少個門，終於有人對我的東西感興趣了，於是我走進房間，打開書包，讓她隨便挑一瓶清潔劑，然後在廚房做實驗。當看到這種清潔劑真的有效的時候，女

主人高興地說：「這東西真靈，我買五瓶。」「這種清潔劑有效期短，過期以後效果就不好了，您先買兩瓶，過兩個星期我會再來！」女主人很奇怪地看著我，也許她覺得有人要多買東西，我[4]**應該**高興**才對**。可是我想我應該誠實。

　　那天回家以後，我發現我實際的收入比應有的收入多了五十塊錢。顯然，一定是有人把錢給錯了。我覺得不應該多拿人家的錢，可是又不知道是誰給錯了。那天只有六個人買了我的東西，所以就決定一家一家地去找，一定能找到。當我把五十塊錢還給顧客的時候，我從他的眼

裏看到了信任，我知道我的決定是正確的。

後來這附近的人都開始用我推銷的清潔劑，而且他們又向他們的朋友推薦我的商品，我的成績因此越來越好，後來我被公司提職，從此不需要像從前那樣

一家一家地去推銷商品，可是我很珍惜那幾年的經歷。後來我也告訴下面的職員，想成功需要兩個條件，[5] **一是**能吃苦，**二是**要誠實，這樣才能贏得信任，最後才能成功。

閱讀理解 Comprehension Check

8. 一般人對推銷員有什麼看法？敘述者認為呢？
9. 敘述者開始推銷東西的時候成功嗎？他感覺怎麼樣？
10. 後來有個家庭主婦覺得他這個推銷員很奇怪，為什麼？
11. 這個推銷員後來做了什麼正確的決定？
12. 這個推銷員後來成功了嗎？為什麼？
13. 他對自己推銷的經歷有什麼感覺？
14. 這個推銷員覺得成功需要哪兩個條件？

推销员也能为顾客着想

每当说起"推销员"的时候，人们免不了会想到那些想尽办法向顾客推销商品的人，认为他们总是想欺骗顾客。然而真正成功的推销员应该是一个诚实、为顾客着想的人。

我开始做推销员的时候是推销一种清洁剂。我记得第一天我去一个公寓推销我的商品。我准备了许多要对顾客说的话，可是得到的却是拒绝。然而为了生活我不能放弃，只能硬着头皮继续。不知道敲了多少个门，终于有人对我的东西感兴趣了，于是我走进房间，打开书包，让她随便挑一瓶清洁剂，然后在厨房做实验。当看到这种清洁剂真的有效的时候，女主人高兴地说："这东西真灵，我买五瓶。""这种清洁剂有效

期短，过期以后效果就不好了，您先买两瓶，过两个星期我会再来！"女主人很奇怪地看着我，也许她觉得有人要多买东西，我[4]**应该**高兴**才对**。可是我想我应该诚实。

那天回家以后，我发现我实际的收入比应有的收入多了五十块钱。显然，一定是有人把钱给错了。我觉得不应该多拿人家的钱，可是又不知道是谁给错了。那天只有六个人买了我的东西，所以就决定一家一家去找，一定能找到。当我把五十块钱还给顾客的时候，我从他的眼里看到了信任，我知道我的决定是正确的。

后来这附近的人都开始用我推销的清洁剂，而且他们又向他们的朋友推荐我的商品，我的成

绩越来越好，后来我被公司提职，从此不需要象从前那样一家一家地去推销商品，可是我很珍惜那几年的经历。后来我也告诉下面职员，想成功需要两个条件，⁵**一是能吃苦，二是要诚实**，这样才能赢得信任，最后才能成功。

阅读理解 Comprehension Check

15. 一般人对推销员有什么看法？叙述者认为呢？
16. 叙述者开始推销东西的时候成功吗？他感觉怎么样？
17. 後来有个家庭主妇觉得他这个推销员很奇怪，为什么？
18. 这个推销员後来做了什么正确的决定？
19. 这个推销员後来成功了吗？为什么？
20. 他对自己推销的经历有什么感觉？
21. 这个推销员觉得成功需要哪两个条件？

敘述生詞 Vocabulary

	繁	简				
17.	推銷	推销	tuīxiāo	V	to promote sale of	[to push-to sell]
18.	著想	着想	zháoxiǎng	V	to consider, to take into consideration	[to feel-to think]
	真正		zhēnzhèng	Adj	genuine, true, real	[true-right]
19.	誠實	诚实	chéngshí	Adj	honest	[honest-real]
	清潔劑	清洁剂	qīngjiéjì	N	detergent	[to clean up-clean-dose]
	公寓		gōngyù	N	flats, apartment	[public-residence]
	硬著頭皮	硬着头皮	yìngzhe tóupí	IE	<口> to brace oneself, to bite the bullet	[hard-(particle)-head-skin]
20.	敲		qiāo	V	to knock	
	實驗	实验	shíyàn	V/N	to experiment, test	[real-to test]
21.	靈	灵	líng	Adj	effective, quick, sharp	
	期		qī	N	period of time, phase, stage (e.g., 有效期、退貨期、危險期)	
22.	過期	过期	guòqī	VO	to expire, to be overdue	[to exceed-period of time]
23.	顯然	显然	xiǎnrán	Adv	obviously, evidently	[obvious-adv marker]

給錯	给错	gěicuò	RV	to make a mistake in giving (money)　→看錯、想錯	[to give-wrong]
24. 信任		xìnrèn	N/V	trust, to have confidence in	[to believe-trust]
25. 正確	正确	zhèngquè	Adj	correct, right, proper	[right-true]
26. 提職	提职	tízhí	VO	\<PRC\> to promote \<TW\> 升職	[to raise-position]
從此	从此	cóngcǐ	Adv	henceforth, thereupon	[from-this]
27. 珍惜		zhēnxī	V	to treasure, to cherish	[to value highly-to cherish]
職員	职员	zhíyuán	N	office worker, staff member	[duty-personnel]
28. 贏得	赢得	yíngdé	V	to win, to gain	[to win-to get]

Characters with Many Strokes

實　潔　劑　寓　敲　靈　顯　確　職　贏

詞彙用法 Words in Context

17. 推銷：向老板推銷自己；推銷商品；推銷不出去；推銷員

推销：向老板推销自己；推销商品；推销不出去；推销员

畢業的時候怎麼樣才能找到一個理想的工作？

毕业的时候怎么样才能找到一个理想的工作？

你會不會買那些別人向你推銷的商品？

你会不会买那些别人向你推销的商品？

18. 著想：為別人著想

着想：为别人着想

你覺得什麼樣的人算是自私的人？

你觉得什么样的人算是自私的人？

我們做什麼事情的時候應該為別人著想？

我们做什么事情的时候应该为别人着想？

19. 誠實：誠實的人；很誠實；不誠實

诚实：诚实的人；很诚实；不诚实

誠實的人有什麼特點？

诚实的人有什么特点？

你覺得商人都是不誠實的嗎？

你觉得商人都是不诚实的吗？

20. 敲：敲門、窗戶、玻璃、桌子　　　　敲：敲门、窗户、玻璃、桌子

如果上課的時候有人隨便說話，　　如果上课的时候有人随便说话，
老師會做什麼？　　　　　　　　　老师会做什么？

你什麼時候會用手指敲自己的　　　你什么时候会用手指敲自己的
頭？　　　　　　　　　　　　　　头？

21. 靈：藥很靈；辦法真靈；不靈　　　灵：药很灵；办法真灵；不灵

這個治感冒的藥怎麼樣？　　　　　这个治感冒的药怎么样？

如果你的電視不清楚，你可以用　　如果你的电视不清楚，你可以用
手敲一敲，你覺得這個辦法有效　　手敲一敲，你觉得这个办法有效
嗎？　　　　　　　　　　　　　　吗？

22. 過期：藥過期了；還沒過期；還　　过期：药过期了；还没过期；还
有三天就過期了　　　　　　　　　有三天就过期了

同一個牌子的牛奶，這一瓶為什　　同一个牌子的牛奶，这一瓶为什
麼這麼便宜？　　　　　　　　　　么这么便宜？

什麼樣的藥吃了以後會有不好的　　什么样的药吃了以后会有不好的
作用？　　　　　　　　　　　　　作用？

23. 顯然：顯然這個想法不靈　　　　　显然：显然这个想法不灵

你怎麼知道你喜歡的人不喜歡　　　你怎么知道你喜欢的人不喜欢
你？　　　　　　　　　　　　　　你？

你為什麼說小王會成為一個成功　　你为什么说小王会成为一个成功
的推銷員？　　　　　　　　　　　的推销员？

24. 信任：信任朋友；得到朋友的信　　信任：信任朋友；得到朋友的信
任；不可信任；不值得信任　　　　任；不可信任；不值得信任

什麼樣的朋友不值得信任？　　　　什么样的朋友不值得信任？

誰是你最信任的人？　　　　　　　谁是你最信任的人？

25. 正確：正確的回答、決定 ↔錯誤　　正确：正确的回答、决定 ↔错误

你覺得自己長大以後做出的最正　　你觉得自己长大以后做出的最正
確的決定是什麼？　　　　　　　　确的决定是什么？

上課的時候，你什麼時候願意主　　上课的时候，你什么时候愿意主

動回答老師的問題？　　　　　　　　动回答老师的问题？

26. 提職：被提職　　　　　　　　　　提职：被提职

在公司工作的人，什麼時候會被　　在公司工作的人，什么时候会被
提職？　　　　　　　　　　　　提职？

提職之後對一個人有什麼好處？　　提职之后对一个人有什么好处？

27. 珍惜：珍惜機會、朋友、經歷；　　珍惜：珍惜机会、朋友、经历；
值得珍惜；值得珍惜的經歷　　　　值得珍惜；值得珍惜的经历

在你的生活中，哪些回憶是值得　　在你的生活中，哪些回忆是值得
珍惜的？　　　　　　　　　　　珍惜的？

如果你有去中國學習的機會，你　　如果你有去中国学习的机会，你
會放棄嗎？　　　　　　　　　　会放弃吗？

28. 贏得：贏得信任、尊敬、友誼　　　赢得：赢得信任、尊敬、友谊

你是怎麼贏得朋友的友誼的？　　　你是怎么赢得朋友的友谊的？

人們為什麼那麼尊敬那位老總　　　人们为什么那么尊敬那位老总
統？　　　　　　　　　　　　　统？

自由發揮與課堂活動 Free Discussion and Class Activities

7. 在你的生活中，你碰到過推銷什　　在你的生活中，你碰到过推销什
麼產品的推銷員？最讓你反感的　　么产品的推销员？最让你反感的
是哪一類？你為什麼對他們很反　　是哪一类？你为什么对他们很反
感？　　　　　　　　　　　　　感？

8. 你會不會買推銷員向你推銷的商　　你会不会买推销员向你推销的商
品？為什麼？　　　　　　　　　品？为什么？

9. 向同學推銷雜誌、減肥藥、清潔　　向同学推销杂志、减肥药、清洁
劑或車子，看誰是最好的推銷　　　剂或车子，看谁是最好的推销
員，誰推銷的最多。　　　　　　员，谁推销的最多。

說明 Exposition

 電視廣告何時了？

「廣告之後我們再見！」如果做個統計，這應該是電視劇迷和球迷們最反感的話，大概也是電視中出現次數最多的話。

當商家[6]以電視為媒體來宣傳產品的時候，廣告就在電視上出現了。但是由於廣告越來越多，而播的時間有限，就形成了一個僧多粥少的情況。那麼誰出的價高就播誰的廣告，這是很符合商業原則的。結果電視台賺了大錢，而觀眾卻得痛苦地忍受無聊的廣告。

有的電視台每十五分鐘插播一次廣告，廣告時間長達七、八分鐘，一個一小時的節目被分為幾個部分。浪費的時間先不談，就節目而言，再精彩也會讓人失去興趣。如果廣告的質量高一點，也許可以把看廣告當作一種享受，無奈的是不少廣告拍得相當差，美女、明星泛濫不說，有的甚至看了半天還讓人覺得莫名其妙。於是人們不禁要問：「電視廣告何時了？」

閱讀理解 Comprehension Check

15. 電視中出現頻率最高的是什麼話？為什麼？
19. 為什麼電視上的廣告這麼多？這對電視台和觀眾有什麼影響？
16. 電視台怎麼插播廣告？
17. 作者認為現在的廣告有哪些問題？

电视广告何时了？

"广告之后我们再见！"如果做个统计，这应该是电视剧迷和球迷们最反感的话，大概也是电视中出现次数最多的话。

当商家6以电视为媒体来宣传产品的时候，广告就在电视上出现了。但是由於广告越来越多，而播的时间有限，就形成了一个僧多粥少的情况。那么谁出的价高就播谁的广告，这是很符合商业原则的。结果电视台赚了大钱，而观众却得痛苦地忍受无聊的广告。

有的电视台每十五分钟插播一次广告，广告时间长达七、八分钟，一个一小时的节目被分为几个部分。浪费的时间先不谈，就节目而言，再精彩也会让人失去兴趣。如果广告的质量高一点，也许可以把看广告当作一种享受，无奈的是不少广告拍得相当差，美女、明星泛滥不说，有的甚至看了半天还让人觉得莫名其妙。於是人们不禁要问："电视广告何时了？"

阅读理解 Comprehension Check

18. 电视中出现频率最高的是什么话？为什么？
20. 为什麼电视上的广告这么多？这对电视台和观众有什么影响？
19. 电视台怎么插播广告？
20. 作者认为现在的广告有哪些问题？

說明生詞 Vocabulary

	了		liǎo	V	to end, to finish, to settle	
29.	之後	之后	zhīhòu	Suf	以後	[of-after]
30.	反感		fǎngǎn	V/N	to be disgusted with, dislike	[to turn over-feeling]
	次數	次数	cìshù	N	number of times, frequency	[occurance-number]
	媒體	媒体	méitǐ	N	media	[medium-form]
31.	宣傳	宣传	xuānchuán	V/N	to give publicity to, propaganda	[to declare-to pass (on)]
32.	產品	产品	chǎnpǐn	N	product	[to produce-goods]
33.	有限		yǒuxiàn	Adj	limited, finite	[to have-limit]
34.	形成		xíngchéng	V	to take shape, to form	[form-to become]
	僧多粥少		sēngduō-zhōushǎo	IE	not enough to go around	[monk-many-porridge-few]
	出價	出价	chūjià	VO	to bid (as in an auction)	[to put out-price]
35.	符合		fúhé	V	to accord/tally with, to conform to	[tally-to accord with]
36.	原則	原则	yuánzé	N	principle	[primary-rule]
37.	痛苦		tòngkǔ	N/Adj	pain, suffering	[painful-bitter]
38.	忍受		rěnshòu	V	to endure, to bear	[to endure-to accept]
39.	插		chā	V	to insert, to interpose	
40.	長達	长达	chángdá	V	to last for (time spent)	[long-to reach]
41.	失去		shīqù	V	to lose	[to lose-to go]
42.	無奈	无奈	wúnài	Ph	沒辦法	[without-what]
43.	相當	相当	xiāngdāng	Adv	quite, fairly, considerably	[mutual-to be equal]
	泛濫	泛滥	fànlàn	V	to overflow, to inundate, to be in flood	[flood-to overflow]
	莫名其妙		mòmíng qímiào	IE	to be baffled, inexplicable	[not-to describe-its-wonder]
44.	不禁		bùjīn	Adv	can't help (doing sth.)	[not-endure]

Characters with Many Strokes

數 媒 體 傳 產 僧 插 粥 達 濫

詞彙用法 Words in Context

29. 之後：考試、宣傳、被提職之後

    考試之後，你一般會做什麼？

    為什麼很多公司願意花那麼多錢
    做廣告？

    之后：考试、宣传、被提职之后

    考试之后，你一般会做什么？

    为什么很多公司愿意花那么多钱
    做广告？

30. 反感：讓人反感；對……很反感

    你覺得什麼樣的人最讓人反感？

    有的人為什麼從來不看恐怖kǒngbù
    電影？

    反感：让人反感；对……很反感

    你觉得什么样的人最让人反感？

    有的人为什么从来不看恐怖电
    影？

31. 宣傳：宣傳產品；宣傳品；向老
    百姓宣傳

    你覺得電視和報紙這些媒體的作
    用是什麼？

    商家花那麼多錢做廣告的目的是
    什麼？

    宣传：宣传产品；宣传品；向老
    百姓宣传

    你觉得电视和报纸这些媒体的作
    用是什么？

    商家花那么多钱做广告的目的是
    什么？

32. 產品：推銷、宣傳產品；重視產
    品質量

    你會不會買推銷員打電話向你推
    銷的產品？

    你覺得哪個公司特別重視產品質
    量？

    产品：推销、宣传产品；重视产
    品质量

    你会不会买推销员打电话向你推
    销的产品？

    你觉得哪个公司特别重视产品质
    量？

33. 有限：時間、空間、條件、能力
    有限

    你很喜歡那份工作，可是為什麼
    沒接受呢？

    你對這個話題挺感興趣，為什麼
    這篇論文卻寫得這麼簡單？

    有限：时间、空间、条件、能力
    有限

    你很喜欢那份工作，可是为什么
    没接受呢？

    你对这个话题挺感兴趣，为什么
    这篇论文却写得这么简单？

34. 形成：形成了一種情況、自己的
    風格、特點；這種觀念是六十年

    形成：形成了一种情况、自己的
    风格、特点；这种观念是六十年

代形成的　　　　　　　　　　代形成的

在就業的時候，僧多粥少的情況
是怎麼形成的？

在就业的时候，僧多粥少的情况
是怎么形成的？

中國人為什麼會有重男輕女的觀
念？

中国人为什么会有重男轻女的观
念？

35. 符合：符合原則、事實、要求

在商業界，競爭非常激烈，但是

微軟公司為什麼會被別的公司
告？

微软公司为什么会被别的公司
告？

人們為什麼說報紙上的報導也不
能全信？

人们为什么说报纸上的报导也不
能全信？

36. 原則：遵守、保持原則；毫無原
則

原则：遵守、保持原则；毫无原
则

在商業界，競爭非常激烈，但是
商人也應該做到什麼？

在商业界，竞争非常激烈，但是
商人也应该做到什么？

什麼樣的人不適合做朋友？

什么样的人不适合做朋友？

37. 痛苦：感到痛苦；十分痛苦；痛
苦的生活、經歷、回憶

痛苦：感到痛苦；十分痛苦；痛
苦的生活、经历、回忆

那個老兵為什麼不願意回憶打仗
時發生的事情？

那个老兵为什么不愿意回忆打仗
时发生的事情？

什麼事情曾經讓你很痛苦？

什么事情曾经让你很痛苦？

38. 忍受：忍受痛苦；忍受了很長時
間；忍受不了；無法忍受

忍受：忍受痛苦；忍受了很长时
间；忍受不了；无法忍受

你覺得很多小孩子離家出走的
原因是什麼？

你觉得很多小孩子离家出走的
原因是什么？

在生活中，你最無法忍受的事情
是什麼？

在生活中，你最无法忍受的事情
是什么？

39. 插：插播廣告；插隊；別插嘴；
沒機會插嘴；插話；插手

插：插播广告；插队；别插嘴；
没机会插嘴；插话；插手

別人說話的時候，什麼樣的行為

别人说话的时候，什么样的行为

是不禮貌的？

你父母會插手管你的事嗎？

40. 長達：長達三個小時、一百多米

這部電影有多長時間？

游泳的時候，你一口氣可以游多遠？

41. 失去：失去朋友、興趣、機會；完全失去

你現在為什麼不看籃球比賽了？

我的成績不好，是不是我沒有進大學的機會了？

42. 無奈：覺得無奈；很無奈；無奈的是

什麼事情讓你覺得很無奈？

不喜歡學外語，可以不學嗎？

43. 相當：相當多、難

三年級的中文課怎麼樣？

電視中插播的廣告多不多？

44. 不禁：不禁要問；不禁哭起來了；不禁想起；不禁感到失望

為什麼一看愛情片你就會哭？

昨天的晚會沒完，你怎麼就走了？

是不礼貌的？

你父母会插手管你的事吗？

长达：长达三个小时、一百多米

这部电影有多长时间？

游泳的时候，你一口气可以游多远？

失去：失去朋友、兴趣、机会；完全失去

你现在为什么不看篮球比赛了？

我的成绩不好，是不是我没有进大学的机会了？

无奈：觉得无奈；很无奈；无奈的是

什么事情让你觉得很无奈？

不喜欢学外语，可以不学吗？

相当：相当多、难

三年级的中文课怎么样？

电视中插播的广告多不多？

不禁：不禁要问；不禁哭起来了；不禁想起；不禁感到失望

为什么一看爱情片你就会哭？

昨天的晚会没完，你怎么就走了？

自由發揮與課堂活動　Free Discussion and Class Activities

10. 和其他國家比，你覺得美國的電視廣告有什麼特點？

和其他国家比，你觉得美国的电视广告有什么特点？

11. 每個人準備一條你最喜歡或者最討厭的報紙或電視廣告給同學看，然後解釋你喜歡或者討厭這個廣告的原因。

每个人准备一条你最喜欢或者最讨厌的报纸或电视广告给同学看，然后解释你喜欢或者讨厌这个广告的原因。

應用詞 Productive Vocabulary

◎By Grammatical Categories

Nouns/Pronouns/Measure Words

廣告	guǎnggào	advertisement		牌子	páizi	brand, trademark, sign
顧客	gùkè	customer, shopper, client		價格	jiàgé	price
痛苦	tòngkǔ	pain, suffering		原則	yuánzé	principle
信任	xìnrèn	trust, to have confidence in		規定	guīdìng	rule, policy, to stipulate, to set
產品	chǎnpǐn	product				
功能	gōngnéng	function				

Verbs/Stative Verbs/Adjectives

退	tuì	to return, to refund		符合	fúhé	to accord/tally with, to conform to
換	huàn	to change, to exchange		忍受	rěnshòu	to endure, to bear
敲	qiāo	to knock		失去	shīqù	to lose
插	chā	to insert, to interpose		毫無	háowú	to completely lack
長達	chángdá	to last for (time spent)		(欺)騙	(qī)piàn	to deceive, to fool
過期	guòqī	to expire, to be overdue		上當	shàngdàng	to be taken in, to be fooled/cheated
開業	kāiyè	<PRC> to start business		反感	fǎngǎn	to be disgusted with, dislike
宣傳	xuānchuán	to give publicity to, propaganda		靈	líng	effective, quick, sharp
推銷	tuīxiāo	to promote sale of		全	quán	whole, entire, completely
著想	zháoxiǎng	to consider, to take into consideration		誠實	chéngshí	honest
看上	kànshàng	to take fancy to, to settle on		可信	kěxìn	trustworthy, reliable
珍惜	zhēnxī	to treasure, to cherish		正確	zhèngquè	correct, right, proper
贏得	yíngdé	to win, to gain		有限	yǒuxiàn	limited, finite
提職	tízhí	<PRC> to promote				
形成	xíngchéng	to take shape, to form				

Adverbs and Others

之後	zhīhòu	later, after, afterwards		相當	xiāngdāng	quite, fairly, considerably
無奈	wúnài	helpless, without choice		不禁	bùjīn	can't help (doing sth.)
顯然	xiǎnrán	obviously, evidently		別提了	bié tí le	Don't even mention it!

理解詞 Receptive Vocabulary

◎ By Grammatical Categories

Nouns/Pronouns/Measure Words

期	qī	period of time, phase	皮衣	píyī	fur/leather clothing
次數	cìshù	frequency	手機	shǒujī	cellular phone
式樣	shìyàng	style, type, pattern	商品	shāngpǐn	commodity, goods
俗話	súhuà	common saying, proverb	收據	shōujù	receipt
媒體	méitǐ	media	老公	lǎogōng	husband
真相	zhēnxiàng	real situation	經理	jīnglǐ	manager
公寓	gōngyù	flats, apartment	職員	zhíyuán	office worker
商場	shāngchǎng	market, bazaar	售貨員	shòuhuòyuán	shop assistant, salesclerk
商家	shāngjiā	Merchant	清潔劑	qīngjiéjì	detergent
襯衣	chènyī	\<PRC>shirt			

Verbs/Stative Verbs/Adjectives

了	liǎo	to end, to finish	出價	chūjià	to bid (as in an auction)
實驗	shíyàn	to experiment, test	泛濫	fànlàn	to overflow
給錯	gěicuò	to make a mistake in giving (money)	真正	zhēnzhèng	genuine, true, real

Adverbs and Others

從此	cóngcǐ	henceforth, thereupon	僧多粥少	sēngduō-zhōu shǎo	not enough to go around
買一送一	mǎi yī sòng yī	buy one, get one free	便宜沒好貨	piányí méi hǎo huò	You get what you pay for.
莫名其妙	mòmíngqí miào	to be baffled, inexplicable			
硬著頭皮	yìngzhe tóupí	to brace oneself, to bite the bullet			

本课词表 Chapter Vocabulary

◎ By Pinyin

Words with asterisk* are productive vocabulary which needs to be memorized and studied for its usage.

(qī)piàn*	（欺）骗	to deceive, to fool	chángdá*	长达	to last for (time spent)
bié tí le*	别提了	Don't even mention it!	chǎnpǐn*	产品	product
bùjīn*	不禁	can't help (doing sth.)	chéngshí*	诚实	honest
chā*	插	to insert, to interpose	chènyī	衬衣	\<PRC> shirt

chūjià	出价	to bid (as in an auction)
cìshù	次数	number of times
cóngcǐ	从此	henceforth
fǎngǎn*	反感	to be disgusted with
fànlàn	泛滥	to overflow
fúhé*	符合	to accord/tally with
gěicuò	给错	to make a mistake in giving (money)
gōngnéng*	功能	function
gōngyù	公寓	flats, apartment
guǎnggào*	广告	advertisement
guīdìng*	规定	rule, policy, to set
gùkè*	顾客	customer, shopper
guòqī*	过期	to expire
háowú*	毫无	to completely lack
huàn*	换	to (ex)change
jiàgé*	价格	price
jīnglǐ	经理	manager
kāiyè*	开业	to start business
kànshàng*	看上	to take fancy to
kěxìn*	可信	trustworthy, reliable
lǎogōng	老公	husband
liǎo	了	to end, to finish
líng*	灵	effective, quick
mǎi yī sòngyī	买一送一	buy one, get one free
méitǐ	媒体	media
mòmíngqímiào	莫名其妙	to be baffled
páizi*	牌子	brand, trademark
piányí méi hǎohuò	便宜没好货	You get what you pay for.
píyī	皮衣	fur/leather clothing
qī	期	period of time, stage
qiāo*	敲	to knock
qīngjiéjì	清洁剂	detergent
quán*	全	whole, completely

rěnshòu*	忍受	to endure, to bear
sēngduō-zhōushǎo	僧多粥少	not enough to go around
shāngchǎng	商场	market, bazaar
shàngdàng*	上当	to be taken in, to be fooled/cheated
shāngjiā	商家	merchant
shāngpǐn	商品	commodity, goods
shīqù*	失去	to lose
shíyàn	实验	to experiment, test
shìyàng	式样	style, type, pattern
shòuhuòyuán	售货员	shop assistant
shǒujī	手机	cellular phone
shōujù	收据	receipt
súhuà	俗话	common saying
tízhí*	提职	<PRC> to promote
tòngkǔ*	痛苦	pain, suffering
tuì*	退	to return, to refund
tuīxiāo*	推销	to promote sale of
wúnài*	无奈	helpless
xiāngdāng*	相当	quite, considerably
xiǎnrán	显然	obviously, evidently
xíngchéng*	形成	to take shape
xìnrèn*	信任	trust, to trust
xuānchuán*	宣传	to give publicity to
yíngdé*	赢得	to win, to gain
yìngzhe tóupí	硬着头皮	to brace oneself, to bite the bullet
yǒuxiàn*	有限	limited, finite
yuánzé*	原则	principle
zháoxiǎng*	着想	to consider
zhèngquè*	正确	correct, right
zhēnxī*	珍惜	to treasure
zhēnxiàng	真相	real situation
zhēnzhèng	真正	genuine, true, real
zhīhòu*	之后	later, after
zhíyuán	职员	office worker

語法和用法 Grammar and Usage

Pay attention to the function of the structure and then study the example sentences.   When blanks are provided, either answer the questions or complete the sentences.

1. Expressing skepticism

難道 S … 不成/嗎 S 難道… 不成/嗎	nándào…bùchéng/ma	Don't tell me that S….; Do you mean to say…?; Can it be that…?

- 難道他們沒有打折不成？

1. 都九點半了，你還不起來，難道今天你不上課了嗎？

   都九点半了，你还不起来，难道今天你不上课了吗？

   It's already nine-thirty and you still aren't up. Don't tell me that you're not going to class today?

   今天我們的老師要開會，所以沒有課，不然我怎麼敢睡到現在？

   今天我们的老师要开会，所以没有课，不然我怎么敢睡到现在？

   Today our teachers have a meeting, so there are no classes. Otherwise, how could I dare sleep till now?

2. 我發現中文越學越難，我不想去上中文課了。

   我发现中文越学越难，我不想去上中文课了。

   I've found that Chinese is getting hard and harder. I don't want to go to Chinese class.

   難道你後悔了不成？我記得你告訴過我，不管中文多難學，你也要堅持下去。

   难道你后悔了不成？我记得你告诉过我，不管中文多难学，你也要坚持下去。

   Don't tell me that you have regrets now? I remember you told me that you would keep studying Chinese no matter how hard it was.

3. 難道你發財了不成，一下子買回來這麼多東西？

   难道你发财了不成，一下子买回来这么多东西？

   Don't tell me that you have made a fortune? How come you've bought so many things all of a sudden?

   今天碰到商場打折，買一百塊錢以上的東西有禮品，

   今天碰到商场打折，买一百块钱以上的东西有礼品，

   Today the mall has discounts. If you spend over 100 dollars, you get something free. So, I bought a bit more.

所以就多買了點。   所以就多买了点。

4. 我發現我愛上了好朋友的男朋   我发现我爱上了好朋友的男朋
   友，你說我該怎麼辦？   友，你说我该怎么办？

   _____

5. 媽媽，可不可以給我500塊錢，   妈妈，可不可以给我500块钱，
   我要去聽張學友的演唱會。   我要去听张学友的演唱会。

   _____

6. 你為什麼突然送我一個禮物，   你为什么突然送我一个礼物，
   今天是什麼日子？   今天是什么日子？

   _____

難道S … 不成/嗎 is a rhetorical structure used to question the integrity of the point raised. In this pattern, 難道 can go before or after the subject. The end of the sentence can be either 嗎 or 不成.

2. Expressing scope

(在) … 以內	yǐnèi	within (time/distance)
(在) … 以外	yǐwài	out of (distance)
(在) … 以上	yǐshàng	over/above (age/height)
(在) … 以下	yǐxià	below/under (age/height)

● 我們的商品在一個月以內可以退換，您的手機已經超過退貨期了，我
  不能給您退。

1. 商家用什麼辦法來   商家用什么办法来   How do store owners
   吸引顧客買更多的   吸引顾客买更多的   encourage customers to buy
   東西？   东西？   even more merchandise?

   為了吸引顧客買更   为了吸引顾客买更   In order to encourage customers
   多的東西，商家的   多的东西，商家的   to buy even more, the store
   新辦法是：如果顧   新办法是：如果顾   owner's new method is: if a
   客買了200塊錢以上   客买了200块钱以上   customer spends over 200
                                                      dollars, the store will give

的商品，商家就送顧客 20 塊錢的東西；如果買的東西在 200 塊錢以下，就不送了。

的商品，商家就送顾客 20 块钱的东西；如果买的东西在 200 块钱以下，就不送了。

him/her 20 dollars worth of merchandise. If the customer spends less than 200 dollars, he/she won't get anything free.

2. 圖書館借回來的書多久要還？

图书馆借回来的书多久要还？

How long before we need to return the books checked out from the library?

從圖書館借書，要在兩個星期以內把書還回去，如果過期不還的話，就會被罰款。

从图书馆借书，要在两个星期以内把书还回去，如果过期不还的话，就会被罚款。

If you check out books from the library, they need to be returned in two weeks. If not, you will be fined.

3. 電腦對我們的生活有什麼好處？

电脑对我们的生活有什么好处？

What benefit have computers brought us?

電腦給我們的生活帶來很多方便，而且通過電腦，我們可以知道美國以外的地方發生了什麼事情。

电脑给我们的生活带来很多方便，而且通过电脑，我们可以知道美国以外的地方发生了什么事情。

Computers have made our lives more convenient and, moreover, through computers we can know what's going on outside of the U.S.

4. 在美國，多大的人可以合法地買酒？合法地開車？

在美国，多大的人可以合法地买酒？合法地开车？

5. 如果我對自己買的東西不滿意，在多長時間以內可以退換？

如果我对自己买的东西不满意，在多长时间以内可以退换？

6.　你每天會花幾個小時學習中　　你每天会花几个小时学习中
　　文？　　　　　　　　　　　　文？

The pattern (在) … 以內/以外/以上/以下 expresses scope. Note that 以內 is often used with time and distance, while 以外 is mostly used with distance. 以上/以下 deals mostly with height and age. To say "those who are over 21 can buy liquor," the following will be used 二十一歲以上的人可以買酒. Think of why the following sentence is odd: 我每天花不到三個小時以上的時間來學中文.

3.　Expressing a minimum extent

| … 毫無 N | háowú N | <書> not at all; in the least |
| … 毫不 V | háobù V | 一點兒也沒/不 |

● 這個規定毫無道理，而且我買的時候你也沒告訴我必須在一個月以內退換。

1.　這部功夫片很好，　　　这部功夫片很好，　　　This martial arts movie is good.
　　你要不要看？　　　　你要不要看？　　　　Would you like to see it?

　　我對功夫片毫無興　　我对功夫片毫无兴　　I have no interest at all in
　　趣，所以不管多好　　趣，所以不管多好　　martial arts movies, so no
　　的功夫片，我都毫　　的功夫片，我都毫　　matter how good it is, I don't
　　不動心。　　　　　不动心。　　　　　want to see it.

2.　大家對奧斯卡獎有　　大家对奥斯卡奖有　　How do people feel about the
　　什麼看法？　　　　什么看法？　　　　Oscar awards?

　　有些人覺得奧斯卡　　有些人觉得奥斯卡　　Some think that the Oscar
　　獎不過是傳媒公司　　奖不过是传媒公司　　awards are only a money-
　　賺錢的工具罷了，　　赚钱的工具罢了，　　making tool for media
　　對普通人來說毫無　　对普通人来说毫无　　companies and have no value
　　價值，但是也有些　　价值，但是也有些　　at all for ordinary people. Yet,
　　人認為，奧斯卡代　　人认为，奥斯卡代　　some people think that the
　　表了電影的最高水　　表了电影的最高水　　Oscars represent the highest
　　平。　　　　　　　平。　　　　　　　level of movie achievement.

3. | 你為什麼對小張這麼反感？ | 你为什么对小张这么反感？ | Why were you so disgusted with Xiao Zhang? |

小張買了一台電腦，用了幾個月後，發現市場上有新的電腦，於是要退掉剛買的，我覺得他的作法毫無道理。　小张买了一台电脑，用了几个月后，发现市场上有新的电脑，于是要退掉刚买的，我觉得他的作法毫无道理。　Xiao Zhang bought a computer and, after using it for a few months, found a new model available. Therefore, he wanted to return the one he had just bought. I think what he did makes no sense at all.

4. 看中文電影的時候，你為什麼要把字幕蓋gài上？　看中文电影的时候，你为什么要把字幕盖上？

---

5. 你可以給大家介紹一下中國現代文學的特點嗎？　你可以给大家介绍一下中国现代文学的特点吗？

---

6. 我打算在爸爸過生日的時候，請他去聽一個搖滾音樂會，你覺得怎麼樣？　我打算在爸爸过生日的时候，请他去听一个摇滚音乐会，你觉得怎么样？

The pattern 毫無N/毫不V expresses a minimum extent. Note that what follows 毫無 is a noun and what follows 毫不 is a verb, and that the noun and verb are always two syllables, e.g., 毫無興趣、研究、了解、意義、價值、幫助、影響、用處、道理/毫不客氣、喜歡、動搖. Adjectives or auxiliary verbs cannot follow 毫無/毫不, so the following are incorrect: 聽錄音帶毫無有用; 我毫不可以給你介紹中國文學. Instead, they should be changed to 聽錄音帶毫無用處; 我對中國文學毫無了解，不能給你介紹 'It's useless to listen to the tapes; I have no understanding of Chinese literature, so I cannot give you an overview.'

4. Expressing an appropriate outcome

S 應該…才對	yīnggāi…cáiduì	It's only right for S to…
S 應該…才是	yīnggāi…cáishì	It's only right for S to…
S 應該…才好	yīnggāi…cáihǎo	It's only good for S to…
S 應該…才行	yīnggāi…cáixíng	It's only fine for S to…

● 也許她覺得有人要多買東西，我應該高興才對。

1. 明天有一個考試，你今晚應該在家裏複習功課才對，為什麼還要出去？

　明天有一个考试，你今晚应该在家里复习功课才对，为什么还要出去？

　Tomorrow there will be a test. You should stay home tonight and review your lesson. Why do you still want to go out?

　我已經複習好了，現在要休息一下，不應該那麼緊張才是。

　我已经复习好了，现在要休息一下，不应该那么紧张才是。

　I'm done with my review, and now I need a break. One shouldn't be so nervous.

2. 我發現今天實際賺的錢比應該賺的錢多，也許是有人把錢給錯了。

　我发现今天实际赚的钱比应该赚的钱多，也许是有人把钱给错了。

　I found that the actual amount I earned today was more than what I expected. Perhaps someone gave me more money by mistake.

　我覺得你應該把別人多給你的錢還給他才是，不然以後別人就不信任你了。

　我觉得你应该把别人多给你的钱还给他才是，不然以后别人就不信任你了。

　I think it is only right for you to return the extra money. Otherwise, no one will trust you later on.

3. 小王工作特別認真，老板應該給他提職才對。

　小王工作特别认真，老板应该给他提职才对。

　Xiao Wang works conscientiously. It's only right that the boss gives him a promotion.

　難道只有他一個人工作認真嗎？我覺得大家都應該提職。

　难道只有他一个人工作认真吗？我觉得大家都应该提职。

　Do you mean to say that he's the only one who works hard? I think everyone should be promoted.

4. 我一直對中國的文化很感興
    趣，你覺得我怎麼樣可以更了
    解中國呢？

    我一直对中国的文化很感兴
    趣，你觉得我怎么样可以更了
    解中国呢？

---

5. 我覺得我父母的想法太落伍，
    我不喜歡和他們聊天。

    我觉得我父母的想法太落伍，
    我不喜欢和他们聊天。

---

6. 小張最近總是沒有精神，我猜
    他大概是因為減肥而營養不
    良！

    小张最近总是没有精神，我猜
    他大概是因为减肥而营养不
    良！

The pattern 應該…才對/才是/才好/才行 expresses an appropriate outcome. Note
that 才對/才是/才好/才行 always occurs at the end of a sentence.

5. Enumerating reasons

| 一是 … ， 二是 … | yīshì... èrshì... | the first reason is…, and the second is… |
| 一來 … ， 二來 … | yīlái... èrlái... | for one thing…, for another… |

• 後來我也告訴下面的職員，想成功需要兩個條件， 一是能吃苦，二
  是要誠實……

1. 為什麼中文對美國
    學生這麼難？

    为什么中文对美国
    学生这么难？

    Why is Chinese so difficult for
    American students?

    對美國學生來說，
    中文很難學，一是
    因為中文有四聲，
    而英語沒有；二是
    因為中文的漢字非
    常複雜。

    对美国学生来说，
    中文很难学，一是
    因为中文有四声，
    而英语没有；二是
    因为中文的汉字非
    常复杂。

    To American students, Chinese
    is hard to learn. For one thing,
    Chinese has four tones and
    English doesn't. For another,
    Chinese characters are very
    complicated.

2. | 為什麼你要退這個手機？ | 为什么你要退这个手机？ | Why do you want to return this celluar phone? |

我要退掉這個手機的原因有二：一是它的價格比其他地方的貴很多，二是它的樣子和功能都過時了。 | 我要退掉这个手机的原因有二：一是它的价格比其他地方的贵很多，二是它的样子和功能都过时了。 | I want to return this celluar phone for two reasons: first, its price is much more expensive than those sold in other places; second, its style and function are out of date.

3. 李明為什麼被老板提職？ | 李明为什么被老板提职？ | Why was Li Ming promoted by his boss?

李明之所以被老板提職，一是因為他工作努力，贏得了老板的信任，二是因為他從來不抱怨。 | 李明之所以被老板提职，一是因为他工作努力，赢得了老板的信任，二是因为他从来不抱怨。 | One reason Li Ming was promoted is because he works hard and has earned his boss' trust. Another reason is he never complains.

4. 在聖誕節過後，很多商品都會打折，這是為什麼呢？ | 在圣诞节过后，很多商品都会打折，这是为什么呢？

5. 我知道你不喜歡經濟，為什麼還要硬著頭皮學下去呢？ | 我知道你不喜欢经济，为什么还要硬着头皮学下去呢？

6. 我覺得現在很多暢銷書的內容並不吸引人，可是它們為什麼暢銷呢？ | 我觉得现在很多畅销书的内容并不吸引人，可是它们为什么畅销呢？

The pattern 一是/一來⋯，二是/二來⋯ is used to enumerate reasons. The clauses after 一是 and 二是 are often in parallel structure, e.g., 我不喜歡他，一是因為他壞

習慣多，二是因為他態度不好 'I don't like him. For one thing, he has many bad habits. For another, his attitude is not good.' The reasons enumerated should provide different information. So, it's odd to say 我不喜歡經濟一是因為這門課沒意思，二是因為這門課很悶.

6. Expressing attribution

以 X(為 Y)(來 V)	yǐ...(wéi...)(lái)	to use X (as Y) (in order to V)
把 X當作/作為 Y	bǎ...dāngzuò/zuòwéi...	to regard X as Y

- 當商家以電視為媒體來宣傳產品的時候……
- 如果廣告的質量高一點，也許可以把看廣告當作一種享受……

1. 很多商家怎麼拒絕顧客退貨的要求？

很多商家怎么拒绝顾客退货的要求？

How do most store owners refuse their customers' requests to return merchandise?

當顧客對商品不滿而要求退貨的時候，很多商家以超過規定的時間為理由，來拒絕顧客的要求。

当顾客对商品不满而要求退货的时候，很多商家以超过规定的时间为理由，来拒绝顾客的要求。

When customers are not happy with a product and ask to return it, many stores use an expiration on return as a reason for refusing a customer's request.

2. 看中文電影只是一種享受嗎？

看中文电影只是一种享受吗？

Is seeing a Chinese movie only a kind of amusement?

我們在看中文電影的時候，除了享受以外，還應該把它當作一種學習語言和了解中國文化的方法。

我们在看中文电影的时候，除了享受以外，还应该把它当作一种学习语言和了解中国文化的方法。

When we see Chinese movies, in addition to having fun, we should also take it as a way of studying language and understanding Chinese culture.

3. 我們應該怎麼分析中美家庭觀念的不同？

我们应该怎么分析中美家庭观念的不同？

How should we analyze the differences between Chinese and American concepts of the family?

中國人和美國人的

中国人和美国人的

There are many differences

家庭觀念有很多不同，我們應該以對孩子的教育為例來分析它們的不同。

家庭观念有很多不同，我们应该以对孩子的教育为例来分析它们的不同。

between Chinese and American concepts of the family. We should use the education of children as an example and analyze their differences.

4. 在美國，年輕人非常崇拜瑪丹娜嗎？他們覺得這位明星怎麼樣？

在美国，年轻人非常崇拜玛丹娜吗？他们觉得这位明星怎么样？

---

5. 我覺得現在流行歌曲的旋律和節奏都很不好，而且歌詞也沒有深度，你不同意我的看法，可是你有什麼理由呢？

我觉得现在流行歌曲的旋律和节奏都很不好，而且歌词也没有深度，你不同意我的看法，可是你有什么理由呢？

---

6. 你覺得商家應該以什麼樣的原則來對待顧客？

你觉得商家应该以什么样的原则来对待顾客？

The pattern 以X為Y來V is a more formal expression to indicate attribution. X can be a noun or VO, and either 為Y or 來V can be omitted, e.g., 很多年輕人以瑪丹娜為偶像 'Many young people idolize Madonna'; 他以唱歌來維持生活 'He sings for a living.' In the sentence 他以電影為教材來提高學生的中文水平 'He uses movies as teaching materials to enhance the Chinese language level of his students,' none is omitted. The pattern 把X當作/作為Y is more colloquial. Y can be a noun or a noun phrase, e.g., 他把聽流行歌曲當作一種享受 'He enjoys listening to popular songs' or 他把聽流行歌曲當作一種了解現代人思想的方法 'He sees listening to popular songs as a way to understand the thoughts of people nowadays.' Don't confuse 以…來… 'use…to…' with 以…來說 'to speak of…'

背景常識 Background Notes

1. 促銷方法：打折是最常見的促銷方法，在節假日前後或者是一個季節快結束的時候，各個大的商場都會用打折的方法推銷商品。「買100送30」是近幾年開始流行的另一種促銷活動。如果一位顧客買了100塊錢的東西，就可以免費得到價格30塊錢的東西。「限時搶購」是一種很刺激的促銷方法，就是在規定的時間內可以用很低的價格購買某個牌子的商品，過了這個時間就不行了。

2. 廣告：在電視上你可以看到各種各樣的廣告，但是也有一些產品的廣告相對來說更多一些。首先就是藥品的廣告，尤其是治療感冒的藥和一些平時吃的補藥；酒的廣告也非常多，有的人甚至批評中國的電視台酒氣沖天。

3. 退換商品：以前，如果不是買了特別有問題的商品，人們一般不會去商店退換，因為退換商品不僅不會得到新的東西，反而可能會受售貨員的氣。現在退換東西比以前簡單多了，但還是需要帶好發票，在規定的退還日期內去商店，而且東西一旦用過也很難退換。

背景常识 Background Notes

1. 促销方法：打折是最常见的促销方法，在节假日前后或者是一个季节快结束的时候，各个大的商场都会用打折的方法推销商品。"买100送30"是近几年开始流行的另一种促销活动。如果一位顾客买了100块钱的东西，就可以免费得到价格30块钱的东西。"限时抢购"是一种很刺激的促销方法，就是在规定的时间内可以用很低的价格购买某个牌子的商品，过了这个时间就不行了。

2. 广告：在电视上你可以看到各种各样的广告，但是也有一些产品的广告相对来说更多一些。首先就是药品的广告，尤其是治疗感冒的药和一些平时吃的补药；酒的广告也非常多，有的人甚至批评中国的电视台酒气冲天。

3. 退换商品：以前，如果不是买了特别有问题的商品，人们一般不会去商店退换，因为退换商品不仅不会得到新的东西，反而可能会受售货员的气。现在退换东西比以前简单多了，但还是需要带好发票，在规定的退还日期内去商店，而且东西一旦用过也很难退换。

第八課　單身貴族煩惱多？

Theme: Love and Marriage

Communicative Objectives
- Urging someone to get married
- Talking with a soon-to-be groom
- Narrating an experience of being on a dating game show

Skill Focus
Comprehending a report on a population poll

Grammar Focus
- 都什麼N了
- S不妨V，(說不定)…
- S儘可能地快/早/多V
- S不再是N了　　S不再VO了
  S再也不/別VO了
- S假如…也/就V
- A向B表示好感/關心/同
  情/歡迎/友好

Problem Scenario

As you are in your late twenties, you are reminded repeatedly, by your parents and friends, that you should get married. Some suggest that you should have an arranged marriage, if you can't find the right person by yourself. Yet, you believe in free love and definitely not "love after marriage." Some suggest that you announce to the world that you are still available and put an ad in a newspaper or solicit help online. What would you do to have a relationship and why?

對話 Dialogue

(1) Urging someone to get married

李明的姑姑李潔勸女兒早一點兒結婚。

母親：　孩子，下個月你就三十歲了，應該想一想你的終身大事了。

女兒：　我不是沒想過，而是到現在為止都沒有碰到一個合適的人。

母親：　趙升叔叔給你介紹的幾個條件不錯的男孩子，你為什麼不去見一見？

女兒：　¹**都**什麼年代**了**，你還讓我去相親？丟死人了！再說，沒有愛情的婚姻不會幸福。

母親：　你們可以先結婚再戀愛，就像我和你爸，你覺得我們不幸福嗎？

女兒：　你們是你們，我是我。反正我相信我的夢中情人在等我呢！

母親：　現在有一個電視徵婚的節目很受歡迎，你²**不妨**也去試一試，**說不定**能找到你的夢中情人。

女兒：　別開玩笑了！我只相信緣分，如果緣分沒到，不管你怎麼找都沒用。

母親：　緣分是要自己創造的。如果你總是等，就算緣分到了你也不一定知道！

女兒：　那我就繼續做單身貴族！

閱讀理解 Comprehension Check

1. 母親要女兒考慮什麼事情？為什麼？
2. 女兒不想結婚嗎？為什麼還沒有男朋友？
3. 女兒覺得母親要自己找男朋友的做法好嗎？為什麼？
4. 母親要女兒參加一個電視徵婚節目，女兒覺得怎麼樣？
5. 女兒覺得找對象要靠什麼？母親覺得對嗎？為什麼？

(1) Urging someone to get married

李明的姑姑李洁劝女儿早一点儿结婚。

母亲：　孩子，下个月你就三十岁了，应该想一想你的终身大事了。

女儿：　我不是没想过，而是到现在为止都没有碰到一个合适的人。

母亲：　赵升叔叔给你介绍的几个条件不错的男孩子，你为什么不去见一见？

女儿：　[1]都什么年代了，你还让我去相亲？丢死人了！再说，没有爱情的婚姻不会幸福。

母亲：　你们可以先结婚再恋爱，就象我和你爸，你觉得我们不幸福吗？

女儿：　你们是你们，我是我。反正我相信我的梦中情人在等我呢！

母亲：　现在有一个电视征婚的节目很受欢迎，你[2]不妨也去试一试，说不定能找到你的梦中情人。

女儿：　别开玩笑了！我只相信缘分，如果缘分没到，不管你怎么找都没用。

母亲：　缘分是要自己创造的。如果你总是等，就算缘分到了你也不一定知道！

女儿：　那我就继续做单身贵族！

阅读理解 Comprehension Check

6.　母亲要女儿考虑什么事情？为什么？

7.　女儿不想结婚吗？为什么还没有男朋友？

8.　女儿觉得母亲要自己找男朋友的做法好吗？为什么？

9.　母亲要女儿参加一个电视征婚节目，女儿觉得怎么样？

10.　女儿觉得找对象要靠什么？母亲觉得对吗？为什么？

對話一生詞 Vocabulary

Study the numbered vocabulary (productive vocabulary) for its usage. The unnumbered items (receptive vocabulary) are to facilitate reading comprehension.

◎**By Order of Appearance**

1.	單身貴族	单身贵族	dānshēn guìzú	N	還沒有結婚的男女	[alone-body-noble-group]
2.	煩惱	烦恼	fánnǎo	N/V	worry, to worry	[to trouble-angry]
	終身大事	终身大事	zhōngshēn dàshì	N	一生中最重要的事：結婚	[eventually-life-big-event]
	叔叔		shūshu/ shúshu	N	father's younger brother, uncle	[uncle-uncle]
	年代		niándài	N	day and age, years, decade	[year-generation]
3.	相親	相亲	xiāngqīn/ xiàngqīn	VO	to get look at prospective spouse before engagement	[to size up by appearance-marriage]
	丟人		diūrén	VO	to lose face	[to lose-people]
4.	婚姻		hūnyīn	N	marriage, matrimony	[to wed-marriage]
5.	幸福		xìngfú	N/Adj	happiness, happy	[luck-blessing]
6.	戀愛	恋爱	liàn'ài	V/N	to love, romantic attachment	[to love-to love]
	夢中情人	梦中情人	mèngzhōng qíngrén	N	dream lover	[dream-in-lover]
7.	徵婚	征婚	zhēnghūn	VO	to advertise for marriage partner	[to solicit-marriage]
	節目	节目	jiémù	N	program, item (on program)	[section-eye]
8.	不妨		bùfáng	IE	might as well, why not (Ving)?	[not-to hinder]
9.	說不定	说不定	shuōbudìng	IE	perhaps, maybe	[to say-not-definite]
10.	緣分	缘分	yuánfèn	N	predestined affinity	[fate-what is within one's rights]
11.	創造	创造	chuàngzào	V	to create, to produce, to bring about	[to initiate-to make]
12.	繼續	继续	jìxù	V	to continue	[to succeed-to continue]

Characters with Many Strokes

貴　婚　福　戀　夢　徵　緣　創　繼　續

詞匯用法 Words in Context

1. 單身貴族：單身漢；單身的生活
   什麼樣的人才能算單身貴族？
   單身貴族的生活有什麼煩惱？

   单身贵族：单身汉；单身的生活
   什么样的人才能算单身贵族？
   单身贵族的生活有什么烦恼？

2. 煩惱：有很多煩惱；為上學煩惱
   最近你在為什麼事情煩惱？
   為什麼很多人都覺得童年最幸
   福？

   烦恼：有很多烦恼；为上学烦恼
   最近你在为什么事情烦恼？
   为什么很多人都觉得童年最幸
   福？

3. 相親：去相親；和別人相親
   你的父母會不會要求你去相親？
   相親的時候應該穿什麼樣的衣
   服？

   相亲：去相亲；和别人相亲
   你的父母会不会要求你去相亲？
   相亲的时候应该穿什么样的衣
   服？

4. 婚姻：幸福的婚姻；婚姻法；維
   持婚姻；婚姻生活
   你覺得什麼樣的婚姻才是幸福
   的？
   父母應該為孩子維持他們的婚姻
   嗎？

   婚姻：幸福的婚姻；婚姻法；维
   持婚姻；婚姻生活
   你觉得什么样的婚姻才是幸福
   的？
   父母应该为孩子维持他们的婚姻
   吗？

5. 幸福：幸福的生活、婚姻；很幸
   福；一點也不幸福
   你覺得單身貴族的生活怎麼樣？
   你覺得自己什麼時候最幸福？

   幸福：幸福的生活、婚姻；很幸
   福；一点也不幸福
   你觉得单身贵族的生活怎么样？
   你觉得自己什么时候最幸福？

6. 戀愛：談戀愛；正在戀愛；戀愛
   關係
   你覺得一個人什麼時候可以談戀
   愛？
   小麗為什麼每天都是那麼高興，
   那麼幸福的樣子？

   恋爱：谈恋爱；正在恋爱；恋爱
   关系
   你觉得一个人什么时候可以谈恋
   爱？
   小丽为什么每天都是那么高兴，
   那么幸福的样子？

7. 徵婚：徵婚廣告；上報紙、電視徵婚

什麼樣的報紙上會有徵婚廣告？

你會不會上電視徵婚？

8. 不妨：（句型）

9. 說不定：說不定他會來；什麼時候離開還說不定；這是一件說不定的事情

你以後會不會做一個單身貴族？

在報上徵婚能找到滿意的對象嗎？

10. 緣分：有、靠、相信緣分；跟我的朋友有緣分

你相信緣分嗎？

你跟誰很有緣分？

11. 創造：創造機會、條件；有、培養創造力

為什麼我總是找不到表現自己的機會？

你覺得學校教育的目的應該是什麼？

12. 繼續：繼續工作、努力、發展；繼續下去；還在繼續

你以後想繼續學習中文嗎？

可口可樂公司和百事公司的競爭什麼時候能結束？

自由發揮與課堂活動 Free Discussion and Class Activities

1. 你會怎麼定義「愛情」？

   你会怎么定义"爱情"？

2. 有人認為愛情是靠緣分的，沒有緣分相愛的人也不一定能生活在一起。這種看法你覺得如何？

   有人认为爱情是靠缘分的，没有缘分相爱的人也不一定能生活在一起。这种看法你觉得如何？

3. 請你給「單身貴族」下個定義。

   请你给"单身贵族"下个定义。

4. 角色扮演
   女兒：三十二歲，未婚，相信緣分，拒絕相親和電視徵婚
   媽媽：勸女兒儘快結婚，要她去相親或者登電視廣告

   角色扮演
   女儿：三十二岁，未婚，相信缘分，拒绝相亲和电视征婚
   妈妈：劝女儿尽快结婚，要她去相亲或者登电视广告

(2) Talking with a soon-to-be groom

李明和快要結婚的表哥周健聊天。

表哥：　下個星期我要結婚了，希望你能來喝我和小葉的喜酒。

小李：　恭喜,恭喜！你真有福氣，聽說你的老婆又漂亮又溫柔。

表哥：　謝謝。希望你也能儘快找到自己的另一半。

小李：　不過聽說你老婆學歷比你高，賺的錢也比你多，而且連你們住的房子都是你老婆的。娶一個女強人，你會不會覺得有壓力？

表哥：　你知道中國人很講究「男主外、女主內」，雖然我覺得男女應該平等，但是我多少還是會有一些壓力。

小李：　不過你們經歷了那麼多挫折，應該好好珍惜現在的幸福。

表哥：　我會的！

閱讀理解 Comprehension Check

6. 表哥請小李來做什麼？什麼時候？
7. 小李怎麼恭喜他？表哥怎麼回答？
8. 小李覺得他們的婚姻會有什麼問題？為什麼？
9. 表哥自己怎麼看他和未來太太的關係？
10. 小李最後怎麼祝福他？表哥怎麼回答？

(2) Talking with a soon-to-be groom

李明和快要结婚的表哥周健聊天。

表哥： 下个星期我要结婚了，希望你能来喝我和小叶的喜酒。

小李： 恭喜,恭喜！你真有福气，听说你的老婆又漂亮又温柔。

表哥： 谢谢。希望你也能尽快找到自己的另一半。

小李： 不过听说你老婆学历比你高，赚的钱也比你多，而且连你们住的房子都是你老婆的。娶一个女强人，你会不会觉得有压力？

表哥： 你知道中国人很讲究"男主外、女主内"，虽然我觉得男女应该平等，但是我多少还是会有一些压力。

小李： 不过你们经历了那么多挫折，应该好好珍惜现在的幸福。

表哥： 我会的！

阅读理解 Comprehension Check

6. 表哥请小李来做什么？什么时候？
7. 小李怎么恭喜他？表哥怎么回答？
8. 小李觉得他们的婚姻会有什么问题？为什么？
9. 表哥自己怎么看他和未来太太的关系？
10. 小李最后怎么祝福他？表哥怎么回答？

對話二生詞 Vocabulary

	喝喜酒		hē xǐjiǔ	VO	to drink at wedding feast, to attend wedding banquet	[to drink-happy event-wine]
	福氣	福气	fúqì	N	happy lot, good fortune	[blessing-air]
13.	娶		qǔ	V	to take a wife, to get married	
14.	溫柔		wēnróu	Adj	gentle and soft	[warm-supple]
	老婆		lǎopó	N	<口>太太、妻子 ↔老公	[prefix-wife]
15.	儘快	尽快	jǐnkuài	Adv	as soon as possible	[utmost-fast]
	另一半		lìngyíbàn	N	先生、妻子	[other-one-half]
16.	女強人	女强人	nǚqiángrén	N	successful career woman	[female-strong-person]
17.	壓力	压力	yālì	N	pressure	[pressure-force]
18.	講究	讲究	jiǎngjiū	V	to pay attention to, to be particular about	[to stress-to look into]
	男主外女主內		nán zhǔ wài nǚ zhǔ nèi	IE	男的在外頭工作，女的在家裏做家務	[man-to manage-outside-woman-to manage-inside]
19.	平等		píngděng	Adj/N	equal, equality	[level-to be equal]
20.	多少		duōshǎo	Adv	somewhat, to some extent	[more-less]
21.	挫折		cuòzhé	N	setback, reverse	[to defeat-to break]

Characters with Many Strokes

娶 溫 柔 婆 儘 強 壓 講 等 挫

詞彙用法 Words in Context

13.　娶：娶老婆；娶不到妻子 ↔嫁　　　　娶：娶老婆；娶不到妻子 ↔嫁
　　你準備娶一個什麼樣的妻子？　　　你准备娶一个什么样的妻子？
　　什麼樣的人娶不到老婆？　　　　　什么样的人娶不到老婆？

14.　溫柔：溫柔的妻子；說話的時候　　溫柔：温柔的妻子；说话的时候

很溫柔；個性很溫柔   很温柔；个性很温柔

你覺得妻子一定應該溫柔嗎？   你觉得妻子一定应该温柔吗？

你覺得服務員說話的聲音怎麼   你觉得服务员说话的声音怎么
樣？   样？

15. 儘快：（句型）   尽快：（句型）

16. 女強人：她是個女強人；做女強   女强人：她是个女强人；做女强
人   人

你會娶一個女強人當老婆嗎？   你会娶一个女强人当老婆吗？

你怎麼看女強人？   你怎么看女强人？

17. 壓力：有很多、大的壓力；面對   压力：有很多、大的压力；面对
壓力；學習、生活壓力大   压力；学习、生活压力大

你現在面對什麼樣的壓力？   你现在面对什么样的压力？

你覺得現在的社會中，什麼人的   你觉得现在的社会中，什么人的
壓力最大？   压力最大？

18. 講究：講究吃、穿；有很多講究   讲究：讲究吃、穿；有很多讲究

你覺得自己在哪些方面特別講   你觉得自己在哪些方面特别讲
究？   究？

吃西餐的時候有什麼講究？   吃西餐的时候有什么讲究？

19. 平等：平等的地位、關係；很平   平等：平等的地位、关系；很平
等；不平等；完全平等   等；不平等；完全平等

你覺得男女現在完全平等了嗎？   你觉得男女现在完全平等了吗？

你覺得你和父母的關係怎麼樣？   你觉得你和父母的关系怎么样？

20. 多少：多少要操點心；多少有點   多少：多少要操点心；多少有点
不滿；多少吃了一點   不满；多少吃了一点

孩子長大以後,父母就可以不為他   孩子长大以后,父母就可以不为他
們操心了吧？   们操心了吧？

你對宿舍的管理很滿意嗎？   你对宿舍的管理很满意吗？

21. 挫折：遇到挫折；有很多挫折；   挫折：遇到挫折；有很多挫折；

有很大的挫折感

你在學中文的時候，遇到了哪些挫折？

每個人在長大的過程中都會經歷什麼？

有很大的挫折感

你在学中文的时候，遇到了哪些挫折？

每个人在长大的过程中都会经历什么？

自由發揮與課堂活動 Free Discussion and Class Activities

5. 在選擇結婚對象的時候，哪些條件最重要？為什麼？

在选择结婚对象的时候，哪些条件最重要？为什么？

6. 辯論：在「男女平等」的社會中，男人的壓力比較大還是女人的壓力比較大？
   - 解釋你們認為什麼是男女平等的社會
   - 在傳統的社會裏男女的責任是什麼
   - 在這樣的社會裏男女各有什麼責任

   男生組：男人的壓力大
   女生組：女人的壓力大

辯论：在"男女平等"的社会中，男人的压力比较大还是女人的压力比较大？
   - 解释你们认为什么是男女平等的社会
   - 在传统的社会里男女的责任是什么
   - 在这样的社会里男女各有什么责任

   男生組：男人的压力大
   女生組：女人的压力大

敘述 Narrative

徵婚廣告還是商品廣告

三十歲以上的未婚男女總是會受到人們特別的「關心」。很不幸，我就是這樣的一個大齡青年，所以好像婚姻 **³不再是**我個人的問題，而是大家的事情。為了不讓大家為我的事情過分操心，我決定儘快解決自己的終身大事，加入電視徵婚的行列。

聽說「非常男女」是一個收視率很高的電視徵婚節目，很多人都通過這個節目找到了自己滿意的對象，所以我決定參加這個節目，我想說不定我也能找到自己的夢中情人。

這個節目分為三個部分。首先，每個參加節目的人要介紹自己的年齡、職業、學歷、興趣、愛好等等。接著主持人會提出一個問題，大家分別談談自己的看法，然後大家可以互相問問題。之所以這樣安排，大概是為了讓大家 **⁴儘可能地多**互相了解。當然最後，也是最關鍵的是要告訴大家你最喜歡的人是誰，假如兩個人互相喜歡，當然很好；**⁵假如** 沒有在節目中找到合適的對象，**也**沒關係。因為看這個節目的人很多，如果有人對你有興趣，他們可以直接和你聯繫。

老實說，參加節目的十位男士無論是外表，還是學歷都很不錯。後來，我主動和其中的一位男士聯繫，**⁶向**他**表示**我的好感，並且約他見面。可是我萬萬 沒想到他卻告訴我，他不能和我約會，因為他已經有女朋友了！「神經病！」我大聲罵他，「有女朋友為什麼還去參加電視徵婚？」「因為這個節目的收視率很高，我的老板覺得那是宣傳我們公司 的好機會。」怪不得拍節目

的那天，他的同事和老板都來了，我開始還以為這個人的「人緣」一定很好。原來這些都是他的老板安排好的計劃。徵婚廣告竟然變成了商業廣告！我**再也**不信什麼電視紅娘了，我還是繼續做我的單身貴族吧！

閱讀理解 Comprehension Check

11. 在中國，什麼樣的人會受到別人特別的關心？敘述者怎麼解決這個問題？

12. 敘述者決定參加什麼節目？為什麼？

13. 那個節目分為哪三個部分？

14. 如果在節目中沒找到合適的對象，有關係嗎？為什麼？

15. 參加那個節目的男士怎麼樣？敘述者主動做了什麼事？結果呢？

16. 為什麼有女朋友的人還去參加那個節目？

17. 最後敘述者決定怎麼辦？為什麼？

征婚广告还是商品广告

三十岁以上的未婚男女总是会受到人们特别的"关心"。很不幸，我就是这样的一个大龄青年，所以好象婚姻 [3]**不再是**我个人的问题，而是大家的事情。为了不让大家为我的事情过分操心，我决定尽快解决自己的终身大事，加入电视征婚的行列。

听说"非常男女"是一个收视率很高的电视征婚节目，很多人都通过这个节目找到了自己满意的对象，所以我决定参加这个节目，我想说不定我也能找到自己的梦中情人。

这个节目分为三个部分。首先，每个参加节目的人要介绍自己的年龄、职业、学历、兴趣、爱好等等。接着主持人会提出一个问题，大家分别谈谈自己的看法，然后大家可以互相问问题。之所以这样安排，大概是为了让大家[4]**尽可能地**多互相了解。当然最后，也是最关键的是要告诉大家你最喜欢的人是谁，假如两个人互相喜欢，当然很好；[5]**假如**没有在节目中找到合适的对象，**也**没关系。因为看这个节目的人很多，如果有人对你有兴趣，他们可以直接和你联系。

老实说，参加节目的十位男士无论是外表，还是学历都很不错。后来，我主动和其中的一位男士联系，[6]**向**他**表示**我的好感，并且约他见面。可是我万万没想到他却告诉我，他不能和我约会，因为他已经有女朋友了！"神经病！"

我大声骂他，"有女朋友为什么还去参加电视征婚？""因为这个节目的收视率很高，我的老板觉得那是宣传我们公司的好机会。"怪不得拍节目的那天，他的同事和老板都来了，我开始还以为这个人的"人缘"一定很好。原来这些都是他的老板安排好的计划。征婚广告竟然变成了商业广告！我**再也**不信什么电视红娘了，我还是继续做我的单身贵族吧！

阅读理解 Comprehension Check

11. 在中国，什么样的人会受到别人特别的关心？叙述者怎么解决这个问题？

12. 叙述者决定参加什么节目？为什么？

13. 那个节目分为哪三个部分？

14. 如果在节目中没找到合适的对象，有关系吗？为什么？

15. 参加那个节目的男士怎么样？叙述者主动做了什么事？结果呢？

16. 为什么有女朋友的人还去参加那个节目？

17. 最后叙述者决定怎么办？为什么？

敘述生詞 Vocabulary

22.	不幸		búxìng	Adv/Adj/N	運氣不好 ↔幸運	[not-luck]
	大齡青年	大龄青年	dàlíng qīngnián	N	<PRC> single young persons over 30	[big-age-youth]
23.	過分	过分	guòfèn	Adv	excessively, over-, undue	[to exceed-what is within one's rights]
24.	操心		cāoxīn	VO	to worry, to trouble about	[to hold-heart]
25.	加入		jiārù	V	to join, to add, to put in	[to add-to enter]
26.	行列		hángliè	N	ranks, procession	[row-column]
	收視率	收视率	shōushìlǜ	N	(TV/etc.) ratings	[to receive-to review-rate]
	年齡	年龄	niánlíng	N	age	[age-years]
27.	職業	职业	zhíyè	N	occupation, profession	[job-employment]
	愛好	爱好	àihào	N	interest, hobby	[to love-to like]

28.	接著	接着	jiēzhe	Adv	next, immediately after, to follow	[to connect-(particle)]
	主持人		zhǔchírén	N	host, anchor, chair	[to direct-to run-person]
29.	提出		tíchū	RV	to put forward, to raise, to pose	[to mention-to vent]
30.	分別		fēnbéi	Adv/N	separately, difference	[to divide-to separate]
31.	假如		jiǎrú	Conj	如果、要是	[conditional-if]
	男士		nánshì	N	man	[man-person]
32.	外表		wàibiǎo	N/Adv	outward appearance, surface	[outside-surface]
33.	主動	主动	zhǔdòng	Adv	on one's own initiative	[to direct-to move]
34.	表示		biǎoshì	V	to show, to express (usually feelings), to indicate	[to indicate-to show]
35.	好感		hǎogǎn	N	favorable impression	[good-feeling]
36.	萬萬	万万	wànwàn	Adv	absolutely (not), by no means (used only in negation)	[ten thousand-ten thousand]
	神經病	神经病	shénjīngbìng	IE	＜口＞(You're) crazy!	[nerve-disease]
	人緣	人缘	rényuán	N	relations with other people	[people-karmic affinity]
	紅娘	红娘	hóngniáng	N	match-maker	[red-elderly married woman

Characters with Many Strokes

齡 操 率 職 業 接 假 動 萬 經

詞匯用法 Words in Context

22. 不幸：很不幸；發生了不幸 不幸：很不幸；发生了不幸

我們這個星期的考試取消了，你 我们这个星期的考试取消了，你
們呢？ 们呢？

大家最近為什麼都在談和飛機有 大家最近为什么都在谈和飞机有
關的話題？ 关的话题？

23. 過分：過分關心、講究；太過分 过分：过分关心、讲究；太过分
了 了

你覺得小麗在穿的方面是不是太
講究了？

你覺得小丽在穿的方面是不是太
讲究了？

你為什麼這麼生氣？

你为什么这么生气？

24. 操心：為孩子操心；愛操心；操
了太多的心

操心：为孩子操心；爱操心；操
了太多的心

你父母常常為誰操心？

你父母常常为谁操心？

你覺得自己是一個愛操心的人
嗎？

你觉得自己是一个爱操心的人
吗？

25. 加入：加入一個組織；加入新的
內容　↔退出

加入：加入一个组织；加入新的
内容　　↔退出

你加入了什麼學生組織？

你加入了什么学生组织？

你的論文不是寫完了嗎，怎麼還
在改？

你的论文不是写完了吗，怎么还
在改？

26. 行列：學生、商人的行列；加
入、進入一個行列

行列：学生、商人的行列；加
入、进入一个行列

現在電腦專業學生的行列為什麼
越來越大？

现在电脑专业学生的行列为什么
越来越大？

你是什麼時候加入學中文的行列
的？

你是什么时候加入学中文的行列
的？

27. 職業：職業運動員

职业：职业运动员

你最喜歡的職業是什麼？

你最喜欢的职业是什么？

這個大學的籃球運動員算不算職
業運動員？

这个大学的篮球运动员算不算职
业运动员？

28. 接著：接著說　＝接下來

接着：接着说　＝接下来

接著該誰上來報告？

接着该谁上来报告？

你已經讀完碩士了，接著要不要
讀博士？

你已经读完硕士了，接着要不要
读博士？

29. 提出：提出問題、要求、條件、

提出：提出问题、要求、条件、

意見；提不出問題

開學的第一堂課，老師一般會做
什麼？

你為什麼不接受那份工作？

30. 分別：分別提出要求；分別談
話；他們的觀點有分別

同學們有問題的時候應該怎麼和
老師談？

你覺得西餐和中餐一樣嗎？

31. 假如：（句型）

32. 外表：重視、講究外表；外表正
常、乾淨 ↔內心

你談戀愛的時候會重視什麼，忽
視什麼？

你覺得那個新同學怎麼樣？

33. 主動：主動要求、學習；態度很
主動；不夠主動 ↔被動

你自己學習中文的態度怎麼樣？

如果父母幫孩子選擇專業，會有
什麼後果？

34. 表示：（句型）

35. 好感：有好感；沒什麼好感
↔反感

你喜歡這個學校嗎？

你為什麼從來不和那個同學講
話？

36. 萬萬：萬萬不能學中文；萬萬沒
想到

一個女孩半夜一個人回家安全嗎？

一个女孩半夜一个人回家安全吗？

你以前知道中文這麼難學嗎？

你以前知道中文这么难学吗？

自由發揮與課堂活動 Free Discussion and Class Activities

7. 你覺得社會中是不是存在歧視大齡青年的現象？請舉例說明。

你觉得社会中是不是存在歧视大龄青年的现象？请举例说明。

8. 如果過了三十歲還沒有結婚，你會不會去相親？為什麼？

如果过了三十岁还没有结婚，你会不会去相亲？为什么？

9. 據你所知，電視上有哪些徵婚的節目？你覺得哪些節目比較好，而哪些不太好？為什麼？

据你所知，电视上有哪些征婚的节目？你觉得哪些节目比较好，而哪些不太好？为什么？

10. 現在人們常常提到「網戀」，你相信通過網絡可以找到真正的愛情嗎？你覺得網絡愛情存在哪些危險？

现在人们常常提到"网恋"，你相信通过网络可以找到真正的爱情吗？你觉得网络爱情存在哪些危险？

11. 辯論：通過相親和徵婚能找到真正的愛情嗎？為什麼？

辩论：通过相亲和征婚能找到真正的爱情吗？为什么？

說明 Exposition

 幾年後男人找不到老婆

　　根據中國第五次人口普查，我們發現中國男女嬰兒的出生比例不平衡，也就是說出生的男嬰比女嬰多。產生這種現象的主要原因，是因中國傳統文化中長期存在重男輕女的觀念；其次人們養兒防老的想法一時也難以改變；此外，也有知道是女嬰後選擇人工流產的現象，但這並不是男嬰出生比例高的主要原因。

　　這個人口問題已經引起了中國政府的重視。除了繼續宣傳男女平等的觀念外，發展經濟無疑是最有效的解決問題的方法。因為只有通過經濟的發展，才能減輕人們生活上的壓力，給人們更多受教育的機會，這樣才能讓老百姓放棄重男輕女、養兒防老的傳統觀念。

閱讀理解 Comprehension Check

18. 中國第五次人口普查的結果怎麼樣？
19. 為什麼中國的男女嬰出生率不平衡？是因為選擇性流產嗎？
20. 作者認為解決中國人口問題的方法有哪些？什麼方法最有效？

几年后男人找不到老婆

　　根据中国第五次人口普查，我们发现中国男女婴儿的出生比例不平衡，也就是说出生的男婴比女婴多。产生这种现象的主要原因，是因中国传统文化中长期存在重男轻女的观念；其次人们养儿防老的想法一时也难以改变；此外，也有知道是女婴后选择人工流产的现象，但这并不是男婴出生比例高的主要原因。

　　这个人口问题已经引起了中国政府的重视。除了继续宣传男女平等的观念外，发展经济无疑是最有效的解决问题的方法。因为只有通过经济的发展，才能减轻人们生活上的压力，给人们更多受教育的机会，这样才能让老百姓放弃重男轻女、养儿防老的传统观念。

阅读理解 Comprehension Check

18. 中国第五次人口普查的结果怎么样？
19. 为什么中国的男女婴出生率不平衡？是因为选择性流产吗？
20. 作者认为解决中国人口问题的方法有哪些？什么方法最有效？

說明生詞 Vocabulary

	普查		pǔchá	N	general survey/ investigation	[widespread-to investigate]
	嬰兒	婴儿	yīng'ér	N	baby, infant	[infant-child]
37.	出生		chūshēng	N/ V	birth, to be born	[to come out-to be born]
38.	比例		bǐlì	N	proportion	[to compare-case]
39.	平衡		pínghéng	N/ Adj	balance, balanced	[level-to measure]
	重男輕女	重男轻女	zhòng nán qīng nǚ	IE	to value boys over girls	[to lay stress on-boy-to neglect-girl]
	養兒防老	养儿防老	yǎng ér fáng lǎo	IE	to raise children to take care of one in one's old age	[to raise-child-guard against-old]
40.	一時	一时	yìshí	N	a short while, now...	[one-time]
41.	此外		cǐwài	Conj	besides, in addition, moreover	[this-outside]
42.	選擇	选择	xuǎnzé	V/ N	to select, to opt, choice	[to choose-to select]
	人工		réngōng	Adj/ N	man-made, manual work	[person-work]
	流產	流产	liúchǎn	N/ VO	abortion, miscarriage, to miscarry	[to flow-to give birth to]
43.	重視	重视	zhòngshì	V	to take sth. seriously, to value	[important-to regard]
44.	減輕	减轻	jiǎnqīng	RV	to lighten, to ease, to mitigate	[to reduce-light]
	機會	机会	jīhuì	N	chance, opportunity	[chance-occasion]

Characters with Many Strokes

普　嬰　例　衡　養　選　擇　產　減　機

詞匯用法 Words in Context

37. 出生：1990年出生；出生在北京；還沒出生；出生率

你是在什麼地方出生的？

和美國比，中國人的出生率怎麼樣？

37. 出生：1990年出生；出生在北京；还没出生；出生率

你是在什么地方出生的？

和美国比，中国人的出生率怎么样？

38. 比例：男女比例；佔比較大的比例

在中文課中，哪些學生佔的比例比較大？

什麼樣的社會可以被稱為老年人的社會？

39. 平衡：比例平衡；保持平衡；平衡能力

在哪些職業中，有男女比例不平衡的問題？

開始學騎自行車的時候，為什麼你總是摔倒？

40. 一時：一時忘了；一時高興、糊塗

你和那個人談了很長時間的話，怎麼不知道他的名字？

你不喜歡旅遊，為什麼同意和小李一起去？

41. 此外：

你為什麼總說自己功課多呢？

大四的學生都在忙什麼？

42. 選擇：選擇專業；有很多選擇

你為什麼會到這兒來念大學？

你畢業之後打算做什麼？

43. 重視：重視外表、環境；受到重視；值得重視

你覺得現在哪些社會問題最值得重視？

你選學校時最重視什麼？

38. 比例：男女比例；佔比较大的比例

在中文课中，哪些学生占的比例比较大？

什么样的社会可以被称为老年人的社会？

39. 平衡：比例平衡；保持平衡；平衡能力

在哪些职业中，有男女比例不平衡的问题？

开始学骑自行车的时候，为什么你总是摔倒？

40. 一时：一时忘了；一时高兴、糊涂

你和那个人谈了很长时间的话，怎么不知道他的名字？

你不喜欢旅游，为什么同意和小李一起去？

41. 此外：

你为什么总说自己功课多呢？

大四的学生都在忙什么？

42. 选择：选择专业；有很多选择

你为什么会到这儿来念大学？

你毕业之后打算做什么？

43. 重视：重视外表、环境；受到重视；值得重视

你觉得现在哪些社会问题最值得重视？

你选学校时最重视什么？

44. 減輕：減輕壓力、負擔、責任、　　減轻：减轻压力、负担、责任、
　　體重、痛苦　　　　　　　　　　体重、痛苦

　　你為什麼每天都去做運動？　　　你为什么每天都去做运动？

　　怎樣能減輕學生的學習壓力？　　怎样能减轻学生的学习压力？

自由發揮與課堂活動　Free Discussion and Class Activities

12. 你覺得在美國的社會中有沒有重　你觉得在美国的社会中有没有重
　　男輕女的現象？舉例說明。　　　男轻女的现象？举例说明。

13. 世界上很多國家都有人口問題，　世界上很多国家都有人口问题，
　　請你選一個國家介紹（比如印　　请你选一个国家介绍（比如印
　　度，意大利，加拿大……）。請　度，意大利，加拿大……）。请
　　說明　　　　　　　　　　　　　说明
　　1) 那個國家有什麼樣的人口問　1) 那个国家有什么样的人口问
　　　題；　　　　　　　　　　　　题；
　　2) 問題產生的原因；　　　　　2) 问题产生的原因；
　　3) 政府用什麼方法解決。　　　3) 政府用什么方法解决。

應用詞 Productive Vocabulary

◎By Grammatical Categories

Nouns/Pronouns/Measure Words

婚姻	hūnyīn	marriage, matrimony
幸福	xìngfú	happiness, happy
煩惱	fánnǎo	worry, to worry
緣分	yuánfèn	predestined affinity
職業	zhíyè	occupation, profession
外表	wàibiǎo	outward appearance, surface
好感	hǎogǎn	favorable impression
壓力	yālì	pressure
挫折	cuòzhé	setback, reverse

行列	hángliè	ranks, procession
一時	yìshí	a short while, now...
比例	bǐlì	proportion
平衡	pínghéng	balance, balanced
出生	chūshēng	birth, to be born
女強人	nǚqiángrén	successful career woman
單身貴族	dānshēn guìzú	unmarried/single adults (lit. single nobles)

Verbs/Stative Verbs/Adjectives

娶	qǔ	to take a wife, to get married
創造	chuàngzào	to create, to produce, to bring about
繼續	jìxù	to continue
加入	jiārù	to join, to add, to put in
提出	tíchū	to put forward, to raise, to pose
表示	biǎoshì	to show, to express (usually feelings), to indicate
重視	zhòngshì	to take sth. seriously, to value
講究	jiǎngjiū	to pay attention to, to be particular about

操心	cāoxīn	to worry, to trouble about
選擇	xuǎnzé	to select, to opt, choice
減輕	jiǎnqīng	to lighten, to ease, to mitigate
戀愛	liàn'ài	to love, romantic attachment
相親	xiāngqīn/ xiàngqīn	to get look at prospective spouse before engagement
徵婚	zhēnghūn	to advertise for marriage partner
溫柔	wēnróu	gentle and soft
平等	píngděng	equal, equality

Adverbs and Others

多少	duōshǎo	somewhat, to some extent
接著	jiēzhe	next, immediately after, to follow
儘快	jǐnkuài	as soon as possible
主動	zhǔdòng	on one's own initiative
過分	guòfèn	excessively, over-
分別	fēnbéi	separately, difference

萬萬	wànwàn	absolutely (not), by no means
不幸	búxìng	unfortunate(ly), misfortune
不妨	bùfáng	might as well, why not (Ving)
假如	jiǎrú	if, supposing, in case
此外	cǐwài	besides, in addition, moreover
說不定	shuōbudìng	perhaps, maybe

理解詞 Receptive Vocabulary

◎By Grammatical Categories

Nouns/Pronouns/Measure Words

年代	niándài	day and age, years	男士	nánshì	man
年齡	niánlíng	age	叔叔	shūshu/ shúshu	father's younger brother, uncle
機會	jīhuì	chance, opportunity	紅娘	hóngniáng	match-maker
節目	jiémù	program, item	主持人	zhǔchírén	host, anchor, chair
愛好	àihào	interest, hobby	收視率	shōushìlǜ	(TV/etc.) ratings
人緣	rényuán	relations with other people	另一半	lìngyíbàn	the other half
福氣	fúqì	happy lot, good fortune	夢中情人	mèngzhōng qíngrén	dream lover
普查	pǔchá	general survey/investigation	大齡青年	dàlíng qīngnián	<PRC> single young persons over 30
流產	liúchǎn	abortion, to miscarry	終身大事	zhōngshēn dàshì	important event in one's life—marriage
嬰兒	yīng'ér	baby, infant			
老婆	lǎopó	wife			

Verbs/Stative Verbs/Adjectives

丟人	diūrén	to lose face	人工	réngōng	man-made, manual work
喝喜酒	hē xǐjiǔ	to attend wedding banquet			

Adverbs and Others

神經病	shénjīngbìng	(You're) crazy!	男主外 女主內	nán zhǔ wài nǔ zhǔ nèi	The man is in charge of work outside and the woman takes care of work in the house.
重男輕女	zhòng nán qīng nǔ	to value boys over girls			
養兒防老	yǎng ér fáng lǎo	to raise children to take care of one in one's old age			

本课词表 Chapter Vocabulary

◎By Pinyin

Words with asterisk* are productive vocabulary which needs to be memorized and studied for its usage.

àihào	愛好	interest, hobby	bùfáng*	不妨	might as well, why not (Ving)
biǎoshì*	表示	to show, to express (usually feelings)	cāoxīn*	操心	to worry
bǐlì*	比例	proportion	chūshēng*	出生	birth, to be born
búxìng*	不幸	unfortunate(ly), misfortune	chuàngzào*	創造	to create, to produce
			cǐwài*	此外	besides, in addition

cuòzhé*	挫折	setback, reverse
dàlíng qīngnián	大龄青年	<PRC>single young persons over 30
dānshēn guìzú*	单身贵族	unmarried/single adults
diūrén	丢人	to lose face
duōshǎo*	多少	somewhat, to some extent
fánnǎo*	烦恼	worry, to worry
fēnbié*	分别	separately, difference
fúqì	福气	happy lot
guòfèn*	过分	excessively, over-
hángliè*	行列	ranks, procession
hǎogǎn*	好感	favorable impression
hē xǐjiǔ	喝喜酒	to attend wedding banquet
hóngniáng	红娘	match-maker
hūnyīn*	婚姻	marriage, matrimony
jiǎngjiū*	讲究	to pay attention to
jiǎnqīng*	减轻	to lighten, to ease
jiǎrú*	假如	if, supposing, in case
jiārù*	加入	to join, to add
jiémù	节目	program, item
jiēzhe*	接着	next, to follow
jīhuì	机会	chance, opportunity
jǐnkuài*	尽快	as soon as possible
jìxù*	继续	to continue
lǎopó	老婆	wife
liàn'ài*	恋爱	to love, romantic attachment
lìngyíbàn	另一半	the other half
liúchǎn	流产	abortion, to miscarry
mèngzhōng qíngrén	梦中情人	dream lover
nán zhǔ wài nǚ zhǔ nèi	男主外女主内	The man is in charge of work outside and the woman takes care of work in the house.
nánshì	男士	man
niándài	年代	day and age, years

niánlíng	年龄	age
nǚqiángrén*	女强人	successful career woman
píngděng*	平等	equal, equality
pínghéng*	平衡	balance, balanced
pǔchá	普查	general survey
qǔ*	娶	to take a wife
réngōng	人工	man-made
rényuán	人缘	relations with other people
shénjīngbìng	神经病	(You're) crazy!
shūshu/ shúshu	叔叔	uncle
shōushìlǜ	收视率	(TV/etc.) ratings
shuōbudìng*	说不定	perhaps, maybe
tíchū*	提出	to put forward
wàibiǎo*	外表	outward appearance
wànwàn*	万万	absolutely (not), by no means
wēnróu*	温柔	gentle and soft
xiāngqīn/ xiàngqīn*	相亲	to get look at prospective spouse before engagement
xìngfú*	幸福	happiness, happy
xuǎnzé*	选择	to select, choice
yālì*	压力	pressure
yǎng ér fáng lǎo	养儿防老	to raise children to take care of one in one's old age
yīng'ér	婴儿	baby, infant
yìshí*	一时	a short while, now...
yuánfèn*	缘分	predestined affinity
zhēnghūn*	征婚	to advertise for marriage partner
zhíyè*	职业	occupation
zhòng nán qīng nǚ	重男轻女	to value boys over girls
zhōngshēn dàshì	终身大事	marriage
zhòngshì*	重视	to take sth. seriously
zhǔchírén	主持人	host, anchor, chair
zhǔdòng*	主动	on one's own initiative

語法和用法 Grammar and Usage

Pay attention to the function of the structure and then study the example sentences. When blanks are provided, either answer the questions or complete the sentences.

1. Expressing a moderate complaint

都什麼N了	dōu shénme…le	It's already N (time)!
都多(大/久/晚)了		N: 時候、年代

● 都什麼年代了，你還讓我去相親？

1. 我男朋友覺得，我們結婚以後應該和他父母住在一起，這樣照顧他們很方便！

    我男朋友觉得，我们结婚以后应该和他父母住在一起，这样照顾他们很方便！

    My boyfriend thinks that after we marry, we should live with his parents. That way it's convenient to take care of them.

    都什麼年代了，他怎麼還有這麼傳統的思想？你們結婚以後應該自己住才對。

    都什么年代了，他怎么还有这么传统的思想？你们结婚以后应该自己住才对。

    In this day and age how could he still have this kind of traditional idea? After you get married, you should live by yourselves.

2. 媽，我的朋友們都勸我登一個徵婚廣告，這樣也許可以找到一個理想的對象，你覺得怎麼樣？

    妈，我的朋友们都劝我登一个征婚广告，这样也许可以找到一个理想的对象，你觉得怎么样？

    Mom, my friends all urge me to run an ad to look for a partner. This way, perhaps I can find an ideal mate. What do you think?

    你都多大了，怎麼自己的事情還要媽媽幫你決定？

    你都多大了，怎么自己的事情还要妈妈帮你决定？

    How old are you? Why do you still need your mother to help you decide your personal affairs?

3. 都什麼時候了，你怎麼還在推銷清潔劑？

    都什么时候了，你怎么还在推销清洁剂？

    Look at the time already! Why are you still selling detergent?

我推銷了一整天，可是大家對我的產品毫無興趣，我只好繼續推銷。

我推销了一整天，可是大家对我的产品毫无兴趣，我只好继续推销。

I have been selling all day, but people have no interest in my product at all, so I just keep on selling it.

4.　我現在還沒決定寒假要不要去夏威夷，你有什麼打算嗎？

我现在还没决定寒假要不要去夏威夷，你有什么打算吗？

5.　媽媽，我的運動鞋你洗乾淨了嗎？

妈妈，我的运动鞋你洗干净了吗？

6.　今天晚上有一場非常精彩的籃球比賽，你要不要和我一起看？

今天晚上有一场非常精彩的篮球比赛，你要不要和我一起看？

The pattern 都什麼 N了/都多 (大、久、晚) 了 expresses a moderate complaint about the lateness or perceived inappropriateness of an action taken by the interlocutor. Note there is always a 了 at the end of the sentence. No subject should be placed before 都什麼 N了, so it's wrong to say 你都什麼時候了，怎麼還不做決定？ Yet, it's all right to have a subject when 都多大了 is used, e.g., 你都多大了，怎麼還不自己做決定？ 'How old are you? Why don't you yourself make a decision?'

2. Expressing a polite suggestion

S 不妨 V，(說不定)⋯ bùfáng…(shuōbudìng)…	It wouldn't hurt for S to V Perhaps…

● 現在有一個電視徵婚的節目很受歡迎，你不妨也去試一試，說不定能找到你的夢中情人。

1.　我很喜歡李明，可是我不敢告訴他我

我很喜欢李明，可是我不敢告诉他我

I like Li Ming very much, but I dare not tell him how I feel

的想法，因為我不知道他對我有沒有感覺。

的想法，因为我不知道他对我有没有感觉。

because I don't know if he has feelings for me or not.

我覺得你不妨向他表示你的好感，說不定他也很喜歡你，只是不好意思說罷了。

我觉得你不妨向他表示你的好感，说不定他也很喜欢你，只是不好意思说罢了。

I think it wouldn't hurt for you to tell him your feelings. Perhaps he likes you, too, but he is too embarrassed to say it.

2. 我最討厭的就是搖滾樂，先不談旋律，就連歌手在唱什麼，我都聽不懂。

我最讨厌的就是摇滚乐，先不谈旋律，就连歌手在唱什么，我都听不懂。

What I dislike the most is rock-and-roll music. To say nothing of the melody, I don't even understand what those singers are singing about.

其實你不妨仔細地聽一聽搖滾樂，說不定你聽懂他們在唱什麼以後，就會喜歡了。

其实你不妨仔细地听一听摇滚乐，说不定你听懂他们在唱什么以后，就会喜欢了。

Actually it wouldn't hurt you to listen to rock-and-roll music carefully. Perhaps after you understand what they are singing about, you will like it.

3. 我上個月買了一個手機，不過現在發現它的功能好像不是很好，不知道還能不能退貨。

我上个月买了一个手机，不过现在发现它的功能好象不是很好，不知道还能不能退货。

Last month I bought a cellular phone, but now it appears that it doesn't function very well. I don't know if I can still return it or not.

你不妨去商店試一試，說不定他們會給你退貨。

你不妨去商店试一试，说不定他们会给你退货。

It wouldn't hurt you to go to the store and give it a try. Perhaps they will let you return it.

4. 我是個相信緣分的人，可是我媽一定要讓我去相親，你說我該怎麼辦？

我是个相信缘分的人，可是我妈一定要让我去相亲，你说我该怎么办？

5. 電視裏總是播很多的廣告，我　　電视里总是播很多的广告，我
　　都煩死了！　　　　　　　　　都烦死了！

---

6. 我以前最反感的就是推銷員，　　我以前最反感的就是推销员，
　　現在我自己卻要作一個推銷　　　现在我自己却要作一个推销
　　員，我真不知道該怎麼向顧客　　员，我真不知道该怎么向顾客
　　推銷商品。　　　　　　　　　推销商品。

To give a polite suggestion, one can use the pattern 不妨 V， (說不定) …. Note that 不妨 should go after the subject. Since the clause that accompanies 說不定 is a conjecture, it often includes an auxiliary verb such as 會 (examples 2 and 3)、能、可以.

3. Expressing a maximum extent

> S 儘可能地快/早/多 V　jǐnkěnéngde kuài/zǎo/duō　to V as quickly/early/much as possible

● 之所以這樣安排，大概是為了讓大家儘可能地多互相了解。

1. 你為什麼現在急著　　你为什么现在急着　　Why are you so anxious to find
　　找對象？　　　　　找对象？　　　　　a partner now?

　　過了三十歲還沒有　　过了三十岁还没有　　I'm over thirty and haven't been
　　結婚，我想我應該　　结婚，我想我应该　　married. I think I should get
　　儘可能地快解決我　　尽可能地快解决我　　married as soon as possible, so
　　的終身大事，省得　　的终身大事，省得　　that people won't worry about
　　大家為我操心。　　大家为我操心。　　me.

2. 你現在怎麼這麼用　　你现在怎么这么用　　How come you work so hard
　　功？　　　　　　　功？　　　　　　　now?

　　雖然下個星期才考　　虽然下个星期才考　　Although I don't have a test till
　　試，但是我覺得還　　试，但是我觉得还　　next week, I think I should
　　　　　　　　　　　　　　　　　　　　prepare for it as soon as

是應該儘可能地早準備，這樣就不會到考試前熬夜。

是应该尽可能地早准备，这样就不会到考试前熬夜。

possible. This way, I won't have to stay up late the night before the test.

3. 為什麼有些顧客對推銷員很反感？

为什么有些顾客对推销员很反感？

Why do some customers dislike salespeople?

有些顧客對推銷員有反感，可能是因為一些推銷員總是希望顧客儘可能地多買他們的商品，而沒有考慮會不會過期的問題。

有些顾客对推销员有反感，可能是因为一些推销员总是希望顾客尽可能地多买他们的商品，而没有考虑会不会过期的问题。

Some customers dislike salespeople. Probably because some salespeople always want their customers to buy as much merchandise as possible, and do not think about whether the goods will expire or not.

4. 我打算聖誕節的時候去旅行，你覺得我什麼時候訂機票比較好？

我打算圣诞节的时候去旅行，你觉得我什么时候订机票比较好？

5. 最近大家都在討論下學期選什麼課，可是我還沒決定。

最近大家都在讨论下学期选什么课，可是我还没决定。

6. 你為什麼每天中午都吃快餐，這會有害於你的健康。

你为什么每天中午都吃快餐，这会有害于你的健康。

The pattern 儘可能地快/早/多V is used to express a maximum extent. Note that 儘可能地快/早/多 is placed after the subject. Since this pattern is often used in a suggestion or for giving advice, one can expect to find 應該 in most cases (examples 1 and 2). 儘可能地快/早 is also lexicalized into 儘快/儘早. In mainland usage, it seems more common to see 地 placed after the adverb 快/早/多 and thus the pattern is 儘可能快/早/多地 V.

4. Expressing obsolescence

S 不再是 N（了）	búzàishì…(le)	S is no longer N
S 不再 VO（了）	búzài…(le)	S no longer VO
S 再也不/別 VO 了	zàiyěbù/bié…le	S will never VO again

- 我就是這樣的一個大齡青年，所以好像婚姻不再是我個人的問題，而是大家的事情。

- 我再也不信什麼電視紅娘了……

1. 年輕人會一直崇拜某個明星嗎？

   年轻人会一直崇拜某个明星吗？

   Do young people keep worshiping a certain star?

   很多年輕人盲目地崇拜一些明星，可是等他們的思想比較成熟以後，這些明星就不再是他們的偶像了。

   很多年轻人盲目地崇拜一些明星，可是等他们的思想比较成熟以后，这些明星就不再是他们的偶像了。

   Many young people worship some stars blindly. Yet, after they become more mature, these stars are no longer their idols.

2. 現代的劇院跟傳統的一樣嗎？大家還在那兒欣賞京劇嗎？

   现代的剧院跟传统的一样吗？大家还在那儿欣赏京剧吗？

   Are modern theaters the same as the traditional ones? Do people still enjoy Beijing opera there?

   現代的戲院雖然保持了傳統的結構，可是不再是人們欣賞京劇的場所了，反而成了人們聚會聊天的地方。

   现代的戏院虽然保持了传统的结构，可是不再是人们欣赏京剧的场所了，反而成了人们聚会聊天的地方。

   Although modern theaters have kept traditional structure, they are no longer a place for people to enjoy Beijing opera. Instead, they've become places for people to hang out and chat.

3. 你還要上電視推銷自己嗎？

   你还要上电视推销自己吗？

   Do you want to go on TV again to promote yourself?

   第一次上電視徵婚，並沒有找到我的夢中情人，我決

   第一次上电视征婚，并没有找到我的梦中情人，我决

   The first time I went on TV to find a date, I couldn't find my dream lover. So, I've decided not to promote myself this way

定再也不用這種方　　定再也不用这种方　　again.
法推銷自己了。　　　法推销自己了。

4.　以前你很喜歡看香港的功夫　　以前你很喜欢看香港的功夫
　　片，最近為什麼不看了？　　　片，最近为什么不看了？

5.　老張說投資股票能賺很多錢，　　老张说投资股票能赚很多钱，
　　可是我買的股票卻讓我賠péi了很　　可是我买的股票却让我赔了很
　　多錢。　　　　　　　　　　　　多钱。

6.　我記得李明上高中的時候很驕　　我记得李明上高中的时候很骄
　　傲，現在他變了嗎？　　　　　　傲，现在他变了吗？

To express obsolescence, one can use the pattern 不再 or 再也不/別. 不再 means
"no longer" and it can be followed by a noun or a verb. When it's followed by a noun,
there is always 是 after 不再. Since 不再 indicates a change of condition, 了 is often
used as well. Note the difference between the following: (1) 我不再是功夫片迷了
'I'm no longer a fan of kungfu films'; (2) 我不再喜歡看功夫片了，我現在喜歡看愛
情片 'I don't like to watch kungfu movies any more; now I like to watch romantic
films.' 再也不/別 means "never again," and there is always a verb phrase after it. 了
is often present to mark the change of condition, e.g., 現在的功夫片都不好看，我再
也不看功夫片了 'The kungfu movies nowadays are not good. I will never watch
another kungfu movie.'

5. Expressing a condition

假如S … 也/就 V	jiǎrú…yě/jiù	If S…, then V

● 假如沒有在節目中找到合適的對象，也沒關係。

1.　我們真有緣！居然　　我们真有缘！居然　　We really are meant to be
　　在這兒認識。　　　　在这儿认识。　　　together. It's such a surprise to
　　　　　　　　　　　　　　　　　　　　　meet you here.

假如這所大學沒有接受我的申請，我們現在就不會成為好朋友。

假如这所大学没有接受我的申请，我们现在就不会成为好朋友。

If this university hadn't accepted my application, we wouldn't have become good friends.

2. 你覺得電視徵婚好嗎？

你觉得电视征婚好吗？

Do you think it is good to go on TV to find a date?

我覺得電視徵婚沒什麼不好的，如果你能找到自己的夢中情人，當然最好；假如沒找到，你至少也可以認識一些新朋友，總之對你沒有壞處。

我觉得电视征婚没什么不好的，如果你能找到自己的梦中情人，当然最好；假如没找到，你至少也可以认识一些新朋友，总之对你没有坏处。

I think there is nothing wrong with going on TV to find a date. If you can find your dream lover, of course that's best. If not, you at least will meet some new friends. In short, this will do you no harm.

3. 老板答應你什麼？

老板答应你什么？

What has the boss promised you?

我的老板告訴我，假如我能在一個月以內推銷出我們公司的商品，她就給我提職。

我的老板告诉我，假如我能在一个月以内推销出我们公司的商品，她就给我提职。

My boss told me that if I can sell our merchandise within one month, she will give me a promotion.

4. 你為什麼每次去旅遊以前，總是要和住在那個地方的朋友聯繫？

你为什么每次去旅游以前，总是要和住在那个地方的朋友联系？

5. 京劇曾經是中國最受歡迎的表演藝術，但是現在人們覺得它的節奏太慢，表演太固定，所以越來越不受年輕人的歡迎。

京剧曾经是中国最受欢迎的表演艺术，但是现在人们觉得它的节奏太慢，表演太固定，所以越来越不受年轻人的欢迎。

6. 現在的電視廣告質量不高，內   現在的电视广告质量不高，内
    容無聊，實在讓人反感。   容无聊，实在让人反感。

The pattern 假如…也/就 V can express either a fateful circumstance (example 1) or a simple condition (examples 2 and 3) and is slightly more formal than 如果、要是. Note 假如 often goes before the subject. If the subject of the second clause is present, it always goes before 也/就.

6. Expressing sentiment

A向B表示好感/關心/同情/歡迎/友好	xiàng…biǎoshì hǎogǎn/guānxīn/tóngqíng/huānyíng/yǒuhǎo	to express favorable impression/concern/sympathy/welcome/good-will

● 我主動和其中的一位男士聯繫，向他表示我的好感，並且約他見面。

1. 中國女孩子會主動   中国女孩子会主动   Do Chinese girls take the
    向男孩子表示好感   向男孩子表示好感   initiative to show their feelings
    嗎？   吗？   to a boy?

    讓中國女孩子主動   让中国女孩子主动   Getting Chinese girls to take
    向男孩子表示好感   向男孩子表示好感   the initiative to express their
    是一件很不容易的   是一件很不容易的   feelings for boys is no easy
    事情。   事情。   task.

2. 為什麼很多人捐款   为什么很多人捐款   Why have many people
    juānkuǎn 給農村？   给农村？   donated to charities in the
                                          countryside?

    在中國的農村，有   在中国的农村，有   In China's countryside, there
    很多的孩子因為窮   很多的孩子因为穷   are many children who can't
    而不能上學，很多   而不能上学，很多   afford to go to school. Many
    人為了表示自己的   人为了表示自己的   people have made a donation
    同情而捐款，這樣   同情而捐款，这样   to express their sympathy.
    可以幫助不少孩子   可以帮助不少孩子   This way they can help a lot of
    得到上學的機會。   得到上学的机会。   children get a chance to go to
                                          school.

3.　中國最近對美國的
　　態度怎麼樣？

　　中国最近对美国的
　　态度怎么样？

What is China's attitide toward the U.S. lately?

　　大熊貓是中國的國
　　寶 guóbǎo，為了向美
　　國表示友好，去年
　　中國政府送給美國
　　兩隻大熊貓。

　　大熊猫是中国的国
　　宝，为了向美国表
　　示友好，去年中国
　　政府送给美国两只
　　大熊猫。

Giant pandas are a Chinese national treasure. In order to show their good-will, last year the Chinese government gave the U.S. two pandas.

4.　聽說昨天有一位很有名的教授
　　來這兒演講，你們怎麼向他表
　　示歡迎？

　　听说昨天有一位很有名的教授
　　来这儿演讲，你们怎么向他表
　　示欢迎？

5.　在大城市的大街上，我經常可
　　以看到一些乞丐 qǐgài 'beggar'，可
　　是我不知道我應不應該給他們
　　錢。

　　在大城市的大街上，我经常可
　　以看到一些乞丐，可是我不知
　　道我应不应该给他们钱。

6.　我在中國留學的時候，總是有
　　一些中國朋友問我每天做什
　　麼、吃什麼、甚至和什麼人在
　　一起。

　　我在中国留学的时候，总是有
　　一些中国朋友问我每天做什
　　么、吃什么、甚至和什么人在
　　一起。

The pattern A 向 B 表示/好感/關心/同情/歡迎/友好 is used to express sentiment. This is often seen in more formal and literary Chinese. So, to put the sentence "他關心我" slightly more formally, one can say "他向我表示關心" 'He showed his concern for me.' The way of indicating one's sentiment can precede the pattern, e.g., 我們準備了很多食物和飲料，來向他表示歡迎 'We prepared a lot of food and beverages to express our hospitality to him.' It can also be framed in a phrase starting with 以, e.g., 我們以晚會的方式，來向他表示歡迎 'We showed our hospitality to him in the form of a dinner party.'

背景常識 Background Notes

1. 相親：以前，中國沒有自由戀愛。男女的婚姻是由父母決定的。有的時候男女雙方和他們的家人會見面，這樣可以看看大家對彼此是否滿意。這樣的聚會就是相親。相親曾經被認為是落伍的現象，但是現在年輕人工作越來越忙，沒有時間接觸更多的人，所以相親又開始流行起來

2. 速配節目：「非常男女」是台灣一個非常有名的結識男女朋友的節目，在大陸也有很多觀眾。一般會有十個男性和十個女性參加，通過互相介紹，回答主持人問題和互相提問來彼此了解。彼此喜歡的人可以互送禮物，沒有找到自己喜歡的人也沒關係，因為有那麼多的觀眾在看這個節目，對他們有興趣的觀眾一定會跟他們聯繫。大陸各個電視台也有類似的節目，收視率都不錯。不過很多參加節目的男女，也並沒有打算在節目中找到自己的夢中情人，他們更多的是把它當作認識新朋友的一種方法。

3. 男主外，女主內：根據傳統的觀念，中國人認為男人應該在外工作，而女人應該留在家裏做家務，照顧孩子。但是由於消費水平高的原因，只靠一個人的收入很難維持比較高的生活水平，所以在中國，夫妻都工作是非常普遍的。儘管如此，一些人還是有這樣的傳統思想。

4. 婚禮：和美國不同，在中國舉行婚禮的費用應該由男方負責。習慣是新郎在中午12點以前去新娘家把新娘接到自己家，而結第二次婚的女人應該在12點以後被新郎接走。現在的習慣則是先把新娘接到舉行婚禮的飯館，婚禮結束之後再回到自己的家。

背景常识 Background Notes

1. 相亲：以前，中国没有自由恋爱。男女的婚姻是由父母决定的。有的时候男女双方和他们的家人会见面，这样可以看看大家对彼此是否满意。这样的聚会就是相亲。相亲曾经被认为是落伍的现象，但是现在年轻人工作越来越忙，没有时间接触更多的人，所以相亲又开始流行起来。

2. 速配节目："非常男女"是台湾一个非常有名的结识男女朋友的节

目，在大陆也有很多观众。一般会有十个男性和十个女性参加，通过互相介绍，回答主持人问题和互相提问来彼此了解。彼此喜欢的人可以互送礼物，没有找到自己喜欢的人也没关系，因为有那么多的观众在看这个节目，对他们有兴趣的观众一定会跟他们联系。大陆各个电视台也有类似的节目，收视率都不错。不过很多参加节目的男女，也并没有打算在节目中找到自己的梦中情人，他们更多的是把它当作认识新朋友的一种方法。

3. 男主外，女主内：根据传统的观念，中国人认为男人应该在外工作，而女人应该留在家里做家务，照顾孩子。但是由于消费水平高的原因，只靠一个人的收入很难维持比较高的生活水平，所以在中国，夫妻都工作是非常普遍的。尽管如此，一些人还是有这样的传统思想。

4. 婚礼：和美国不同，在中国举行婚礼的费用应该由男方负责。习惯是新郎在中午12点以前去新娘家把新娘接到自己家，而结第二次婚的女人应该在12点以后被新郎接走。现在的习惯则是先把新娘接到举行婚礼的饭馆，婚礼结束之后再回到自己的家。

第九課　誰是好學生？

Theme: Education and Career

Communicative Objectives
- Talking about student behavior
- Talking about the high school experience
- Narrating the experience of trying to get ahead of others in school

Skill Focus
- Reading a commentary on the job search by recent college graduates

Grammar Focus
- S 一 V 就是 NP
- S VO V個不/沒 停/完
- 瞧/看你V/Adj的
- S在V_1O_1的同時，也 V_2O_2
- S不僅不/沒V_1O_1，(甚至/反而)還V_2O_2
- …，況且S (也/還/又)VO

Problem Scenario
　　You have two children, one is still in high school and the other is about to graduate from college. Your younger child is very active and loves to help others, including his teachers, but is labeled "a teacher's pet." Your older child is very shy and self-conscious, particularly over her appearance. How would you help them know what is important and what is superficial? What advice do you have for them?

對話 Dialogue

(1) Talking about student behavior

李明的鄰居孫太太和吳太太在討論孩子的問題。

孫太太：這麼早，去哪兒啊？

吳太太：孩子的老師病了，我得去看看。

孫太太：買這麼多東西，我以為你去給領導送禮呢！

吳太太：本來我也覺得去看看隨便帶點兒東西就可以了，可是孩子不同意。他說別的同學給老師送禮[1]—送就是幾百塊錢的東西，我們禮送輕了還不如不送呢！

孫太太：現在的孩子真是早熟，這麼小就知道拍老師的馬屁。

吳太太：可不是。上個月我孩子的老師上課的時候打了一個學生的耳光，學校調查的時候，大部分學生卻替老師說話。

孫太太：他們說老師沒打學生嗎？

吳太太：那倒沒有，不過他們都說那個被打的學生上課表現不好，總是說話說[2]個不停，老師打他是為了不影響其他人。

孫太太：我的孩子也是這樣，有時候我想告訴他不應該這麼做，可是別人都做，你不做，反而對孩子不好。

吳太太：這也不能怪孩子，我覺得大家都有責任。

閱讀理解 Comprehension Check

1. 吳太太要上哪兒去？為什麼？
2. 為什麼孫太太以為吳太太要去給領導送禮？
3. 為什麼吳太太要拿這麼多東西？她的孩子怎麼說？
4. 吳太太怎麼說明現在的學生很會拍老師的馬屁？
5. 孫太太不讓她的孩子拍馬屁嗎？為什麼？

👥 (1)Talking about student behavior

李明的邻居孙太太和吴太太在讨论孩子的问题。

孙太太： 这么早，去哪儿啊？

吴太太： 孩子的老师病了，我得去看看。

孙太太： 买这么多东西，我以为你去给领导送礼呢！

吴太太： 本来我也觉得去看看随便带点东西就可以了，可是孩子不同意。他说别的同学给老师送礼[1]一送**就是**几百块钱的东西，我们礼送轻了还不如不送呢！

孙太太： 现在的孩子真是早熟，这么小就知道拍老师的马屁。

吴太太： 可不是。上个月我孩子的老师上课的时候打了一个学生的耳光，学校调查的时候，大部分学生却替老师说话。

孙太太： 他们说老师没打学生吗？

吴太太： 那倒没有，不过他们都说那个被打的学生上课表现不好，总是说话说[2]**个不停**，老师打他是为了不影响其他人。

孙太太： 我的孩子也是这样，有时候我想告诉他不应该这么做，可是别人都做，你不做，反而对孩子不好。

吴太太： 这也不能怪孩子，我觉得大家都有责任。

阅读理解 Comprehension Check

1. 吴太太要上哪儿去？为什么？
2. 为什么孙太太以为吴太太要去给领导送礼？
3. 为什么吴太太要拿这么多东西？她的孩子怎么说？
4. 吴太太怎么说明现在的学生很会拍老师的马屁？
5. 孙太太不让她的孩子拍马屁吗？为什么？

對話一生詞 Vocabulary

Study the numbered vocabulary (productive vocabulary) for its usage. The unnumbered items (receptive vocabulary) are to facilitate reading comprehension.

◎By Order of Appearance

1.	領導	领导	lǐngdǎo	N	leader, leadership	[to lead-to guide]
	送禮	送礼	sòng lǐ	VO	送人禮物	[to give-present]
2.	早熟		zǎoshú ✓	Adj	early-maturing, precocious	[early-ripe]
3.	拍馬屁	拍马屁	pāi mǎpì	IE	<口> to flatter, butter up	[to clap-horse-buttocks]
	打耳光		dǎ ěrguāng	VO	<口> to slap sb. in the face, to box sb.'s ears	[to hit-ear-scene]
4.	調查	调查	diàochá ✓	V/N	to investigate, to look into	[to tune-to examine]
5.	替…說話	替…说话	tì…shuōhuà ✓	IE	<口> to speak for (sb.)	[for-say-words]
	反而		fǎn'ér	Adv	on the contrary, instead (used after subject)	[to counter-and]
6.	怪		guài	V	to blame	
7.	責任	责任	zérèn ✓	N	duty, responsibility, blame	[duty-task]

Characters with Many Strokes

領 導 禮 特 殊 顧 熟 調 替 責

詞匯用法 Words in Context

1. 領導：國家的領導；在他的領導下；領導能力

   工作以後，你會給領導送禮嗎？

   你覺得怎麼樣才能培養 péiyǎng 一個人的領導能力？

   领导：国家的领导；在他的领导下；领导能力

   工作以后，你会给领导送礼吗？

   你觉得怎么样才能培养一个人的领导能力？

2. 早熟：孩子、思想早熟；比較早熟

   你猜「窮人的孩子早當家」這句

   早熟：孩子、思想早熟；比较早熟

   你猜"穷人的孩子早当家"这句

話的意思是什麼？

你覺得早熟的孩子和普通孩子有什麼不同？

3. 拍馬屁：拍領導的馬屁；很會拍馬屁

他總是拍誰的馬屁？

你為什麼對那個女孩說她穿的衣服很漂亮？

4. 調查：調查一件事；接受調查；調查清楚、結果；社會調查

怎麼才能知道自行車被誰偷走了？

你做過社會調查嗎？

5. 替……說話：替我說好話

老師批評你的同學的時候，你會不會替他說話？

走後門的人可能會用什麼方法找工作？

6. 怪：不要怪別人；怪交通太糟

如果你對自己的專業不滿意，你會怪誰？

你怎麼又遲到了？

7. 責任：有、負責任；責任很大；減輕責任

我們的環境越來越不好，誰應該負責任？

你覺得家庭主婦的工作不重要嗎？

话的意思是什么？

你觉得早熟的孩子和普通孩子有什么不同？

拍马屁：拍领导的马屁；很会拍马屁

他总是拍谁的马屁？

你为什么对那个女孩说她穿的衣服很漂亮？

调查：调查一件事；接受调查；调查清楚、结果；社会调查

怎么才能知道自行车被谁偷走了？

你做过社会调查吗？

替……说话：替我说好话

老师批评你的同学的时候，你会不会替他说话？

走后门的人可能会用什么方法找工作？

怪：不要怪别人；怪交通太糟

如果你对自己的专业不满意，你会怪谁？

你怎么又迟到了？

责任：有、负责任；责任很大；减轻责任

我们的环境越来越不好，谁应该负责任？

你觉得家庭主妇的工作不重要吗？

自由發揮與課堂活動 Free Discussion and Class Activities

1. 你喜歡什麼樣的老師？為什麼？　你喜欢什么样的老师？为什么？

2. 你贊成不贊成體罰學生？為什麼？　你赞成不赞成体罚学生？为什么？

(2) Talking about the high school experience

吳成和何信是初中同學，上高中的時候有一天他們在書店碰到。

吳成：　小何，這麼巧，你也來買書嗎？

何信：　我今天沒什麼事，就來看看有沒有什麼好看的小說？

吳成：　小說？難道你還有時間看小說嗎？看來考上了重點中學就是不一樣，你根本不用為考大學操心了，可是我這個普通中學的學生每天都還過著兩點一線、上課考試的生活，連週末都不能休息。

何信：　³瞧你說的，就算是重點中學的學生，也得參加競爭激烈的高考，而且家裏人覺得我們是重點中學的學生就應該考上好大學，所以我們的壓力更大。

吳成：　對了，政府現在一直宣傳要減輕中學生的負擔，我們現在下午只有兩堂課了，你們呢？

何信：　我們還是有四堂課，不過其中兩堂是不需要考試的，大家可以根據自己的興趣去選擇上什麼課，比如讀小說、作社會調查什麼的，沒什麼限制。

吳成：　聽起來真有意思。我每天下午不是去電子遊戲廳打遊戲，就是去網吧上網。為了避免這樣的情況，我爸媽就給我安排別的功課，所以我的負擔沒有減輕。

何信：　我爸媽倒是一直鼓勵我看課本以外的書，他們不希望我只會考試，不會思考。

吳成：　假如我們不用「考大學」，而是像其他國家那樣「申請大學」，也許我們就可以花更多的時間去看課本以外的書了。

何信：　有道理，不管怎麼樣，現在對我們來說成績還是最重要的。

吳成：　你說的對，我還是好好的準備高考吧！

閱讀理解 Comprehension Check

6. 吳成覺得和重點中學的學生比，自己的生活怎麼樣？何信呢？
7. 吳成每天下午上幾堂課？他的負擔輕嗎？為什麼？
8. 吳成和何信認為「申請大學」有什麼好處？現在該做的是什麼？

(2) Talking about the high school experience

吴成和何信是初中同学，上高中的时候有一天他们在书店碰到。

吴成：　小何，这么巧，你也来买书吗？

何信：　我今天没什么事，就来看看有没有什么好看的小说？

吴成：　小说？难道你还有时间看小说吗？看来考上了重点中学就是不一样，你根本不用为考大学操心了，可是我这个普通中学的学生每天都还过着两点一线、上课考试的生活，连周末都不能休息。

何信：　³瞧你说的，就算是重点中学的学生，也得参加竞争激烈的高考，而且家里人觉得我们是重点中学的学生就应该考上好大学，所以我们的压力更大。

吴成：　对了，政府现在一直宣传要减轻中学生的负担，我们现在下午只有两堂课了，你们呢？

何信：　我们还是有四堂课，不过其中两堂是不需要考试的，大家可以根据自己的兴趣去选择上什么课，比如读小说、作社会调查什么的，没什么限制。

吴成：　听起来真有意思。我每天下午不是去电子游戏厅打游戏，就是去网吧上网。为了避免这样的情况，我爸妈就给我安排别的功课，所以我的负担没有减轻。

何信：　我爸妈倒是一直鼓励我看课本以外的书，他们不希望我只会考试，不会思考。

吴成：　假如我们不用"考大学"，而是象其他国家那样"申请大学"，也许我们就可以花更多的时间去看课本以外的书了。

何信：　有道理，不管怎么样，现在对我们来说成绩还是最重要的。

吴成：　你说的对，我还是好好地准备高考吧！

阅读理解 Comprehension Check

6.　吴成觉得和重点中学的学生比，自己的生活怎么样？何信呢？

7. 吳成每天下午上几堂课？他的负担轻吗？为什么？

8. 吳成和何信认为"申請大學"有什么好处？现在该做的是什么？

對話二生詞 Vocabulary

8.	巧		qiǎo	Adv	coincidentally	
	考上		kǎoshang	RV	to pass an entrance examination	[to take test-able]
9.	重點	重点	zhòngdiǎn	N	key, focal point, emphasis	[important-place]
	線	线	xiàn	N	line, thread	
10.	瞧		qiáo	V	看	
11.	競爭	竞争	jìngzhēng	N	competition, to compete	[to compete-to vie]
12.	激烈		jīliè	Adj	intense, sharp, fierce	[surge-strong]
	高考		gāokǎo	N	colleges entrance examination <TW> 大學聯考	[high-exam]
	政府		zhèngfǔ	N	govenment	[government-seat of government]
13.	負擔	负担	fùdān	N	burden, load	[to shoulder-to undertake]
	比如		bǐrú	Adv	比方說	[to compare-if]
	社會	社会	shèhuì	N	society	[society-union]
14.	鼓勵	鼓励	gǔlì	V	to encourage, to urge	[drum-to encourage]
	以外		yǐwài	Suf	beyond, outside, other than	[from a point on-outside]
15.	成績	成绩	chéngjī	N	grade, result, achievement	[to accomplish-achievement]

Characters with Many Strokes

點 線 瞧 算 競 激 擔 鼓 勵 績

詞匯用法 Words in Context

8. 巧：特別巧；很不巧   巧：特别巧；很不巧

我們明天有個晚會，你能參加   我们明天有个晚会，你能参加
嗎？   吗？

你昨天怎麼會碰到那個中學的同   你昨天怎么会碰到那个中学的同

學？   学？

9. 重點：重點中學、問題   重点：重点中学、问题

    在美國是否有重點中學？他們和   在美国是否有重点中学？他们和
    普通中學有什麼不同？   普通中学有什么不同？

    在我們的課本裏哪些詞是重點   在我们的课本里哪些词是重点
    詞？   词？

10. 瞧：（句型）   瞧：（句型）

11. 競爭：和別人競爭；競爭不過   竞争：和别人竞争；竞争不过
    他；競爭很激烈；競爭的壓力；   他；竞争很激烈；竞争的压力；
    競爭力很強   竞争力很强

    為什麼現在大學生找工作這麼   为什么现在大学生找工作这么
    難？   难？

    哪個公司在電腦市場的競爭力最   哪个公司在电脑市场的竞争力最
    強？   强？

12. 激烈：競爭、辯論、戰爭、比賽   激烈：竞争、辩论、战争、比赛
    很激烈；過分激烈；激烈地反對   很激烈；过分激烈；激烈地反对

    昨天的足球比賽怎麼樣？   昨天的足球比赛怎么样？

    什麼樣的政策受到大家激烈地反   什么样的政策受到大家激烈地反
    對？   对？

13. 負擔：學習、生活、家庭負擔；   负担：学习、生活、家庭负担；
    負擔重、輕   负担重、轻

    在大學裏哪些專業的學習負擔比   在大学里哪些专业的学习负担比
    較重，哪些專業的負擔比較輕？   较重，哪些专业的负担比较轻？

    哪些人的生活負擔最重？   哪些人的生活负担最重？

14. 鼓勵：鼓勵學生；受到鼓勵   鼓励：鼓励学生；受到鼓励

    你的父母是否鼓勵你和別的同學   你的父母是否鼓励你和别的同学
    競爭？   竞争？

    如果你的父母希望你學醫，而你   如果你的父母希望你学医，而你
    喜歡學語言，你希望你的父母怎   喜欢学语言，你希望你的父母怎

麼做？   么做？

15. 成績：成績很好；重視成績   成绩：成绩很好；重视成绩

高中畢業以後，成績好的學生一
定能上好大學嗎？

你父母對你每次的考試成績有什
麼要求嗎？

高中毕业以后，成绩好的学生一
定能上好大学吗？

你父母对你每次的考试成绩有什
么要求吗？

自由發揮與課堂活動　Free Discussion and Class Activities

3. 你覺得現在的中小學生和你小的
時候有哪些相同和不相同的地
方？

你觉得现在的中小学生和你小的
时候有哪些相同和不相同的地
方？

4. 回想並介紹自己中學的生活，比
比看誰的壓力和負擔更重。

回想并介绍自己中学的生活，比
比看谁的压力和负担更重。

5. 在美國現在流行父母自己在家教
育孩子，你覺得這樣的教育方法
對孩子有哪些好處和壞處？

在美国现在流行父母自己在家教
育孩子，你觉得这样的教育方法
对孩子有哪些好处和坏处？

6. 任何一個中國的小學生都知道根
號2等于1.414，可是大部分的美
國小學生恐怕都不知道。你覺得
這反映出中美教育的哪些差別？

任何一个中国的小学生都知道根
号2等于1.414，可是大部分的美
国小学生恐怕都不知道。你觉得
这反映出中美教育的哪些差别？

敘述 Narrative

我要比他強

　　我的爸媽和李明的爸媽是大學的同學和好朋友，非常巧的是，我和李明又考上了同一所中學，這對他們來說大概是一個好消息，可是對我來說⁴**在**多了一個朋友**的同時，也**多了一個競爭對手。因為不管碰到什麼事情，爸媽總會拿我和李明比，不幸的是，每一次我都比不過李明。

　　三年以後我們又考上了同一所大學。上學的第一天我就下了決心，一定要比李明強，決不再做第二。我說到做到，為了得第一，我放棄了休息和娛樂的時間。每天早上第一個去教室，晚上最後一個離開。週末別人在逛街或者泡吧的時候，我仍然堅持在圖書館學習。「功夫不負有心人」，每次考試我的成績總是第一。我知道老師對我的表現非常滿意，而且不少同學也都把我當成他們學習的榜樣。

　　李明在做什麼呢？我想他的行為一定讓他的父母十分失望。自從上了大學以後，他好像一切「向錢看」！剛上大一的時候，他就在學校裏推銷書，據他自己說每賣出一本就可以賺幾塊錢。寒暑假他也從來不學習，而是去公司打工，大概一個假期的收入就是他一個學期的生活費。可是他的父母一直反對他在上學的時候打工，我也勸過他，家裏又不是沒錢，難道還需要自己打工賺錢嗎？可是對大家的勸告，李明總是一個耳朵進，一個耳朵出。不管是老師還是同學，都為他感到遺憾，從前那個有前途的學生，怎麼會變成這樣呢？就連我也不希望看到他這種變化。

　　四年的大學生活很快就過去了。雖然學校不再為畢業生分配工作，但是父母對我抱了很大的希望，我對自己也信心十足。然而當我面對現實的時候才發現，每年畢業的博士、碩士一大堆，我們這些小本科生只能找人家剩下的工作。找工作的競爭比高考還激烈。為了能引起別人的注意，我只好和大家一樣，通過簡歷、服裝來包裝自己。當大家都忙著找工作的時候，李明[5]**不僅不像大家一樣包裝自己，還**比平時更放鬆了。　這個人就是這麼怪，到了該工作的時候，他反而沒什麼反應，一點兒也不著急！

　　後來我在報上看到了一家公司請人的廣告，那家公司雖然不大，但是小有名氣，而且聽說老板是一個年輕人。我相信這樣的公司需要年輕人，也會重視年輕人。他們對我的簡歷很感興趣，並約我面試。面試那天，我穿著新買的西裝，希望給老板一個好印象。秘書小姐帶我來到老板的辦公室，並為我打開門，我走進去，發現坐在裏面的竟然是李明！

閱讀理解 Comprehension Check

9. 「我」喜歡和李明做同學嗎？為什麼？
10. 上了大學以後，「我」做了什麼決定？他怎麼努力學習？
11. 李明上大學的時候，都在做什麼？大家對他有什麼看法？他聽別人的勸告嗎？
12. 大四的時候，「我」對將來有什麼看法？那時李明在做什麼？
13. 「我」後來去哪兒找工作？為什麼？
14. 面試那天，「我」怎麼準備？結果發現了什麼？

我要比他强

我的爸妈和李明的爸妈是大学的同学和好朋友，非常巧的是，我和李明又考上了同一所中学，这对他们来说大概是一个好消息，可是对我来说[4]**在**多了一个朋友**的同时**，也多了一个竞争对手。因为不管碰到什么事情，爸妈总会拿我和李明比，不幸的是，每一次我都比不过李明。

三年以后我们又考上了同一所大学。上学的第一天我就下了决心，一定要比李明强，决不再做第二。我说到做到，为了得第一，我放弃了休息和娱乐的时间。每天早上第一个去教室，晚上最后一个离开。周末别人在逛街或者泡吧的时候，我仍然坚持在图书馆学习。"功夫不负有心人"，每次考试我的成绩总是

第一。我知道老师对我的表现非常满意，而且不少同学也都把我当成他们学习的榜样。

李明在做什么呢？我想他的行为一定让他的父母十分失望。自从上了大学以后，他好象一切"向钱看"！刚上大一的时候，他就在学校里推销书，据他自己说每卖出一本就可以赚几块钱。寒暑假他也从来不学习，而是去公司打工，大概一个假期的收入就是他一个学期的生活费。可是他的父母一直反对他在上学的时候打工，我也劝过他，家里又不是没钱，难道还需要自己打工赚钱吗？可是对大家的劝告，李明总是一个耳朵进，一个耳朵出。不管是老师还是同学，都为他感到遗憾，从前

那个有前途的学生，怎么会变成这样呢？就连我也不希望看到他这种变化。

四年的大学生活很快就过去了。虽然学校不再为毕业生分配工作，但是父母对我抱了很大的希望，我对自己也信心十足。然而当我面对现实的时候才发现，每年毕业的博士、硕士一大堆，我们这些小本科生只能找人家剩下的工作。找工作的竞争比高考还激烈。为了能引起别人的注意，我只好和大家一样，通过简历、服装来包装自己。当大家都忙着找工作的时候，李明[5]不仅不象大家一样包装

自己，还比平时更放松了。这个

人就是这么怪，到了该工作的时候，他反而没什么反应，一点儿也不着急！

后来我在报上看到了一家公司请人的广告，那家公司虽然不大，但是小有名气，而且听说老板是一个年轻人。我相信这样的公司需要年轻人，也会重视年轻人。他们对我的简历很感兴趣，并约我面试，面试那天，我穿着新买的西装，希望给老板一个好印象。秘书小姐带我来到老板的办公室，并为我打开门，我走进去，发现坐在里面的竟然是李明！

阅读理解 Comprehension Check

9. "我"喜欢和李明做同学吗？为什么？

10. 上了大学以后，"我"做了什么决定？他怎么努力学习？

11. 李明上大学的时候，都在做什么？大家对他有什么看法？他听别人的劝告吗？

12. 大四的时候，"我"对将来有什么看法？那时李明在做什么？
13. "我"后来去哪儿找工作？为什么？
14. 面试那天，"我"怎么准备？结果发现了什么？

敘述生詞 Vocabulary

16. 強	强	qiáng	Adj	strong, better	
同一		tóngyī	Adj	same, identical	[same-one]
所		suǒ	M	for houses/schools	
17. 同時	同时	tóngshí	Conj/ Adv	simultaneously with…, at the same time, meanwhile	[same-time]
18. 對手	对手	duìshǒu	N	opponent, adversary, match	[opposite-person skilled in sth.]
19. 決	决	jué	Adv	一定	
說到做到	说到做到	shuōdàozuòdào	IE	to keep one's promise	[to say-towards-to do-towards]
娛樂	娱乐	yúlè	N	entertainment, amusement	[to amuse-happy]
泡吧		pào bā	VO	to go to bars to have fun	[to soak-bar]
功夫不負有心人	功夫不负有心人	gōngfu bú fù yǒuxīnrén	IE	努力就會有結果 <TW> 皇天不負苦心人	[effort-not-betray-have-heart-person]
20. 榜樣	榜样	bǎngyàng	N	example, model	[notice-sample]
21. 行為	行为	xíngwéi	N	action, behavior, conduct	[to go-to act as]
22. 十分		shífēn	Adj	非常、很	[ten-percent]
向錢看	向钱看	xiàngqiánkàn	IE	to care only about money, a pun of "向前看"	[towards-money-look]
假期		jiàqī	N	vacation, holiday	[holiday-time period]
反對	反对	fǎnduì	V/N	不贊成 to oppose, to be against	[to oppose-opposite]
23. 勸告	劝告	quàngào	N	advice	[to advise-to tell]
一個耳朵進，一個耳朵出	一个耳朵进，一个耳朵出	yí ge ěrduo jìn, yí ge ěrduo chū	IE	in one ear and out the other	[one-ear-in-one-ear-out]
24. 感到		gǎndào	RV	to feel, to sense	[to feel-to]
25. 遺憾	遗憾	yíhàn	N/Adj	regret, pity	[to leave behind-sorry]

26.	前途		qiántú	N	future, prospects	[front-route]
	畢業	毕业	bìyè	V/N	to graduate, graduation →畢業生	[to conclude-school studies]
27.	分配		fēnpèi	V	to allot, to assign, to distribute	[to divide-to match]
28.	抱		bào	V	to hold, to embrace, to hug	
	信心		xìnxīn	N	confidence, faith	[to believe-heart]
	十足		shízú	Adj	100 percent, out-and-out	[ten-foot]
	博士		bóshì	N	Ph.D.	[abundant-scholar]
	碩士	硕士	shuòshì	N	Master (of Arts), M.A.	[large-scholar]
	本科生		běnkēshēng	N	undergraduate student	[current-branch of study-student]
	簡歷	简历	jiǎnlì	N	<PRC> curriculum vitae, résumé <TW> 履歷 lǚlì	[simple-experience]
	服裝	服装	fúzhuāng	N	dress, clothing	[clothes-outfit]
29.	反應	反应	fǎnyìng	N/V	reaction, response, to react	[to return-answer]
30.	著急	着急	zhāojí	Adj	anxious	[to feel-urgent]
	名氣	名气	míngqì	N	reputation, fame, name	[fame-air]
	老板		lǎobǎn	N	boss	[prefix-board]
31.	面試	面试	miànshì	N/V	interview, to interview	[face-test]
	西裝	西装	xīzhuāng	N	Western-style clothes	[west-outfit]
	秘書	秘书	mìshū	N	secretary	[secret-clerk]

Characters with Many Strokes

強　對　娛　樂　榜　樣　勸　遺　憾　畢

詞匯用法 Words in Context

16. 強：能力、想像力強；這的空氣　　強：能力、想像力强；这的空气
比大城市強多了　　　　　　　　　比大城市强多了
小孩子的哪些能力比較強？　　　　小孩子的哪些能力比较强？
美國的足球隊和中國的足球隊哪　　美国的足球队和中国的足球队哪

個更好？

个更好？

17. 同時：（句型）

同时：（句型）

18. 對手：競爭、比賽對手；不是我
的對手；當作對手

对手：竞争、比赛对手；不是我
的对手；当作对手

微軟公司最強的競爭對手是誰？

微软公司最强的竞争对手是谁？

你覺得那個大學的籃球隊能打贏
我們嗎？

你觉得那个大学的篮球队能打赢
我们吗？

19. 決：決不是你的對手；決不/沒/
非

决：决不是你的对手；决不/没/
非

沒到二十一歲的學生能不能喝
酒？

没到二十一岁的学生能不能喝
酒？

他是一個說到做到的人嗎？

他是一个说到做到的人吗？

20. 榜樣：好榜樣；把爸爸當作榜
樣；是我的榜樣

榜样：好榜样；把爸爸当作榜
样；是我的榜样

在你的心目中，誰是你的榜樣？

在你的心目中，谁是你的榜样？

一般美國的年輕人會把什麼樣的
人當作榜樣？

一般美国的年轻人会把什么样的
人当作榜样？

21. 行為：注意自己的行為；不道
德、非法的行為；行為很小心、
可笑

行为：注意自己的行为；不道
德、非法的行为；行为很小心、
可笑

什麼樣的行為是非法的？

什么样的行为是非法的？

你很注意自己平時的行為嗎？

你很注意自己平时的行为吗？

22. 十分：十分高興、失望、生氣

十分：十分高兴、失望、生气

你昨天為什麼沒有等晚會結束就
離開了？

你昨天为什么没有等晚会结束就
离开了？

小李為什麼做什麼事情都那麼小
心？

小李为什么做什么事情都那么小
心？

23. 勸告：勸告朋友不要抽煙；不

劝告：劝告朋友不要抽烟；不

聽、聽不進去別人的勸告

在什麼事情上你會聽朋友的勸告？

朋友開始有了不好的行為，你會做什麼？

24. 感到：感到高興、失望、難過；能感到他不高興

你覺得這兒的生活怎麼樣？

你最近為什麼很少和小李一起去娛樂？

25. 遺憾：很遺憾；感到遺憾；遺憾的是；沒什麼可遺憾的

最讓你遺憾的事情是什麼？

你沒去聽昨天的音樂會，不遺憾嗎？

26. 前途：光明的前途；很有前途；沒什麼前途；有前途的專業

什麼樣的專業最有前途？

在你看來，哪家電腦公司的前途比較光明？

27. 分配：分配工作、房子；由政府分配

你畢業以後，政府有沒有給你分配工作的責任？

什麼東西是由政府分配的？

28. 抱：抱著當明星的理想；抱著樂觀的態度；抱孩子；抱著書進教室

你對政府減稅的政策抱什麼態

度？

為什麼很多年輕的演員都想去好萊塢？

为什么很多年轻的演员都想去好莱坞？

29. 反應：沒什麼反應；反應很慢

反应：没什么反应；反应很慢

為什麼老年人開車的危險會比較大？

为什么老年人开车的危险会比较大？

你勸小李別抽煙時，他有什麼反應？

你劝小李别抽烟时，他有什么反应？

30. 著急：為孩子著急；別著急；著什麼急；十分著急

着急：为孩子着急；别着急；着什么急；十分着急

你昨天在路上碰到我，為什麼連招呼都不跟我打就走了？

你昨天在路上碰到我，为什么连招呼都不跟我打就走了？

你會為誰著急？

你会为谁着急？

31. 面試：面試找工作的人；誰給你面試；參加面試

面试：面试找工作的人；谁给你面试；参加面试

在找工作的時候誰得參加面試？

在找工作的时候谁得参加面试？

面試的時候要做哪些準備？

面试的时候要做哪些准备？

自由發揮與課堂活動 Free Discussion and Class Activities

7. 談一談在你的國家裏，什麼樣的學生被認為是好學生？

谈一谈在你的国家里，什么样的学生被认为是好学生？

8. 有一句話說：「學理的人是拿螺絲刀的，而學文的人則是管那些拿螺絲刀的。」你覺得這句話的意思是什麼？你怎麼看這句話？

有一句话说："学理的人是拿螺丝刀的，而学文的人则是管那些拿螺丝刀的。"你觉得这句话的意思是什么？你怎么看这句话？

9. 辯論：大學生打工好還是不好？

辩论：大学生打工好还是不好？

10. 大家一起看幾份中文簡歷，討論中英文簡歷的內容和寫法有什麼不同。

大家一起看几份中文简历，讨论中英文简历的内容和写法有什么不同。

說明 Exposition

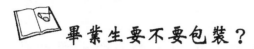 畢業生要不要包裝？

儘管離畢業還有一段時間，但是為了在競爭中吸引更多的注意，包裝自己已經成為現階段畢業生們的主要任務。

教育專家認為這種現象的存在並非好事。大學生們努力表現自己，有助於請人的單位全面了解學生，但是很可能浪費了大量的金錢和時間。⁶**況且**對外表的過分包裝**還**可能反映出一個人對自己的信心不足，這對找工作反而會起負面的作用。不少公司也表示，自信才是公司選擇人才的第一條件，因為人越自信越說明他有實力，不必靠外表的包裝來贏得工作。

與此相反，畢業生的家長卻贊成孩子們的做法。他們認為畢業是走向社會的第一步，雖然畢業後找到的第一份工作也許只是暫時的，但是不管如何，這對孩子的一生可能都會有很大的影響；而且面試的時間一般都很短，所以外表的包裝十分必要。不管花多少錢，他們都會儘可能地支持。

閱讀理解 Comprehension Check

15. 現在快畢業的中國大學生特別注意什麼？為什麼？
16. 教育專家對「包裝自己」有什麼看法？為什麼？
17. 很多公司認為，找工作的時候，什麼最重要？
18. 畢業生的家長對「包裝自己」有什麼看法？為什麼？

毕业生要不要包装？

尽管离毕业还有一段时间，但是为了在竞争中吸引更多的注意，包装自己已经成为现阶段毕业生们的主要任务。

教育专家认为这种现象的存在并非好事。大学生们努力表现自己，有助于请人的单位全面了解学生，但是很可能浪费了大量的金钱和时间。⁶况且对外表的过分包装还可能反映出一个人对自己的信心不足，这对找工作反而会起负面的作用。不少公司也表示，自信才是公司选择人才的第一条件，因为人越自信越说明他有实力，不必靠外表的包装来赢得工作。

与此相反，毕业生的家长却赞成孩子们的做法。他们认为毕业是走向社会的第一步，虽然毕业后找到的第一份工作也许只是暂时的，但是不管如何，这对孩子的一生可能都会有很大的影响；而且面试的时间一般都很短，所以外表的包装十分必要。不管花多少钱，他们都会尽可能地支持。

阅读理解 Comprehension Check

15. 现在快毕业的中国大学生特别注意什么？为什么？
16. 教育专家对"包装自己"有什么看法？为什么？
17. 很多公司认为，找工作的时候，什么最重要？
18. 毕业生的家长对"包装自己"有什么看法？为什么？

说明生詞 Vocabulary

32.	階段	阶段	jiēduàn	N	stage, phase	[stage-section]
33.	任務	任务	rènwù	N	assignment, task, job	[to appoint-task]
	專家	专家	zhuānjiā	N	expert, specialist	[special-person]
34.	現象	现象	xiànxiàng	N	phenomenon	[current-appearance]

35.	存在		cúnzài	V/N	to exist, existence	[to keep-to live]
36.	單位	单位	dānwèi	N	unit in organization (one works in/for) or measurement	[single-position]
37.	全面		quánmiàn	Adj	comprehensive, all-round	[entire-surface]
	大量		dàliàng	N	large quantity, mass	[big-amount]
	金錢	金钱	jīnqián	N	money, wealth	[gold-money]
	非		fēi	Adj/Adv/Pref	not, no, non	
38.	況且	况且	kuàngqiě ✓	Conj	而且	[circumstance-moreover]
	不足		bùzú	V	to be not sufficient	[not-enough]
39.	負面	负面	fùmiàn ✓	Adj	negative	[negative-side]
40.	自信		zìxìn	N/V	對自己的信心	[self-to believe]
	人才		réncái	N	person of ability/talent	[people-talent]
	實力	实力	shílì	N	actual strength, substance	[solid-strength]
41.	贊成	赞成	zànchéng ✓	V	同意	[to support-to become]
42.	暫時	暂时	zànshí ✓	Adj/Adv	temporary, temporarily	[for a short time-time]
43.	必要		bìyào	Adj/N	necessary, indispensable, need	[must-shall]
44.	支持		zhīchí	V/N	to support, to back	[branch-to hold]

Characters with Many Strokes

階 段 務 專 單 量 錢 實 贊 暫

詞匯用法 Words in Context

32. 階段：初級、高級階段；發展到什麼階段；分成幾個階段

學習外語可以分成幾個階段？

你的中文水平在哪個階段？

阶段：初级、高级阶段；发展到什么阶段；分成几个阶段

学习外语可以分成几个阶段？

你的中文水平在哪个阶段？

33. 任務：分配、完成任務；首要任務

最近你被分配了什麼任務？

任务：分配、完成任务；首要任务

最近你被分配了什么任务？

什麼是你現在的首要任務？　　　　　什么是你现在的首要任务？

34. 現象：有這種現象　　　　　　　　現象：有这种现象

據你的了解，還有哪個國家有留　　据你的了解，还有哪个国家有留
學生不願意回國的現象？　　　　　学生不愿意回国的现象？

你相信地球已經有了越來越熱的　　你相信地球已经有了越来越热的
現象嗎？　　　　　　　　　　　　现象吗？

35. 存在：存在…問題、不同；外星　　存在：存在…问题、不同；外星
人存在嗎？　　　　　　　　　　　人存在吗？

你覺得自己的中文發音存在什麼　　你觉得自己的中文发音存在什么
問題？　　　　　　　　　　　　　问题？

你覺得中國人和美國人的習慣一　　你觉得中国人和美国人的习惯一
樣嗎？　　　　　　　　　　　　　样吗？

36. 單位：工作單位；由單位負責；　　单位：工作单位；由单位负责；
分配單位　　　　　　　　　　　　分配单位

在以前的中國，老百姓為什麼不　　在以前的中国，老百姓为什么不
需要自己買房子？　　　　　　　　需要自己买房子？

老人退休了以後，誰負責給他退　　老人退休了以后，谁负责给他退
休金？　　　　　　　　　　　　　休金？

37. 全面：全面了解情況；全面發　　全面：全面了解情况；全面发
展；考慮得很全面　　　　　　　　展；考虑得很全面

在你家裏，誰考慮問題的時候比　　在你家里，谁考虑问题的时候比
較全面？　　　　　　　　　　　　较全面？

你認為現在政府能不能做到經濟　　你认为现在政府能不能做到经济
的全面發展？　　　　　　　　　　的全面发展？

38. 況且：（句型）　　　　　　　　况且：（句型）

你覺得什麼樣的政策會給社會帶　　你觉得什么样的政策会给社会带
來負面影響？　　　　　　　　　　来负面影响？

40. 自信：很、特別、過分有自信；
不要太自信；缺乏自信

你是一個很有自信的人嗎？

他為什麼沒去那家公司面試？

自信：很、特别、过分有自信；
不要太自信；缺乏自信

你是一个很有自信的人吗？

他为什么没去那家公司面试？

41. 贊成：贊成你的觀點、做法、態
度；完全贊成

我覺得政府不應該規定二十一歲
以下的人不可以喝酒，你覺得
呢？

老師說我們應該每天考聽寫，你
覺得這個做法怎麼樣？

赞成：赞成你的观点、做法、态
度；完全赞成

我觉得政府不应该规定二十一岁
以下的人不可以喝酒，你觉得
呢？

老师说我们应该每天考听写，你
觉得这个做法怎么样？

42. 暫時：暫時的名字、現象；暫時
獨立；暫時落後

現在我們籃球隊的分數比對手
低，會不會輸啊？

你會一直用你現在的中文名字
嗎？

暂时：暂时的名字、现象；暂时
独立；暂时落后

现在我们篮球队的分数比对手
低，会不会输啊？

你会一直用你现在的中文名字
吗？

43. 必要：有討論的必要；沒有發表
的必要；很有必要；是非常必要
的

現在的大學生是否應該學習外
語？

你在選擇專業的時候要不要和父
母討論？

必要：有讨论的必要；没有发表
的必要；很有必要；是非常必要
的

现在的大学生是否应该学习外
语？

你在选择专业的时候要不要和父
母讨论？

44. 支持：支持我的觀點；支持總
統；謝謝你的支持；支持者

你怎麼看環保主義者讓人們騎自
行車的建議？

你是不是總統的支持者？為什
麼？

支持：支持我的观点；支持总
统；谢谢你的支持；支持者

你怎么看环保主义者让人们骑自
行车的建议？

你是不是总统的支持者？为什
么？

自由發揮與課堂活動　Free Discussion and Class Activities

11.　介紹一次你自己找工作的經歷，並說明你認為那一次成功和失敗的地方是什麼。

介绍一次你自己找工作的经历，并说明你认为那一次成功和失败的地方是什么。

12.　你的朋友正在找工作，請給他一些建議。

你的朋友正在找工作，请给他一些建议。

13.　一個人在準備自己的簡歷的時候，應該注意哪些方面？什麼樣的簡歷才能引起別人的注意？

一个人在准备自己的简历的时候，应该注意哪些方面？什么样的简历才能引起别人的注意？

14.　從網上找到招聘英文老師的廣告，然後1）請學生閱讀並了解工作要求；2）三、四個同學一組，根據招聘廣告寫一份簡歷。

从网上找到招聘英文老师的广告，然后1）请学生阅读并了解工作要求；2）三、四个同学一组，根据招聘广告写一份简历。

應用詞 Productive Vocabulary

◎By Grammatical Categories

Nouns/Pronouns/Measure Words

領導	lǐngdǎo	leader, leadership
對手	duìshǒu	opponent, adversary
榜樣	bǎngyàng	example, model
責任	zérèn	duty, responsibility
負擔	fùdān	burden, load
競爭	jìngzhēng	competition, to compete
行為	xíngwéi	action, behavior
反應	fǎnyìng	reaction, response, to react
自信	zìxìn	self-confidence, to be self-confident
勸告	quàngào	advice

遺憾	yíhàn	regret, pity
重點	zhòngdiǎn	key, focal point
成績	chéngjī	grade, result, achievement
單位	dānwèi	unit in organization (one works in/for) or measurement
面試	miànshì	interview, to interview
前途	qiántú	future, prospects
階段	jiēduàn	stage, phase
任務	rènwù	assignment, task, job
現象	xiànxiàng	phenomenon

Verbs/Stative Verbs/Adjectives

怪	guài	to blame
抱	bào	to hold, to hug
瞧	qiáo	to look, to see
感到	gǎndào	to feel, to sense
鼓勵	gǔlì	to encourage, to urge
支持	zhīchí	to support, to back
贊成	zànchéng	to approve, to endorse
調查	diàochá	to investigate, to look into
分配	fēnpèi	to allot, to assign, to distribute
存在	cúnzài	to exist, existence

強	qiáng	strong, better
早熟	zǎoshú	early-maturing, precocious
激烈	jīliè	intense, sharp, fierce
十分	shífēn	very, fully, utterly
著急	zhāojí	anxious
全面	quánmiàn	comprehensive, all-round
負面	fùmiàn	negative
暫時	zànshí	temporary, temporarily
必要	bìyào	necessary, indispensable, need

Adverbs and Others

巧	qiǎo	coincidentally
決	jué	definitely (not)
同時	tóngshí	simultaneously with…, at the same time, meanwhile
況且	kuàngqiě	moreover, besides

拍馬屁	pāi mǎpì	to flatter, butter up
替…說話	tì…shuōhuà	to speak for (sb.)

理解詞 Receptive Vocabulary

◎By Grammatical Categories

Nouns/Pronouns/Measure Words

所	suǒ	for houses/schools		信心	xìnxīn	substance confidence, faith
線	xiàn	line, thread		大量	dàliàng	large quantity, mass
政府	zhèngfǔ	govenment		金錢	jīnqián	money, wealth
社會	shèhuì	society		專家	zhuānjiā	expert, specialist
娛樂	yúlè	entertainment, amusement		人才	réncái	person of ability/talent
假期	jiàqī	vacation, holiday		老板	lǎobǎn	boss
高考	gāokǎo	college entrance examination		秘書	mìshū	secretary
簡歷	jiǎnlì	<PRC> curriculum vitae, résumé		博士	bóshì	Ph.D.
服裝	fúzhuāng	dress, clothing		碩士	shuòshì	Master (of Arts), M.A.
西裝	xīzhuāng	Western-style clothes		本科生	běnkēshēng	undergraduate student
名氣	míngqì	reputation, fame, name				
實力	shílì	actual strength,				

Verbs/Stative Verbs/Adjectives

考上	kǎoshang	to pass an entrance examination		泡吧	pào bā	to go to bars to have fun
畢業	bìyè	to graduate, graduation		打耳光	dǎ ěrguāng	to slap sb. in the face, to box sb.'s ears
不足	bùzú	to be not sufficient		同一	tóngyī	same, identical
反對	fǎnduì	to oppose, to be against		十足	shízú	100 percent, out-and-out
送禮	sòng lǐ	to give sb. a present				

Adverbs and Others

非	fēi	not, no, non		功夫不負有心人	gōngfu bú fù yǒuxīn rén	Those who work hard are rewarded.
以外	yǐwài	beyond, outside, other than				
反而	fǎn'ér	on the contrary, instead (used after subject)		一個耳朵進，一個耳朵出	yí ge ěrduo jìn, yí ge ěrduo chū	in one ear and out the other
比如	bǐrú	for example				
向錢看	xiàngqián kàn	to care only about money, a pun of "向前看"				
說到做到	shuōdàozuòdào	to keep one's promise				

本课词表 Chapter Vocabulary

◎ By Pinyin

Words with asterisk* are productive vocabulary which needs to be memorized and studied for its usage.

bǎngyàng*	榜样	example, model
bào*	抱	to hold, to embrace, to hug
běnkēshēng	本科生	undergraduate student
bǐrú	比如	for example
bìyào*	必要	necessary, indispensable, need
bìyè	毕业	to graduate, graduation
bóshì	博士	Ph.D.
bùzú	不足	to be not sufficient
chéngjī*	成绩	grade, result, achievement
cúnzài*	存在	to exist, existence
dǎ ěrguāng	打耳光	to slap sb. in the face, to box sb.'s ears
dàliàng	大量	large quantity, mass
dānwèi*	单位	unit in organization (one works in/for) or measurement
diàochá*	调查	to investigate, to look into
duìshǒu*	对手	opponent, adversary, match
fǎn'ér	反而	on the contrary, instead (used after subject)
fǎnduì	反对	to oppose, to be against
fǎnyìng*	反应	reaction, response, to react
fēi	非	not, no, non
fēnpèi*	分配	to allot, to assign, to distribute
fúzhuāng	服装	dress, clothing
fùdān*	负担	burden, load
fùmiàn*	负面	negative
gǎndào*	感到	to feel, to sense
gāokǎo	高考	college entrance examination

gōngfu bú fù yǒuxīn rén	功夫不负有心人	Those who work hard are rewarded.
guài*	怪	to blame
gǔlì*	鼓励	to encourage, to urge
jiǎnlì	简历	<PRC> curriculum vitae, résumé
jiàqī	假期	vacation, holiday
jiēduàn*	阶段	stage, phase
jīliè*	激烈	intense, sharp, fierce
jìngzhēng*	竞争	competition, to compete
jīnqián	金钱	money, wealth
jué*	决	definitely (not)
kǎoshang	考上	to pass an entrance examination
kuàngqiě*	况且	moreover, besides
lǎobǎn	老板	boss
lǐngdǎo*	领导	leader, leadership
miànshì*	面试	interview, to interview
míngqì	名气	reputation, fame, name
mìshū	秘书	secretary
pāi mǎpì*	拍马屁	to flatter, butter up
pào bā	泡吧	to go to bars to have fun
qiáng*	强	strong, better
qiántú*	前途	future, prospects
qiáo*	瞧	to look, to see
qiǎo*	巧	coincidentally
quàngào*	劝告	advice
quánmiàn*	全面	comprehensive, all-round
réncái	人才	person of ability/talent

rènwù*	任务	assignment, task, job
shèhuì	社会	society
shífēn*	十分	very, fully, utterly
shílì	实力	actual strength, substance
shízú	十足	100 percent, out-and-out
shuōdàozuòdào	说到做到	to keep one's promise
shuòshì	硕士	Master (of Arts), M.A.
sòng lǐ	送礼	to give sb. a present
suǒ	所	for houses/schools
tì...shuōhuà*	替...说话	to speak for (sb.)
tóngshí*	同时	simultaneously with..., at the same time, meanwhile
tóngyī	同一	same, identical
xiàn	线	line, thread
xiàngqiánkàn	向钱看	to care only about money
xiànxiàng*	现象	phenomenon
xíngwéi*	行为	action, behavior, conduct
xìnxīn	信心	confidence, faith
xīzhuāng	西装	Western-style clothes

yí ge ěrduo jìn, yí ge ěrduo chū	一个耳朵进，一个耳朵出	in one ear and out the other
yíhàn*	遗憾	regret, pity
yǐwài	以外	beyond, outside, other than
yúlè	娱乐	entertainment, amusement
zànchéng*	赞成	to approve, to endorse
zànshí*	暂时	temporary, temporarily
zǎoshú*	早熟	early-maturing, precocious
zérèn*	责任	duty, responsibility, blame
zhāojí*	着急	anxious
zhèngfǔ	政府	govenment
zhīchí*	支持	to support, to back
zhòngdiǎn*	重点	key, focal point, emphasis
zhuānjiā	专家	expert, specialist
zìxìn*	自信	self-confidence, to be self-confident

語法和用法 Grammar and Usage

Pay attention to the function of the structure and then study the example sentences. When blanks are provided, either answer the questions or complete the sentences.

1. Expressing a compulsion

S 一 V 就是 NP	yī…jiùshì…	Whenever S does something, S does something a lot

- 他說別的同學給老師送禮物一送就是幾百塊錢的東西，我們禮送輕了還不如不送呢！

1. 學生都喜歡上網玩遊戲嗎？玩多久？

   学生都喜欢上网玩游戏吗？玩多久？

   Do students like to play games on the internet? How long do they play?

   很多學生都特別喜歡上網玩遊戲，而且一玩就是一個下午。

   很多学生都特别喜欢上网玩游戏，而且一玩就是一个下午。

   Many students like to play games on the internet and when they do, they spend the whole afternoon playing.

2. 你常去逛街買東西嗎？會花很多錢嗎？

   你常去逛街买东西吗？会花很多钱吗？

   Do you often buy things window-shopping? Do you spend a lot of money?

   我平時不經常逛街買東西，但是一買就是幾百塊錢的。

   我平时不经常逛街买东西，但是一买就是几百块钱的。

   I don't usually buy things window-shopping, but when I do, I spend several hundred dollars.

3. 你每個星期都洗衣服嗎？

   你每个星期都洗衣服吗？

   Do you do your laundry every week?

   我平時太忙了，沒有時間每個星期洗衣服，所以一洗就是幾袋子。

   我平时太忙了，没有时间每个星期洗衣服，所以一洗就是几袋子。

   Ordinarily I'm too busy and don't have time to do my laundry every week; so when I do, I have several bags of dirty clothes.

4. 你回家的時候，媽媽是不是會做　　你回家的时候，妈妈是不是会做

很多的菜？	很多的菜？

5. 你和好朋友聊天的時候會聊很長 時間嗎？ | 你和好朋友聊天的时候会聊很长 时间吗？

6. 你每天都會運動很長時間嗎？ | 你每天都会运动很长时间吗？

The pattern S 一 V就是⋯ expresses a person's tendency to act compulsively. What follows 就是 is a noun phrase specifying excessiveness of an action (e.g., duration). So, it is wrong to say 我一去就是運動一個下午 'Whenever I go, I work out all afternoon.' A sentence such as 我一運動就是很長時間 'Whenever I work out, it takes a long time' is better phrased as 我一運動就是三個小時 'Whenever I work out, it takes three hours.' Compare this pattern with 不VO⋯，一VO⋯ (就/才) (L6, G4).

2. Expressing continuous action

S VOV個不停/沒完 ge bù tíng/ méi wán	S keeps Ving

• 不過他們都說那個被打的學生上課表現不好，總是說話說個不停⋯⋯

1. 小明又在和朋友打 電話聊天，咱們先 吃飯吧，別等他 了！ | 小明又在和朋友打 电话聊天，咱们先 吃饭吧，别等他 了！ | Xiao Ming is chatting with his friend on phone again. Let's eat first and not wait for him.

這個孩子太不像 話，每次打電話都 打個沒完，不知道 他哪兒有那麼多可 聊的。 | 这个孩子太不象 话，每次打电话都 打个没完，不知道 他哪儿有那么多可 聊的。 | This child is really outrageous. Each time he's on the phone, he never hangs up. I don't know how he can have so much to talk about.

2. 這部電影非常好 笑，看的時候所有 | 这部电影非常好 笑，看的时候所有 | This movie is hilarious. When they saw it, the whole audience

的觀眾都笑個不停。	的观众都笑个不停。	couldn't stop laughing.
這麼好的電影，如果不看的話，我一定會非常遺憾。	这么好的电影，如果不看的话，我一定会非常遗憾。	If I don't go see such a good movie, I'll certainly regret it.

3.
你最近為了找工作已經有好幾個面試了，有沒有找到一個讓你滿意的？	你最近为了找工作已经有好几个面试了，有没有找到一个让你满意的？	You've had several job interviews lately. Did you find one you're satisfied with?
哎！面試的時候，那些用人單位的人有很多問題，總是問個沒完，我根本沒有時間提問。	哎！面试的时候，那些用人单位的人有很多问题，总是问个没完，我根本没有时间提问。	Well, when having an interview, those personnel people had many questions and never finished asking them. I didn't have time to raise any questions at all.

4.
鄰居的那隻狗怎麼了，為什麼最近沒聽見它的叫聲？	邻居的那只狗怎么了，为什么最近没听见它的叫声？

5.
你為什麼不看ABC電視台的電影？	你为什么不看ABC电视台的电影？

6.
老張和他的太太又吵架了嗎？	老张和他的太太又吵架了吗？

The expression S VO V個不/沒 停/完 indicates continuous action. V is often an action that can go on and on, e.g., 說、唱、吵、打、叫、播. If an object is present, the verb should be repeated. 停 or 完 is often at the end of the sentence. Note that this pattern is used to describe a continuous action, not an intention to continue doing something. So, it's odd to say 那一台的節目很有意思，我一定要看電視看個不停 'The programs of that station are very interesting. I will certainly keep watching their programs.' Compare this with V (得/不) 下去 (L3, G5) which also expresses the continuation or progression of an action.

3. Expressing a reproach

瞧/看 你 V/Adj 的	qiáo/kàn nǐ…de	Look at what you V/Adj!

● 瞧你說的，就算是重點中學的學生，也得參加競爭激烈的高考……

1. 昨天老板批評我的時候，你替我說話，我不知道該怎麼感謝你才對？　　昨天老板批評我的时候，你替我说话，我不知道该怎么感谢你才对？　　Yesterday when the boss criticized me, you spoke up for me. I don't know how to thank you?

瞧你說的，我們是同事，互相幫助是應該的，有什麼好謝的？　　瞧你说的，我们是同事，互相帮助是应该的，有什么好谢的？　　Look at what you've said. We are colleagues and should help each other. What's the point of thanking me?

2. 瞧你睏kùn的，連眼睛都睜不開了，昨晚是不是又熬夜了？　　瞧你困的，连眼睛都睁不开了，昨晚是不是又熬夜了？　　My, how sleepy you look! You can't even open your eyes. Did you stay up late last night?

那還用說嗎？今天有大考，不複習怎麼行？　　那还用说吗？今天有大考，不复习怎么行？　　It goes without saying. Today I have an exam, so how would it do to not review?

3. 我簡直不能相信，老師竟然會因為學生上課說話而打學生的耳光！　　我简直不能相信，老师竟然会因为学生上课说话而打学生的耳光！　　I simply can't believe the teacher would slap a student because he spoke in class.

瞧你氣的，有話好好說，生氣也不能解決問題。　　瞧你气的，有话好好说，生气也不能解决问题。　　Look at how mad you are. Slow down if you have something to say. Getting angry won't solve the problem.

4. 我已經寄出去幾十份簡歷了，為　　我已经寄出去几十份简历了，

什麼到現在還沒有公司約我面試　　为什么到现在还没有公司约我
呢？　　　　　　　　　　　　面试呢？

---

5. 我今天去體育館做了一個小時的　　我今天去体育馆做了一个小时
運動，我需要好好休息一下。　　的运动，我需要好好休息一
　　　　　　　　　　　　　　　下。

---

6. 太不像話了，父母的話他總是一　　太不象话了，父母的话他总是
個耳朵進，一個耳朵出！　　　　一个耳朵进，一个耳朵出！

The colloquial expression 瞧/看你 V/Adj 的 is used to indicate a reproach. What
follows 你 is often a one-syllable verb like 說 (example 1)、睡、吃 or adjective like
睏 (example 2)、氣(example 3)、累、餓、急. 的 is always at the end of this
expression and it cannot be substituted by anything else, so it's wrong to say 瞧你氣了.

4. Expressing simultaneous action

S 在 V_1O_1 的同時，　也V_2O_2	zài...de tóngshí,　S V_2O_2 while V_1O_1
在 V_1O_1 的同時，S 也V_2O_2	yě...

- 對我來說在多了一個朋友的同時，也多了一個競爭對手。

1. 父母應該怎麼教養　　父母应该怎么教养　　How should parents teach their
   孩子？　　　　　　　孩子？　　　　　　　children?

   父母在看到孩子的　　父母在看到孩子的　　When parents see a child make
   錯誤時，總是想嚴　　错误时，总是想严　　a mistake, they always want to
   屬地批評，可是在　　厉地批评，可是在　　criticize the child harshly. Yet,
   批評的同時，也應　　批评的同时，也应　　while criticizing, they should
   該告訴孩子正確的　　该告诉孩子正确的　　also tell their child what the
   作法是什麼。　　　　作法是什么。　　　　right way of doing things is.

2. 怎麼樣可以成為一　　怎么样可以成为一　　How can one become a

個成功的推銷員？

個成功的推銷員？

successful salesman?

要成為一個成功的推銷員，在向顧客推銷商品的同時，也應該為顧客著想。

要成为一个成功的推销员，在向顾客推销商品的同时，也应该为顾客着想。

In order to become a successful salesman, while you promote your products, you should also think from the customer's perspective.

3. 現在的明星能紅多久？

現在的明星能紅多久？

How long can today's stars stay popular?

現在很多的明星在公司的包裝下，一夜之間出名，但是不久以後就會被人們忘記；所以我想在包裝的同時，也應該注意培養péiyǎng他們的藝術修養xiūyǎng。

现在很多的明星在公司的包装下，一夜之间出名，但是不久以后就会被人们忘记；所以我想在包装的同时，也应该注意培养他们的艺术修养。

Nowadays many stars, packaged by their companies, have become famous overnight, but people will soon forget about them. So, I think while packaging these stars, the company should also pay attention to improving the mastery of their art.

4. 我覺得婚姻是一種緣分，除了感覺以外，什麼都不應該考慮。

我觉得婚姻是一种缘分，除了感觉以外，什么都不应该考虑。

5. 感恩節過後，各個商場都會有打折商品，到時候我們又可以大購物了。

感恩节过后，各个商场都会有打折商品，到时候我们又可以大购物了。

6. 你覺得什麼樣的書算是好書，暢銷就可以了嗎？

你觉得什么样的书算是好书，畅销就可以了吗？

The pattern 在V$_1$O$_1$ 的同時，也 V$_2$O$_2$ is used to express simultaneous action. The subject either goes before 在V$_1$O$_1$的同時 or before 也V$_2$O$_2$. The two simultaneous actions should indicate different aspects of the subject. So, it's odd to say 書在暢銷的同時，也要有好的內容 'While books are selling well, they should have good contents as well.' Rather, it's better to say something like 書在娛樂讀者的同時，也應該有教育意義 'While books entertain the reader, they should have educational value as well' or 我們在看書的銷售量的同時，也應該注意書的質量 'While we pay attention to a book's sales, we should also be concerned about its quality.'

5. Expressing contradiction

S 不僅不/沒 V$_1$O$_1$，（甚至/反而）還V$_2$O$_2$	bùjǐnbù/méi…(shènzhì/fǎn'ér) hái	S not only not V$_1$O$_1$, but even V$_2$O$_2$

- 當大家都準備畢業、忙著找工作的時候，李明不僅不包裝自己，還比平時更放鬆了。

1. 為什麼你對那個老師那麼反感？

   为什么你对那个老师那么反感？

   Why do you dislike that teacher so much?

   老師上課的時候打了學生的耳光，當家長向老師表示不滿時，老師不僅沒道歉，還批評被打的學生太淘氣 táoqì。

   老师上课的时候打了学生的耳光，当家长向老师表示不满时，老师不仅没道歉，还批评被打的学生太淘气。

   That teacher slapped his student in class. When the parents indicated their discontent, the teacher not only did not apologize, but even criticized the slapped student for being too naughty.

2. 很多女性怎麼減肥？

   很多女性怎么减肥？

   How do most women lose weight?

   很多年輕的女性為了減肥而節食，這樣做不僅不會有助於減肥，還會有害於身體健康。

   很多年轻的女性为了减肥而节食，这样做不仅不会有助于减肥，还会有害于身体健康。

   Many young women are on a diet in order to lose weight. But this way is not only not helpful for losing weight, but harms one's health.

3. 王小姐過了三十歲還沒結婚，她自己著急嗎？

王小姐过了三十岁还没结婚，她自己著急吗？

Ms. Wang is over thirty and not yet married. Is she herself worried about it?

大家都勸她應該儘可能地早解決自己的終身大事，可是她不僅不著急，還很享受現在的單身生活。

大家都劝她应该尽可能地早解决自己的终身大事，可是她不仅不着急，还很享受现在的单身生活。

Everyone urges her to get married as soon as possible. Yet, she is not only not anxious, but instead enjoys her currently single life very much.

4. 期末考試就快到了，_____

期末考试就快到了，_____

_____

5. 我找到工作以後，打算請大家到麥當勞去吃飯，_____

我找到工作以后，打算请大家到麦当劳去吃饭，_____

_____

6. 電影《臥虎藏龍》受到了美國觀眾的喜愛，可是在中國_____

电影《卧虎藏龙》受到了美国观众的喜爱，可是在中国_____

_____

The pattern 不僅不/沒 V_1O_1, (甚至/反而) 還 V_2O_2 is used to express contradiction. 不僅不/沒 goes after the subject. If the action is current and habitual, 不僅不 is used. If the action occurred in the past, 不僅沒 is used. V_1O_1 indicates what is normally expected of the subject given the circumstance, and V_2O_2 is the unexpected, contrary or outrageous action taken. Thus, V_1O_1 and V_2O_2 should not have identical or similar meaning, and it's odd to say 人們不僅不太喜歡這部電影，反而還討厭這部電影 'People not only don't like this movie, they hate it.' It's more appropriate to have something such as 這部電影不僅不能吸引人們的興趣，還受到很多觀眾的批評 'This movie not only could not pique people's interest, but was criticized by many viewers as well.'

6. Linking reasons

> …，況且 S(也/還/又) VO   kuàngqiě (yě/hái/ yòu)   …, and besides SVO

- 但是很可能浪費了大量的金錢和時間。況且對外表的過分包裝還可能反映出一個人對自己的信心不足……

1. 你覺得年輕人應該接受父母的批評嗎？	你觉得年轻人应该接受父母的批评吗？	Do you think young people should accept their parents'criticism?
我覺得年輕人對父母的批評，不應該一個耳朵進一個耳朵出，因為父母的經驗畢竟比我們的豐富，況且他們之所以批評我們，也是為了我們好。	我觉得年轻人对父母的批评，不应该一个耳朵进一个耳朵出，因为父母的经验毕竟比我们的丰富，况且他们之所以批评我们，也是为了我们好。	I think that young people shouldn't disagree with their parents'criticism because parents, after all, have more experience than we do. Besides, their criticism of us is for our own good.
2. 在中國為什麼中學生不可以談戀愛？	在中国为什么中学生不可以谈恋爱？	In China, why can't middle school students go on date?
在中國中學生不可以談戀愛，因為十幾歲的孩子思想還不成熟，不了解愛是什麼，況且上學的時候談戀愛，也會影響學習成績。	在中国中学生不可以谈恋爱，因为十几岁的孩子思想还不成熟，不了解爱是什么，况且上学的时候谈恋爱，也会影响学习成绩。	In China, middle school students can't go on date, because teenagers are not mature enough and don't understand what love is; besides, if they have dates when going to school, this will affect their grades.
3. 你覺得電視上應該有廣告嗎？	你觉得电视上应该有广告吗？	Do you think there should be commercials on TV?
我覺得電視台根本不應該播放廣告，我從來不會根據廣告的好壞來決定買什麼東西，況且很多廣告拍	我觉得电视台根本不应该播放广告，我从来不会根据广告的好坏来决定买什么东西，况且很多广告拍	I think that TV stations shouldn't have commercials at all. I never buy a product based on the commercials I see. Besides, many

得很差，也不可能讓　　得很差，也不可能让　　commericials are poorly
人對他們的商品感興　　人对他们的商品感兴　　shot, and don't arouse
趣。　　　　　　　　趣。　　　　　　　　people's interest in their
　　　　　　　　　　　　　　　　　　　　product.

4.　我很少聽現在的流行音樂，＿＿　　我很少听现在的流行音乐，＿＿

_____

5.　我有不少朋友是電腦迷，可是我　　我有不少朋友是电脑迷，可是我
　　自己卻從來不上網，＿＿＿＿＿　　自己却从来不上网，＿＿＿＿＿

_____

6.　週末的時候，我的同屋總是要到　　周末的时候，我的同屋总是要到
　　外面吃飯，可是我卻喜歡在家裏　　外面吃饭，可是我却喜欢在家里
　　自己做飯，＿＿＿＿＿＿＿＿　　自己做饭，＿＿＿＿＿＿＿＿

_____

The pattern 況且S (也/還/又) VO is used to link reasons, so there is always another
clause preceding 況且. In the second clause, if the subject is present, it goes after 況且
and 也/還/又 goes before the verb. It's odd to say 我喜歡在家做飯，況且自己做飯
比較好吃，又有營養 'I like to cook at home. Besides, the food I make is better
tasting and more nutritious.' The sentence should be rephrased as 我喜歡在家做飯，
自己做飯比較好吃，況且又有營養 'I like to cook at home. The food I make is quite
tasty; plus home-cooked food is more nutritious.'

背景常識 Background Notes

1.　重點中學：中學可以分為重點中學和普通中學。這兩種學校的最大差
　　別在於老師的質量、學校的設備和學生來源。由於老師和學生的素質
　　都比較高，所以重點中學的學生考上大學的比例就比較大，很多學生
　　都把考上重點中學當成是考大學的第一步。

2.　高考：因為每年的高考是在7月7、8、9三天，所以有黑色七月說法。從
　　2003年起，因為7月的天氣太熱，所以高考改到了6月7、8、9三天。一
　　個學生上了12年學，就要靠這三天的考試來決定自己是否能上大學，

也有人用「千軍萬馬過獨木橋」來形容高考。

3. 大學生：在進入大學之前，學生們就應該決定自己的專業，以前在大學換專業非常難，現在的情況有一些改變，但是上大學以後換專業的學生還是少數。現在的大學生除了讀自己的專業以外，還會選擇很多的選修課，這樣在畢業以後選擇工作的機會就會更大。當然電腦和外語是大學生最關心的兩門課。近幾年，大學生打工的現象越來越普遍，大家都覺得在大學打工不但可以解決一些經濟上的問題，更重要的是儘早的開始積累工作經驗，為今後的工作做準備。

背景常识 Background Notes

1. 重点中学：中学可以分为重点中学和普通中学。这两种学校的最大差别在于老师的质量、学校的设备和学生来源。由于老师和学生的素质都比较高，所以重点中学的学生考上大学的比例就比较大，很多学生都把考上重点中学当成是考大学的第一步。

2. 高考：因为每年的高考是在7月7、8、9三天，所以有黑色七月说法。从2003年起，因为7月的天气太热，所以高考改到了6月7、8、9三天。一个学生上了12年学，就要靠这三天的考试来决定自己是否能上大学，也有人用"千军万马过独木桥"来形容高考。

3. 大学生：在进入大学之前，学生们就应该决定自己的专业，以前在大学换专业非常难，现在的情况有一些改变，但是上大学以后换专业的学生还是少数。现在的大学生除了读自己的专业以外，还会选择很多的选修课，这样在毕业以后选择工作的机会就会更大。当然电脑和外语是大学生最关心的两门课。近几年，大学生打工的现象越来越普遍，大家都觉得在大学打工不但可以解决一些经济上的问题，更重要的是尽早的开始积累工作经验，为今后的工作做准备。

✐我的問題：

第 十 課　芒果女人

Theme: Social Commentary

Communicative Objectives
- Discussing a work of literature

Skill Focus
- Reading an authentic text with little glossary aid
- Synthesizing reading and study skills acquired from previous chapters

Grammar Focus
- O S V得/不著
  S V得/不了O
- V 了一N$_1$ 的N$_2$
- 往輕點說是…，重說是…
- 不單單是A，B還/都/也…
- …，…以V
- A為B（所）V

Problem Scenario

Have you ever been abroad for a while only to return to your home country and, by way of comparison, notice something your country could improve upon? If so, how would you respond? Would you voice your opinion no matter how trivial or even controversial the subject? Which type of person are you: the silence majority or the outspoken minority?

芒果女人 作者：畢淑敏

第一部分（繁）Part 1

Who is the protagonist? _____

What is the setting of the story? _____

Why is the protagonist here? _____

What is her/his personality? _____

What is the main issue discussed in this section? _____

　　小學同學檬從北美回來探親，因國內已無親人，她要求以前的同學除了敘舊以外，就是陪她逛街購物吃飯，於是大家安排好時間，今日是張三明日是李四，好像醫院陪床一般，每人陪她一天。

　　檬的先生在外發了財，檬家有花園洋房游泳池，檬的女兒在讀博士，檬真是吃穿不愁。可是檬依然很樸素，就像當年在鄉下插隊時一般。檬說：「我這麼多年主要是當家庭婦女，每日修剪草坪和購物。要說有什麼本領，就是學會了如何當一名消費者。」檬說中國的商家已經學會了賺錢，可很多人還不知道錢要賺得有道理。中國老百姓也已經知道了，錢可以買來服務。可這服務是什麼質量的，心裡卻不太了解。

　　和檬坐出租汽車。司機一邊開車，一邊用打火機點著了煙。檬對我

檬	méng	a person's name
探親	tànqīn	to visit relatives
敘舊	xùjiù	to reminisce
陪	péi	
張三	zhāngsān	John Doe
陪床	péichuáng	to keep sb. company in a hospital
洋房	yángfáng	Western-style building
吃穿不愁	chīchuān bù chóu	not worried about making a living
依然	yīrán	still, as before
樸素	pǔsù/púsù	simple, plain
鄉下	xiāngxià	countryside
插隊	chāduì	to go to countryside
修剪	xiūjiǎn	to prune, to trim
草坪	cǎopíng	lawn
本領	běnlǐng	
消費	xiāofèi	
打火機	dǎhuǒjī	(cigarette) lighter
點	diǎn	

說，你抽煙嗎？我躲著煙霧說，不抽。艨說，我也不抽。然後是誰也不說話，只有發動機的聲音。等了一會兒，艨對司機說，師傅，我本來是想委婉地提醒您一下，沒想到您不明白。那我就得明說了，請您把煙熄了。司機愣了一下，好像沒聽懂她的話，想了想，還算和氣地說，起得早，睏。抽一支，提提神。我這車，不禁煙，沒看不貼禁止吸煙的標誌嗎？艨說，這跟禁煙標誌無關，而是您抽煙並沒有得到我們的同意啊。司機說，新鮮。抽煙這事，連老婆都[1]管不著，幹嘛要你們的同意？

艨說，你老婆給你錢嗎？

司機說，新鮮。我老婆給我什麼錢？是我給她錢。

艨又說，這就對了。你老婆和你是私事，你可聽也可不聽。我們出了錢，從一上車，我們就買了你的服務。我們是你的雇主，你在車內吸煙，怎能不問主人的意見呢？

躲	duǒ	
煙霧	yānwù	smoke, mist
發動機	fādòngjī	engine
聲音	shēngyīn	sound, voice
委婉	wěiwǎn	tactful
明說	míngshuō	to speak frankly
熄	xí	to put out
愣	lèng	
和氣	héqi	kind, amiable
睏	kùn	
提神	tíshén	to perk up
禁煙	jìnyān	to ban smoking
貼	tiē	
禁止	jìnzhǐ	
標誌	biāozhì	to mark, mark
管	guǎn	
幹嘛	gànmá	
私事	sīshì	private affair
雇主	gùzhǔ	employer
捏一把汗	niē yì bǎ hàn	to break into a cold sweat
火	huǒ	to be mad
評書	píngshū	story-telling
氣氛	qìfen	
尷尬	gāngà	embarrassed

我捏了一把汗，怕司機火起來，沒想到他拿著煙想了半天，把沒抽完的烟丟到車窗外面了。過了一會，司機看看錶，把車上的收音機打開，開始聽評書，使車內的氣氛不那麼尷尬。

籐的**眉頭皺**起來，這一次，她不再委婉地提醒司機，而是直接說，師傅，我**心臟**不好，不能聽這麼大的聲音，請您關了收音機。

司機生氣地說，**怎麼著**？這評書我是每天都聽的，**莫非**今天拉了你，就得壞了我的**規矩**？你這個女人腦子有毛病！

我雖從**感情**上**向著**籐，但司機的話也**不無道理**。我忙**打圓場**說，師傅，我這位朋友愛靜，就請您把聲音**擰**小點，大家**將就**一下吧。

沒想到首先反對我的是籐。她說，這不是可以將就的事。師傅願意聽評書，可以。您把車停了，自個兒坐在**樹蔭**下，愛怎麼聽就怎麼聽，那是你的自由。既然您是在**從事**服務性的工作，就得以顧客為**上帝**。

司機**故意**讓車**顛簸**起來，**冷笑**著說，怎麼著？我就是聽，你能把我如何？說完把聲音擰到**震耳欲聾**。

籐**毫不示弱**地說，那你把車停下。我們下車！

司機說，我就不停，你有什麼辦法？莫非你還敢跳車？！

籐說，我為什麼要跳車？我坐車，就是為了方便。我付了錢，就該得到好的服務，你無法**提供**讓人滿意的服務，我就不付你**報酬**。這件事情，走遍天下我也有理。

眉頭	méitóu	brows
皺	zhòu	to wrinkle
心臟	xīnzàng	heart
怎麼著	zěnmezhe	What about?
莫非	mòfēi	can it be that
規矩	guījǔ	
感情	gǎnqíng	
向著	xiàngzhe	
不無道理	bù wú dàolǐ	not without reason
打圓場	dǎyuán chǎng	to smooth things over
擰	níng	to twist
將就	jiāngjiù	to make do
樹蔭	shùyìn	shade (of a tree)
從事	cóngshì	
上帝	shàngdì	God
故意	gùyì	
顛簸	diānbǒ	to bump
冷笑	lěngxiào	to sneer
震耳欲聾	zhèn ěr yù lóng	deafening
毫不	háobù	not at all
示弱	shìruò	to not take sth. lying down
提供	tígōng	to provide
報酬	bàochóu	

我以為司機一定會**大怒**，把我們**扔**在公路上。沒想到在艨的**邏輯**面前，他真的把收音機關了，雖然**臉色**黑得好似被**微波爐烤焦**的**蝦餅**。

司機終於把我們平安拉到了目的地。下車後，我**心有餘悸**。 艨卻說，這個司機肯定會記住這件事的，以後也許會懂得**尊重乘客**。

大怒	dànù	rage
扔	rēng	
邏輯	luójí	logic
臉色	liǎnsè	look
微波爐	wéibōlú	microwave oven
烤焦	kǎojiāo	to toast and burn
蝦餅	xiābǐng	shrimp cracker
心有餘悸	xīn yǒu yújì	to have lingering fears
尊重	zūnzhòng	
乘客	chéngkè	passenger

閱讀理解 Comprehension Check

1. 艨的同學每天要陪她做什麼？為什麼？
2. 艨現在的家庭情況怎麼樣？這對她有什麼影響？
3. 艨認為自己現在最會做什麼？為什麼？
4. 艨覺得中國的老百姓對什麼沒有概念？
5. 出租汽車司機做了什麼讓艨生氣？艨怎麼跟司機講道理？
6. 我覺得艨的做法怎麼樣？司機對還是艨對？
7. 司機生氣以後做什麼？他把艨和她的朋友扔在公路上嗎？

第一部分（简）Part 1

Who is the protagonist? _____

What is the setting of the story? _____

Why is the protagonist here? _____

What is her/his personality? _____

What is the main issue discussed in this section? _____

小学同学**朦**从北美回来**探亲**，因国内已无亲人，她要求以前的同学除了**叙旧**以外，就是**陪**她逛街购物吃饭，于是大家安排好时间，今日是**张三**明日是李四，好象医院**陪床**一般，每人陪她一天。

朦的先生在外发了财，朦家有花园**洋房**游泳池，朦的女儿在读博士，朦真是**吃穿不愁**。可是朦**依然**很**朴素**，就象当年在**乡下插队**时一般。朦说："我这么多年主要是当家庭妇女，每日**修剪草坪**和购物。要说有什么**本领**，就是学会了如何当一名**消费者**。"

朦说中国的商家已经学会了赚钱，可很多人还不知道钱要赚得有道理。中国老百姓也已经知道了，钱可以买来服务。可这服务是什么质量的，心里却不太了解。

和朦坐出租汽车。司机一边开车，一边用**打火机点**着了烟。朦对我

朦	méng	a person's name
探亲	tànqīn	to visit relatives
叙旧	xùjiù	to reminisce
陪	péi	
张三	zhāngsān	John Doe
陪床	péichuáng	to keep sb. company in a hospital
洋房	yángfáng	Western-style building
吃穿不愁	chīchuān bù chóu	not worried about making a living
依然	yīrán	still, as before
朴素	pǔsù/púsù	simple, plain
乡下	xiāngxià	countryside
插队	chāduì	to go to countryside
修剪	xiūjiǎn	to prune, to trim
草坪	cǎopíng	lawn
本领	běnlǐng	
消费	xiāofèi	
打火机	dǎhuǒjī	(cigarette) lighter
点	diǎn	

说，你抽烟吗？我**躲着烟雾**说，不抽。藤说，

我也不抽。然后是谁也不说话，只有**发动机**的

声音。等了一会儿，藤对司机说，师傅，我本

来是想**委婉**地提醒您一下，没想到您不明白。

那我就得**明说**了，请您把烟**熄**了。司机**愣**了一

下，好象没听懂她的话，想了想，还算**和气**地

说，起得早，**困**。抽一支，提**提神**。我这车，

不**禁烟**，没看不**贴禁止**吸烟的**标志**吗？藤说，

这跟禁烟标志无关，而是您抽烟并没有得到我

们的同意啊。司机说，新鲜。抽烟这事，连**老**

婆都[1]**管不著**，干嘛要你们的同意？

藤说，你老婆给你钱吗？

司机说，新鲜。我老婆给我什么钱？是我

给她钱。

藤又说，这就对了。你老婆和你是**私事**，

你可听也可不听。我们出了钱，从一上车，我

们就买了你的服务。我们是你的**雇主**，你在车

内吸烟，怎能不问主人的意见呢？

我**捏**了**一把汗**，怕司机**火**起来，没想到他拿着烟想了半天，把没抽完

的烟丢到车窗外面了。过了一会，司机看看表，把车上的收音机打开，开

始听**评书**，使车内的**气氛**不那么**尴尬**。

藤的**眉头皱**起来，这一次，她不再委婉地提醒司机，而是直接说，师

傅，我**心脏**不好，不能听这么大的声音，请您关了收音机。

躲	duǒ	
烟雾	yānwù	smoke, mist
发动机	fādòngjī	engine
声音	shēngyīn	sound, voice
委婉	wěiwǎn	tactful
明说	míngshuō	to speak frankly
熄	xí	to put out
愣	lèng	
和气	héqi	kind, amiable
困	kùn	
提神	tíshén	to perk up
禁烟	jìnyān	to ban smoking
贴	tiē	
禁止	jìnzhǐ	
标志	biāozhì	to mark, mark
管	guǎn	
干吗	gànmá	
私事	sīshì	private affair
雇主	gùzhǔ	employer
捏一把汗	niē yì bǎ hàn	to break into a cold sweat
火	huǒ	to be mad
评书	píngshū	story-telling
气氛	qìfen	
尴尬	gāngà	embarrassed
眉头	méitóu	brows
皱	zhòu	to wrinkle
心脏	xīnzàng	heart

司机生气地说，**怎么着**？这评书我是每天都听的，**莫非**今天拉了你，就得坏了我的**规矩**？你这个女人脑子有毛病！

我虽从**感情**上**向着**蘩，但司机的话也**不无道理**。我忙**打圆场**说，师傅，我这位朋友爱静，就请您把声音**拧**小点，大家**将就**一下吧。

没想到首先反对我的是蘩。她说，这不是可以将就的事。师傅愿意听评书，可以。您把车停了，自个儿坐在**树荫**下，爱怎么听就怎么听，那是你的自由。既然您是在**从事**服务性的工作，就得以顾客为**上帝**。

司机**故意**让车**颠簸**起来，**冷笑**着说，怎么着？我就是听，你能把我如何？说完把声音拧到**震耳欲聋**。

蘩**毫不示弱**地说，那你把车停下。我们下车！

司机说，我就不停，你有什么办法？莫非你还敢跳车？！

蘩说，我为什么要跳车？我坐车，就是为了方便。我付了钱，就该得到好的服务，你无法**提供**让人满意的服务，我就不付你**报酬**。这件事情，走遍天下我也有理。

我以为司机一定会**大怒**，把我们**扔**在公路上。没想到在蘩的**逻辑**面

怎么着	zěnmezhe	What about?
莫非	mòfēi	can it be that
规矩	guījǔ	
感情	gǎnqíng	
向着	xiàngzhe	
不无道理	bù wú dàolǐ	not without reason
打圆场	dǎyuán chǎng	to smooth things over
拧	níng	to twist
将就	jiāngjiù	to make do
树荫	shùyìn	shade (of a tree)
从事	cóngshì	
上帝	shàngdì	God
故意	gùyì	
颠簸	diānbǒ	to bump
冷笑	lěngxiào	to sneer
震耳欲聋	zhèn ěr yù lóng	deafening
毫不	háobù	not at all
示弱	shìruò	to not take sth. lying down
提供	tígōng	to provide
报酬	bàochóu	
大怒	dànù	rage
扔	rēng	
逻辑	luójí	logic

前，他真的把收音机关了，虽然**脸色**黑得好似
被**微波炉烤焦**的**虾饼**。

司机终于把我们平安拉到了目的地。下
车后，我**心有余悸**。 朦却说，这个司机肯定
会记住这件事的，以后也许会懂得**尊重乘客**。

脸色	liǎnsè	look
微波炉	wéibōlú	microwave oven
烤焦	kǎojiāo	to toast and burn
虾饼	xiābǐng	shrimp cracker
心有余悸	xīn yǒu yújì	to have lingering fears
尊重	zūnzhòng	
乘客	chéngkè	passenger

阅读理解 Comprehension Check

1. 朦的同学每天要陪她做什么？为什么？
2. 朦现在的家庭情况怎么样？这对她有什么影响？
3. 朦认为自己现在最会做什么？为什么？
4. 朦觉得中国的老百姓对什么没有概念？
5. 出租汽车司机做了什么让朦生气？朦怎么跟司机讲道理？
6. 我觉得朦的做法怎么样？司机对还是朦对？
7. 司机生气以后做什么？他把朦和她的朋友扔在公路上吗？

詞匯用法 Words in Context

1. 陪：

   你週末的時候會陪父母吃飯嗎？

   如果出國旅遊，你需要有一個有經驗的朋友陪你嗎？

   陪：

   你周末的时候会陪父母吃饭吗？

   如果出国旅游，你需要有一个有经验的朋友陪你吗？

2. 本領：有本領；本領很大

   在競爭激烈的社會裏，什麼樣的人才能成功？

   朦在美國學到了什麼樣的本領？

   本领：有本领；本领很大

   在竞争激烈的社会里，什么样的人才能成功？

   朦在美国学到了什么样的本领？

3. 消費：消費水平；消費者

   這兒的消費水平在美國算高嗎？

   消费：消费水平；消费者

   这儿的消费水平在美国算高吗？

你覺得消費者該有哪些權利？　　　你觉得消费者该有哪些权利？

4. 　點：點烟、點火；點得著、點　　点：点烟、点火；点得着、点
　　不著；點菜　　　　　　　　　　不着；点菜

　　打火機是用來做什麼的？　　　　打火机是用来做什么的？
　　吃燒烤之前應該先做什麼？　　　吃烧烤之前应该先做什么？

5. 　躲：躲起來；能躲就躲；躲著　　躲：躲起来；能躲就躲；躲着
　　老板　　　　　　　　　　　　　老板

　　你最近為什麼老躲著你的女朋　　你最近为什么老躲着你的女朋
　　友？　　　　　　　　　　　　　友？

　　我聽說你的同屋在家裏養病，　　我听说你的同屋在家里养病，是
　　是真的嗎？　　　　　　　　　　真的吗？

6. 　楞：愣了一下；愣住了　　　　　楞：愣了一下，愣住了

　　那個人叫你名字的時候，你為　　那个人叫你名字的时候，你为什
　　什麼愣了一下？　　　　　　　　么愣了一下？

　　你怎麼知道那個學生沒準備？　　你怎么知道那个学生没准备？

7. 　睏：很睏；睏死了　　　　　　　困：很困，困死了

　　你今天上課的時候為什麼那麼　　你今天上课的时候为什么那么
　　睏？　　　　　　　　　　　　　困？

　　你覺得喝茶可以讓你不那麼睏　　你觉得喝茶可以让你不那么困了
　　了嗎？　　　　　　　　　　　　吗？

8. 　貼：貼郵票；把畫貼在牆上　　　贴：贴邮票；把画贴在墙上

　　你寄的信為什麼被退回來了？　　你寄的信为什么被退回来了？
　　你站在桌子上做什麼？　　　　　你站在桌子上做什么？

9. 　禁止：禁止抽煙、停車、左轉　　禁止：禁止抽烟、停车、左转
　　彎　　　　　　　　　　　　　　弯

　　在麥當勞吃飯可以抽煙嗎？　　　在麦当劳吃饭可以抽烟吗？

　　你為什麼要把車停在離辦公室　　你为什么要把车停在离办公室这

這麼遠的地方？　　　　　　　么远的地方？

10. 管：管得很嚴；什麼事情都管　　管：管得很严；什么事情都管

我不知道應該和誰討論怎麼選　我不知道应该和谁讨论怎么选
課？　　　　　　　　　　　課？

買衣服的時候，你覺得牌子重　买衣服的时候，你觉得牌子重要
要還是價格重要？　　　　　还是价格重要？

11. 幹嘛：　　　　　　　　　　干嘛：

你幹嘛不陪你媽媽去逛街呢？　你干嘛不陪你妈妈去逛街呢？

你不喜歡同屋總是把音樂的聲　你不喜欢同屋总是把音乐的声音
音放得很大，那你幹嘛不直接　放得很大，那你干嘛不直接告诉
告訴他呢？　　　　　　　　他呢？

12. 氣氛：氣氛緊張、輕鬆、很好　气氛：气氛紧张、轻松、很好

你覺得中文課的氣氛怎麼樣？　你觉得中文课的气氛怎么样？

什麼課讓你覺得氣氛特別緊　什么课让你觉得气氛特别紧张？
張？

13. 規矩：守規矩；有規矩；沒規　规矩：守规矩；有规矩；没规
矩；規矩多　　　　　　　　矩；规矩多

為什麼不可以隨便去看病人？　为什么不可以随便去看病人？

你為什麼不喜歡去別人家裏吃　你为什么不喜欢去别人家里吃
飯？　　　　　　　　　　　饭？

14. 感情：對北京很有感情；動了　感情：对北京很有感情；动了
感情；感情很好　　　　　　感情；感情很好

你對哪個城市最有感情？為什　你对哪个城市最有感情？为什
麼？　　　　　　　　　　　么？

看哪部電影的時候你動了感　看哪部电影的时候你动了感情？
情？為什麼？　　　　　　　为什么？

15. 向著：向著人　　　　　　　向着：向着人

如果我和別的同學發生矛盾，　如果我和别的同学发生矛盾，我

我媽媽總是覺得是別人的錯，你知道為什麼嗎？

媽媽总是觉得是别人的错，你知道为什么吗？

你覺得父母總是向著自己的孩子好不好？

你觉得父母总是向着自己的孩子好不好？

16. 從事：從事教育工作

从事：从事教育工作

你畢業以後打算從事什麼樣的工作？

你毕业以后打算从事什么样的工作？

你覺得從事什麼工作的人會被別人看不起？

你觉得从事什么工作的人会被别人看不起？

17. 故意：（不）是故意的；故意遲到

故意：（不）是故意的；故意迟到

你會為一些小事和父母發生糾紛嗎？

你会为一些小事和父母发生纠纷吗？

你只遲到了幾分鐘，老師為什麼那麼生氣？

你只迟到了几分钟，老师为什么那么生气？

18. 報酬：付報酬；很高的報酬

报酬：付报酬；很高的报酬

我想請一個英文輔導，我應該付給他多少報酬呢？

我想请一个英文辅导，我应该付给他多少报酬呢？

在美國，從事什麼工作會得到比較高的報酬？

在美国，从事什么工作会得到比较高的报酬？

19. 扔：扔垃圾；亂扔；別扔；把東西扔了

扔：扔垃圾；乱扔；别扔；把东西扔了

你把我昨天穿的那件破舊的襯衣放在哪兒了，為什麼我找不到？

你把我昨天穿的那件破旧的衬衣放在哪儿了，为什么我找不到？

為什麼旅遊地區的環境和衛生都不太好？

为什么旅游地区的环境和卫生都不太好？

20. 尊重：尊重父母；受人尊重；尊重別人的觀點、選擇、決定

尊重：尊重父母；受人尊重；尊重别人的观点、选择、决定

在你看來，什麼是不尊重父母 | 在你看来，什么是不尊重父母的
的做法？ | 做法？

舉一個例子說明你的父母非常 | 举一个例子说明你的父母非常尊
尊重你的選擇。 | 重你的选择。

自由發揮與課堂活動 Free Discussion and Class Activities

1. 把學生分成幾組，分別扮演司 | 把学生分成几组，分别扮演司
    機、朦、和朋友的角色。 | 机、朦、和朋友的角色。

第二部分（繁）Part 2

What do you think will be the issue discussed in this section? _____

Do you think the protagonist will "fight" again this time? _____

Would you ever do something similar in your own society? _____

If you were being challenged, as the protagonist is in this section, what would you do? _____
_____

Why do you think the protagonist behaves in such a way? _____

　　吃飯時去了**籐挑選**的小飯館，她很**熟練**地點了**招牌菜**。籐說**此次**回國，除了見老朋友，最重要的是讓自己的胃享**享福**，它被洋餐**折磨**得太久太痛苦了。菜上得很快，籐高興地動了筷子，入了口，臉上卻變了顏色，叫來小姐。

　　你們的**大廚**，是不是得了重**感冒**？不舒服，休息就是，不應該再給客人做飯的。籐很**嚴肅**地說。

　　小姐馬上跑到廚房去，很快回來報告說，大廚人很健康，沒有病的。我也有些怪籐**多此一舉**，你也不是**防疫站**的**官員**，管得真**寬**。忙說，快吃快吃，要不菜就**涼**了。

　　籐又[2]**夾了一筷子菜**，吃了以后說，既然大廚沒生病，那就一定是換了**廚師**。這菜的味道和往日不一樣，**鹽擱**得尤其多。我原以為是廚師生了感冒，**辨不出鹹淡**，現在可**確定**是換了人。對嗎？

熟練	shúliàn	
招牌菜	zhāopáicài	specialty dish
此次	cǐcì	this time
享福	xiǎngfú	to enjoy a life of ease and comfort
折磨	zhémó	
大廚	dàchú	chef
感冒	gǎnmào	cold
嚴肅	yánsù	
多此一舉	duō cǐ yì jǔ	to make an unnecessary move
防疫站	fángyìzhàn	epidemic-prevention station
官員	guānyuán	official
寬	kuān	
涼	liáng	
夾	jiā/jiá	
廚師	chúshī	cook
鹽	yán	salt
擱	gē	
辨不出	biànbùchū	cannot distinguish
鹹淡	xiándàn	salty or bland
確定	quèdìng	to confirm

小姐一下子變得很尷尬，不過馬上又有幾分**佩服**地說，你的**舌頭**真是**神**。大廚今天有**急事**沒來，菜是**二廚代炒**的。真對不起。

小姐的**態度**很**親切**，我覺得大**可到此為止**。不想籐根本**不吃這一套**，慢慢地說，在飯店裡，是不應該說「對不起」這幾個字的。

籐說，如果我享受了你的服務，出門的時候，不付錢，只說一聲「對不起」，行嗎？

小姐不語，答案顯然是**否定**的。

籐又說，在你這裡，我所要的一切都是**付費**的。用「對不起」這種話安慰客人，[3]**往輕點說是數衍，重說就是欺騙。**

這時一個胖胖的男人走過來，和氣地說，我是這裡的老板，你們的談話我都聽到了，有什麼要求，就同我說吧。是菜不夠熱，還是不新鮮？您要是覺得太鹹的話，我這就叫

佩服	pèifú	
舌頭	shétóu	tongue
神	shén	magical
急事	jíshì	urgent matter
二廚	èrchú	assistant chef
代炒	dàichǎo	to fill in for the cook
態度	tàidù	
親切	qīnqiè	
到此為止	dào cǐ wéi zhǐ	to this point, thus far, up to now
不吃這一套	bù chī zhè yí tào	to not allow oneself to be pushed around
否定	fǒudìng	
付費	fùfèi	to pay
敷衍	fūyǎn	to be perfunctory
欺騙	qīpiàn	to cheat
盤	pán	dish, tray
壓	yā	to restrain
怒火	nùhuǒ	(flames of) fury
菜譜	càipǔ	menu
殺價	shājià	to slash prices
常客	chángkè	regular visitor
若	ruò	if
看得起	kàndeqǐ	to think highly of

廚房再炒一**盤**，您以為如何？

我想，籐總該接受這個建議了吧。沒想到籐說，我想要少付你錢。

老板**壓**著**怒火**說，菜的價錢是寫在**菜譜**上的，你點了這道菜，就是接受了它的價錢，怎麼能吃了之後**殺價**呢？看來您是**常客**，**若**還**看得起**小店，這道菜我可以送

你，少收錢卻是不能**開例**的。

開例	kāilì	to create a precedent
不慌不忙	bùhuāng bù máng	composedly

艨不慌不忙地說，菜譜上是有價錢，可那

是大廚炒的菜，現在換了二廚，他炒的菜的確不如大廚，你就不能收一樣的錢。因為你付給大廚的報酬和付給二廚的報酬是不一樣的。

艨這樣一說，道理就很明白了。於是艨達到了目的。

閱讀理解 Comprehension Check

8. 艨回國除了見朋友，最想做什麼？為什麼？
9. 艨問飯館的小姐什麼問題？為什麼？
10. 飯館的廚師生病了嗎？到底是什麼問題？
11. 服務小姐怎麼應付艨問的問題？艨接受她的道歉嗎？為什麼？
12. 飯館老板打算怎麼解決問題？艨接受嗎？為什麼？
13. 艨到底想做什麼？她達到目的了嗎？怎麼達到的？

第二部分 （简） Part 2

What do you think will be the issue discussed in this section? _____

Do you think the protagonist will "fight" again this time? _____

Would you ever do something similar in your own society? _____

If you were being challenged, as the protagonist is in this section, what would you do? _____

_____

Why do you think the protagonist behaves in such a way? _____

　　吃饭时去了藤挑选的小饭馆，她很熟练地点了招牌菜。藤说此次回国，除了见老朋友，最重要的是让自己的胃享享福，它被洋餐折磨得太久太痛苦了。菜上得很快，藤高兴地动了筷子，入了口，脸上却变了颜色，叫来小姐。

　　你们的大厨，是不是得了重感冒？不舒服，休息就是，不应该再给客人做饭的。藤很严肃地说。

　　小姐马上跑到厨房去，很快回来报告说，大厨人很健康，没有病的。我也有些怪藤多此一举，你也不是防疫站的官员，管得真宽。忙说，快吃快吃，要不菜就凉了。

　　藤又²夹了一筷子菜，吃了以后说，既然大厨没生病，那就一定是换了厨师。这菜的味道和往日不一样，盐搁得尤其多。我原以为是厨师生了感冒，辨不出咸淡，现在可确定是换了人。对吗？

熟练	shúliàn	
招牌菜	zhāopáicài	specialty dish
此次	cǐcì	this time
享福	xiǎngfú	to enjoy a life of ease and comfort
折磨	zhémó	
大厨	dàchú	chef
感冒	gǎnmào	cold
严肃	yánsù	
多此一举	duō cǐ yì jǔ	to make an unnecessary move
防疫站	fángyìzhàn	epidemic-prevention station
官员	guānyuán	official
宽	kuān	
凉	liáng	
夹	jiā/jiá	
厨师	chúshī	cook
盐	yán	salt
搁	gē	
辨不出	biànbùchū	cannot distinguish
咸淡	xiándàn	salty or bland
确定	quèdìng	to confirm

小姐一下子变得很尴尬，不过马上又有几分**佩服**地说，你的**舌头**真是**神**。大厨今天有**急事**没来，菜是**二厨代炒**的。真对不起。

小姐的**态度**很**亲切**，我觉得大可**到此为止**。不想藤根本**不吃这一套**，慢慢地说，在饭店里，是不应该说"对不起"这几个字的。

藤说，如果我享受了你的服务，出门的时候，不付钱，只说一声"对不起"，行吗？

小姐不语，答案显然是**否定**的。

藤又说，在你这里，我所要的一切都是**付费**的。用"对不起"这种话安慰客人，[3]**往轻点说是敷衍，重说就是欺骗**。

这时一个胖胖的男人走过来，和气地说，我是这里的老板，你们的谈话我都听到了，有什么要求，就同我说吧。是菜不够热，还是不新鲜？您要是觉得太咸的话，我这就叫厨房再炒一**盘**，您以为如何？

我想，藤总该接受这个建议了吧。没想到藤说，我想要少付你钱。

老板**压**着**怒火**说，菜的价钱是写在**菜谱**上的，你点了这道菜，就是接受了它的价钱，怎么能吃了之后**杀价**呢？看来您是**常客**，**若**还**看得起**小店，这道菜我可以送你，少收钱却是不能**开例**的。

藤**不慌不忙**地说，菜谱上是有价钱，可那是大厨炒的菜，现在换了

佩服	pèifú	
舌头	shétóu	tongue
神	shén	magical
急事	jíshì	urgent matter
二厨	èrchú	assistant chef
代炒	dàichǎo	to fill in for the cook
态度	tàidù	
亲切	qīnqiè	
到此为止	dào cǐ wéi zhǐ	to this point, thus far, up to now
不吃这一套	bù chī zhè yí tào	to not allow oneself to be pushed around
否定	fǒudìng	
付费	fùfèi	to pay
敷衍	fūyǎn	to be perfunctory
欺骗	qīpiàn	to cheat
盘	pán	dish, tray
压	yā	to restrain
怒火	nùhuǒ	(flames of) fury
菜谱	càipǔ	menu
杀价	shājià	to slash prices
常客	chángkè	regular visitor
若	ruò	if
看得起	kàndeqǐ	to think highly of
开例	kāilì	to create a precedent
不慌不忙	bùhuāng bù máng	composedly

二厨，他炒的菜的确不如大厨，你就不能收一样的钱。因为你付给大厨的
报酬和付给二厨的报酬是不一样的。

　　艨这样一说，道理就很明白了。于是艨达到了目的。

阅读理解 Comprehension Check

8.　艨回国除了见朋友，最想做什么？为什么？
9.　艨问饭馆的小姐什么问题？为什么？
10.　饭馆的厨师生病了吗？到底是什么问题？
11.　服务小姐怎么应付艨问的问题？艨接受她的道歉吗？为什么？
12.　饭馆老板打算怎么解决问题？艨接受吗？为什么？
13.　艨到底想做什么？她达到目的了吗？怎么达到的？

詞匯用法 Words in Context

21.　熟練：技術熟練；很熟練地V

　　如果和朋友一起出去玩，你可以
　　負責開車嗎？為什麼？

　　如果一個人很熟練地給別人點
　　煙，這說明什麼？

熟练：技术熟练；很熟练地V

如果和朋友一起出去玩，你可以
负责开车吗？为什么？

如果一个人很熟练地给别人点
烟，这说明什么？

22.　折磨：折磨人；被折磨；別折磨
　　他了；快被折磨死了；……是一
　　種折磨

　　對你來說，做什麼事情是一種折
　　磨？

　　你為什麼不把這件事告訴他？

折磨：折磨人；被折磨；別折磨
他了；快被折磨死了；……是一
種折磨

对你来说，做什么事情是一种折
磨？

你为什么不把这件事告诉他？

23.　嚴肅：老師很嚴肅；嚴肅地說
　　話；嚴肅的人、態度

　　你見過我們的老師笑嗎？

　　什麼時候你父母會和你嚴肅地說
　　話？

严肃：老师很严肃；严肃地说
话；严肃的人、态度

你见过我们的老师笑吗？

什么时候你父母会和你严肃地说
话？

24. 寬：汽車、馬路、河比較寬　　　　　寬：汽车、马路、河比较宽

你的汽車後面能坐三個人嗎？　　　你的汽车后面能坐三个人吗？

你覺得你的老師管得寬不寬？為　　你觉得你的老师管得宽不宽？为
什麼？　　　　　　　　　　　　什么？

25. 涼：菜、天氣涼了；涼菜；涼茶　　　凉：菜、天气凉了；凉菜；凉茶

在這兒，什麼時候天氣會開始變　　在这儿，什么时候天气会开始变
涼？　　　　　　　　　　　　　凉？

根據中國的習慣，吃飯的時候應　　根据中国的习惯，吃饭的时候应
該先吃涼菜還是先吃熱菜？　　　该先吃凉菜还是先吃热菜？

26. 夾：夾菜；夾起來；夾不起來；　　　夹：夹菜；夹起来；夹不起来；
夾不住　　　　　　　　　　　　夹不住

你不會用筷子嗎？為什麼總夾不　　你不会用筷子吗？为什么总夹不
起東西來？　　　　　　　　　　起东西来？

吃麵條的時候應該用筷子還是勺　　吃面条的时候应该用筷子还是勺
子？為什麼？　　　　　　　　　子？为什么？

27. 擱：擱鹽、醋、醬油；把書擱在　　　搁：搁盐、醋、酱油；把书搁在
桌子上　　　　　　　　　　　　桌子上

吃餃子的時候，你喜歡擱醋嗎？　吃饺子的时候，你喜欢搁醋吗？

平時你把你的電腦擱在哪兒？　　平时你把你的电脑搁在哪儿？

28. 佩服：讓人佩服；值得佩服；很　　　佩服：让人佩服；值得佩服；很
佩服喬丹　　　　　　　　　　　佩服乔丹

你覺得哪個籃球運動員最讓人佩　　你觉得哪个篮球运动员最让人佩
服？　　　　　　　　　　　　　服？

在你看來，哪位總统最值得佩　　　在你看来，哪位总统最值得佩
服？　　　　　　　　　　　　　服？

29. 態度：態度好、差；有（抱　　　　态度：态度好、差；有（抱
著）……態度；服務態度　　　　着）……态度；服务态度

你覺得麥當勞的服務態度怎麼　　　你觉得麦当劳的服务态度怎么
樣？　　　　　　　　　　　　　样？

你覺得對朋友應該抱著什麼樣的 | 你觉得对朋友应该抱着什么样的
態度？ | 态度？

30. 親切：態度親切，感到親切 | 亲切：态度亲切，感到亲切

你覺得麥當勞的服務態度怎麼 | 你觉得麦当劳的服务态度怎么
樣？ | 样？

在外國看到從自己國家來的人， | 在外国看到从自己国家来的人，
你會有什麼樣的感覺？ | 你会有什么样的感觉？

31. 否定：答案是否定的；建議被否 | 否定：答案是否定的；建议被否
定；否定別人的能力 | 定；否定别人的能力

如果你問老師可不可以不考試， | 如果你问老师可不可以不考试，
你猜答案是什麼？ | 你猜答案是什么？

如果一個人失業了，是不是說明 | 如果一个人失业了，是不是说明
他的能力比較差？ | 他的能力比较差？

自由發揮與課堂活動 Free Discussion and Class Activities

2. 你覺得朦是不是一個挑剔的人？ | 你觉得朦是不是一个挑剔的人？
為什麼？ | 为什么？

3. 飯店老板剛開始決定怎麼解決朦 | 饭店老板刚开始决定怎么解决朦
的問題？你覺得他解決問題的方 | 的问题？你觉得他解决问题的方
法合理嗎？為什麼？ | 法合理吗？为什么？

4. 如果你在飯館吃飯的時候，發現 | 如果你在饭馆吃饭的时候，发现
他們做的飯不如以前的好吃，你 | 他们做的饭不如以前的好吃，你
會怎麼做？為什麼？ | 会怎么做？为什么？

5. 分角色表演朦、我、飯館的服務 | 分角色表演朦、我、饭馆的服务
小姐和老板。 | 小姐和老板。

第三部分（繁）Part 3

What do you think will be the issue discussed in this section? _____

Do you think the protagonist will "fight" again this time? _____

Would you ever do something similar in your own society? _____

If you ran into the problem, as described in this section, what would you do? _____

_____

Why do you think the protagonist behaves in such a way? _____

和籐上公共廁所，籐**感嘆**地說，真**豪華**啊，廁所像**宮殿**，這好像是中國改變最大的地方。

女洗手間裡每一**扇**廁所的門都關著，每个門外都站著一隊人。

我和籐各選了一隊，耐心地等。我的那扇門還好，不斷地開關，不一會就**輪到**了我。籐可**慘**了，那門總是關着。我受不了裏面的味道，就到外面去等籐，便出去了。等了許久，許多比籐晚進去的女人，都出來了，籐還在等⋯⋯等籐終於解決問題了以後，我對籐說，可惜你**站錯**了隊啊。

籐笑著說，麻煩你陪我去找一下公共廁所的**負責**人。

我說，就是門口發**手紙**的老大媽。籐說，你別**欺負**我出國多年，這點規矩還是記得的。她管不了事。我要找一位負責公共**設施**的官員。

我不知道這**類**事情該找誰。籐想了一會兒，找來報紙，毫不**猶豫**地**撥**打了上面的**市長**電話。

感嘆	gǎntàn	to sigh
豪華	háohuá	luxurious
宮殿	gōngdiàn	palace
洗手間	xǐshǒujiān	toilet
扇	shàn	measure word for door
輪到	lúndào	to be one's turn
慘	cǎn	
站錯	zhàncuò	to stand in the wrong line
負責	fùzé	
手紙	shǒuzhǐ	toilet paper
欺負	qīfù	
設施	shèshī	facilities
類	lèi	kind, type
猶豫	yóuyù	to hesitate
撥	bō	to dial
市長	shìzhǎng	mayor

我嚇得用手壓住電話，說艨你瘋了，太不注意國情！

艨說，我正是相信政府是為人民辦事的啊。

我說，一個廁所，哪裡值得如此興師動眾？

艨說，[4]不單單是廁所。還有郵局、銀行、售票處等等，中國凡是有窗口和門口的地方，只要排隊，都存在這個問題。每個工作人員速度不同，需要服務的人所花的時間也不同，在後面等的人不能預先知道哪個隊快哪個隊慢。比如我剛才不能一個個地問排在前面的

嚇	xià	
壓	yā	
瘋	fēng ✓	crazy
國情	guóqíng	condition of a country
如此	rúcǐ	thus, like this
興師動眾	xīngshī dòngzhòng ✓	to drag in many people (to do sth.)
單單	dāndān	
售票處	shòupiào chù	ticket office
排隊	páiduì ✓	
預先	yùxiān ✓	
解大手	jiědàshǒu	to defecate
革命	gémìng ✓	revolution
設	shè ✓	to set up, to found
一米線	yìmǐxiàn	the waiting line (lit., one meter line)
效率	xiàolǜ ✓	

女人，你是解大手還是解小手，[5]以確定我該排在哪一隊後⋯⋯

我說，艨你打算在廁所裡搞一場什麼樣的革命？

艨說，要求市長在廁所裡畫條一米線，排隊的人都在線外等，這樣就避免了排錯隊的問題，提高效率，大家心情愉快。北美就是這樣的。

我說，艨，你在國內還會上幾次廁所？還會給誰寄錢或者寄信？我們生活在其中都不管，你又何必管得這麼寬？你已是一個北美人，馬上就要回北美去，還是到那裡享受你的廁所一米線吧！

閱讀理解 Comprehension Check

14. 艨覺得中國改變最大的地方是什麼？

15. 艨的朋友為什麼說艨慘了？她覺得這個問題是誰的責任？

16. 艨打算找誰談她遇到的問題？為什麼？最後她找了誰？

17. 艨的朋友同意她的做法嗎？為什麼？

18. 艨覺得她自己遇到的問題應該怎麼解決？她的朋友認為這種問題需要解決嗎？為什麼？

第三部分（简） Part 3

What do you think will be the issue discussed in this section?_____

Do you think the protagonist will "fight" again this time?_____

Would you ever do something similar in your own society?_____

If you ran into the problem, as described in this section, what would you do?_____

_____

Why do you think the protagonist behaves in such a way?_____

和藤上公共厕所，藤**感叹**地说，真**豪华**啊，厕所象**宫殿**，这好象是中国改变最大的地方。

女**洗手间**里每一**扇**厕所的门都关着，每个门外都站着一队人。

我和藤各选了一队，耐心地等。我的那扇门还好，不断地开关，不一会就**轮到**了我。藤可**惨**了，那门总是关着。我受不了裹面的味道，就到外面去等藤，便出去了。等了许久，许多比藤晚进去的女人，都出来了，藤还在等……等藤终于解决问题了以后，我对藤说，可惜你**站错**了队啊。

藤笑着说，麻烦你陪我去找一下公共厕所的**负责**人。

我说，就是门口发**手纸**的老大妈。藤说，你别**欺负**我出国多年，这点规矩还是记得的。她管不了事。我要找一位负责公共**设施**的官员。

我不知道这**类**事情该找谁。藤想了一会儿，找来报纸，毫不**犹豫**地**拨**打了上面的**市长**电话。

感叹	gǎntàn	to sigh
豪华	háohuá	luxurious
宫殿	gōngdiàn	palace
洗手间	xǐshǒujiān	toilet
扇	shàn	measure word for door
轮到	lúndào	to be one's turn
惨	cǎn	
站错	zhàncuò	to stand in the wrong line
负责	fùzé	
手纸	shǒuzhǐ	toilet paper
欺负	qīfù	
设施	shèshī	facilities
类	lèi	kind, type
犹豫	yóuyù	to hesitate
拨	bō	to dial
市长	shìzhǎng	mayor

我**吓**得用手**压**住电话，说藤你**疯**了，太不注意**国情**！

藤说，我正是相信政府是为人民办事的啊。

我说，一个厕所，哪里值得**如此兴师动众**？

藤说，[4]**不单单**是厕所。还有邮局、银行、**售票处**等等，中国凡是有窗口和门口的地方，只要排队，都存在这个问题。每个工作人员速度不同，需要服务的人所花的时间也不同，在后面等的人不能**预先**知道哪个队快哪个队慢。比如我刚才不能一个个地问排在前面的女人，你是**解大手**还是解小手，[5]**以**确定我该排在哪一队后……

我说，藤你打算在厕所里搞一场什么样的**革命**？

藤说，要求市长在厕所里画条**一米线**，排队的人都在线外等，这样就避免了排错队的问题，提高**效率**，大家心情愉快。北美就是这样的。

我说，藤，你在国内还会上几次厕所？还会给谁寄钱或者寄信？我们生活在其中都不管，你又何必管得这么宽？你已是一个北美人，马上就要回北美去，还是到那里享受你的厕所一米线吧！

吓	xià	
压	yā	
疯	fēng	
国情	guóqíng	condition of a country
如此	rúcǐ	thus, like this
兴师动众	xīngshī dòngzhòng	to drag in many people (to do sth.)
单单	dāndān	
售票处	shòupiào chù	ticket office
排队	páiduì	
预先	yùxiān	
解大手	jiědàshǒu	to defecate
革命	gémìng	revolution
设	shè	to set up, to found
一米线	yìmǐxiàn	the waiting line (lit.,one meter line)
效率	xiàolǜ	

阅读理解 Comprehension Check

14. 藤觉得中国改变最大的地方是什么？
15. 藤的朋友为什么说藤惨了？她觉得这个问题是谁的责任？
16. 藤打算找谁谈她遇到的问题？为什么？最后她找了谁？
17. 藤的朋友同意她的做法吗？为什么？
18. 藤觉得她自己遇到的问题应该怎么解决？她的朋友认为这种问题需

要解决吗？为什么？

詞彙用法 Words in Context

32. 慘：累慘了；把……害慘了

你今天怎麼一直睡覺睡到下午才
起床？

美國經濟不景氣對老百姓有很大
的影響嗎？

惨：累惨了；把……害惨了

你今天怎么一直睡觉睡到下午才
起床？

美国经济不景气对老百姓有很大
的影响吗？

33. 負責：對……負責；由……負
責；負責一件事情；負責人

你覺得照顧父母應該由誰負責？

開晚會的時候我負責買東西，你
打算負責什麼？

负责：对……负责；由……负
责；负责一件事情；负责人

你觉得照顾父母应该由谁负责？

开晚会的时候我负责买东西，你
打算负责什么？

34. 欺負：欺負別人；受欺負

在學校裏，什麼樣的學生容易受
別人的欺負？

你覺得艨有沒有欺負那個出租車
司機？

欺负：欺负别人；受欺负

在学校里，什么样的学生容易受
别人的欺负？

你觉得艨有没有欺负那个出租车
司机？

35. 嚇：嚇人；嚇了我一大跳；被嚇
了一跳

你剛剛為什麼在門外大叫了一
聲？

你覺得昨天晚上的恐怖電影怎麼
樣？

吓：吓人；吓了我一大跳；被吓
了一跳

你刚刚为什么在门外大叫了一
声？

你觉得昨天晚上的恐怖电影怎么
样？

36. 壓：壓住火；壓住电话

你特別生氣的時候，有什麼辦法
可以壓住火？

把書壓在筆記本電腦上有沒有什
麼壞處？

压：压住火；压住电话

你特别生气的时候，有什么办法
可以压住火？

把书压在笔记本电脑上有没有什
么坏处？

37. 瘋：瘋了；氣瘋了；玩得很瘋   疯：疯了；气疯了；玩得很疯

    什麼時候，學生都會玩得很瘋？   什么时候，学生都会玩得很疯？

    你曾經被什麼事情氣瘋了？   你曾经被什么事情气疯了？

38. 單單：（句型）   单单：（句型）

39. 排隊：排長隊   排队：排长队

    在排隊的時候，你喜歡做什麼？   在排队的时候，你喜欢做什么？

    在什麼地方經常需要排隊？   在什么地方经常需要排队？

40. 預先：預先安排、計劃、約定   预先：预先安排、计划、约定

    去看醫生的時候，你需要做什麼？   去看医生的时候，你需要做什么？

    去外國旅遊之前，你應該做什麼？   去外国旅游之前，你应该做什么？

41. 效率：有效率；效率高；提高效率；降低效率   效率：有效率；效率高；提高效率；降低效率

    你覺得在郵局工作的人怎麼樣？   你觉得在邮局工作的人怎么样？

    你覺得電腦可以提高工作效率嗎？   你觉得电脑可以提高工作效率吗？

自由發揮與課堂活動 Free Discussion and Class Activities

6. 請你談談在中國排隊的地方存在什麼樣的問題？羕的建議是什麼？你覺得她的建議是否合理？為什麼？   请你谈谈在中国排队的地方存在什么样的问题？羕的建议是什么？你觉得她的建议是否合理？为什么？

7. 如果你對你的城市的某些方面不是很滿意，你會不會給市長打電話？為什麼？   如果你对你的城市的某些方面不是很满意，你会不会给市长打电话？为什么？

8. 你覺得普通人對社會中存在的問題有什麼樣的責任？   你觉得普通人对社会中存在的问题有什么样的责任？

9. 你猜市長接到艬的電話會有什麼
    反應？為什麼？

10. 表演：如果艬有機會和市長見
    面，你猜他們會談什麼問題？市
    長會說什麼？

你猜市长接到艬的电话会有什么
反应？为什么？

表演：如果艬有机会和市长见
面，你猜他们会谈什么问题？市
长会说什么？

第四部分（繁）Part 4

How does the essay conclude?_____

Do you agree with the way the protagonist achieves her end? Why or why not ?

_____

Can you figure out the meaning of the title of this essay by now? What does "mango woman"

really stand for?_____

報效	bàoxiào	to repay one's country
高明	gāomíng	brilliant
英雄	yīngxióng	hero
主張	zhǔzhāng	
舉動	jǔdòng	movement, act
標準	biāozhǔn	standard, criterion
苦心	kǔxīn	trouble taken
感動	gǎndòng	
溫飽	wēnbǎo	to be warmly dressed and well-fed
充滿	chōngmǎn	
瑣事	suǒshì	trivial matter
文明	wénmíng	civilization
公正	gōngzhèng	just, fair

藤說，這些年，我在國外，沒有什麼本事，就是買買東西、上上街。我不像別的留學生，有很多**報效**國家的能力。我只是一個家庭婦女，覺得那裏有些比咱**高明**的地方，就想讓這邊學了來。這幾天我讓你們陪我，是想讓你們明白我的心。我不是**英雄**，沒法宣傳我的**主張**；也不是作家，不會寫了文章，讓更多的人知道我的想法。我只有讓你們從我的**舉動**裏，感覺到這世上有一個更合理的**標準**存在著，可以學習。

我[6]**為**藤的**苦心感動**，但還是說，就算你說的有理，這些事也太小了。要知道中國有些地方連**溫飽**都沒有解決啊。

藤說，我對中國**充滿**信心。溫飽解決之後，馬上就會碰到這些問題。身邊的**瑣事**標誌著**文明**的水平。現代化不是表面的進步，而是一個更美好更**公正**的社會。

我拿開了壓在電話上的手，讓藤去完

成找市長的計劃。那個電話打了很長，艨講了許多她以為中國可以**改進**的地方。

　　分手的時候，艨說，有些中國人入了外國**籍**以後，就認為自己是個「**香蕉**人」，意思是自己除了外皮是黃色的，**內心**已變得**雪白**。而我是一個「**芒果**人」。

　　我說「芒果人」，好新鮮，怎麼講？

　　艨說，芒果**皮**是黃的，**瓤**也是黃的。我永遠愛我的**祖國**。

山子摘自《深圳青年》1997年第8期；中華書庫，亦凡公益圖書館(shuku.net)

改進	gǎijìn	to improve
分手	fēnshǒu	to part company
入籍	rùjí	to become naturalized
標榜	biāobǎng	to boast
香蕉	xiāngjiāo	banana
內心	nèixīn	heart, inner being
雪白	xuěbái	snow-white
芒果	mángguǒ	mango
瓤	ráng	pulp, interior
祖國	zǔguó	homeland

閱讀理解 Comprehension Check

19. 艨覺得她自己遇到的問題應該怎麼解決？她的朋友認為這種問題需要解決嗎？為什麼？

20. 艨為什麼要堅持自己的做法？她的目的是什麼？

21. 艨的朋友覺得那些問題是大問題嗎？為什麼？

22. 艨認為現代化指的是什麼？她的朋友最後同意她的做法了嗎？

23. 什麼是「香蕉人」？為什麼艨說自己是個「芒果人」？

第四部分（简）Part 4

How does the essay conclude?_____

Do you agree with the way the protagonist achieves her end? Why or why not ?

_____

Can you figure out the meaning of the title of this essay by now? What does "mango woman"
really stand for?_____

报效	bàoxiào	to repay one's country
高明	gāomíng	brilliant
英雄	yīngxióng	hero
主张	zhǔzhāng	
举动	jǔdòng	movement, act
标准	biāozhǔn	standard, criterion
苦心	kǔxīn	trouble taken
感动	gǎndòng	
温饱	wēnbǎo	to be warmly dressed and well-fed
充满	chōngmǎn	
琐事	suǒshì	trivial matter
文明	wénmíng	civilization
公正	gōngzhèng	just, fair
改进	gǎijìn	to improve

　　籐说，这些年，我在国外，没有什么本事，就是买买东西、上上街。我不象别的留学生，有很多**报效**国家的能力。我只是一个家庭妇女，觉得那里有些比咱**高明**的地方，就想让这边学了来。这几天我让你们陪我，是想让你们明白我的心。我不是**英雄**，没法宣传我的**主张**；也不是作家，不会写了文章，让更多的人知道我的想法。我只有让你们从我的**举动**里，感觉到这世上有一个更合理的**标准**存在着，可以学习。

　　我[6]为籐的**苦心感动**，但还是说，就算你说的有理，这些事也太小了。要知道中国有些地方连**温饱**都没有解决啊。

　　籐说，我对中国**充满**信心。温饱解决之后，马上就会碰到这些问题。身边的**琐事**标志着**文明**的水平。现代化不是表面的进步，而是一个更美好更**公正**的社会。

　　我拿开了压在电话上的手，让籐去完成找市长的计划。那个电话打了很长，籐讲了许多她以为中国可以**改进**的地方。

分手的时候，艨说，有些中国人入了外国籍以后，就认为自己是个"香蕉人"，意思是自己除了外皮是黄色的，**内心**已变得**雪白**。而我是一个"芒果人"。

我说"芒果人"，好新鲜，怎么讲？

艨说，芒果**皮**是黄的，**瓤**也是黄的。我永远爱我的祖国。

分手	fēnshǒu	to part company
入籍	rùjí	to become naturalized
标榜	biāobǎng	to boast
香蕉	xiāngjiāo	banana
内心	nèixīn	heart, inner being
雪白	xuěbái	snow-white
芒果	mángguǒ	mango
瓤	ráng	pulp, interior
祖国	zǔguó	homeland

山子摘自《深圳青年》1997年第8期；中华书库，亦凡公益图书馆(shuku.net)

阅读理解 Comprehension Check

8. 艨觉得她自己遇到的问题应该怎么解决？她的朋友认为这种问题需要解决吗？为什么？
9. 艨为什么要坚持自己的做法？她的目的是什么？
10. 艨的朋友觉得那些问题是大问题吗？为什么？
11. 艨认为现代化指的是什么？她的朋友最后同意她的做法了吗？
12. 什么是"香蕉人"？为什么艨说自己是个"芒果人"？

詞匯用法 Words in Context

42. 主張：主張男女平等；主張做…；我的主張是

克林頓和布希的政治主張有什麼不同的地方？

你覺得女人結婚以後應該待在家裏照顧孩子，還是應該出去工作？

42. 主张：主张男女平等；主张做…；我的主张是

克林顿和布什的政治主张有什么不同的地方？

你觉得女人结婚以后应该待在家里照顾孩子，还是应该出去工作？

43. 感動：讓人感動；很感動

最讓你感動的電影是哪一部？

43. 感动：让人感动；很感动

最让你感动的电影是哪一部？

什麼樣的事情會讓你感動？

什么样的事情会让你感动？

44. 充滿：充滿希望、信心、快樂

明天的考試你覺得能考好嗎？

你覺得我們的將來會怎麼樣？

充满：充满希望、信心、快乐

明天的考试你觉得能考好吗？

你觉得我们的将来会怎么样？

自由發揮與課堂活動　Free Discussion and Class Activities

11. 你覺得「香蕉人」、「芒果人」
這種比喻bǐyù 'metaphor, analogy'合適
嗎？你聽過別的對不同種類的人
的比喻嗎？你覺得自己是個什麼
「人」？

你觉得"香蕉人"、"芒果人"
这种比喻bǐyù 'metaphor, analogy'合适
吗？你听过别的对不同种类的人
的比喻吗？你觉得自己是个什么
"人"？

12. 小品表演：全班分成三組，每組
選擇文章中的一幕表演。

小品表演：全班分成三组，每组
选择文章中的一幕表演。

13. 做一個挑剔的人！這個學校也一
定有一些可以改進的地方，請你
模仿藜，指出一些不合理的方
面，並提出你改進的建議和理
由。

做一个挑剔的人！这个学校也一
定有一些可以改进的地方，请你
模仿藜，指出一些不合理的方
面，并提出你改进的建议和理
由。

應用詞 Productive Vocabulary

◎ By Grammatical Categories

Nouns/Pronouns/Measure Words

氣氛	qìfen	atmosphere, ambience		效率	xiàolǜ	efficiency, productiveness
感情	gǎnqíng	emotion, feeling		規矩	guīju	rule, custom, social etiquette
態度	tàidù	manner, attitude		報酬	bàochóu	reward, pay
本領	běnlǐng	skill, ability				

Verbs/Stative Verbs/Adjectives

陪	péi	to accompany		佩服	pèifú	to admire
點	diǎn	to light, dot		向著	xiàngzhe	to side with, to be partial to
管	guǎn	to bother about, to be in charge of		充滿	chōngmǎn	to be brimming/ permeated with
嚇	xià	to frighten, to scare		折磨	zhémó	to torment
壓	yā	to pressure		禁止	jìnzhǐ	to prohibit, to ban
躲	duǒ	to hide (oneself), to dodge, to avoid		否定	fǒudìng	to negate, deny, negation
貼	tiē	to stick, to paste		欺負	qīfù	to browbeat, to take advantage of, to pick on
扔	rēng	to throw, to toss		排隊	páiduì	to stand in line
夾	jiā/jiá	to press, to squeeze, to clip		睏	kùn	tired
擱	gē	to put		愣	lèng	distracted, stupefied
消費	xiāofèi	to consume		慘	cǎn	tragic
從事	cóngshì	to go in for, to be engaged in (a profession or career)		瘋	fēng	crazy
				寬	kuān	wide, broad
主張	zhǔzhāng	to advocate, to maintain		涼	liáng	cool, cold
負責	fùzé	to be responsible for, to be in charge of		熟練	shúliàn	skilled, proficient
尊重	zēnzhòng	to respect, to value		親切	qīnqiè	cordial, warm
感動	gǎndòng	to move, to touch, to be moved		嚴肅	yánsù	serious, solemn

Adverbs and Others

故意	gùyì	intentionally, willfully		預先	yùxiān	in advance, beforehand
單單	dāndān	only, alone		幹嘛	gànmá	What are you doing? What's up?

理解詞 Receptive Vocabulary

◎By Grammatical Categories

Nouns/Pronouns/Measure Words

鄉下	xiāngxià	countryside		英雄	yīngxióng	hero
標準	biāozhǔn	standard, criterion		乘客	chéngkè	passenger
感冒	gǎnmào	cold				

Verbs/Stative Verbs/Adjectives

皺	zhòu	to wrinkle		欺騙	qīpiàn	to cheat
撥	bō	to dial		輪到	lúndào	to be one's turn
確定	quèdìng	to confirm		站錯	zhàncuò	to stand in the wrong line
提供	tígōng	to provide		殺價	shājià	to slash prices
改進	gǎijìn	to improve		看得起	kàndeqǐ	to think highly of
將就	jiāngjiù	to make do		樸素	pǔsù/púsù	simple, plain
猶豫	yóuyù	to hesitate		和氣	héqi	kind, amiable
敷衍	fūyǎn	to be perfunctory		尷尬	gāngà	embarrassed

Adverbs and Others

依然	yīrán	still, as before		到此為止	dào cǐ wéi zhǐ	to this point, thus far, up to now
如此	rúcǐ	thus, like this		捏一把汗	niē yì bǎ hàn	to break into a cold sweat
毫不	háobù	not at all		不吃這一套	bù chī zhè yí tào	to not allow oneself to be pushed around
莫非	mòfēi	can it be that				
怎麼著	zěnmezhe	What about?				
多此一舉	duō cǐ yì jǔ	to make an unnecessary move				

本课词表 Chapter Vocabulary

◎By Pinyin

Words with asterisk* are productive vocabulary which needs to be memorized and studied for its usage.

bàochóu*	报酬	reward, pay		bù chī zhè yí tào	不吃这一套	to not allow oneself to be pushed around
běnlǐng*	本领	skill, ability				
biāozhǔn	标准	standard, criterion		cǎn*	惨	tragic
bō	拨	to dial		chéngkè	乘客	passenger

chōngmǎn*	充满	to be brimming with	niē yì bǎ hàn	捏一把汗	to break into a cold sweat
cóngshì*	从事	to be engaged in (a profession or career)	páiduì*	排队	to stand in line
dāndān*	单单	only, alone	péi*	陪	to accompany
dào cǐ wéi zhǐ	到此为止	to this point, thus far, up to now	pèifú*	佩服	to admire
diǎn*	点	to light, dot	pǔsù/púsù	朴素	simple, plain
duō cǐ yì jǔ	多此一举	to make an unnecessary move	qìfen*	气氛	atmosphere
			qīfù*	欺负	to pick on
duǒ*	躲	to hide (oneself)	qīnqiè*	亲切	cordial, warm
fēng*	疯	crazy	qīpiàn*	欺骗	to cheat
fǒudìng*	否定	to negate, negation	quèdìng	确定	to confirm
fūyǎn	敷衍	to be perfunctory	rēng*	扔	to throw, to toss
fùzé*	负责	to be responsible for	rúcǐ	如此	thus, like this
gǎijìn	改进	to improve	shājià	杀价	to slash prices
gǎndòng*	感动	to move, to touch, to be moved	shúliàn*	熟练	skilled, proficient
gāngà	尴尬	embarrassed	tàidù*	态度	manner, attitude
gànmá*	干嘛	What's up?	tiē*	贴	to stick, to paste
gǎnmào	感冒	cold	tígōng	提供	to provide
gǎnqíng*	感情	emotion, feeling	xià*	吓	to frighten, to scare
gē*	搁	to put	xiāngxià	乡下	countryside
guǎn*	管	to bother about, to be in charge of	xiàngzhe*	向着	to side with
guījǔ*	规矩	rule, social etiquette	xiāofèi*	消费	to consume
gùyì*	故意	intentionally	xiàolǜ*	效率	efficiency
háobù	毫不	not at all	yā*	压	to pressure
héqi	和气	kind, amiable	yánsù*	严肃	serious, solemn
jiā/jiá*	夹	to press, to squeeze	yīngxióng	英雄	hero
jiāngjiù	将就	to make do	yīrán	依然	still, as before
jìnzhǐ*	禁止	to prohibit, to ban	yóuyù	犹豫	to hesitate
kàndeqǐ	看得起	to think highly of	yùxiān*	预先	in advance
kuān*	宽	wide, broad	zěnmezhe	怎么着	What about?
kùn*	困	tired	zēnzhòng*	尊重	to respect, to value
lèng*	愣	distracted, stupefied	zhàncuò	站错	to stand in the wrong line
liáng*	凉	cool, cold	zhémó*	折磨	to torment
lúndào	轮到	to be one's turn	zhòu	皱	to wrinkle
mòfēi	莫非	can it be that	zhǔzhāng*	主张	to advocate

語法和用法 Grammar and Usage

Pay attention to the function of the structure and then study the example sentences. When blanks are provided, either answer the questions or complete the sentences.

1. Expressing the limit/ability to handle something

| O S V 得/不著 | ...de/bù zháo | S is (un)able to VO |
| S V 得/不了 O | ...de/bù liǎo | S is (un)able to VO |

- 抽煙這事，連老婆都管不著，幹嘛要你們的同意？
- 她管不了事。我要找一位負責公共設施的官員。

1. 你媽媽不是不讓你抽煙嗎？你怎麼不聽她的話呢？

   你妈妈不是不让你抽烟吗？你怎么不听她的话呢？

   Your mom doesn't let you smoke, does she? Why don't you listen to her?

   我已經18歲了，可以決定自己要做什麼。我的事別人管不著。

   我已经18岁了，可以决定自己要做什么。我的事别人管不着。

   I'm eighteen years old. I can decide what I want to do on my own and no one else can tell me what to do.

2. 你兒子抽煙，你怎麼也不管一管呢？

   你儿子抽烟，你怎么也不管一管呢？

   Your son smokes. Why don't you discipline your son?

   他已經大了，我管不了他了。

   他已经大了，我管不了他了。

   He has grown up and I can't control him any more.

3. 氣死我了，我們的環境污染問題越來越嚴重了！

   气死我了，我们的环境污染问题越来越严重了！

   I'm so furious. Our problem with environmental pollution is becoming more and more serious.

   這些市政府應該管的事情，你又管不了，著急也沒用。

   这些市政府应该管的事情，你又管不了，着急也没用。

   These are matters for the city government to handle. You can't do anything about it. There is no use in worrying about it.

4. 你的這本英漢辭典真有用，我也打算買一

   你的这本英汉辞典真有用，我也打算买一

   Your English-Chinese dictionary is really useful. I plan to buy one, too.

本。   本。

這本辭典是在北京買   这本辞典是在北京买   I bought this dictionary in
的，在美國恐怕買不   的，在美国恐怕买不   Beijing. You probably won't
著。   着。   be able to get it in the U.S.

5.   如果看到有人買東西的時候不   如果看到有人买东西的时候不
     排隊，你會不會勸他們排隊？   排队，你会不会劝他们排队？
     為什麼？   为什么？

6.   你父母對你的考試成績會不會   你父母对你的考试成绩会不会
     有一些要求？為什麼？   有一些要求？为什么？

7.   你每次上課的時候為什麼都要   你每次上课的时候为什么都要
     坐在第一排呢？   坐在第一排呢？

8.   你覺得美國是否應該攻打伊拉   你觉得美国是否应该攻打伊拉
     克？為什麼？   克？为什么？

The pattern S V得/不著 or S V得/不了 'to be (un)able to V' expresses basically the
limit or ability to do something. Yet, V得/不著 focuses more on the "limit/range of
authority" or "within/beyond one's control, reach, access, etc." V得/不了 focuses
more on the capacity/ability of doing something. Compare the following: 1) 父母不在
身邊，管不著我 'My parents are far away so they don't have any say over me;' 2) 父
母年紀大了，管不了我 'My parents are old and can't help me.' This subtle
difference is also present when other verbs are used, e.g., "這書在美國已經絕版了，
買不著" 'This book is out of print in the U.S., and cannot be purchased.'; "我才學了
三年中文，還看不了小說" 'I have only studied Chinese for three years and can't read
a novel yet.'

To say "can't fall asleep" or "can't hear," one can say 睡不著、聽不著. To say "can't win" or "can't pursuade," one can say 贏不了、勸不了. Note that the object for V不了 usually follows the phrase, while the object of V不著, if it's long, is often topicalized and placed at the beginning of the sentence, e.g., 父母管不了我 and 我的事父母管不著.

2. Expressing the measure of something

V了一N$_1$ (的) N$_2$	le yí...(de)...	V a N$_1$-full of N$_2$

- 縢又夾了一筷子菜，吃了以後說，既然大廚沒生病，那就一定是換了廚師。

1.	你要不要再喝點什麼？	你要不要再喝点什么？	Would you like anything else to drink?
	我已經喝了一肚子啤酒，不能再喝了。	我已经喝了一肚子啤酒，不能再喝了。	I have already had a belly full of beer. I can't drink any more.
2.	你怎麼又在洗澡？	你怎么又在洗澡？	Why are you taking another bath?
	我剛剛跑完步，出了一身汗，當然要再洗一個澡了。	我刚刚跑完步，出了一身汗，当然要再洗一个澡了。	I've just finished jogging and am sweating all over. Of course, I need to take another bath.
3.	哎呀，我吃了一大口冰淇淋，涼死我了！	哎呀，我吃了一大口冰淇淋，涼死我了！	Wow, I just ate a mouthful of ice cream. It's so cold.
	又沒有人跟你搶，你吃得那麼急幹什麼？	又没有人跟你抢，你吃得那么急干什么？	No one is going to fight you over this. Why did you eat it in such a hurry?
4.	你的書包那麼重，裏面裝的是什麼？	你的书包那么重，里面装的是什么？	

5.	你每兩個星期去買一次菜，那每次一定都買很多吧？	你每两个星期去买一次菜，那每次一定都买很多吧？

6. 今天上課的時候你的老師在黑板　　今天上课的时候你的老师在黑板
    上寫了很多生詞嗎？　　　　　　　上写了很多生词吗？

The pattern V 了一N₁ (的) N₂ uses ordinary nouns to express the measure of
something. The noun after 一 works as a measure and is often the location or container
for N₂, e.g., 一黑板的生詞 'a blackboard full of new words' 一屋子的水 'a roomful of
water,' 一冰箱的菜 'a refrigerator full of vegetables,' 一車子的東西 'a cartful of
stuff,' 一手的糖 'a handful of candy.' 的 between N₁ and N₂ can be omitted.

3. Expressing reproach with a negative rebuttal

往輕點說是⋯，重說是⋯	wǎng qīngdiǎn shuō shì..., zhòng shuō shì	To put sth. mildly/take sth. lightly/to say the least...; to put it more seriously, ...

● 用「對不起」這種話安慰客人，往輕點說是敷衍，重說就是欺騙。

1. 我忘了今天是我媽媽
    的生日。

    我忘了今天是我妈妈
    的生日。

    I forgot that today is my
    mother's birthday.

    什麼？這你怎麼可以
    忘呢？往輕點說是忘
    了，重說是你根本不
    重視你媽媽。

    什么？这你怎么可以
    忘呢？往轻点说是忘
    了，重说是你根本不
    重视你妈妈。

    What? How could you forget
    about that? To say that you
    forgot is to put it mildly; to put
    it more seriously, you don't
    respect your mother at all.

2. 我昨天和朋友去酒吧
    喝酒了。

    我昨天和朋友去酒吧
    喝酒了。

    I went to the bar with my
    friend yesterday and drank.

    天哪，你這麼做往輕
    點說是不聽話，重說
    是犯法。

    天哪，你这么做往轻
    点说是不听话，重说
    是犯法。

    My god! Your behavior was
    "disobedient" to say the least,
    to put it more seriously you
    were "breaking the law."

3. 昨天我上課的時候睡
    著了。

    昨天我上课的时候睡
    着了。

    Yesterday I fell asleep in class.

    你這麼做往輕點說是

    你这么做往轻点说是

    To put it mildly, you are not

不好好上課，重說是　不好好上课，重说是　doing well in class; to put it
不尊敬老師。　　　　　不尊敬老师。　　　　seriously, you don't respect
　　　　　　　　　　　　　　　　　　　　your teachers.

4.　我還沒有駕駛執照，可是我昨天　我还没有驾驶执照，可是我昨天
　　開車去飛機場接了我的朋友。　　开车去飞机场接了我的朋友。

5.　我昨天沒做我的功課。　　　　我昨天没做我的功课。

6.　我花了100塊美金買了一件襯衣。　我花了100块美金买了一件衬衣。

The pattern 往輕點說是…，重說是… expresses reproach with a negative rebuttal. So
what goes after 輕點說是 or 重說是 is a comment rather than a fact. To spend money
unwisely can be viewed as "wasteful" 浪費 or "detrimental to the family" 敗家. To
not do one's homework can be viewed as "lazy" 懶惰 or "irresponsible" 不負責任.

4. Expressing an additional condition

不單單是A，B還/都/也…	bù dāndān (shì)…,	Not just A, B also…
S不單單V₁O₁，還/也V₂O₂	hái/dōu/yě	S not just V_1O_1 but also V_2O_2

- 不單單是廁所。還有郵局、銀行、售票處等等，中國凡是有窗口和門
  口的地方，只要排隊，都存在這個問題。

1.　昨天我去郵局寄信，　昨天我去邮局寄信，　Yesterday I went to the post
　　發現大家都在一米線　发现大家都在一米线　office to send mail and noticed
　　以外排隊。　　　　　以外排队。　　　　　that everyone was standing in
　　　　　　　　　　　　　　　　　　　　line.

　　不單單是郵局，還有　不单单是邮局，还有　It's not just at the post office;
　　很多地方都有了一米　很多地方都有了一米　many other places now have
　　線。　　　　　　　　线。　　　　　　　　waiting lines as well.

2.　我發現現在好像所有　我发现现在好象所有　I found that nowadays it seems

的快餐店都禁止抽煙了。	的快餐店都禁止抽烟了。	that all of the fast-food restaurants ban smoking.
不單單是快餐店，很多飯館都禁止抽煙了。	不单单是快餐店，很多饭馆都禁止抽烟了。	Not just fast food restaurants ban smoking; many other restaurants do so as well.

3.

我覺得中國環境污染的問題太嚴重了。	我觉得中国环境污染的问题太严重了。	I think China's problem with environmental pollution is way too serious.
不單單是中國有這個問題，很多國家都有。	不单单是中国有这个问题，很多国家都有。	It's not just China that has this problem. Many other countries do too.

4.

星期一上課的時候我都快睏死了！	星期一上课的时候我都快困死了！

5.

真麻煩，沒想到看病以前還要跟醫生預先約定時間。	真麻烦，没想到看病以前还要跟医生预先约定时间。

6.

他真是一個很有本領的人，他修車的技術非常熟練。	他真是一个很有本领的人，他修车的技术非常熟练。

The pattern 不單單…，還/都/也… expresses an additional condition. When it's used to conjoin two different subjects, 是 goes after 不單單 and the second subject goes before 還/都/也. When it's used to conjoin two actions taken by someone, the subject can go either before 不單單 or before 還/也. A sentence such as 在美國不單單是跟醫生得預先約定時間，也得跟牙醫約定時間 should be rephrased as 在美國不單單跟醫生，跟牙醫也得預先約定時間 'In the States one has to make an appointment in advance not only with doctors, but also with dentists.'

5. Expressing a purpose

…，…以 V	…, yǐ…	…, …in order to V

- 比如我剛才不能一個個地問排在前面的女人，你是解大手還是解小手，以確定我該排在哪一隊後……

1. 在這兒我去看病以前應該做什麼？

   在这儿我去看病以前应该做什么？

   What should I do here before I see a doctor?

   去看病以前應該和醫生預先約定，以確定醫生有時間。

   去看病以前应该和医生预先约定，以确定医生有时间。

   Before you can see a doctor, you have to make an appointment with the doctor to make sure that he is available.

2. 我來上課以前應該做什麼？

   我来上课以前应该做什么？

   What should I do before I come to class?

   上課以前檢查一下書包，以保證沒有忘記功課。

   上课以前检查一下书包，以保证没有忘记功课。

   Before you come to class, you should check your shool bag and make sure that you did not forget to bring your homework.

3. 你為什麼要我跟他談一談？

   你为什么要我跟他谈一谈？

   Why did you ask me to talk to that person?

   出國旅遊以前和有經驗的朋友討論，以了解那個地方的情況。

   出国旅游以前和有经验的朋友讨论，以了解那个地方的情况。

   Before you go on a trip you need to talk with friends who have some experience to make sure that you understand the situation there.

4. 去旅遊之前為什麼應該預先確定機票？

   去旅游之前为什么应该预先确定机票？

5. 朦為什麼要給市長打電話？

   朦为什么要给市长打电话？

6. 考試的時候老師為什麼要學生把　　考试的时候老师为什么要学生把
　　書放在椅子下面？　　　　　　　　书放在椅子下面？

The pattern "…以V" expresses a purpose in more formal and literary Chinese. The verbs after 以 are often two-syllable, abstract ones such as 防止 'prevent,' 確定 'ascertain,' 保證 'guarantee,' 避免 'avoid,' 宣傳 'promote,' 表達 'express,' 改進 'improve,' etc. Thus, it's inappropriate to say 她給市長打電話，以讓市長知道排隊的問題 because the colloquial expression 讓 is mixed with a formal element 以. 好, a colloquial counterpart of 以, would be more appropriate in this case, e.g., 她給市長打電話，好讓市長知道排隊的問題 'She called the mayor, so as to let the mayor know about the problem of long lines.' The following is an appropriate use of 以: 她給市長打電話，以表達自己對政府制度的不滿 'She called the mayor to express her dissatisfaction with the governmental system.'

6. Expressing Passive Voice

A 為B（所）V	wéi…(suǒ)…	A is V-ed by B

• 我為籐的苦心感動，但還是說，就算你說的有理，這些事也太小了。

1. 現在中國人對西方文　　現在中国人对西方文　　In China today, what kind of
　　化抱什麼態度？　　　　化抱什么态度？　　　　attitude do the people have
　　　　　　　　　　　　　　　　　　　　　　　toward Western culture?

　　隨著東西方交流的擴　　随着东西方交流的扩　　Along with the expanded
　　展，西方文化慢慢地　　展，西方文化慢慢地　　contact between East and West,
　　為越來越多的中國人　　为越来越多的中国人　　Western culture is gradually
　　所接受。　　　　　　　所接受。　　　　　　　becoming accepted by more
　　　　　　　　　　　　　　　　　　　　　　　and more Chinese.

2. 人們怎麼看消防員所　　人们怎么看消防员所　　How do people see the work
　　從事的工作？　　　　　从事的工作？　　　　　being done by firefighters?

　　九一一事件以後，消　　九一一事件以后，消　　Since September 11th, people
　　防員從事的工作更為　　防员从事的工作更为　　respect the job being done by
　　人們所尊重。　　　　　人们所尊重。　　　　　firefighters even more.

3. 他的工作態度怎麼　　　他的工作态度怎么　　　How is his attitude toward
　　樣？大家有什麼看　　　样？大家有什么看　　　work? What is everyone's
　　　　　　　　　　　　　　　　　　　　　　　opinion?

法？   法？

他對工作認真負責的   他对工作认真负责的   His conscientious and
態度為人們所佩服。   态度为人们所佩服。   responsible work attitude is
                                                          really admired by people.

4. 你覺得人們現在對同性戀的態度   你觉得人们现在对同性恋的态度
    是怎麼樣的？   是怎么样的？

_____

5. 在美國，從事什麼工作的人為人   在美国，从事什么工作的人为人
    們所尊重？   们所尊重？

_____

6. 在你看來，歌手小甜甜為什麼樣   在你看来，歌手小甜甜为什么样
    的人所喜愛？   的人所喜爱？

_____

The pattern A 為 B (所) V expresses passive voice in very formal and literary Chinese. Though both 被 and 為 are passive markers, 被 often marks less desirable actions while 為 tends to be more associated with positive actions and verbs. 所 goes before the verb and can be omitted. Compare 從事教育工作的人為人們所尊重 'Those who are engaged in education are well-respected' and 他經常被老師罵 'He was often scolded by his teacher.'

背景常識 Background Notes

1. 排隊：在北京由於人多，所以在銀行、郵局等很多地方都需要排隊。一般來說，排隊的方法和美國的有些不同。以銀行為例，如果有五個窗口為大家服務的話，就會有五個隊。每個窗口的服務是一樣的，所以人們可以隨便選擇排哪個隊。這樣的做法有一個不方便的地方就是，如果排在你前邊的人有比較麻煩的事情，你就需要等很久。而和你一起來，但是選了不同隊的人可能很快就辦完了事情。

2. 出租車：在北京有很多出租車每天都在馬路上開來開去，所以坐出租車非常方便，根本不需要給出租汽車公司打電話。不管是早上還是晚

上，只要一招手，就會有出租車。根據車的好壞，出租車的價格也不
太一樣。

3. 公共廁所：在購物中心、飯館還有大街上都可以找到公共廁所，不過
   在大街上的公共廁所需要收費。過去中國的公共廁所裏沒有衛生紙，
   所以在門口會有一個人負責收錢，並且給人們衛生紙。

背景常识 Background Notes

1. 排队：在北京由于人多，所以在银行、邮局等很多地方都需要排队。
   一般来说，排队的方法和美国的有些不同。以银行为例，如果有五个
   窗口为大家服务的话，就会有五个队。每个窗口的服务是一样的，所
   以人们可以随便选择排哪个队。这样的做法有一个不方便的地方就
   是，如果排在你前边的人有比较麻烦的事情，你就需要等很久。而和
   你一起来，但是选了不同队的人可能很快就办完了事情。

2. 出租车：在北京有很多出租车每天都在马路上开来开去，所以坐出租
   车非常方便，根本不需要给出租汽车公司打电话。不管是早上还是晚
   上，只要一招手，就会有出租车。根据车的好坏，出租车的价格也不
   太一样。

3. 公共厕所：在购物中心、饭馆还有大街上都可以找到公共厕所，不过
   在大街上的公共厕所需要收费。过去中国的公共厕所里没有卫生纸，
   所以在门口会有一个人负责收钱，并且给人们卫生纸。

Appendix 1. Vocabulary from *Connections*

The following is the summary of vocabulary introduced in ***Connections I-II***. This material represents the entry level knowledge required for users of ***Encounters I-II***. Although some of the more difficult vocabulary are repeated in ***Encounters I-II*** as new vocabulary, it is assumed that much of the vocabulary from ***Connections I-II*** is already familiar. Review the following and focus on those items you have already forgotten. Entries with * indicate lexical items used in Mini-Dialogues instead of the Texts and of possible interest for supplemental study.

◎ By Pinyin

Pinyin	Character	English
A		
ài	唉	Oh!
àihào	愛好/爱好	hobby, interest
àiqíng	愛情/爱情	romantic love
àiren	愛人/爱人	spouse
àishang	愛上/爱上	to fall in love with
ānpái	安排	to arrange, to plan
ānquán	安全	safe, security
(àn)zhào	按照	according to
B		
bài	拜	to worship
báirén	白人	Caucasian
báitiān	白天	daytime, day
bàn	辦/办	to handle
bànfǎ	辦法/办法	way, means
bāngzhù	幫助/帮助	help, to assist
bàntiān	半天	a long time
bǎo	飽/饱	full
bǎochí	保持	to keep, to maintain
bǎohù	保護/保护	protection, to protect
bǎomǔ*	褓姆/保姆	housekeeper, nanny
bǎoshǒu	保守	conservative
bàoyuàn	抱怨	to complain, to grumble
bèi	倍	times, -fold
bèidòng	被動/被动	passive
bēiguān*	悲觀/悲观	pessimistic
bèijǐng	背景	background

Pinyin	Character	English
bèn*	笨	stupid
běnlái	本來/本来	originally
bǐ	筆/笔	measure word for money
biànhuà	變化/变化	change
biǎomiàn	表面	surface, appearance
biǎoyǎn	表演	performance exhibiton, to perform
biāozhǔn	標準/标准	standard
bǐbushàng	比不上	can't compare with
biérén	別人	other people
bǐfāng shuō	比方说/比方说	for example
bìng	並/并	actually (not)
bīng*	冰	to ice, ice
bìngrén*	病人	patient
bìxū	必須/必须	must
bú jiàn bú sàn*	不見不散/不见不散	Be there or be square.
búdàn	不但	not only
búduàn*	不斷/不断	continuously, uninterrupted
bówùguǎn	博物館/博物馆	museum
bùdé bù	不得不	cannot but
bùfen	部分	part, section
bùguǎn	不管	regardless of
bùmǎn	不滿/不满	dissatisfied
bǔpǐn	補品/补品	tonic

bùtíng	不停	incessantly
bǔxíbān	補習班/补习班	supplemental studies program
bùxíng	不行	to be no good

C

càidān*	菜單/菜单	menu
cāidào	猜到	to figure out
cǎn	慘/惨	miserable
cānguān	參觀/参观	to visit, to tour
cāntīng	餐廳/餐厅	restaurant
cāochǎng	操場/操场	practice field
chà	差	poor, inferior
cháng	嚐/尝	to taste
chángcháng	常常	often
chángjǐnglù*	長頸鹿/长颈鹿	giraffe
chángtú*	長途/长途	long distance
chǎo	炒	to stir-fry
cháodài*	朝代	dynasty
chǎojià	吵架	to quarrel
chénggōng	成功	successful, to succeed, success
chéngjī/jì	成績/成绩	grade
chéngjiù	成就	achievement
chéngshì	城市	town, city
chēngzàn	稱讚/称赞	to praise
chī dòufu*	吃豆腐	to eat bean-curd, to flirt with
chīcù	吃醋	to be jealous (of rival in love)
chījīng	吃驚/吃惊	to be shocked
chīkǔ	吃苦	to bear hardship
chīkuī	吃虧/吃亏	to suffer loss, to come to grief
chīlì	吃力	strenuous
chīsù*	吃素	to be a vegetarian
chūfā	出發/出发	to set out
chúfēi	除非	only if
chūguó	出國/出国	to go abroad
chūkǒu	出口	exit

chūmíng*	出名	famous, well-known
chóngbài	崇拜	to worship
chōngtū	衝突/冲突	conflict, clash
chǒngwù	寵物/宠物	pet
chūnjié	春節/春节	Spring Festival
chūntiān*	春天	spring
chòu*	臭	smelly, foul
chūxiàn	出現/出现	to appear, to emerge
chūzū qìchē	出租汽車/出租汽车	<PRC> taxi
chuáng	床	bed
chuānghu*	窗戶	window
chuánshuō	傳說/传说	it is said
chuántǒng	傳統/传统	traditional, tradition
chuīniú	吹牛	to brag
cí	辭/辞	to quit, to decline
cí*	辭/辞	to quit (a job)
cōngming	聰明/聪明	intelligent
cóngxiǎo	從小/从小	from childhood
cūxīn*	粗心	careless, thoughtless

D

dǎ kēshuì	打瞌睡	to doze off, to nod
dǎ zhāohu	打招呼	to greet
dǎbàn	打扮	to dress/make up
dǎdī	打的	to hire a taxi
dàfāng	大方	elegant and composed
dàgài	大概	probably, approximate
dài	戴	to wear (glasses, etc.)
dài	帶/带	to look after, to bring
dàigōu	代溝/代沟	generation gap
dàijià*	代價/代价	price, cost
dàlù	大陸/大陆	mainland China
dàngāo	蛋糕	cake
dāngshí	當時/当时	at that time, then
dānwèi*	單位/单位	(work) unit
dào	倒	instead
dào	倒	to dump (rubbish), to pour (water, tea)

dàochù	到處/到处	everywhere
dàodǐ	到底	after all
Dàojiào	道教	Daoism (as a religion)
dàolǐ	道理	reason, sense, argument
dàolǐ*	道理	reason, sense
dǎoyǎn	導演/导演	director
dǎrǎo	打擾/打扰	to disturb
dàren	大人	adult
dàrén*	大人	adult
dǎtōng	打通	to get through (phone call)
dàxiàng*	大象	elephant
dàxióngmāo	大熊貓/大熊猫	giant panda
dēng	燈/灯	lamp
děngděng	等等	and so on, etc.
dēngjīpái*	登機牌/登机牌	boarding pass
diǎn*	點/点	to order (dishes)
diǎnxīn	點心/点心	pastry
diànzǐ	電子/电子	electronic
diàoyú*	釣魚/钓鱼	to fish
diē/dié	跌	fall, tumble
dìfang	地方	place
dìng	訂/订	to book, to subscribe to
diūliǎn	丟臉/丢脸	to lose face
díquè	的確/的确	certainly, surely
dìtǎn	地毯	carpet, rug
dìtú	地圖/地图	map
dòngbudòng	動不動/动不动	easily, at the slightest provocation
dōngtiān	冬天	winter
dòngwù yuán*	動物園/动物园	zoo
dòngwù	動物/动物	animal
dòujiāng	豆漿/豆浆	soybean milk
duàn	段	period (of time), paragraph (of article)

duì…lái shuō	對…来说/对…来说	concerning
duìbuqǐ	對不起/对不起	to let sb. down
duìhuà	對話/对话	to carry on dialogue
duìmiàn	對面/对面	opposite
duìniú-tánqín	對牛彈琴/对牛弹琴	to cast pearls before swine
duìxiàng	對象/对象	boy/girlfriend
duō(me)	多麼/多么	how, what
E		
ér-nǚ	兒女/儿女	children
èrshǒuyān	二手煙/二手烟	second-hand smoke
értóng	兒童/儿童	children
érzi	兒子/儿子	son
F		
fā	發/发	to issue
fācái	發財/发财	to get rich
fādá	發達/发达	developed
fāmíng	發明/发明	invention
fǎn'ér	反而	on the contrary
fàndiàn*	飯店/饭店	hotel, restaurant
fǎnduì	反對/反对	to oppose
fāngbiàn miàn*	方便麵/方便面	\<PRC\> instant noodles
fāngbiàn*	方便	to go to the restroom, convenient
fāngfǎ	方法	method, means
fángjiān	房間/房间	room
fāngmiàn	方面	aspect, side
fàngqì	放棄/放弃	to give up
fāngxiàng	方向	direction
fāngyán	方言	dialect
fángzū*	房租	rent
fánróng	繁榮/繁荣	prosperous
fánshì	凡事	everything
fánshì	凡是	every, any, all
fántǐzì	繁體字/	traditional characters

	繁体字	
fānyì	翻譯/翻译	translation, to translate, translator
fànzuì	犯罪	crime, to commit a crime
fāpàng*	發胖/发胖	to gain weight
fāshēng	發生/发生	to happen
fāyīn	發音/发音	pronunciation, to pronounce
fāzhǎn	發展/发展	to develop, development
fēi...bùkě	非…不可	must
Fēizhōu	非洲	Africa
fēn	分	fraction, one-tenth, percent, to divide
fèn(r)	份(兒)/份(儿)	measure word for jobs, copies, etc.
fēng	封	measure word for letters
fēngfù	豐富/丰富	rich, enrich
fènglí*	鳳梨/凤梨	pineapple
fēngshui	風水/风水	landscape geomancy
fēnshǒu	分手	to break up
fēnxī	分析	to analyze, analysis
fū	夫	husband
Fójiào	佛教	Buddhism
fúqi*	福氣/福气	happy lot
fǒuzé	否則/否则	otherwise
fúwù	服務/服务	to serve, service
fùxí	複習/复习	to review
fùzá	複雜/复杂	complicated
G		
gǎi	改	to change
gǎigé	改革	to reform, reform
gān	乾/干	dry
gǎn	敢	to dare
gǎn	感	sense
gǎn xìngqù	感興趣/感兴趣	to be interested in
gānbēi	乾杯/干杯	bottoms up
gāngqín	鋼琴/钢琴	piano
gānjìng	乾淨/干净	clean

gǎnjué	感覺/感觉	feeling
gǎnqíng	感情	feeling
gǎnrén	感人	touching
gǎnxiǎng	感想	reflections, thoughts
gǎnxiè	感謝/感谢	to thank, to be grateful
gǎo	搞	to do
gāodà	高大	tall and big
gāojí	高級/高级	high in rank
gè	各	each
gēnběn	根本	simply
gèng	更	even
gēnjù	根據/根据	on the basis of, according to, basis
gèrénzhǔyì	個人主義/个人主义	individualism
gètǐhù	個體戶/个体户	individual entrepreneur
gòngchǎnzhǔyì	共產主義/共产主义	communism
gōnggòng*	公共	public
gōnglì	公立	public
gōngrén	工人	worker
gōngsī	公司	company
gòngtóng	共同	common
gòngxiàn	貢獻/贡献	contribution
gōngyuán	公園/公园	park
gōngzuò	工作	job, to work
gūniang	姑娘	girl
gōutōng	溝通/沟通	to communicate
guā	瓜	melon
guāfēng	刮風/刮风	the wind blows
guāi	乖	well-behaved
guài	怪	to blame
guǎi*	拐	to turn
guàibude	怪不得	no wonder
guàiwu	怪物	monster, freak
guǎn xiánshì	管閒事/管闲事	to meddle

guǎngbō	廣播/广播	broadcast, to air
guǎngchǎng	廣場/广场	public square
guāngshì	光是	merely, just
guānniàn	觀念/观念	concept
guānxīn	關心/关心	to be concerned about
guānyú	關於/关于	about, with regard to
gǔdài	古代	ancient times
guǐ	鬼	ghost
gǔlì	鼓勵/鼓励	encouragement
guò	過/过	to pass
guòfèn	過分/过分	excessive, over-
guójiā	國家/国家	country, state, nation
guòjié	過節/过节	to celebrate a festival
guónèi	國內/国内	internal, domestic
guònián	過年/过年	to celebrate New Year
guòqù	過去/过去	past
guǒrán	果然	as expected, sure enough
guówài	國外/国外	internal, overseas, abroad
guōzi*	鍋子/锅子	wok, pan
gǔpiào	股票	stock
gùshi	故事	story, tale
gǔzhǎng*	鼓掌	to clap hands
H		
hāhā	哈哈	haha (sound of laughter)
hǎi	海	sea
hài	害	to do harm to, cause trouble to
hǎiguān	海關/海关	customs
hàipà	害怕	to be afraid/ scared
hǎixiá	海峽/海峡	strait
hǎochu	好處/好处	benefit
hǎogǎn	好感	favorable impression
hàomǎ*	號碼/号码	number
hàoqí	好奇	curious
hǎoróngyì	好容易	with great difficulty, to have a hard time (doing sth.)
hǎoyùn	好運/好运	good luck

hǎozài	好在	fortunately
hébì	何必	there is no need
héshang	和尚	Buddhist monk
hézuò	合作	to cooperate, cooperation
hú	湖	lake
hóngbāo	紅包/红包	red paper bag with gift money
hūrán	忽然	suddenly
hútòng	胡同	lane
hútu	糊塗/糊涂	muddled, confused
hòu	厚	thick
hóuzi	猴子	monkey
huáchuán*	划船	to row a boat
huàhuàr	畫畫兒/画画儿	to draw pictures
huáiyí	懷疑/怀疑	to doubt, to suspect
huàjiā	畫家/画家	painter
huánjìng	環境/环境	environment
huānyíng*	歡迎/欢迎	to welcome
Huáyì	華裔/华裔	ethnic Chinese of other nationalities
huāyuán	花園/花园	flower garden
huàzhuāng*	化妝/化妆	to apply makeup
huídá	回答	to reply, to answer
Huíjiào	回教	Islam
huíxìn	回信	to write in reply
huǒchē	火車/火车	train
huódòng	活動/活动	activity, to exercise
huǒtuǐ*	火腿/火腿	ham
hùxiāng	互相	mutually
hùzhào	護照/护照	passport
J		
jǐ	擠/挤	crowded, to squeeze
jì...yě	既···也···	not only... but also...
jià	嫁	(of a woman) to marry
jiācháng biànfàn	家常便飯/家常便饭	simple meal
jiājiào	家教	home tutoring, upbringing, tutor

jiājù	家具	furniture			advantage of (opportunity /etc.)
jiǎndān	簡單/简单	simple	jiēchù	接觸/接触	to come into contact with
jiàndào	見到/见到	to see	jiéguǒ	結果/结果	result
jiāng	江	river	jiějué	解決/解决	to solve, to settle
jiǎng	講/讲	to stress, to speak	jièkǒu	藉口/借口	excuse
jiǎngjiu	講究/讲究	to be particular about	jièkǒu*	藉口/借口	excuse
jiānglái	將來/将来	future	jiémù	節目/节目	program
jiàngyóu*	醬油/酱油	soy sauce	jiérì	節日/节日	festival, holiday
jiànjiàn	漸漸/渐渐	gradually	jiěshì	解釋/解释	analysis, to expound
jiànkāng	健康	health	jiēshòu	接受	to accept
jiǎnlì	簡歷/简历	curriculum vitae	jiéshù	結束/结束	to end
jiànmiàn	見面/见面	to meet, to see	jīhū	幾乎/几乎	almost
jiǎntǐzì	簡體字/简体字	simplified characters	jìhuà	計劃/计划	plan, project
jiànyì	建議/建议	suggestion	-jíle	極了/极了	extremely
jiànzhù	建築/建筑	architecture, to build	jīliè	激烈	intense, fierce
jiāo	交	to make (friends), to hand over	jǐmǎn	擠滿/挤满	to be filled to overflowing
jiàocái	教材	teaching materials	jìmò	寂寞	lonely
jiàoshì	教室	classroom	jīn	金	gold, blonde
jiàoshòu*	教授	professor	jīn*	斤	half a kilogram
jiāotōng	交通	traffic	jīnfànwǎn	金飯碗/金饭碗	well-paid job
jiàoxun	教訓/教训	lesson, to lecture sb.			
jiàoyù	教育	education	jīngcǎi	精彩	brilliant
jiātíng	家庭	family	jīngcháng	經常/经常	frequently, often
jiāwù	家務/家务	household duties	jīngguò	經過/经过	to pass
jiāyóu*	加油	Cheers! Go!	jīngjì	經濟/经济	economical
jiāzhǎng	家長/家长	parent of school children	jīngjìxuéjiā	經濟學家/经济学家	economist
jīběn	基本	basic, essential	jīnglǐ*	經理/经理	manager
jīchē	機車/机车	<TW> motor-cycle	jìngrán	竟然	unexpectedly
jìchéngchē	計程車/计程车	<TW> taxi	jǐngsè*	景色	scenery, view
jīchǔ	基礎/基础	foundation, basic	jìngshàng	敬上	respectfully submitted
jīdàn*	雞蛋/鸡蛋	hen's egg	jǐnguǎn	儘管/尽管	even though
Jīdūjiào	基督教	Christianity	jìngzhēng	競爭/竞争	competition, to compete
jiē	接	to pick sb. up	jìniànpǐn	紀念品/纪念品	souvenir
jiē	接	to pick up (phone call), to welcome			
jiè	藉/借	to make use of, take	jǐnzhāng	緊張/紧张	in short supply

jǐnzhāng	緊張/紧张	nervous, tense	kèfú	克服	to surmount
jiūjìng	究竟	actually, after all, in the end	kējì	科技	science and technology
jīpiào	機票/机票	plane ticket	kělián	可憐/可怜	pitiable, poor
jìrán	既然	since, now that	kěndìng	肯定	<PRC> definitely, positive, to affirm
jíshǐ	即使	even, even if/though			fearful, terrible
jiùsuàn	就算	even if	kěpà	可怕	fearful, terrible
jūrán	居然	unexpectedly	kèqi	客氣/客气	to be polite
júzi*	橘子/桔子	orange	kèren	客人	visitor, guest
jù	句	sentence	késou	咳嗽	to cough
juǎn	捲/卷	to roll, to curl	kèwài	課外/课外	extra-curricular
juézhǒng	絕種/绝种	to become extinct	kèwén	課文/课文	text
jùlí	距離/距离	distance	kěxī	可惜	It's a pity!
jùxíng	句型	sentence pattern	kěxiào	可笑	funny
K			kōngtiáo	空調/空调	air-conditioning
kāfēiguǎn	咖啡館/咖啡馆	café	kǒuyīn	口音	regional accent
			kǒuyǔ	口語/口语	spoken/vernacular language
kāi yèchē	開夜車/开夜车	to burn the midnight oil	kuàicān	快餐	fast food
kāifàng	開放/开放	to open to the world, to open to traffic or public use	kùnnán	困難/困难	difficulty
			L		
			la	啦	indicating excitement/doubt (le 了 plus 啊)
kāiqiāng	開槍/开枪	to shoot			
kāishuǐ	開水/开水	boiling/boiled water	lā guānxi	拉關係/拉关系	to saddle up to
kāixīn	開心/开心	to feel happy			
kàn rènao	看熱鬧/看热闹	to go where crowds are (for fun/ excitement)	lādùzi	拉肚子	to have diarrhea
			láibují	來不及/来不及	can't do sth. in time
kànbuqǐ	看不起	to scorn			
kànfǎ	看法	view	lājī, lèsè	垃圾	garbage
kànyàngzi	看樣子/看样子	it seems, it looks as if	làngfèi	浪費/浪费	to waste, extravagant
			lǎo	老	tough, overdone
kào	靠	to rely on, to lean on	lǎo	老	always
kǎojuàn*	考卷	test paper	lǎobǎixìng	老百姓	common people, civilians
kǎolǜ	考慮/考虑	to consider, to think over	lǎobǎn	老板	boss
kǎoshàng	考上	to pass an entrance examination	lǎodà*	老大	eldest child (in a family)
kǎoshì	考試/考试	test, to test	lǎohǔ*	老虎	tiger
kě	渴	thirsty	láojià*	勞駕/劳驾	excuse me
kě'ài	可愛/可爱	lovely	lǎojiā*	老家	native place
kèběn	課本/课本	textbook	lǎorén	老人	old man/woman

lǎoshíshuō	老實說/老实说	to tell the truth	mà	罵/骂	to call names, to scold
lǎoshǔ*	老鼠	mouse, rat	mángbuguòlái	忙不過來/忙不过来	too busy to deal with
lǎowài	老外	foreigner	mǎnyì	滿意/满意	satisfied
lèguān	樂觀/乐观	optimistic, hopeful	mào	冒	to risk, to brave
liàng*	輛/辆	measure word for cars	máobing	毛病	shortcoming
liǎng'àn	兩岸/两岸	both sides (Chinese Mainland and Taiwan)	máodùn	矛盾	contradictory, contradiction
liánxì	聯繫/联系	to contact	měi	美	beautiful
liǎobuqǐ	了不起	amazing, terrific	méiguānxi	沒關係/没关系	it doesn't matter
liǎojiě	了解	to understand	mèimei	妹妹	younger sister
lìhai	厲害/厉害	sharp	méitǐ	媒體/媒体	media
líhūn	離婚/离婚	divorce	méixiǎngdào	沒想到	unexpectedly
lǐjiě	理解	to understand	mèng	夢/梦	dream
líkāi	離開/离开	to leave, to depart from	ménpiào*	門票/门票	admission ticket
lǐmào	禮貌/礼貌	polite	mí	迷	to be enchanted with
línjū	鄰居/邻居	neighbor	miǎnbuliǎo	免不了	to be unavoidable
liú*	留	to keep	miànqián	面前	in front of
liúxué	留學/留学	to study abroad	miàntán	面談/面谈	to discuss face to face
liúyán	留言	to leave message	miànzi	面子	face
lìrú	例如	for instance, such as	miào	廟/庙	temple
lìshǐ	歷史/历史	history	mìmì	秘密	secret
liùniǎo*	遛鳥/遛鸟	to take a bird on a stroll	míngshènggǔjī	名勝古蹟/名胜古迹	places of historic interest and scenic beauty
lìwài	例外	exception	míngxiào	名校	famous school
lǐxiǎng	理想	ideal	míngxīng	明星	star
lìyòng	利用	to use, to take advantage of	míngxìnpiàn	明信片	postcard
lìzi	例子	example, case	mínzhǔ	民主	democracy
lǚkè*	旅客	traveller, passenger	mínzú	民族	ethnic group /minority, nation
lǚxíngshè	旅行社	travel agent	míxìn	迷信	superstition, to have blind faith in
lǚyóutuán	旅遊團/旅游团	tour group	mùdì	目的	purpose, aim, goal
luàn	亂/乱	chaotic, messy	mùqián	目前	at present
luōsuo	囉嗦/罗嗦	wordy, longwinded	mǔqin	母親/母亲	mother
lǜdòutāng	綠豆湯/绿豆汤	mung bean soup	**N**		
M			nándào	難道/难道	Do you mean to say that…?
			nándé	難得/难得	rare

nánguài	難怪/难怪	no wonder		pàomiàn*	泡麵/泡面	\<TW> instant noodles
nánháir	男孩兒/男孩儿	boy		páshān*	爬山	to climb mountain
nán-nǔ-lǎo-shào	男女老少	men and women, old and young		pī	批	batch, lot, group
				piān	篇	piece of writing
nánzǐhàn	男子漢/男子汉	a real man		piàn	騙/骗	to deceive, to cheat, to swindle
nào xiàohua	鬧笑話/闹笑话	to make a fool of oneself		piānjiàn	偏見/偏见	bias
				piānzi	片子	film
nàozhōng	鬧鐘/闹钟	alarm clock		píng	瓶	bottle
nèiróng	内容	content		píng'ān	平安	safe and sound
nénggàn	能幹/能干	competent		píngděng	平等	equal
nénggòu	能夠	can, be able to		píngguǒ	蘋果/苹果	apple
nénglì	能力	ability, capacity		pīngpāng qiú*	乒乓球	ping-pong
néngyuán	能源	energy		píngshí	平時/平时	in ordinary times
nì	膩/腻	greasy, tired of		pīnmìng	拼命	to make a do-or-die effort
niánjì	年紀/年纪	age		pǔbiàn	普遍	universal, widespread
niánqīng	年輕/年轻	young		pǔtōnghuà	普通話/普通话	Mandarin Chinese
niánqīngrén	年輕人/年轻人	young people				
				Q		
nìngkě	寧可/宁可	would rather, better		qí	騎/骑	to ride
niú	牛	ox		qǐ zuòyòng	起作用	to have an effect
niúròumiàn	牛肉麵/牛肉面	beef noodles		qiáng	強	strong, powerful, better
nóngmín	農民/农民	peasant		qiángdiào	強調/强调	to stress
nǔháir	女孩兒/女孩儿	girl		qiántú	前途	future, prospects
				qiānwàn	千萬/千万	by all means
nǔxìng	女性	woman		qiānzhèng	簽證/签证	visa
nuǎnhuo	暖和	(nice and) warm		qǐchuáng	起床	to get up (from bed)
O				qiézi	茄子	eggplant
Ōuzhōu	歐洲/欧洲	Europe		qìgōng	氣功/气功	deep breathing exercises
P				qīng-shàonián	青少年	young people and teenagers, youths
pá*	爬	to climb, to crawl		qīngchu	清楚	clear
pāi	拍	to shoot film, to take a picture		qǐngjià	請假/请假	to ask for leave
páigǔ	排骨	spareribs		qǐngjiào	請教/请教	to seek advice
pàng	胖	fat, plump		qǐngkè	請客/请客	to treat sb. (to meal/show/etc.)
pǎo	跑	to run		qíngkuàng	情況/情况	situation, circumstances
pǎobù	跑步	to jog		qīngnián	青年	youth

qǐngtiě*	請帖／请帖	invitation card
qìngzhù	慶祝／庆祝	to celebrate
qīnqiè	親切／亲切	cordial
qióngguāng dàn	窮光蛋／穷光蛋	poor wretch
qiūtiān*	秋天	autumn
qíshì	歧視／歧视	discrimination
qítā	其他	other, the rest
qīzi	妻子	wife
quàn	勸／劝	to advise
quánlì	權利／权利	right, privilege
quánqiúhuà	全球化	globalization
quē	缺	to be short of, to lack, opening
què	卻／却	however, yet
quēdiǎn	缺點／缺点	shortcoming, defect

R

rán'ér	然而	even so, but
rèmén	熱門／热门	in great demand
rèn	認／认	to recognize
rěnbuzhù	忍不住	can't help but do sth.
rènhé	任何	any
rénkǒu	人口	population
rénmen	人們／人们	people, the public
rénmín	人民	the people
Rénmínbì*	人民幣／人民币	R.M.B.
rénshān-rénhǎi*	人山人海	huge crowds of people, a sea of people
rènwéi	認爲／认为	to think that
rènzhēn	認眞／认真	earnest, serious, to take for real
rèqíng	熱情／热情	enthusiastic, warm
rìcháng	日常	day-to-day
rìyòngpǐn	日用品	articles for daily use
rìzi	日子	day, days
Rújiā	儒家	Confucian school
ruǎn*	軟／软	soft
ruǎntǐ*	軟體／软体	<TW> software

S

sāichē	塞車／塞车	traffic jam
sànbù	散步	to take a walk
shā	殺／杀	to kill
shāfā	沙發／沙发	sofa
shāng	商	business
shàng	上	to submit (a letter)
shàngcì	上次	last time
shàngdàng	上當／上当	to be taken in
shāngdiàn	商店	shop
shànghuǒ	上火	to suffer excessive internal heat
shāngliang	商量	to consult
shāngxīn	傷心／伤心	to be sad/ grieved
shānshuǐ	山水	landscape (painting)
shāo	燒／烧	to cook, to roast, to burn
shāobǐng	燒餅／烧饼	baked sesame seed flatcake
shěbude	捨不得／舍不得	to loathe to part with or use
shén	神	god, super-natural, magical
shēn	深	deep
shēng	生	raw, green
shěng	省	province, to save
shēngcí	生詞／生词	new word
shēngdòng*	生動／生动	lively, vivid
shēngmìng	生命	(physical) life
shēngxué	升學／升学	to enter higher school
shēngyi	生意	business, trade
shēngyīn	聲音／声音	sound
shénhuà	神話／神话	myth, mythology
shénmede	什麼的／什么的	and so on
shēnqǐng	申請／申请	to apply for
shènzhì	甚至	so much so that
shétou	舌頭／舌头	tongue
shī	詩／诗	poem
shídài*	時代	times, age, era

shīfu*	師傅/师傅	master worker		shùnzhe	順著/顺着	to go along
shíjì	實際/实际	practical, reality		shuōbudìng	説不定/	perhaps
shìjì	世紀/世纪	century			说不定	
shíjì*	實際/实际	practical		shuōlái huà cháng	説來話長/	it's a long story
shìjiè	世界	world			说来话长	
shímáo	時髦/时髦	fashionable		shuōmíng	説明/说明	to explain, illustration
shìqing	事情	affair, matter		shǔtiáor	薯條兒/	french fries
shīwàng	失望	to become disappointed			薯条儿	
shìwēi	示威	to march, demonstration		shùzì	數字/数字	numeral, digit
shíwù	食物	food		sǐ	死	dead, to die
shíxiàn	實現/实现	to realize		sìhéyuàn	四合院	compound with houses around a courtyard
shìyè	事業/事业	career		sījīn	絲巾/丝巾	silk scarf
shìyìng	適應/适应	to get used to		sīxiǎng	思想	thought, thinking, ideology
shízài	實在/实在	indeed, really				
shīzi*	獅子/狮子	lion		suàn	算	to regard as
shūdāizi	書呆子/书呆子	bookworm		suànle*	算了	let it be, let it pass
shūfǎjiā	書法家/书法家	calligrapher		suànmìng	算命	fortune-telling, to tell fortune
shūmiàn yǔ	書面語/书面语	written/ literary language		suān-tián-kǔ-là	酸甜苦辣	all flavors
shōu	收	put away, take back		suíbiàn	隨便/随便	carelessly, casually, to do as one pleases
shòu	瘦	thin, lean		suídì	隨地/随地	anywhere
shǒu*	首	measure word for songs, poems		suíshēn*	隨身/随身	(take) with one, (carry) on one's person
shòudào	受到	to receive		suíshí	隨時/随时	at any time
shǒudū	首都	capital		suízhe	隨著/随着	along with, in the wake of
shǒujī*	手機/手机	cellular phone		suǒ	所	that, which
shōurù	收入	income		suǒwèi	所謂/所谓	so-called
shòushāng	受傷/受伤	to be injured/ wounded		suǒyǒu	所有	all
shōushi	收拾	to pack, to put in order		**T**		
				tàidu	態度/态度	attitude, manner
shúxī	熟悉	familiar		táifēng*	颱風/台风	typhoon
shù	樹/树	tree		tàijíquán	太極拳/太极拳	a kind of shadow-boxing
shuài	帥/帅	handsome				
shuǐguǒ	水果	fruit		tàikōngrén	太空人	astronaut
shùnbiàn	順便/顺便	conveniently, in passing		tàitai	太太	wife, Mrs.
shùnlì	順利/顺利	smooth		Táiwān	台灣/台湾	Taiwan

tàiyáng	太陽/太阳	sun, sunshine			推荐信	letter
tán liàn'ài	談戀愛/ 谈恋爱	to court	tuō'érsuǒ*	托兒所/ 托儿所	child-care center
tán*	彈/弹	to play	tuōyùn*	托運/托运	consign for shipment, to check (baggage)
tào	套	set			
Táohuāyuán	桃花源	utopia	**W**		
tǎojià- huánjià	討價還價/ 讨价还价	to bargain	wàidìrén	外地人	non-local people
			wàihào	外號/外号	nickname
táolǐ mǎn tiānxià	桃李滿天下 桃李满天下	to have pupils everywhere	wàixīngrén	外星人	an extra-terrestrial
			wǎn'ān	晚安	Good night!
tǎolùn	討論/讨论	to discuss, discussion	wǎndiǎn	晚點/晚点	late
tǎoyàn	討厭/讨厌	to be disgusted with	wǎnfàn	晚飯/晚饭	supper, dinner
tèsè	特色	distinguishing feature/quality	wǎng	網/网	net
			wǎngyǒu	網友/网友	net pal
tī*	踢	to kick	wǎngzhàn*	網站/网站	web site
tiānliàng	天亮	daybreak	wàngzǐ chénglóng	望子成龍/ 望子成龙	to hope one's children will have bright future
Tiānzhǔjiào	天主教	Catholicism			
tiáo	條/条	measure word for sth. long and narrow	wánquán	完全	completely
tiào	跳	to jump	wěidà	偉大/伟大	great
tiáojiàn	條件/条件	condition	wèile	爲了/为了	for
tiāotì	挑剔	nitpicky, to nitpick	wèishēngzhǐ	衛生紙/ 卫生纸	toilet paper
tiàowǔ	跳舞	to dance			
tídào	提到	to mention	wēixiǎn	危險/危险	danger, dangerous
tígāo	提高	to raise, to enhance	wéiyī	唯一	only, sole
tīngdào	聽到/听到	to hear	wéizhǐ	爲止/为止	up to, till
tīnghuà	聽話/听话	obedient	wènhǎo	問好/问好	to say hello to
tíqián	提前	in advance	wénhuà	文化	culture
tíxǐng	提醒	to remind	wénmáng	文盲	an illiterate, illiteracy
tóngqíng	同情	to sympathize with	wēnróu	溫柔	gentle and soft
tóngshí	同時/同时	(at) the same time	wénwù	文物	cultural/historical relics
tóngshì	同事	colleague	wénxué	文學/文学	literature
tóngyì	同意	to agree	wénzhāng	文章	essay, article
tōngzhī*	通知	to notify, notice	wénzì	文字	characters, script
tūrán	突然	suddenly	wúlùn	無論/无论	no matter what/how, regardless of
tōudù	偷渡	to steal across international border	wūrǎn	污染	pollution, to contaminate
tóuténg	頭疼/头疼	headache	wòshǒu	握手	to shake/clasp hands
tǔbāozi	土包子	rube, hick	wù*	霧/雾	fog
tuījiànxìn	推薦信/	recommendation			

wùhuì	誤會/误会	to mis-understand				habit
wùjià	物價/物价	commodity prices	xǐjiǔ	喜酒	wedding feast
X			xǐng	醒	to wake up
xì	系	department (in a college)	xìngfú	幸福	happiness
xià	嚇/吓	to scare	xíngli	行李	luggage
xiàbān*	下班	to get off work	xìnjiào	信教	to profess a religion
xián	鹹/咸	salty	xīnqíng	心情	mood
xián	嫌	to dislike the fact that	xīnshǎng	欣賞/欣赏	to appreciate
xiāng	香	fragrant	xīnshì	心事	weight on one's mind, worry
xiǎng	響/响	to ring	xīnshui	薪水	salary, wages
xiàng	向	towards (direction)	xīnwén	新聞/新闻	news
xiāng'ài	相愛/相爱	to love each other	xìnxīn	信心	confidence, faith
xiāngfǎn	相反	opposite	xǐwǎn	洗碗	to do dishes
xiǎngjiā	想家	to be homesick	xìxīn*	細心/细心	careful
xiànglái	向來/向来	always, all along	xīyǐn	吸引	to attract, to draw
xiǎngniàn	想念	to miss	xūyào	需要	to need
xiàngsheng	相聲/相声	cross talk, comical dialogue	xuǎnzé	選擇/选择	to select
xiǎngshòu	享受	to enjoy, enjoyment	xuéxí	學習/学习	to study, to learn
xiǎngxiàng	想像/想象	to imagine, to fancy	xùnliàn	訓練/训练	training, to train
xiāngxìn	相信	to believe	**Y**		
xiànmù	羨慕/羡慕	to envy	yālì	壓力/压力	pressure
xiànshí	現實/现实	reality	yán*	鹽/盐	salt
xiànxiàng	現象/现象	phenomenon	yáng	羊	sheep
xiǎofàn	小販/小贩	peddler	yǎnghuo	養活/养活	to support
xiǎoháir	小孩兒/小孩儿	child	yángrén	洋人	foreigner
xiǎohuǒzi	小伙子	young fellow	yānhuǒ	煙火/烟火	fireworks
			yǎnjìng	眼鏡/眼镜	glasses
xiǎoqi	小氣/小气	stingy	yánjiūshēng	研究生	graduate student
xiāoxi	消息	news	yǎnxì	演戲/演戏	to act in a play
xiāoyè	宵夜	midnight snack	yánzhòng	嚴重/严重	serious, grave
xiǎoyìsi*	小意思	small token of kindly feelings	yào	藥/药	medicine
			(yào)bùrán	(要)不然	otherwise
xiàoyuán	校園/校园	campus	yàobushì	要不是	if it were not for, but for
xiàqí	下棋	to play chess	yàomìng	要命	extremely
xiàxuě*	下雪	to snow	yèshì	夜市	night market
xiàyǔ*	下雨	to rain	yěxǔ	也許/也许	perhaps
xiézi	鞋子	shoes	yéye*	爺爺/爷爷	(paternal) grandfather
xíguàn	習慣/习惯	to be accustomed to,	yī	醫/医	medical science

yìbān	一般	ordinary		yóujiàn	郵件/邮件	postal matter, mail
yíbèizi	一輩子/ 一辈子	all one's life		yóukè	遊客/游客	tourist
				yǒulì	有利	(to be) advan-tageous
yīfu	衣服	clothing		yǒulì*	有力	strong, powerful
-yǐlái	以來/以来	since		yǒumíng	有名	famous
yílù	一路	whole journey		yōumò	幽默	humorous
yímín	移民	emigrant/immigrant		yǒuqù	有趣	interesting
yīncǐ	因此	therefore, consequently		yóutiáo	油條/油条	deep-fried twisted dough sticks
yìng*	硬	hard		yóuxíng	遊行/游行	to demonstrate, parade
yǐngxiǎng	影響/影响	influence, to influence		yóuyú	由於/由于	owing/due/ thanks to
yíngyǎng*	營養/营养	nutrition		yóuyǒng	游泳	to swim
yǐnqǐ	引起	to give rise to, to lead to		yǒuyòng	有用	useful
yìnxiàng	印象	impression		yuán	圓/圆	round
yīnyuèhuì*	音樂會/ 音乐会	concert		yuángù	緣故/缘故	cause, reason
				yuánlái	原來/原来	as it turns out
yīnyuèjiā*	音樂家/ 音乐家	musician		yuànyi	願意/愿意	to be willing
				yuányīn	原因	reason
yìqǐ	一起	together, in the same place		yuànzi*	院子	yard
yíqiè	一切	all, everything		yùdào	遇到	to run into
yìshù	藝術/艺术	art		yuèbǐng	月餅/月饼	moon cake
yìsi	意思	meaning		yuèdǐ	月底	end of month
yìwài	意外	unexpected, accident		yuèdú	閱讀/阅读	reading com- prehension
yíxiàzi	一下子	at once				
yízhènzi	一陣子/ 一阵子	a while, a short period of time		yuēhuì	約會/约会	to date
				yuèliang	月亮	moon
yǐzi	椅子	chair		yuèqiú	月球	moon
yúkuài	愉快	happy		yùnqi	運氣/运气	fortune, luck
yúlè	娛樂/娱乐	entertainment		yǔqí	與其/与其	rather than
yún*	雲/云	cloud		yùshì*	浴室	bathroom, shower room
yǒngyuǎn	永遠/永远	forever		yùxí	預習/预习	to prepare lessons before class
yúshì	於是/于是	thereupon, hence		**Z**		
yóu	由	by, through, from		zài...kànlái	在…看來/ 在…看来	in sb.'s view
yóu	油	oily, oil				
yǒudeshì	有的是	to have plenty of		zàihu	在乎	to care about, to mind
yōudiǎn	優點/优点	merit		zàishuō	再說/再说	besides
				zànchéng	贊成/赞成	to approve
yǒuhǎo	友好	friendly		zāng	髒/脏	dirty

zǎodiǎn	早點/早点	breakfast			中国城	
zěnme huí shì	怎麼回事/怎么回事	what's going on?		zhōngjiān	中間/中间	center, middle
				zhòngshì	重視/重视	to value
zérèn	責任/责任	duty, responsibility		Zhōng-wài	中外	China and foreign countries
zhá	炸	to deep-fry		zhōngxīn	中心	center, heart
zhàdàn	炸彈/炸弹	bomb		zhǒngzú	種族/种族	race, ethnic group
zhàn	佔/占	to occupy		zhōuwéi	周圍/周围	surrounding, all around
zhǎng	漲/涨	to rise, to go up		zhù	祝	to express good wishes
zhǎngdà	長大/长大	to grow up				
zhānglíng*	蟑螂	cockroach		zhǔ	煮	to cook, to boil
zhǎnlǎn	展覽/展览	show, to exhibit		zhù*	祝	to wish
zhànxiàn*	佔線/占线	the (phone) line is busy		zhuāng	裝/装	to pack, to hold, to install
zhàogù	照顧/照顾	to look after		zhuǎnjī	轉機/转机	to change planes
zhāopai	招牌	shop sign		zhuānmén	專門/专门	special, specialized
zhēng	睜	to open the eyes		zhǔfù	主婦/主妇	housewife
zhēng	爭/争	to fight for		zhuōzi	桌子	table, desk
zhèngfǔ	政府	government		zhǔyào	主要	main, principal
zhěnglǐ	整理	to put in order		zhùyì	注意	to pay attention to
zhēnglùn	爭論/争论	to argue, dispute		zībǐnzhǔyì	資本主義/资本主义	capitalism
zhěngqí	整齊/整齐	neat, tidy				
zhèngshū	證書/证书	certificate		zìcóng	自從/自从	since
zhèngzhì	政治	politics		zìrán	自然	natural, naturally, nature
zhēnzhèng	真正	genuine, true, real		zìxíngchē	自行車/自行车	bicycle
zhéxué	哲學/哲学	philosophy				
zhī jiān	之間/之间	between		zìyóu	自由	freedom, free
zhídào	直到	until, up to		zōngjiào	宗教	religion
zhíde	值得	to deserve, to merit		zǒngsuàn	總算/总算	at long last, finally
zhìdù	制度	system		zǒngzhī	總之/总之	in a word
zhíjiē	直接	direct, immediate		zūnjìng	尊敬	to respect
zhǐyào	只要	so long as		zúqiú	足球	soccer
zhíyè	職業/职业	occupation		zǒu hòumén	走後門/走后门	to secure sth. through pull or influence
zhīyī	之一	one of				
zhìyú	至於/至于	as for/to, (go) so far as to		zuǐ	嘴	mouth
zhǐyǒu	只有	only, alone		zuì	醉	drunk
zhūjiǎo	豬腳/猪脚	pig feet		zuìhǎo	最好	had better, it would be best
zhǒng	種/种	kind, sort, type		zuìhòu	最後/最后	final
Zhōngguó chéng	中國城/	Chinatown		zuòfǎ	做法	way of doing sth.

| zuòjiā | 作家 | writer | zuòzhě | 作者 | author |
| zuòpǐn | 作品 | works (of literature/art) | zǔxiān | 祖先 | ancestors |

Appendix 2. Modern Chinese Punctuation

The following is a summary of the punctuation marks used in modern Chinese.   Some marks
are similar in shapes and functions to those of English ones, while others are uniquely Chinese.
Pay special attention to marks that are similar in shape but different in functions, e.g., the use
of a Chinese comma. Detailed explanation of the usage of modern Chinese punctuation can be
found in the first chapter of *Reading Chinese Newspapers: Tactics and Skills* by Stanley
Mickel (1991).

I. Uniquely Chinese Punctuation Marks

Marker	Chinese Name	English Name	Usage
、	頓號/顿号	enumerative comma	mark series of items
。	句號/句号	period mark	mark end of sentence
「」 『』	引號/引号	quotation mark used in Taiwan	mark direct and indirect speech, special language usage, or literary titles
《》 〈〉	書名號/书名号	title mark	mark literary titles
[ ]	括號/括号	parentheses mark	mark parenthetical items
……………	著重號/着重号	emphasis mark	mark emphasis and is placed under the text

II. Graphemically Identical, Functionally Similar Punctuation Marks

Marker	Chinese Name	English Name	Usage
?	問號/问号	question mark	mark interrogative sentences
!	感嘆號/感叹号	exclamation mark	mark exclamations
" " ' '	引號/引号	quotation mark used in P.R.C.	mark direct and indirect speech, special language usage, or literary titles
:	冒號/冒号	colon mark	mark following explanatory items
;	分號/分号	semi- colon mark	mark series, stress, separation
——	破折號/破折号	dash mark	mark parenthetical material
( )	括號/括号	parentheses mark	mark parenthetical material

III. Graphemically Identical Punctuation Marks with Different Usages

Marker	Chinese Name	English Name	Usage
•	間隔號/间隔号	solid dot mark	mark divisions in foreign names, literary titles, addresses, etc.; mark emphasis, ellipsis
,	逗號/逗号	comma mark	mark pauses and emphasis

Index 1. Vocabulary

Productive vocabulary that requires active learning is given with an exact number reference.   Receptive vocabulary is given with a general lesson reference.   The number before a Chinese character indicates its frequency, as categorized in *Frequency List of Chinese Vocabulary and Characters* 漢語水平詞匯與漢字 等級大綱 (1992), one being most common, two belonging to the second category, and so on.

◎By Pinyin

Pinyin	F	Character		Part of Speech	English	L., #
A						
àihào	2	愛好	爱好	N	interest, hobby	8
ānjìng	1	安靜	安静	Adj	quiet, peaceful	3.05
ānpái	1	安排		V/N	to arrange, to plan, to fix up	2.43
ānwèi	2	安慰		V/N	to comfort, consolation	4.43
B						
bái	2	白		Adv	free of charge, to do sth. in vain	2.21
bàle		罷了	罢了	Suf	(indicating limitation)	5.42
bǎngyàng	2	榜樣	榜样	N	example, model	9.20
bào	1	抱		V	to hold, to embrace, to hug	9.28
bǎochí	2	保持		V	to keep (up a good thing going)	1.44
bàochóu	3	報酬	报酬	N	reward, pay	10.18
bāokuò	2	包括		V	to include	2.14
bàolì	4	暴力		N	violence	5
bàoyuàn	4	抱怨		V	to complain, to grumble	6.27
bāozhuāng	4	包裝	包装	V/N	to pack, to dress up, package	5.44
bēi	2	背		V	to carry on the back	2.35
bēibāo	3	背包		N	knapsack, backpack	2
běnkēshēng		本科生		N	undergraduate student	9
běnlǐng	2	本領	本领	N	skill, ability	10.02
běnshēn	3	本身		N	itself, oneself, per se	6.40
biànchéng	1	變成	变成	RV	to change into	1
biǎoshì	1	表示		V	to show, to express (usually feelings), to indicate	8.33
biǎoxiàn	1	表現	表现	V/N	to display, performance	5.06
biāozhǔn	2	標準	标准	N	standard, criterion	10
bǐcǐ	3	彼此		Adv	mutually	1.26
bié kāi wánxiào le!		別開玩笑了！	别开玩笑了！	IE	<口> Stop joking around!	1
bié tí le		別提了		IE	<口> Don't even mention it!	7.04
bǐlì	2	比例		N	proportion	8.38
bìmiǎn	2	避免		V	to avoid	2.40

bìngdú	4	病毒		N	virus	4
bǐrú	2	比如		Adv	for example	9
bìyào	2	必要		Adj/N	necessary, indispensable, need	9.43
bìyè	2	畢業	毕业	V/N	to graduate, graduation	9
bō	4	播		V	to broadcast	6.06
bō	3	撥	拨	V	to dial	10
bú jiàn bú sàn		不見不散	不见不散	IE	Be there or be square.	1
bú xiànghuà	3	不像話	不象话	IE	ridiculous, outrageous, unreasonable	3.02
búduàn	2	不斷	不断	Adv	unceasingly, continuously	6.35
búguò		不過	不过	Adv	merely, no more than	5.41
bújiànde	3	不見得	不见得	Adv	not necessarily/likely	4.07
bóshì	3	博士		N	Ph.D.	9
búshì...ma	2	不是…嗎	不是…吗	IE	<口>Isn't it right?	3.06
búwàihū		不外乎		V	to be nothing more than	5.28
búxìng		不幸		Adv/ Adj/N	unfortunate(ly), misfortune	8.22
bù chī zhè yí tào		不吃這一套	不吃这一套	IE	to not allow oneself to be pushed around	10
bù zhīdào zěnme gǎo de		不知道怎麼搞的	不知道怎么搞的	IE	I don't know how this happened.	4
bùfáng		不妨		IE	might as well, why not (Ving)	8.08
bùjīn	3	不禁		Adv	can't help (doing sth.)	7.44
bùjǐn	2	不僅	不仅	Conj	not only	2.04
bùliáng	2	不良		Adj	bad, harmful	6
bùmǎn	3	不滿	不满	N/Adj	discontent, unsatisfied	1.23
bùtíng	3	不停		Adv	without stopping, incessantly	5.20
bùzhī-bùjué		不知不覺	不知不觉	Adv	unconsciously, unaware	6
bùzú	3	不足		V	to be not sufficient	9
C						
cāi	2	猜		V	to guess	1
càidān	4	菜單	菜单	N	menu	6
cǎifǎng	4	採訪	采访	V	to cover, to interview (for news report), to gather news	5.15
cǎn	3	慘	惨	Adj	tragic	10.32
cānjiā	1	參加	参加	V	to join, to attend, to take part in	3
cānyù	4	參與	参与	V	to participate in	6.16
cāoxīn	3	操心		VO	to worry, to trouble about	8.24
céngjīng	2	曾經	曾经	Adv	once, ever	3.41
chā	2	插		V	to insert, to interpose	7.39
chābié	3	差別		N	difference	2.39
chángdá		長達	长达	V	to last for (time spent)	7.40
chángduǎn	4	長短	长短	N	length	6

chángqī	2	長期	长期	Adj/ N	long-term, long period of time	3.36
chàngxiāo	4	暢銷	畅销	V	to sell well	6.33
chǎnpǐn	2	產品	产品	N	product	7.32
chǎnshēng	2	產生	产生	V	to create (problems, influence) , to emerge	4.19
chǎo	2	吵		V	to quarrel	2.25
cháoshī	3	潮濕	潮湿	Adj	wet, moist, damp	2.07
chèn	2	趁		V/ Conj	to take advantage of (sth.), while (doing sth. else)…	3.01
chēng	2	稱	称	V	to call, to say, to weigh	2.02
chéngjī	1	成績	成绩	N	grade, result, achievement	9.15
chéngkè	3	乘客		N	passenger	10
chéngrèn	2	承認	承认	V	to admit, to acknowledge, to recognize	5.09
chéngshí	2	誠實	诚实	Adj	honest	7.19
chéngwéi	2	成為	成为	V	to become, to turn into (+N) cp. 變成+ Adj	2.33
chènyī	2	襯衣	衬衣	N	<PRC> shirt <TW>襯衫	7
chūbǎn	2	出版		V	to publish, to come out	5
chúcǐ yǐwài	4	除此以外		IE	except for this, in addition	1
chūjià		出價	出价	VO	to bid (as in an auction)	7
chún	3	純	纯	Adj	pure	5
chóngbài	4	崇拜		V	to worship, to adore	5
chōngmǎn	2	充滿	充满	V	to be brimming/ permeated with	10.44
chūshēng	2	出生		N/V	birth, to be born	8.37
chòu	2	臭		Adj	<PRC> foul, stinking, <TW>爛làn	3.14
chūxiàn	1	出現	出现	V	to appear, to arise, to emerge	6.37
chuàngzào	2	創造	创造	V	to create, to produce, to bring about	8.11
chǔlǐ	2	處理	处理	V	to handle, to deal with, to dispose of	4.05
cìshù	4	次數	次数	N	number of times, frequency	7
cǐwài	2	此外		Conj	besides, in addition, moreover	8.41
cún	2	存		V	to save, to deposit (money), to keep, to accumulate	4.04
cóngcǐ	2	從此	从此	Adv	henceforth, thereupon	7
cóngshì	2	從事	从事	V	to go in for, to be engaged in (a profession or career)	10.16
cúnzài	2	存在		V/N	to exist, existence	9.35
cuòzhé	3	挫折		N	setback, reverse	8.21

D

dǎ chē		打車	打车	VO	to take a taxi <TW>搭計程車	6
dǎ ěrguāng		打耳光		VO	<口> to slap sb. in the face, to box sb.'s ears	9
dǎ zhāohu	3	打招呼		VO	to say hello, to greet sb.	3.40
dá'àn	2	答案		N	solution, answer, key	4.30

dǎbàn	2	打扮		V/N	to dress/make up, to pose as	1.03
dàbǎo ěrfú		大飽耳福	大饱耳福	IE	to have a treat for the ears, to listen to good music	5
dádào	2	達到	达到	V	to achieve, to reach, to attain	3.09
dǎdǔ		打賭	打赌	VO	to make a bet, to bet	6.10
dài	2	代		N	generation	6
dàijià	2	代價	代价	N	price, cost	5.22
dǎkāi		打開	打开	V	to open, to unfold, to turn on	4
dàliàng	2	大量		N	large quantity, mass	9
dàlíng qīngnián		大齡青年	大龄青年	N	<PRC> single young persons over 30	8
dāndān		單單	单单	Adv	only, alone	10.38
dānshēn guìzú		單身貴族	单身贵族	N	unmarried/single adults (lit. single nobles)	8.01
dānwèi	2	單位	单位	N	unit in organization (one works in/for) or measurement	9.36
dào cǐ wéi zhǐ	3	到此為止	到此为止	IE	to this point, thus far, up to now	10
dàodé	2	道德		N	morality, ethics, morals	6.28
dàoli	1	道理		N	reason, rationality, the right way	5
dàoqiàn	2	道歉		VO	to apologize	4.44
dǎoyǎn	3	導演	导演	N/V	director, to direct (film/play/etc.)	5.08
dǎoyóu	4	導遊	导游	N	tour guide	2
dǎsuàn	1	打算		N/V	plan, to plan	2.12
dàyī		大一		N	freshman	2
dāying	2	答應	答应	V	to agree to do sth., to promise, to answer	3.12
dàyuē	2	大約	大约	Adv	probably, about, around	3.31
dǎzhé		打折		VO	to have a discount	6.02
déjiǎng	2	得獎	得奖	VO	to win a prize	5.02
diǎn	1	點	点	V	to order (dishes), to check one by one, to hint	1.11
diǎn	1	點	点	V/N	to light, dot	10.04
diànshìjù		電視劇	电视剧	N	TV series	6
diànshìtái	2	電視台	电视台	N	TV station	6
diàochá	2	調查	调查	V/N	to investigate, to look into	9.04
dìng	2	訂	订	V	to book (seats), to order (books, etc.)	1.17
diū	1	丟		V/N	to lose, to misplace	1.15
diūrén	4	丟人		VO	to lose face	8
dìqū	2	地區	地区	N	area, region	2.38
díquè	2	的確	的确	Adv	certainly, indeed	4.09
dìwèi	2	地位		N	position, status	1
dúpǐn	4	毒品		N	drugs, narcotics	4.25
dúzhě	2	讀者	读者	N	reader	6.11

duī	3	堆		N/M/V	pile, heap, to pile up	6.01
duìfu	2	對付	对付	V	to deal/cope with, to tackle, to make do	4.06
duìshǒu	4	對手	对手	N	opponent, adversary, match	9.18
duǒ	2	躲		V	to hide (oneself), to dodge, to avoid	10.05
duō cǐ yì jǔ		多此一舉	多此一举	IE	to make an unnecessary move	10
duōshǎo		多少		Adv	somewhat, to some extent	8.20

F

fābiǎo	2	發表	发表	V	to publish, to issue	6.12
fāmíng	2	發明	发明	V/N	to invent, invention	4.36
fǎn'ér	3	反而		Adv	on the contrary, instead (used after subject)	9
fǎnduì	1	反對	反对	V/N	to oppose, to be against	9
fǎngǎn	4	反感		V/N	to be disgusted with, dislike	7.30
fǎngfú	2	彷彿	仿佛	V	to seem, as if, to be more or less the same	6.24
fàngqì	2	放棄	放弃	V	to give up, to abandon	3.38
fāngshì	2	方式		N	way, fashion, pattern	4.12
fàngsōng	3	放鬆	放松	RV	to relax, to loosen	5.24
fànlàn	3	泛濫	泛滥	V	to overflow, to inundate, to be in flood	7
fánnǎo	4	煩惱	烦恼	N/V	worry, to worry	8.02
fǎnyìng	2	反映		V	to reflect, to dreport	5.32
fǎnyìng	2	反應	反应	N/V	reaction, response, to react	9.29
fāzhǎn	1	發展	发展	N/V	to develop, to expand	1.42
fēi	3	非		Adj/Adv/Pref	not, no, non	9
fēnbié	2	分別		Adv/N	separately, difference	8.29
fèng	4	縫	缝	V	to sew	2
fēng	3	瘋	疯	Adj	crazy	10.37
fēngfù	1	豐富	丰富	V/Adj	to enrich, rich, abundant	3.11
fēnggé	3	風格	风格	N	style	5
fēnpèi	2	分配		V	to allot, to assign, to distribute	9.27
fēnxī	2	分析		V/N	to analyze, analysis	5.38
fúhé	2	符合		V	to accord/tally with, to conform to	7.35
fúqì		福氣	福气	N	happy lot, good fortune	8
fǒudìng	2	否定		V/N	to negate, deny, negation	10.31
fūyǎn	4	敷衍		V	to be perfunctory	10
fúzhuāng	4	服裝	服装	N	dress, clothing	9
fùchū	4	付出		V	to expend (time, efforts, life (but not money))	5.21
fùdān	3	負擔	负担	N	burden, load	9.13

fùjìn	1	附近		N/	vicinity, nearby	1
fùmiàn		負面	负面	Adj	negative	9.39
Fùqīnjié		父親節	父亲节	N	Father's Day	6
fùzé	1	負責	负责	V	to be responsible for, to be in charge of	10.33
fùzhàng		付帳	付帐	VO	to pay a bill	1
G						
gǎibiān	3	改編	改编	V	to adapt, to rearrange, to revise	6.08
gǎibiàn	1	改變	改变	V	to change, to transform	3.25
gǎijìn	2	改進	改进	V	to improve	10
gān	2	乾	干	Adj	dry	2.08
gǎn	1	敢		V	to dare	6.09
gāncuì	2	乾脆	干脆	Adv	simply, to make a quick decision to V	5.35
gǎndào	1	感到		RV	to feel, to sense	9.24
gǎndòng	2	感動	感动	V	to move, to touch, to be moved	10.43
gāngà		尷尬	尴尬	Adj	embarrassed	10
gǎnkǎi/gǎnkài	4	感慨		N/V	feelings, to sign with emotion	6
gànmá	2	幹嘛	干吗	IE	What are you doing? What's up?	10.11
gǎnmào	1	感冒	感冒	N	cold	10
gǎnqíng	2	感情		N	emotion, feeling	10.14
gǎnrén		感人		Adj	touching, moving	5
gāojí	3	高級	高级	Adj	high in rank/grade/quality	1
gāokǎo	4	高考		N	college entrance examination <TW>大學聯考	9
gāolóu		高樓	高楼	N	tall building	6
gāoyuán	2	高原		N	plateau, highland	2
gē	2	擱	搁	V	to put	10.27
gěicuò		給錯	给错	RV	to make a mistake in giving (money)	7
gēnpìchóng		跟屁蟲	跟屁虫	N	a tagalong [follow-buttocks-worm]	3
gēshǒu	4	歌手		N	singer, vocalist	5
gèzi	2	個子	个子	N	height, stature, build	1
gūjì	2	估計	估计	V	to estimate, to appraise, to reckon	3.17
gōngfu	2	功夫		N	martial art, skill	5
gōngfu bú fù yǒuxīnrén		功夫不負有心人	功夫不负有心人	IE	Those who work hard are rewarded. <TW>皇天不負苦心人	9
gōnggong		公公		N	father-in-law	3
gōngjù	2	工具		N	tool	2
gōngkāi	2	公開	公开	V	to make public	5.19
gōngnéng	3	功能		N	function	7.11
gōngyù		公寓		N	flats, apartment	7
gòumǎi	3	購買	购买	V	to purchase	4.08

gōutōng	4	溝通	沟通	V	to communicate	2.11
guà	1	掛	挂	V	to hang, to put up	3.18
guài	3	怪		V	to blame	9.06
guǎn	2	管		V	to bother about, to be in charge of	10.10
guǎnggào	2	廣告	广告	N	advertisement	7.01
guāngpán		光盤	光盘	N	V.C.D. <TW>光碟guāngdié	5
guānjiàn	2	關鍵	关键	N	key, crux	6.43
guānniàn	3	觀念	观念	N	concept	6.29
guānzhòng	2	觀眾	观众	N	spectator, audience	5
guǐ	2	鬼		Suf	term of abuse (e.g., 小氣鬼、酒鬼), ghost	1
guīdìng	2	規定		N/V	rule, policy, to stipulate, to set	7.15
guīgōngyú		歸功於	归功于	V	to attribute success to, to give credit to	5.12
guījǔ	3	規矩	规矩	N	rule, custom, social etiquette	10.13
gùkè	2	顧客	顾客	N	customer, shopper, client	7.07
gǔlì	2	鼓勵	鼓励	V	to encourage, to urge	9.14
guóchǎn	4	國產	国产	N	domestically made	5
guòfèn	3	過分	过分	Adv	excessively, over-, undue	8.23
guójìhuà		國際化	国际化	V/N	to internationalize, internationalization	1
guòqī		過期	过期	VO	to expire, to be overdue	7.22
Guóqìngjié	3	國慶節	国庆节	N	National Day	2
guǒrán	2	果然		Adv	really, as expected, sure enough	6.23
guòshí		過時	过时	Adj	out-of-date	5
gǔpiào	4	股票		N	stock	6.30
gùrán	3	固然		Conj	although	2.22
gùyì	2	故意		Adv	intentionally, willfully	10.17

H

hǎibào		海報	海报	N	poster, playbill	5
hángliè	3	行列		N	ranks, procession	8.26
háobù	2	毫不	毫不	Adv	not at all	10
hǎogǎn	4	好感		N	favorable impression	8.34
hàomǎ	2	號碼	号码	N	(serial) number	3.44
hàoqíxīn	3	好奇心		N	curiosity	4.29
hǎorén yǒu hǎo bào		好人有好報	好人有好报	IE	One good turn deserves another.	2
háowú	2	毫無	毫无	V	to completely lack	7.16
hé	4	何		Pron/Adv	who?, what?, why?, how? (e.g., 何時、何地、何必)	6.38
hē xǐjiǔ		喝喜酒		VO	to drink at wedding feast, to attend wedding banquet	8

hēi	1	黑		Adj	greedy, wicked	6.26
hēikè		黑客		N	<PRC>hacker　<TW>駭客hàikè	4
hélǐ	2	合理		Adj	rational, reasonable, equitable	5.25
héqi	4	和氣	和气	Adj	kind, amiable	10
héshì	1	合適	合适	Adj	suitable, appropriate, right	3.30
hèsuìpiàn		賀歲片	贺岁片	N	films that celebrate Chinese New Year	5
hóngniáng		紅娘	红娘	N	match-maker	8
hūnyīn	2	婚姻		N	marriage, matrimony	8.04
hūrán	1	忽然		Adv	suddenly	4.20
hūshì	3	忽視	忽视	V	to overlook, to neglect, to ignore	3.32
húshuō	3	胡說	胡说	IE	<口> to talk nonsense	1.10
huábǎn		滑板		N	skateboard	3
huàidàn	3	壞蛋	坏蛋	N	scoundrel	4
huáiyí	3	懷疑	怀疑	V/N	to suspect, doubt	4.21
huàn	1	換	换	V	to change, to exchange	7.13
huánghūnliàn		黃昏戀	黄昏恋	N	love between the elderly (lit. sunset love)	3
huánjìng	2	環境	环境	N	environment, surroundings	1
huānyíng	1	歡迎	欢迎	V	to welcome	1.07
huíqǐng		回請	回请	V	to return hospitality, to give return banquet	1
huíyì	2	回憶	回忆	N/V	recollection, to recall	6.17
huópō	2	活潑	活泼	Adj	lively, vivacious	1.02
J						
jí	2	集		M	volume, episode (as in a TV series)	6
jiā/jiá	2	夾	夹	V	to press, to squeeze, to clip	10.26
jiàgé	2	價格	价格	N	price	7.14
jiǎnchá	1	檢查	检查	N/V	examination, to check	3.23
jiānchí	1	堅持	坚持	V	to persist in, to insist on	3.35
jiǎnféi		減肥	减肥	VO	to lose weight	3.19
jiǎngjiū	3	講究	讲究	V	to pay attention to, to be particular about	8.18
jiāngjiù		將就	将就	V	to make do	10
jiǎnlì		簡歷	简历	N	<PRC> curriculum vitae, résumé <TW>履歷lǚlì	9
jiànlì	2	建立		V	to establish, to set up	1.41
jiǎnqīng	2	減輕	减轻	RV	to lighten, to ease, to mitigate	8.44
jiànshēn		健身		VO	to keep fit	3.04
jiànyì	2	建議	建议	V	to suggest	2.24
jiǎnzhí	3	簡直	简直	Adv	simply	6.25
jiāo'ào	2	驕傲	骄傲	Adj/N	arrogant, conceited, to be proud, pride	1
jiāojìwǔ		交際舞	交际舞	N	ballroom/social dancing	3

jiàqī	3	假期		N	vacation, holiday	9
jiǎrú	3	假如		Conj	if, supposing, in case	8.30
jiārù	3	加入		V	to join, to add, to put in	8.25
jiàzhí	2	價值	价值	N	value, worth	5.37
jiēchù	2	接觸	接触	V	to come into contact with, to get in touch with	5.27
jièdiào		戒掉		RV	to stop/kick (bad habit)	4.26
jiēduàn	2	階段	阶段	N	stage, phase	9.32
jiéhé	2	結合	结合	V	to combine, to unite, to integrate	6.22
jiémù	1	節目	节目	N	program, item (on program)	8
jiéshí		節食	节食	VO	to go on diet	5
jiéshù	1	結束	结束	V	to end	2.30
jiézhàng		結帳	结帐	VO	to settle accounts	1.39
jiēzhe	1	接著	接着	Adv	next, immediately after, to follow	8.28
jièzhù		借住		V	to stay over at sb. else's place	2
jīhuì	1	機會	机会	N	chance, opportunity	8
jījí	2	積極	积极	Adj	active, energetic, positive	3.16
jìjié	2	季節	季节	N	season	2.05
jīliè	2	激烈		Adj	intense, sharp, fierce	9.12
jímáng	2	急忙		Adv	in haste, hurriedly	3.43
jīn	1	斤		N	half of a kilogram	3
jǐn	1	緊	紧	Adj	tight	3.21
jīngcǎi	1	精彩		Adj	brilliant, splendid	3.13
jǐngdiǎn		景點	景点	N	scenic spot	2.15
jīngguò	1	經過	经过	Prep/V	after, through, as a result of, to go through	4.39
jīnglǐ	2	經理	经理	N	manager	7
jīnglì	2	經歷	经历	V/N	to experience, experience	2.19
jǐngqì		景氣	景气	N/Adj	prosperity, boom	5.39
jìngrán	3	竟然		Adv	unexpectedly, to one's surprise	5
jīngshén	1	精神		N	spirit, mind	6.36
jǐnguǎn	2	儘管	尽管	Conj	even though, despite	5.05
jìngzhēng	3	競爭	竞争	N	competition, to compete	9.11
jǐnjǐn	2	僅僅	仅仅	Adv	only, merely	6.15
jìnkǒu	2	進口	进口	V	to import, to enter port	5.26
jǐnkuài	4	儘快	尽快	Adv	as soon as possible	8.15
jīnqián	4	金錢	金钱	N	money, wealth	9
jìnzhǐ	3	禁止		V	to prohibit, to ban	10.09
jíshǐ	3	即使		Conj	even, even if/though	1.43
jìsuàn	2	計算	计算	V/N	to compute, planning	4.32
jiǔbā		酒吧		N	bar	3
jiǔdiàn	3	酒店		N	hotel	1

jìxù	1	繼續	继续	V	to continue	8.12
jūzhù	3	居住		N	living	2.37
jué	2	決	决	Adv	definitely (not)	9.19
jùhuì	4	聚會	聚会	N	gathering, to get together	1
jùjué	2	拒絕	拒绝	V	to refuse, to reject, to decline	6.18
jùyuàn	3	劇院	剧院	N	theater	6
K						
kāiyè		開業	开业	VO	\<PRC\> to start business \<TW\>開張	7.02
kǎlā OK		卡拉OK		N	karaoke	1
kàndeqǐ		看得起	看得起	RV	to think highly of	10
kànshàng		看上		RV	to take fancy to, to settle on	7.06
kǎolǜ	2	考慮	考虑	V	to think over, to consider	1.13
kǎoshang		考上		RV	to pass an entrance examination	9
kěxī	3	可惜		Adj/ Ph	unfortunately, It's a pity!	3.15
kěxìn		可信		Adj	trustworthy, reliable	7.08
kēxuéjiā	2	科學家	科学家	N	scientist	4
kǒngpà	2	恐怕		Adv	perhaps, I think, I'm afraid	2.13
kǒudài	2	口袋		N	pocket	2
kuàicān	3	快餐		N	quick meal, fast food	1
kuān	2	寬	宽	Adj	wide, broad	10.24
kuàngqiě	3	況且	况且	Conj	moreover, besides	9.38
kùn	2	睏	困	Adj	tired	10.07
L						
láizì	2	來自	来自	V	to come/stem from	5
lǎnduò	4	懶惰	懒惰	Adj	lazy, indolent	3
làngfèi	2	浪費	浪费	V/Adj	to waste, to squander, extravagant	4.14
lǎobǎixìng	2	老百姓		N	common people, civilians	3.10
lǎobǎn	2	老板		N	boss	9
lǎobàn		老伴		N	one's spouse, my wife/husband	6
lǎodiàoyá		老掉牙		Adj	old and shabby, obsolete	6
lǎogōng		老公		N	husband	7
lǎopó	3	老婆		N	\<口\> wife	8
lǎotóur	2	老頭兒	老头儿	N	\<口\> old man/chap	3
Léi Fēng		雷鋒	雷锋	N	a model citizen who is always ready to help others	2
lèng	3	愣		SV	distracted, stupefied	10.06
lèqù	4	樂趣	乐趣	N	delight, pleasure, joy	2
liàn'ài	2	戀愛	恋爱	V/N	to love, romantic attachment	8.06
liáng	2	涼	凉	Adj	cool, cold	10.25
liánluò	3	聯絡	联络	V	to contact	1.40
liǎo	1	了		V	to end, to finish, to settle	7

líng	4	靈	灵	Adj	effective, quick, sharp	7.21
língdǎo	1	領導	领导	N	leader, leadership	9.01
línghuāqián		零花錢	零花钱	N	pocket money <TW>零用錢	1
língshí		零食		N	between-meal nibbles, snacks	3
lìngyíbàn		另一半		N	the other half	8
línjū	2	鄰居	邻居	N	neighbor	2
liúchǎn		流產	流产	N/VO	abortion, miscarriage, to miscarry	8
lìwài	4	例外		N	exception	1
lìyì	2	利益		N	interest, benefit, profit	5.17
lǚyóu	3	旅遊	旅游	N	tour, tourism	2
luàn	1	亂	乱	Adv	(to do something) carelessly, randomly	1.31
lúndào		輪到	轮到	V	to be one's turn	10
luànqībāzāo	4	亂七八糟	乱七八糟	IE	at sixes and sevens, in a mess	5.14
luòwǔ		落伍		Adj	to be outdated	3.03

M

mǎi yī sòngyī		買一送一	买一送一	IE	buy one, get one free	7
mǎnyì	1	滿意	满意	Adj	satisfied, pleased	5.23
mǎnzú	2	滿足	满足	V	to satisfy, to be contented	5.31
máodùn	2	矛盾		Adj/	contradictory, contradiction	1
méi shénme dàbùliǎode		沒什麼大不了的	没什么大不了的	IE	No big deal.	4
méitǐ		媒體	媒体	N	media	7
mèn/mēn	3	悶	闷	Adj/V	bored, depressed, stuffy, to cover tightly	5.30
mèngzhōng qíngrén		夢中情人	梦中情人	N	dream lover	8
ménpiào		門票	门票	N	admission fee	2
miǎnbuliǎo		免不了		RV	to be unavoidable, to be bound to	3.07
miǎnfèi	4	免費	免费	Adj/VO	to be free of charge	1
miànshì		面試	面试	N/V	interview, to interview	9.31
miáotiáo		苗條	苗条	Adj	slim, slender	3
mìmǎ		密碼	密码	N	password	4
míngqì		名氣	名气	N	reputation, fame, name	9
míngxiǎn	2	明顯	明显	Adj	clear, obvious	6.41
míngzhù		名著		N	famous book/work	6
mínzú	1	民族		N	ethnic group, nationality	2
mìqiè	2	密切		Adj	close, intimate	1
mìshū	3	秘書	秘书	N	secretary	9
mòfēi		莫非		IE	can it be that	10
mòmíngqímiào	4	莫名其妙		IE	to be baffled, inexplicable	7
mǒu	2	某		Pre/Adj	certain, some	6.14

mùdì	2	目的		N	purpose, aim, goal	5.43
N						
ná...kāixīn		拿⋯開心	拿⋯开心	IE	to make fun of...	3
nàixīn	2	耐心		N	patience	1
nán zhǔ wài nǚ zhǔ nèi		男主外女主內		IE	The man is in charge of work outside and the woman takes care of work in the house.	8
nándào	2	難道	难道	MA	Do you really mean to say that...?	1.14
nánshì		男士		N	man	8
nánshòu	2	難受	难受	Adj	to feel unwell/unhappy/pained	5
nánwàng		難忘	难忘	Adj	unforgettable, memorable	2.44
nányǐ	3	難以	难以	V	to be difficult to...	5.36
nèiyī		內衣		N	underwear	2
nì		膩	腻	Adj	bored/tired of ...	5.29
niándài	2	年代		N	day and age, years, decade	8
niánlíng	2	年齡	年龄	N	age	8
niē yì bǎ hàn		捏一把汗		IE	to break into a cold sweat	10
nóngcūn	1	農村	农村	N	rural area, countryside	5
nǚqiángrén		女強人	女强人	N	successful career woman	8.16
O						
ǒuxiàng		偶像		N	image, idol, model	5
P						
pāi	1	拍		V	to shoot film	5.03
pāi mǎpì		拍馬屁	拍马屁	IE	<口> to flatter, butter up	9.03
páiduì	4	排隊	排队	VO	to stand in line	10.39
páihángbǎng		排行榜		N	a rating board	6
páizi	3	牌子		N	brand, trademark, sign	7.12
pànduàn	2	判斷	判断	V	to judge, to determine	1.38
pào bā		泡吧		VO	to go to bars to have fun	9
péi	2	陪		V	to accompany	10.01
pèifú	3	佩服		V	to admire	10.28
pèngdào	2	碰到		RV	to run into	2.18
piàn	1	片		N	films	5
piányí méi hǎohuò		便宜沒好貨	便宜没好货	IE	You get what you pay for.	7
piàofáng		票房		N	box office	5
piàojià		票價	票价	N	ticket price	5
píngděng	2	平等		Adj/N	equal, equality	8.19
pínghéng	3	平衡		N/Adj	balance, balanced	8.39
pīpíng	1	批評	批评	V/N	to criticize, criticism	5.11
píyī		皮衣		N	fur/leather clothing	7
pòhuài	2	破壞	破坏	V	to destroy, to wreck	4.15

pǔchá	4	普查		N	general survey/investigation	8
pǔsù/púsù	2	樸素	朴素	Adj	simple, plain	10

Q

(qī)piàn	2	（欺）騙	（欺）骗	V	to deceive, to fool	7.05
qī	2	期		N	period of time, phase, stage (e.g., 有效期、退貨期、危險期)	7
qiàdàng	3	恰當	恰当	Adj	appropriate, fitting, proper, suitable	6.04
qiáng	2	強	强	Adj	strong, better	9.16
qiǎng	2	搶	抢	V	to fight with, to snatch	6.07
qiántú	2	前途		N	future, prospects	9.26
qiáo	2	瞧		V	to look, to see	9.10
qiāo	2	敲		V	to knock	7.20
qiǎo	2	巧		Adv	coincidentally	9.08
qícì	2	其次		Adv	second	2.42
qìfen	3	氣氛	气氛	N	atmosphere, ambience	10.12
qīfu	3	欺負	欺负	V	to browbeat, to take advantage of, to pick on	10.34
qìhòu	2	氣候	气候	N	climate, situation	2.03
qīngcháo		清朝		N	Qing dynasty (1644–1911)	6
qīngjiéjì		清潔劑	清洁剂	N	detergent	7
qǐngkè	2	請客	请客	VO	to treat sb. (to meal/show/etc.)	1
qíngshū		情書	情书	N	love letter	4
qǐngwèn	1	請問	请问	N	May I ask…?	2.01
qīngxián		清閑	清闲	Adj	at leisure, idle	3
qíngxù	2	情緒	情绪	N	emotions, feelings, mood	4
qīnqiè	2	親切	亲切	Adj	cordial, warm	10.30
qīnrén	3	親人	亲人	N	close relatives, dear ones	1
qiúduì	4	球隊	球队	N	sports team	3
qiúmí	4	球迷		N	sports fan	3
qīpiàn	2	欺騙	欺骗	V	to cheat	10
qízhōng	2	其中		N	in/among (it/them/which/etc.)	1.09
qúnzi	2	裙子		N	skirt	3
qǔ	2	取		V	to take, to get, to fetch	2.23
qǔ	3	娶		V	to take a wife, to get married	8.13
quán	1	全		Adj/Adv	whole, entire, completely	7.03
quàngào	3	勸告	劝告	N	advice	9.23
quánlì	3	權力	权力	N	power, authority	5
quánmiàn	2	全面		Adj	comprehensive, all-round	9.37
quèdìng	2	確定	确定	V	to confirm	10

R

rè	1	熱	热	N	craze, fad	6.39

rěnbuzhù	3	忍不住		RV	can't bear, can't help but do sth.	5.01
réncái	2	人才		N	person of ability/talent	9
rēng	2	扔		V	to throw, to toss	10.19
réngōng	2	人工		Adj/N	man-made, manual work	8
réngrán	2	仍然		Adv	still, yet	1.36
rènhé	1	任何		Adj	any, whatever	3.33
rěnshòu	3	忍受		V	to endure, to bear	7.38
rènwù	2	任務	任务	N	assignment, task, job	9.33
rényuán		人緣	人缘	N	relations with other people	8
rèqíng	1	熱情	热情	Adv	enthusiastically	2.31
rèzhōngyú		熱衷於	热衷于	V	to be keen on, to be very fond of	2.16
rìqī	2	日期		N	date	4
rúcǐ	3	如此		Adv	thus, like this	10
rúhé	2	如何		Adv	how, how about it	2.32
ruǎnjiàn	4	軟件	软件	N	<PRC> software,　<TW>軟體	4
S						
sēngduō-zhōushǎo		僧多粥少		IE	not enough to go around	7
sèqíng		色情		N/Adj	pornography, pornographic	4
shājià		殺價	杀价	VO	to slash prices	10
shāngchǎng	2	商場	商场	N	market, bazaar	7
shàngdàng	2	上當	上当	VO	to be taken in, to be fooled/cheated	7.09
shāngjiā		商家		N	merchant, business person	7
shāngpǐn	2	商品		N	commodity, goods, merchandise	7
shàngwǎng		上網	上网	VO	to log on　　　　↔下網	4
shāngyè	2	商業	商业	N	business, commerce	5
shǎoshù	2	少數	少数	N	small number, few, minority	2.09
shěbùdé	3	捨不得	舍不得	RV	to begrudge doing sth., to loathe to part with or use	1.30
shèhuì	1	社會	社会	N	society	9
shèjì	2	設計	设计	V/N	to design, plan	5.16
shēncái	3	身材		N	figure, stature	3.20
shēndù	3	深度		N	profundity, depth	5
shěng	2	省		V	to save	2.17
shèng(xià)	1	剩(下)		V	to be left (over), to remain	1.25
shěngde	3	省得		Conj	lest	1.12
shénjīngbìng		神經病	神经病	IE	<口> (You're) crazy!	8
shènzhì	3	甚至		Conj	even (to the point of), so much so that	3.26
shì	1	市		N	market (e.g., 書市、花市、菜市、魚市), city	6
shífēn	1	十分		Adj	very, fully, utterly	9.22
shìhé	2	適合	适合	V	to suit, to fit	5.13

shíjì	2	實際	实际	Adj/N	practical, reality	6.05
shíkèbiǎo	2	時刻表	时刻表	N	timetable, schedule	2
shílì	4	實力	实力	N	actual strength, substance	9
shímáo	4	時髦	时髦	Adj	fashionable, in vogue	1
shīqù	2	失去		V	to lose	7.41
shīwàng	2	失望		V/Adj	to become disappointed, to lose (hope)	2.26
shíyàn	2	實驗	实验	V/N	to experiment, test	7
shìyàng	4	式樣	式样	N	style, type, pattern	7
shìyè	2	事業	事业	N	career, undertaking	1.37
shǐyòng	1	使用		V	to use, to employ, to apply	4.38
shǐzhōng	2	始終	始终	Adv	from beginning to end	4.35
shízú	4	十足		Adj	100 percent, out-and-out	9
shūcài	2	蔬菜		N	vegetables, greens	3.29
shúliàn	2	熟練	熟练	Adj	skilled, proficient	10.21
shūshu/shúshu	2	叔叔		N	father's younger brother, uncle	8
shōuhuò	2	收穫	收获	N	gains, results	1.34
shòuhuòyuán		售貨員	售货员	N	shop assistant, salesclerk	7
shǒujī		手機	手机	N	cellular phone	7
shōujù		收據	收据	N	receipt	7
shōushìlǜ		收視率	收视率	N	(TV/etc.) ratings	8
shǒuxiān	2	首先		Adv	first	2.36
shǒuyǎngyang		手癢癢	手痒痒	IE	<口> to have an itch to do sth.	4.24
shǔ	1	數	数	V	<口> to count, to be reckoned as	1.04
shuǐhú		水壺	水壶	N	kettle, watering can	6
shuōbudìng	3	說不定	说不定	IE	perhaps, maybe	8.09
shuōdàozuòdào		說到做到	说到做到	IE	to keep one's promise	9
shuōmíng	1	說明	说明	N/V	explanation, to explain	1.35
shuòshì		碩士	硕士	N	Master (of Arts), M.A.	9
sǐjī		死機	死机	VO	<PRC> to crash (computer), <TW> 當機	4
sīkǎo	3	思考		V	to ponder over, to reflect on	4.18
súhuà	3	俗話	俗话	N	common saying, proverb	7
sòng lǐ	3	送禮	送礼	VO	to give sb. a present	9
suànle	2	算了		IE	<口> Let it be. Forget it.	2.29
sùdù	2	速度		N	speed	4.33
suíbiàn	2	隨便	随便	Adv	casually, to do as one pleases	2.27
suíshí	2	隨時	随时	Adv	at any time, whenever necessary	4.03
suǒ	2	所		M	for houses/schools	9
suǒwèi	2	所謂	所谓	Adj	so-called	4.16

T

| tàidù | 1 | 態度 | 态度 | N | manner, attitude | 10.29 |

Pinyin	Tone	Traditional	Simplified	Type	Definition	Lesson
Tàijíquán		太極拳	太极拳	N	a kind of shadowboxing	3
tān	4	貪	贪	V	to have an insatiable desire for, to covet	1.06
tān	3	攤	摊	N	bookstall, bookstand	6.34
tì…shuōhuà		替…說話	替…说话	IE	<口> to speak for (sb.)	9.05
tián	2	填		V	to fill in (form)	4.10
tiāo	2	挑		V	to choose	1.27
tiāotì		挑剔		Adj	nitpicking	5.34
tíchū		提出		RV	to put forward, to raise, to pose	8.36
tiē	2	貼	贴	V	to stick, to paste	10.08
tígāo	1	提高		V	to raise, to heighten, to enhance	4.34
tígōng	2	提供	提供	V	to provide	10
tǐng	1	挺		Adv	<口> quite, very	1.21
tǐtiē	4	體貼	体贴	Adj	showing consideration for	4
tízhí		提職	提职	VO	<PRC> to promote <TW>升職	7.25
tōngguò	1	通過	通过	Prep/V	by (means/way of), to pass, to carry (motion)	4.37
tòngkǔ	2	痛苦		N/Adj	pain, suffering	7.37
tóngshí	1	同時	同时	Conj/Adv	simultaneously with…, at the same time, meanwhile	9.17
tóngyī	4	同一		Adj	same, identical	9
túpiàn	4	圖片	图片	N	picture, photograph	4
tōulǎn		偷懶	偷懒	V	to slack off, to shirk one's duty	3.34
tóuzī	4	投資	投资	VO	to invest	6.31
tuì	1	退		V	to return, to refund	7.10
tuīxiāo	4	推銷	推销	V	to promote sale of	7.17
tuìxiū	3	退休		VO	to retire	6.32
W						
wàibiǎo	4	外表		N/Adv	outward appearance, surface	8.31
wǎngbā		網吧	网吧	N	Internet café <TW>網咖	3
wǎngluò		網絡	网络	N	<PRC> the net, the internet <TW>網路	4.01
wǎngyǒu		網友	网友	N	netpal	4
wǎngzhàn		網站	网站	N	website	4.31
wànwàn	3	萬萬	万万	Adv	absolutely (not), by no means (used only in negation)	8.35
wéichí	3	維持	维持	V	to keep, to maintain (a modicum of sth.)	5.18
wèihé		為何	为何	QW	why	1
wēixiǎn	1	危險	危险	N/Adj	danger, dangerous	4.13
wèizi		位子		N	seat, place	1
wénjiàn	2	文件		N	documents, file	4
wēnnuǎn	2	溫暖		Adj	warm	2.06

wēnróu	4	溫柔		Adj	gentle and soft	8.14
wénzhāng	1	文章		N	essay, article, literary works	6
wúliáo	4	無聊	无聊	Adj	bored, senseless, silly	3.08
wúnài		無奈	无奈	Ph	helpless, without choice	7.42
wúyí	3	無疑	无疑	Adv	undoubtedly	5.40
wǔhuì	3	舞會	舞会	N	dancing party	2
wǔtái	3	舞台		N	stage, arena	6
wǔxīngjí		五星級	五星级	N	five-star	1

X

xià	1	嚇	吓	V	to frighten, to scare	10.35
xià dìngyì	4	下定義	下定义	VO	to give a definition of, to define	6.03
xiákè		俠客	俠客	N	a person adept in martial arts and given to chivalrous conduct (in old times), chivalrous warrior	4
xián	3	嫌		V	to dislike that…	1.24
xiàn	2	線	线	N	line, thread	9
xiàndàihuà	2	現代化	现代化	V/N	to modernize, modernization	6.19
xiāngdāng	2	相當	相当	Adv	quite, fairly, considerably	7.43
Xiānggǎng		香港		N	Hong Kong	5
xiàngqiánkàn		向錢看	向钱看	IE	to care only about money, a pun of "向前看"	9
xiāngqīn/xiàngqīn		相親	相亲	VO	to get look at prospective spouse before engagement	8.03
xiǎngshòu	2	享受		N/V	to enjoy	3.24
xiāngxià	2	鄉下	乡下	N	countryside	10
xiàngzhe	1	向著	向着	V	to side with, to be partial to	10.15
xiǎnrán	2	顯然	显然	Adv	obviously, evidently	7.23
xiànshí	2	現實	现实	N/Adj	reality, practical	5.33
xiànxiàng	2	現象		N	phenomenon	9.34
xiāofèi	2	消費	消费	V	to consume	10.03
xiàoguǒ	2	效果		N	effect, result	3.37
xiàohuà	2	笑話	笑话	V/N	to laugh at, joke	1.18
xiàolǜ	2	效率		N	efficiency, productiveness	10.41
xiǎoqi		小氣	小气	Adj	stingy, mean	1.01
xiāoshòuliàng	4	銷售量	销售量	N	sales volume	6
xiàzǎi		下載	下载	V	to download	4
xīcān zhōng chī		西餐中吃		N	to eat Western-style food in the Chinese way	1
xíngchéng	2	形成		V	to take shape, to form	7.34
xìngfú	1	幸福		N/Adj	happiness, happy	8.05
xìnggé	2	性格		N	nature, disposition, temperament	1.05
xìngkuī	3	幸虧	幸亏	Adv	fortunately, luckily	4.02
xíngwéi	3	行為	行为	N	action, behavior, conduct	9.21

xíngxiàng	2	形象		N	image	5.10
xìngyùn	4	幸運	幸运	Adj	lucky	2.20
xīnkǔ	1	辛苦		Adj	hard, laborious	1.29
xìnrèn	3	信任		N/V	trust, to have confidence in	7.28
xīnxiān	2	新鮮	新鲜	Adj	novel, new, fresh	4.28
xìnxīn	2	信心		N	confidence, faith	9
xìnyòngkǎ		信用卡		N	credit card	4
xǐshǒujiān		洗手間	洗手间	N	bathroom	2
xīyǐn	2	吸引		V	to attract, to draw, to fascinate	5.07
xīzhuāng		西裝	西装	N	Western-style clothes	9
xuānchuán	2	宣傳	宣传	V/N	to give publicity to, propaganda	7.31
xuǎnzé	2	選擇	选择	V/N	to select, to opt, choice	8.42
xuélì	4	學歷	学历	N	record of formal schooling	4.27
xùnliàn	2	訓練	训练	N/V	training, to drill	4.40
xùshù	3	敘述	叙述	N/V	narration, to narrate	1.19

Y

yā	2	壓	压	V	to pressure	10.36
yālì	3	壓力	压力	N	pressure	8.17
yáng	3	洋		Adj	foreign	1
yǎng ér fáng lǎo		養兒防老	养儿防老	IE	to raise children to take care of one in one's old age	8
yǎnjì		演技		N	acting	5
yǎnqián	2	眼前		N	before one's eyes, at present	6.21
yánqíng		言情		N	love and romance	6
yánsù	2	嚴肅	严肃	Adj	serious, solemn	10.23
yǎnyuán	2	演員	演员	N	performer	5
yàome	4	要麼	要么	Conj	either, or	1.20
Yàzhōu		亞洲	亚洲	N	Asia	5
yěxǔ	1	也許	也许	Adv	perhaps, maybe	1.32
yí ge ěrduo jìn, yí ge ěrduo chū		一個耳朵進，一個耳朵出	一个耳朵进，一个耳朵出	IE	in one ear and out the other	9
yì kǒu chību chū ge pàngzi		一口吃不出個胖子	一口吃不出个胖子	IE	<口> one can't get fat after only one bite	3
yìbān		一般		Adj	general, ordinary, common	5.04
yídàn	4	一旦		Conj	once, some time or other	4.41
yíhàn	3	遺憾	遗憾	N/Adj	regret, pity	9.25
yījǐnhuánxiāng		衣錦還鄉	衣锦还乡	IE	to return home after making good	1
yīn rén ér yì		因人而異		IE	different people do things in different ways, here: to change one's manner of speaking depending on whom he is addressing.	3

yīng'ér	3	嬰兒	婴儿	N	baby, infant	8
yíngdé	4	贏得	赢得	V	to win, to gain	7.27
yīngxióng	2	英雄		N	hero	10
yíngyǎng	2	營養	营养	N	nutrition, nourishment	1
yìngzhe tóupí		硬著頭皮	硬着头皮	IE	<口> to brace oneself, to bite the bullet	7
yǐnqǐ	2	引起		V	to give rise to, to lead to	1.22
yǐnshí	4	飲食	饮食	N	food and drink, diet	2
yǐnsī		隱私	隐私	N	personal secrets, privacy	5
yīrán	3	依然	依然	Adv	still, as before	10
yìshí	2	一時	一时	N	a short while, now…	8.40
yìshù	1	藝術	艺术	N	art	5
yǐwài	2	以外		Suf	beyond, outside, other than	9
yúlè	3	娛樂	娱乐	N	entertainment, amusement	9
yǒu liǎngxiàzi		有兩下子	有两下子	IE	<口> to know one's stuff	4
yǒuchéng		有成		VO	to have achieved success	1
yǒuhàiyú		有害於	有害于	VP	to be harmful	3.27
yóuqí	1	尤其		Adv	especially	1.08
yǒusuǒ		有所		Adv	to some extent, somewhat	6.44
yóuxì	3	遊戲	游戏	N/V	game, to play	4
yǒuxiàn	3	有限		Adj	limited, finite	7.33
yǒuxiào	2	有效		Adj	effective, valid	3.22
yóuyù	3	猶豫	犹豫	V	to hesitate	10
yuánfèn		緣分	缘分	N	predestined affinity	8.10
yuángù	3	緣故	缘故	N	reason	3
yuánliàng	1	原諒	原谅	V	to excuse, to pardon	1.33
yuánzé	2	原則	原则	N	principle	7.36
yùxiān	3	預先	预先	Adv	in advance, beforehand	10.40

Z

zànchéng	2	贊成	赞成	V	to approve, to endorse	9.41
zànshí	2	暫時	暂时	Adj/Adv	temporary, temporarily	9.42
zǎoliàn		早戀	早恋	N	puppy love	1
zǎoshú		早熟		Adj	early-maturing, precocious	9.02
zázhì	3	雜誌	杂志	N	magazine	2
zé	2	則	则	Adv	then, in that case	3.42
zēngjiā	1	增加		V	to increase	2.41
zěnmezhe	4	怎麼著	怎么着	IE	What about?	10
zūnzhòng	3	尊重		V	to respect, to value	10.20
zérèn	2	責任	责任	N	duty, responsibility, blame	9.07
zhàn	1	佔	占	V	to occupy	2.10
zhàncuò		站錯	站错	RV	to stand in the wrong line	10

zhāojí	1	著急	着急	Adj	anxious	9.30
zháoxiǎng		著想	着想	V	to consider, to take into consideration	7.18
zhémó	3	折磨		V/N	to torment	10.22
zhèng	3	掙	挣	V	to earn	1.28
zhèng	4	證	证	N	certificate, card, credentials (e.g., 學生證)	2.28
zhèngfǔ	1	政府		N	govenment	9
zhēnghūn		徵婚	征婚	VO	to advertise for marriage partner	8.07
zhèngquè	1	正確	正确	Adj	correct, right, proper	7.24
zhēnshí	2	真實	真实	Adj	true, real	5
zhēnxī	3	珍惜		V	to treasure, to cherish	7.26
zhēnxiàng	4	真相		N	real situation, the real facts/truth	7
zhēnzhèng	1	真正		Adj	genuine, true, real	7
zhī	3	之		Part	of	2
zhǐ	1	指		V	to point at, to refer to	4.17
zhì		AA制		IE	to go Dutch treat, to each pay his ow	1
zhīchí	2	支持		V/N	to support, to back	9.44
zhíde	2	值得		Adj/V	to merit, to deserve	3.39
zhīhòu	2	之後	之后	Suf	later, after, afterwards	7.29
zhíjiē	2	直接		Adj/ Adv	direct, immediate	6.20
zhǐliàng	2	質量	质量	N	<PRC> quality <TW>品質 pǐnzhí	6.42
zhìshǎo	2	至少		Adv	at (the) least	1.16
zhíyè	2	職業	职业	N	occupation, profession	8.27
zhíyuán	3	職員	职员	N	office worker, staff member	7
zhòng nán qīng nǚ		重男輕女	重男轻女	IE	to value boys over girls	8
zhòngdiǎn	2	重點	重点	N	key, focal point, emphasis	9.09
zhōngshēn dàshì		終身大事	终身大事	N	important event in one's life—marriage	8
zhòngshì	2	重視	重视	V	to take sth. seriously, to value	8.43
zhōngyú	2	終於	终于	Adv	finally	4.22
zhòu	3	皺	皱	V	to wrinkle	10
zhuānjí		專輯	专辑	N	album, special issue/collection of periodicals/films, etc.	5
zhuānjiā	2	專家	专家	N	expert, specialist	9
zhuānmén	2	專門	专门	Adj	special, specialized	6.13
zhǔchírén	3	主持人		N	host, anchor, chair	8
zhǔdòng	2	主動	主动	Adv	on one's own initiative	8.32
zhǔjué		主角		N	leading role, lead, protagonist	5
zhǔyào	1	主要		Adj	main, chief, principal, major	3.28
zhǔzhāng	2	主張	主张	V/N	to advocate, to maintain	10.42
zìdòng	2	自動	自动	Adj	automatic	4.42

zìgǔ yǐlái	4	自古以來	自古以来	IE	since ancient times	1
zīliào	2	資料	资料	N	data, material	4.11
zìmù		字幕		N	subtitle, caption	5
zìxìn	3	自信		N/V	self-confidence, to be self-confident	9.40
zìzhù cāntīng		自助餐廳	自助餐厅	N	restaurant that serves buffet	1
zìzhuàn		自傳	自传	N	autobiography	6
zú	4	族		N	a group of, clan	2.34
zuòjiā	2	作家		N	writer	6
zuòrén		做人		VO	to conduct oneself, to behave, to be an upright person	6
zuòyòng	2	作用		N	effect	4.23

Index 2. Grammar and Usage

◎By Pinyin

(de/bú)xiàqù	O S V（得／不）下去	S (is able to) continue to VO	3.5
xiānbùtán, jiù…láikàn/ éryán	先不談X，就Y來看／而言 X先不談，就Y來看／而言	to say nothing of X, just looking at Y	6.5
xiàng…biǎoshì hǎogǎn/ guānxīn/tóngqíng/ huānyíng/yǒuhǎo	A向B表示好感／關心／同 情／歡迎／友好	to express favorable impression/ concern/ sympathy/welcome/good-will	8.6
xìngkuī…bùrán	幸虧S…，不然…	Fortunately S…, otherwise…	4.1

Y

(zài)…yǐnèi	（在）…以內	within (time/distance)	7.2
(zài)…yǐwài	（在）…以外	out of (distance)	
(zài)…yǐshàng	（在）…以上	over/above (age/height)	
(zài)…yǐxià	（在）…以下	below/under (age/height)	
yàoma…yàoma	S要麼VO，要麼VO	either…or…	1.4
yǐ	…，…以V	…, …in order to V	10.5
yǐ…wéi	S以…為N	to take … to be N	5.6
yǐ…wéilì	S以…為例	to take…as an example	
yǐ…wéishēng	S以…為生	to take…for a living	
yǐ…wéizhǔ	S以…為主	to take…as main part or primary	
yǐ…wéizhòng(xīn)	S以…為重（心）	to take…as more important	
yǐ…(wéi…)lái	以X（為Y）來V	to use X as Y in order to V	7.6
yī…jiùshì…	S 一V就是NP	Whenever S does something, S does something a lot	9.1
yídàn…jiù/yě	S 一旦…，就/也…	If (once) S…, then S will	4.5
yīn…ér…	S 因…而VO	because of …, S VO	4.6
yīnggāi…cáiduì	S 應該…才對	It's only right for S to…	7.4
yīnggāi…cáishì	S 應該…才是	It's only right for S to…	
yīnggāi…cáihǎo	S 應該…才好	It's only good for S to…	
yīnggāi…cáixíng	S 應該…才行	It's only fine for S to…	
yīshì…èrshì…	一是…，二是…	the first reason is…, and the second is; for	7.5
yīlái…èrlái…	一來…，二來…	one thing…, for another	
yú	A Adj 於B	A is more/less Adj than B	1.5
dīyú	A 低於B	A is lower than B	
gāoyú	A 高於B	A is higher than B	
duōyú	A 多於B	A is more than B	
shǎoyú	A 少於B	A is lesser than B	
xiǎoyú	A 小於B	A is smaller than B	
dàyú	A 大於B	A is bigger than B	
yú	S V於…		2.3
rèzhōngyú	S 熱衷於VO	S is very fond of …	
xíguànyú	S 習慣於VO	S is used to…	
shēngyú	S 生於Place/Time	S was born in…	